TRANSFORMATION
IN
CHRIST

WORKS BY DIETRICH VON HILDEBRAND

IN ENGLISH

In Defense of Purity
Marriage: The Mystery of Faithful Love†
Liturgy and Personality†
Transformation in Christ†
Fundamental Moral Attitudes
Ethics
The New Tower of Babel
Situation Ethics
Graven Images
What is Philosophy?
Not as the World Gives
Man and Woman
The Heart
The Trojan Horse in the City of God
The Devastated Vineyard
Celibacy and the Crisis of Faith
The Encyclical *Humanae Vitae*
Satan at Work

IN GERMAN

Die Idee der sittlichen Handlung
Sittlichkeit und ethische Werterkenntnis
Metaphysik der Gemeinschaft
Das katholische Berufsethos
Engelbert Dollfuss: Ein katholischer Staatsmann
Zeitliches im Lichte des Ewigen
Der Sinn philosophischen Fragens und Erkennens
Die Menschheit am Scheideweg
Mozart, Beethoven, Schubert
Heiligkeit und Tüchtigkeit
Das Wesen der Liebe
Die Dankbarkeit
Ästhetik I & II
Moralia
Der Tod

†*Available from Sophia Institute Press*

Dietrich von Hildebrand

TRANSFORMATION
IN
CHRIST

SOPHIA INSTITUTE PRESS
Manchester, New Hampshire

Transformation in Christ was first published in German in 1940 as *Die Umgestaltung in Christus*. Because Dietrich von Hildebrand was at that time proscribed from publishing by the Nazis, Benziger Verlag (Einsiedeln/Köln) published the book using the pseudonym Peter Ott for the author. Longmans, Green and Co. published the first English edition in 1948. Franciscan Herald Press reprinted it in 1974. This 1990 edition is published by Sophia Institute with permission of Alice von Hildebrand.

As this book was first published long before the liturgical changes instituted by Vatican Council II, it sometimes refers to prayers or other acts that are no longer in use in the Liturgy. However, familiarity with the pre-Vatican II Liturgy is not necessary to understand these passages: their context suffices to explain them.

References to the Psalms are based on the psalm and verse numeration found in the Vulgate, which numeration is slightly different today.

Sophia Institute Press
Box 5284, Manchester, NH 03108
1-800-888-9344

Library of Congress Cataloging-in-Publication Data
Von Hildebrand, Dietrich, 1889-1977
 [Umgestaltung in Christus. English]
 Transformation in Christ / by
  Dietrich von Hildebrand.
   Translation of: Die Umgestaltung in Christus.
   Reprint. Originally published: New York: Longmans, Green, 1948.
 ISBN 0-918477-09-3 Cloth
  1. Spiritual life — Catholic authors.   I. Title.
 BX2350.V5913 1989   248.4'82 — dc20   89-11453 CIP

10 9 8 7 6 5 4

TABLE OF CONTENTS

Introduction

by *Alice von Hildebrand, Ph.D.*

"WE MUST have an unconditional *readiness to change* in order to be transformed in Christ." These are the very first words I heard from Dietrich von Hildebrand, the man who was later to become my husband.

His words were a revelation for me. Even though I had been raised a Catholic, I had never been concretely taught how to relate my beliefs to everyday life. There was something sadly lacking in my education: it is not enough for us to believe; we must know *how to live* our beliefs.

This book transformed my spiritual life

Dietrich von Hildebrand — a layman — gave me the key that was to open for me the treasures of the spiritual life. Thanks to his lecture that day, I understood that my soul should become malleable like wax in God's hands, so that I could become what He wanted me to become (and what I was so far from being): *transformed in Christ.*

The impression Dietrich von Hildebrand's words made on me was so strong that I returned home *soberly inebriated.* Finally I had found what I had unconsciously been seeking: a concrete way of living my faith. That day — November 27, 1942 — was one of the most decisive days of my life.

Alas, I was too soon to learn that enthusiasm for a virtue does not guarantee possession of that virtue; and that a clear perception of the beauty of *spiritual transformation* can coexist with a deep reluctance to let oneself be re-formed by Christ.

But I also soon learned that "The Readiness to Change" was the title of the first chapter of *Transformation in Christ*, a book in German by Dietrich von Hildebrand. At the time, *Transformation in Christ* was available only in German, so I dedicated myself to learning German so I could profit from the treasures contained in this book.

Later, my husband often told me that *Transformation in Christ* was "the book of his heart" because it considered the theme he loved most: the glow of supernatural virtues made possible through Christian revelation. It also became *the book of my heart*: reading it opened up for me completely new vistas of spirituality which, until then, had remained totally closed to me.

I could now understand why the German reviewers had called *Transformation in Christ* a "modern *Imitation of Christ*." Like this perennial classic, *Transformation in Christ* is timeless, for it maps out the path leading to holiness: the "one thing necessary," the one unchanging thing in the tempest of changes that characterize our earthly situation.

Regardless of our circumstances and regardless of the age or place in which we live, we are all called to sanctity. Our guide is Christian wisdom, which is not subject to time but rather should shape the time in which it is found. *Transformation in Christ* helps us to achieve sanctity in *our* time because its roots lie in the ageless tradition of Christian spirituality which goes back to Christ Himself. This wisdom retains its full validity from age to age. Being anchored in eternity, it conquers time.

No one would dream of scaling a mountain without an experienced guide; no one should try to ascend the mountain of holiness without the help of someone knowledgeable in things spiritual, who points out dangers that threaten to jeopardize our ascent towards the mountain which is Christ.

Transformation in Christ became such a guide for me. Again and again as I read it, I was led to realize how often I had fallen into illusions about myself, and how often I had followed a path that actually had led me away from the true goal: to be transformed in Christ. It was as if scales had fallen from my eyes.

I discovered that my own readiness to change was highly selective, for whereas I was willing to improve in some areas of my life, I wanted to remain in command and to determine myself the scope and limits of my transformation. Rare are those (and they are properly known as *saints*) whose readiness to change is total, absolute, unconditional, and who let the Divine Master decide how deeply the marble is to be chiselled.

How difficult is it for us fallen men to will what God wills, for much as we believe we love God, we are tempted to love our own will more. How hard it is for us — the sons of Adam — to speak truly and fully the words of Christ: "not as I will, but as Thou wilt." And yet, this absolute and unconditional readiness to change ought to be the very basis of our spiritual life, so that we may become "new men" in Christ.

I learned how difficult it can be in the spiritual life to discriminate between things which seem similar but which are, in fact, profoundly different. How tempting it is for us to believe, for example, that we possess the readiness to change because, lacking in continuity, we follow every fashionable trend of the time. How often we believe that we are truly forgiving when in fact we are really too thick-skinned to notice offenses or we find it advantageous to make peace. How often we assume that we are spiritually recollected because we can concentrate fully on a task, when, in fact, we are merely capable of efficient mental concentration, which is radically different from recollection. To help us see such important differences in ourselves and to help us avoid other pitfalls, *Transformation in Christ* provides spiritual guidance for those who are serious about making progress toward holiness, enabling them to discern more clearly the path to holiness.

Since first reading *Transformation in Christ* and having my eyes opened by it, I have discovered that my experience has been duplicated in the lives of very many other people. Over the years, my husband received innumerable letters from persons testifying that reading *Transformation in Christ* profoundly changed their lives.

Reviewers of the book have also been unanimous in recognizing the extraordinary spiritual wisdom it contains. In 1949, a year after its American publication, it received the *Golden Book Award of the Catholic Writers Guild.*

Transformation in Christ awakens our longing for supernatural virtues

Too often, well-intentioned spiritual authors believe that in order to make the supernatural more palatable, they must water it down and use a vocabulary borrowed from down-to-earth, trivial experiences. This often creates a spiritual hiatus, a false note which is painful to those whose spiritual ear is attuned to the music of the angels.

One of the striking characteristics of this book is that the author never uses a word which is not in perfect harmony with the sublimity of his topic. With an unfailing holy instinct, he always pulls us upward toward a higher sphere clouded over today by our secularized anti-culture which constantly pulls us downward. From this point of view *Transformation in Christ* is a much needed spiritual medicine. It will inevitably sharpen our sense for the supernatural and reawaken the deep longing which exists in every human heart for *what is above*. Indeed, this was the call that St. Paul addressed to us: "Seek the things that are above."

Transformation in Christ illuminates in a unique way the nature of the supernatural virtues which can blossom only in and through Christ. Much as my husband had loved moral values prior to his conversion, it was through the lives of the saints that he discovered a new, higher morality — the supernatural morality — the one embodied in those whose very souls mirror the infinite beauty of the God-Man.

What a chasm lies between the *natural* virtue of modesty — an objective awareness of one's own limitations — and the *supernatural* virtue of humility which (as exemplified in St. Catherine of Siena) makes one rejoice over the fact that *God is everything and man is nothing*. What an abyss separates the *natural* warmth and friendliness which a good pagan possesses, from the ardent, burning *supernatural* charity which characterizes the saints.

It was the beauty of supernatural values which first touched my husband's soul, stirred within it love and longing, and brought him into the Church; it is just this beauty that he eloquently celebrates in *Transformation in Christ*.

Transformation in Christ reveals the splendor of God through the majesty of created things

Much as *Transformation in Christ* deserves to be compared to *The Imitation of Christ*, there is, however, an important difference between these two works which share the very same aim: to help the soul on her path to holiness. For whereas *The Imitation of Christ* (particularly in its first three books) stresses the dangers that natural goods constitute for man on his way to God, *Transformation in Christ* — while fully acknowledging these dangers — shows how these goods, if properly understood as being reflections of God's infinite goodness and beauty, can actually lead us closer to Him by being used as stepping stones leading to Him.

From this point of view, *Transformation in Christ* is strongly marked by the spirit of St. Francis who understood nature and creation to be singers of the glory of the Great King. Created by God's bounty, natural goods are to be loved — but God is to be loved more. That is to say, all created goods should be loved not *above* God, not *outside* of God, not *apart from* God, but *in* God, and should kindle our loving gratitude toward Him as the Giver of all gifts. Indeed, heaven and earth are filled with the glory of the Lord, and are footprints of His greatness.

Transformation in Christ is deep but not complicated

At first sight, *Transformation in Christ* may strike the reader as a long and complicated book, written for a small minority of scholarly people. But this difficulty is only apparent. True, *Transformation* is written by a German, but a German born and raised in Italy, whose mind has been formed and benefited by the clarity of the Latin spirit. In fact, *Transformation in Christ* is luminous throughout, but like all great things, it calls for close and constant attention.

Too many are those who believe that a deep book must be complicated and therefore above the head of the average reader. But *deep* does not mean "complicated" and complication does not guarantee depth. It is true, there are books which hide the penury of their contents by using highly esoteric language which is not only confused but confusing as well. There are thinkers who major in this: their language is so tortuous, so ambiguous, that they cheat people into believing that their message is deep. But the reading of the greatest of all books, the *Gospel*, should reveal to us that a book can be of sublime depth and yet be understood by any man whose heart is open to Truth.

Introduction

Granted: *Transformation in Christ* was written by "an intellectual" — and even by one who had studied under some of the very great thinkers of this century (including Husserl, Scheler and Reinach). Nonetheless, we should keep in mind that Dietrich von Hildebrand put his intellectual talents in God's service and that in writing this book, he wanted to address himself not to a few pundits, but to every Christian who is, like Daniel, "a man of longing."

Therefore, *Transformation in Christ* does not require the reader to have a painstaking philosophical training or to know a special technical vocabulary. It will richly fecundate anyone who has purity of heart, and who longs for the truth. Effort will be required, but it will be rewarded abundantly by the fruits to be harvested.

Transformation in Christ is not meant to be hastily read. No, it should be read slowly, meditatively, and should always be concretely related to your own personal life. Half a page, sometimes a few lines can nourish your soul, illumine your mind, and inflame your heart.

Transformation in Christ is not the fruit of scholarship, but of the author's experiences

Just as *Transformation in Christ* was not written as a scholarly tome, so it is not the fruit of a mind such as we find in some scholars, who unfortunately spend innumerable hours in a library, perusing dusty manuals on spirituality and then couch the ideas harvested there in an abstract, impersonal language.

On the contrary, *Transformation in Christ* was conceived and born of personal experiences. The author had an extraordinarily rich life: he knew royalty; he knew commoners; he knew saintly people; he knew great sinners; he knew great minds; and he knew those whose endowments were mediocre. He was privileged to meet some who had ascended *high on the holy mountain of the Lord* and whose lives were marked by a deep humility; he knew some who lived in complete illusions about themselves, and yet believed themselves to be close to sanctity; he knew some who were still groping in the darkness of sin and error.

Through faith, Dietrich von Hildebrand saw in all of them the image of God and longed to share with them what he himself had received. For much as he loved books, he loved people more; and it is from the wealth of his Christian experiences, enriched and fecundated by his own readings and meditations, that he learned the wisdom found in this book.

It is the wealth of these experiences that he shares with us in this work; it is real people that we meet in *Transformation in Christ* — and in many of them we shall recognize ourselves, our own frailties, our own dangers, our own illusions. (At times, we are even tempted to believe that the author knew us personally when he wrote the book, and that he was sketching our own character and our own faults.)

This serene spiritual classic was written at the peak of the author's dangerous battle against Nazism

Transformation in Christ emanates such a serene spiritual atmosphere that the reader is likely to assume that it was written at a particularly contemplative and peaceful period of the author's life. In truth, however, the book was written in the midst of his heroic and dramatic fight against Nazism. This work — which sings the beauty of supernatural life — was composed at a time when the author knew great hardships and was threatened by constant dangers because of his opposition to Nazism.

Transformation in Christ testifies to the victory of Dietrich von Hildebrand's spiritual life over the powers of evil unleashed by National Socialism. It also implicitly proclaims the final victory of good over evil, of God over Satan. Having left Germany voluntarily when Hitler came to power — because von Hildebrand refused to live in a country headed by a criminal — he first sought refuge in his sister's house in Florence, but upon seeing that Chancellor Engelbert Dollfuss of Austria was the only clear-sighted European politician who had fully gauged the horror of Nazism, von Hildebrand went to Vienna, and offered Dollfuss his intellectual services. With the Chancellor's support, he founded and directed an anti-Nazi, anti-totalitarian weekly newspaper which was published from December 1933 until the Anschluss on March 11, 1938.

Deeply convinced that he was responding to a divine call to unmask the anti-Christian character of Nazism, he fully realized that in so doing, he would have to abandon the intellectual joy of his heart: his philosophical and religious writings. He felt very keenly the sacrifice that responding to this mission entailed, and yet he never hesitated for a moment. For he was convinced that any religious writer worthy of the name was now called upon to be in the forefront of a combat waged against an anti-Christ.

Since his conversion, von Hildebrand's greatest joy had been to meditate and to write about the *new world of Christianity* which he had discovered in reading the lives of the saints. Now, in Vienna, plunged into an anti-Nazi political fight which to him was a hairshirt, Dietrich von Hildebrand lived under such pressure that — apart from his courses at the University — he was forced to devote all his time and all his energies to his task as a journalist.

Moreover, after the assassination of Chancellor Dollfuss in July 1934, the new government headed by Schuschnigg adopted a policy of *détente* with Hitler, and refused to help finance von Hildebrand's anti-Nazi weekly. Fundraising was added to his list of onerous duties.

To make matters worse, only a few people understood and agreed with his primary purpose of showing the intrinsic incompatibility of Christianity and Nazism. Von Hildebrand was persecuted by the pro-Nazis; he was flouted by the anti-Catholics (who resented the deeply religious tone of his weekly); and he was rejected by the anti-semites who refused to acknowledge that anti-semitism was, to quote Léon Bloy, a slap in the face of the Holy Virgin by the hands of the Christians.

Dietrich von Hildebrand stood alone.

Moreover, he was warned by the Chief of Police that the Nazi underground planned to assassinate him and he lived constantly under this sword of Damocles. Harassed by financial difficulties, forced to spend much of his time and energy fundraising (a work for which he was the most untalented of men), von Hildebrand knew little respite.

Two brief moments of peace were given him, however. During the months of August 1936 and 1937, a group of German friends (who missed terribly the lectures von Hildebrand used to give them in his house in Munich) invited him to Florence to give them a series of lectures on spirituality; they rented his sister's villa for that purpose.

What a joy it was for him to put down temporarily the crushing burden he was carrying and, once again, surrounded by friends whom he could trust, breathe the pure, spiritual air of prayer and contemplation.

Transformation in Christ is the fruit of these eighteen lectures given in the city of his birth. Too soon thereafter — when he escaped from the clutches of the Gestapo by taking the very last train leaving Austria for Czechoslovakia before the Nazi takeover — he was forced to live the painful life of a refugee: first in Switzerland, and then in France.

In the midst of this turmoil, he decided to publish his eighteen lectures from Florence, and confided them to Benziger Publishers in Switzerland. At that time von Hildebrand's works were forbidden both in Germany and Austria (possession of any of his writings could send a person to a concentration camp). Therefore, Benziger Publishers insisted that *Transformation in Christ* be printed under a pseudonym: Peter Ott. The book was an immediate success. It was only after the war, when the nightmare of Nazism was over, that a second edition of *Transformation in Christ* appeared, published under von Hildebrand's own name.

From reading it, no one could ever guess that this great book on spirituality was written under such dramatic circumstances. Clearly, the author's manifold sufferings did not deprive him of his inner peace or of his constant longing to deepen his spiritual life. Nazism or not, for Dietrich von Hildebrand, transformation in Christ remained the one, glorious theme of human existence, and of his own existence.

Obviously, he could not have completed this monumental work in just two brief summers without the benefit of the earlier graces he had so abundantly received, of the Christian experiences he had accumulated, of his spiritual readings, and of his own prayer life. Also, it is quite likely that in the mysterious plan of God's Providence, the sufferings Dietrich von Hildebrand endured in Vienna were the price he had to pay to be instrumental in helping so many souls to come closer to Christ by their inner transformation in Him and through the Cross.

Transformation in Christ ends with a prayer. This is appropriate, since the whole book is prayerful: a hymn of praise, a song of gratitude. Dietrich von Hildebrand's deepest wish was that this book would inflame its readers to be ever more transformed in Christ. He knew that our Savior came to bring fire on this earth, and it was His desire that it should be kindled.

Author's Introduction

Traham eos in vinculis charitatis. (Hosea 11:4)

GOD has called upon us to become new men in Christ. In holy Baptism, He communicates a new supernatural life to us; He allows us to participate in His holy life. This new life is not destined merely to repose as a secret in the hidden depths of our souls; rather it should work out in a transformation of our entire personality.

For the goal which the gratuitous mercy of God has called us to attain is not merely a moral perfection qualitatively identical with natural morality, owing its supernatural meaning only to a super-additive gift of grace; it is Christ's supernatural wealth of virtue, which in its very quality represents something new and quite distinct from all merely natural virtue. "That you may declare his virtues, who hath called you out of darkness into His marvelous light" (1 Peter 2:9).

Almost all the prayers of the ecclesiastical year refer to the succession of stages that leads from Baptism, imparting the principle of supernatural life, to our actual transformation in Christ — to the full victory in us of Him whose name is holiness.

In our treatment of the subject of a transformation in Christ, the theological foundations and dogmatic presuppositions of this mystery will be taken for granted. We are conscious of being in complete accord with the classic tradition as established by the Fathers of the Church, and above all, by St. Augustine and by the Angelic Doctor, St. Thomas Aquinas.

Our own theme in these pages is exclusively the operation of supernatural life in the sphere of personal morality: the shaping of that life which lights up the face of the "new man in Christ." Here, again, that aspect of the transformation in Christ which is related to the zone of mystical experience does not come within our scope.

Our purpose is to analyze in their essence some of the spiritual attitudes which are characteristic of the "new man in Christ," thereby indicating the course we must follow, and in particular, the goal we are called upon to reach. The full import of that Call addressed to the Christian is not always fully appreciated; what God expects from us is too often minimized and taken lightly.

While we start, in our description, from the types of attitudes which, as it were, mark the initial stages of the road in question, the order of succession in which the supernatural virtues will be considered here cannot claim a strictly systematic character. The supernatural virtues are so interrelated as to make each of them appear a precondition to the other in one respect and its fruit in another. Hence, the succession of the virtues we are about to examine is meant not so much to reflect the process of the transformation in Christ, as to manifest the abundance of life implicit in that process of transformation.

Again and again we shall encounter on our way the *coincidentia oppositorum* inherent in the divine essence: the mutual interpenetration and unity of perfections which are ostensibly inconsistent with one another and cannot appear on the natural plane except in mutual separation.

The present study is restricted to a selection of the spiritual attitudes and virtues which constitute the treasure yielded by a life in Christ, the understanding of which may reveal the intrinsic, the *qualitative* newness of supernatural morality. It does not pretend to completeness, not even to that completeness in a limited sense which an inexhaustible subject of this kind might admit; even in regard to the scope of its contents, it cannot claim to be comprehensive.

The purpose of this book will be fulfilled if it succeeds in evoking the mystic grandeur of the Call implied in the words of the Lord, "Follow me," and rousing in the hearts of some the desire to be transformed in Christ. For, before all else, it is necessary for us to grasp the "height, breadth, and depth" of our vocation, and fully to comprehend the message of the Gospel which invites us not merely to become disciples of Christ and children of God, but to enter into a process of transformation in Christ. "But we all, beholding the glory of the Lord with open face, are transformed into the same image from glory to glory, even as by the Spirit of the Lord" (2 Cor. 3:18).

TRANSFORMATION
IN
CHRIST

The Readiness to Change

Put off the old man who is corrupted according to
the desire of error, and be renewed in the spirit of your
mind: and put on the new man, who according to God
is created in justice and holiness of truth. (Eph. 4:22-24)

THESE words of St. Paul are inscribed above the gate through which all must pass who want to reach the goal set us by God. They implicitly contain the quintessence of the process which baptized man must undergo before he attains the unfolding of the new supernatural life received in Baptism.

All true Christian life, therefore, must begin with a deep yearning to become a new man in Christ, and an inner readiness to "put off the old man" — a readiness to become something fundamentally different.

All good men desire to change

Even though he should lack religion, the will to change is not unknown to man. He longs to develop and to perfect himself. He believes he can overcome all vices and deficiencies of his nature by human force alone. All morally aspiring men are conscious of the necessity of a purposeful self-education which should cause them to change and to develop. They, too, — as contrasted to the morally indifferent man who lets himself go and abandons himself passively to his natural dispositions — reveal a certain readiness to change. But for this, no spiritual and moral growth would exist at all.

Yet, when man is touched by the light of Revelation, something entirely new has come to pass. The revelation of the Old Testament alone suffices to make the believer aware of man's metaphysical situation and the terrible wound inflicted upon his nature by original sin. He knows that no human force can heal that wound; that he is in *need of redemption*. He grasps the truth that repentance is powerless to remove the guilt of sin which separates him from God, that good will and natural moral endeavor will fail to restore him to the beauty of the paradisiac state. Within him lives a deep yearning for the Redeemer, who by divine force will take the guilt of sin and bridge the gulf that separates the human race from God.

Throughout the Old Testament that yearning resounds: "Convert us, O God: and show us Thy face, and we shall be saved" (Ps. 79:4). We perceive the desire for purification which enables us to appear before God, and to endure the presence of the unspeakably Holy One: "Thou shalt sprinkle me with hyssop, and I shall be cleansed: Thou shalt wash me, and I shall be made whiter than snow" (Ps. 50:9).

God calls us to change

The New Testament, however, reveals to us a *call* which far transcends that *yearning*. Thus Christ speaks to Nicodemus: "Amen, amen, I say to thee, unless a man be born again, he cannot see the kingdom of God" (John 3:3).

Christ, the Messiah, is not merely the Redeemer who breaks apart the bond and cleanses us from sin. He is also the Dispenser

4

of a new divine life which shall wholly transform us and turn us into new men: "Put off the old man who is corrupted according to the desire of error, and be renewed in the spirit of your mind; and put on the new man, who according to God is created in justice and holiness of truth." Though we receive this new life in Baptism as a free gift of God, it may not flourish unless we cooperate. "Purge out the old leaven, that you may be a new paste," says St. Paul.

A strong desire must fill us to become different beings, to mortify our old selves and rearise as new men in Christ. This desire, this readiness to decrease so that "He may grow in us," is the first elementary precondition for the transformation in Christ. It is the primal gesture by which man reacts to the *light of Christ* that has reached his eyes: the original gesture directed to God. It is, in other words, the adequate consequence of our consciousness of being *in need of redemption* on the one hand, and our comprehension of being *called* by Christ on the other. Our surrender to Christ implies a readiness to let Him fully transform us, without setting any limit to the modification of our nature under His influence.

Readiness to change vs. natural optimism

In regard to their respective readiness to change, the difference between the Christian and the natural idealist is obvious. The idealist is suffused with optimism concerning human nature as such. He underestimates the depth of our defects; he is unaware of the wound, incurable by human means, with which our nature is afflicted. He overlooks our impotence to erase a moral guilt or to bring about autonomously a moral regeneration of ourselves. Moreover, his infatuation with activity prevents him from understanding even the necessity of a *basic* renewal. He fails to sense the *essential* inadequacy of all natural morality, as well as the incomparable superiority of virtue supernaturally founded, let alone the full presence of such virtue — holiness.

His readiness to change will differ, therefore, from that of the Christian, above all in the following respects. First, he has in mind a relative change only: an evolution immanent to nature. His endeavor is not, as is the Christian's, to let his nature as a whole be transformed from above, nor to let his character be stamped with a new coinage, a new face, as it were, whose features far transcend human nature and all its possibilities. His object is not to be reborn: to become radically — from the root, that is — another man; he merely wants to perfect himself within the framework of his natural dispositions. He is intent on ensuring an unhampered evolution of these dispositions and potentialities. Sometimes even an express approval of his own nature is implicit therein, and a self-evident confidence in the given tendencies of his nature as they are before being worked upon by conscious self-criticism. Such was, for instance, Goethe's case. Invariably in the idealist, the readiness to change is limited to a concept of nature's immanent evolution or self-perfection: its scope remains *exclusively* human. Whereas, with the Christian, it refers to a basic transformation and redemption of things human by things divine: to a supernatural goal.

A second point of difference is closely connected with this. The idealist's readiness to change is aimed at certain details or aspects only, never at his character as a whole. The aspiring man of natural morality is intent on eradicating *this* defect, on acquiring *that* virtue; the Christian, however, is intent on becoming another man in *all* things, in regard to both what is bad and what is *naturally good* in him. He knows that what is naturally good, too, is insufficient before God: that it, *too*, must submit to supernatural transformation — to a re-creation, we might say, by the new principle of supernatural life conveyed to him by Baptism.

Thirdly, the man of natural moral endeavor, willing as he may be to change in one way or another, will always stick to the firm ground of Nature. How could he be asked to relinquish that foothold, tumbling off into the void? Yet it is precisely this firm ground which the Christian *does* leave. His readiness to change impels him to break with his unredeemed nature as a whole: he *wills* to lose the firm ground of unredeemed nature under his feet and to tumble, so to speak, into the arms of Christ. Only he who may say with St. Paul, "I know in whom I have believed" can risk the enormous adventure of dying unto himself and of relinquishing the natural foundation.

Not all possess the radical readiness to change

Now this radical readiness to change, the necessary condition for a transformation in Christ, is not actually possessed by *all* Catholic believers. It is, rather, a distinctive trait of those who have grasped the *full* import of the Call, and without reserve have decided upon an imitation of Christ.

There are many religious Catholics whose readiness to change is merely a conditional one. They exert themselves to keep the commandments and to get rid of such qualities as they have recognized to be sinful. But they lack the will and the readiness to become new men all in all, to break with all purely natural standards, to view all things in a supernatural light. They prefer to evade the act of *metanoia*: a true conversion of the heart. Hence with undisturbed consciences they cling to all that appears to them legitimate by natural standards.[1]

Their conscience permits them to remain entrenched in their self-assertion. For example, they do not feel the obligation of loving their enemies; they let their pride have its way within certain limits; they insist on the right of giving play to their natural

[1]For the time being we disregard the case, very typical also, in which the call for a radical change is perceived to some extent but meets with a more or less conscious opposition. We are dealing here with the case of a more deeply hidden resistance to the demand of full conversion, which prevents the subject from adequately assessing the import of the required change, so that he may restrict his compliance without being troubled by his conscience.

reactions in answer to any humiliation. They maintain as self-evident their claim to the world's respect, they dread being looked upon as *fools of Christ*; they accord a certain role to human respect, and are anxious to stand justified in the eyes of the world also.

They are not ready for a total breach with the world and its standards; they are swayed by certain conventional considerations; nor do they refrain from letting themselves go within reasonable limits. There are various types and degrees of this reserved form of the readiness to change; but common to them all is the characteristic of a merely conditional obedience to the Call and an ultimate abiding by one's natural self. However great the differences of degree may be, the decisive cleavage is that which separates the unreserved, radical readiness to change from the somehow limited and partial one.

Transformation in Christ requires unqualified readiness to change

The full readiness to change — which might even better be termed *readiness to become another man* — is present in him only who, having heard the call "Follow me" from the mouth of the Lord, follows Him as did the Apostles, "leaving everything behind." To do so, he is not required literally to relinquish everything in the sense of the evangelical counsels: this would be in answer to another, more particular call. He is merely required to relinquish his old self, the natural foundation, and all purely natural standards, and open himself entirely to Christ's action — comprehending and answering the call addressed to *all* Christians: "Put on the new man, who according to God is created in justice and holiness of truth."

Readiness to change, taken in this sense, is the first prerequisite for the transformation in Christ. But, in addition thereto, more is needed: a glowing desire to become a new man in Christ; a passionate will to give oneself over to Christ. And this, again, presupposes a state of fluidity, as it were: that we should be like soft wax, ready to receive the imprint of the features of Christ. We must be determined not to entrench ourselves in our nature, not to maintain or assert ourselves, and above all, not to set up beforehand — however unconsciously — a framework of limiting or qualifying factors for the pervasive and re-creative light of Christ. Rather we must be filled with an unquenchable thirst for regeneration in all things. We must fully experience the bliss of flying into Christ's arms, who will transform us by His light beyond any measure we might ourselves intend. We must say as did St. Paul on the road to Damascus: "Lord, what wilt Thou have me to do?"

Moral progress requires unqualified readiness to change

But the unreserved readiness to change, as here outlined, is not merely the condition for embarking on our journey towards our supernatural goal. It also constitutes the permanent basis for continual progress on our road. It is an attitude we must always preserve so long as we are *in statu viae* — until we have reached the safe harbor of the *status finales*, where there is no longer any task proposed to our will, and where our souls will rest unchangeably in the boundless bliss of communion with God. Should that readiness to change and that passionate will to surrender ever cease, we would no longer have the proper religious disposition. That unlimited readiness to change is not only necessary for the transformation in Christ: even as such, it represents the basic and relevant response to God. It reflects our unreserved devotion to God, our consciousness of our infinite weakness before Him, our habitude of living by the Faith, our love and yearning for God. It finds its highest expression in these words of the Blessed Virgin: "Behold the handmaid of the Lord; be it done to me according to thy word" (Luke 1:38).

In his *Discourses for Mixed Congregations*, Cardinal Newman points out the danger inherent in believing oneself to have attained a satisfactory degree of spiritual progress — no matter how high a degree it actually is — and to be entitled now to discontinue the struggle against one's own nature. The example of the saints teaches us that spiritual progress implies no hardening of that fluidity of which we have spoken, no weakening of the steady will for transformation by Christ. The more one is transformed in Christ, the deeper and more unlimited his readiness to change beyond the point reached, the more he understands the dimension of depth in which that transformation must extend, and the necessity for him to place himself *anew* in God's hands, again and again, so as to lie shaped anew by Christ.

Never, *in statu viae*, will he cease to say with Michelangelo, "Lord, take me away from myself, and make me pleasing to Thee." In his earthly life the Christian must never let the process of dying unto himself and rising again in Christ come to a standstill: he should always preserve that inner fluidity which is an ultimate expression of the situation implied in the *status viae*. Thus spoke the thief on the cross: "We are punished justly, for we receive the due reward of our deeds; but this man hath done no evil. Lord, remember me when Thou shalt come into Thy kingdom." In that moment, a bursting through toward things divine took place in his soul, which bore a connotation of unlimited love. And, because this unlimited surrender was the last act of his life before expiring, in spite of all his imperfections he received this answer from the Lord: "Amen, I say to thee, this day thou shalt be with me in paradise" (Luke 23:42-43).

That unlimited readiness to change is necessary not only for the sinner in the narrower sense of the word, but also for the guarded, the pure, the graced, whom God has drawn unto Himself from youth onwards: not only for a St. Augustine but also for a St. John. The saints are classed sometimes in two categories: on the one hand, the great converts like St. Paul or St. Mary Magdalene; on the other, men and women in whom a continuous slow maturing of grace is clearly observable: such souls as St. John the Evangelist or St. Catherine of Siena. Yet the necessity of what is here described as *readiness to change* applies by no means only to him who has gone through a conversion and who therefore evidently cannot but repent of his former life, but even to such as have never definitely and gravely trespassed against God's commandments. They, too, must be willing to rise above their nature and hold themselves ready for coinage by the spirit of Christ.

Supernatural readiness to change vs. malleability

However, it would mean a grievous misunderstanding of this indispensable basic attitude to interpret it as a state of fluidity as such, a general disposition to change in no matter what direction. In fact, what we have in mind is exclusively the readiness to let ourselves be shaped by Christ, and by whatever speaks of Him and of the "Father of all lights." The change we have in view is merely the change implied in the continual process of dying unto ourselves, and being reformed by Christ. Moreover, that state of fluidity which makes this process possible is linked, on the other hand, to an attitude of *consolidation in Christ* and in the goods we receive from Him. With the postulate of soft receptiveness susceptible to the formative influences from above corresponds, as a logical complement, the postulate of an increasing rigidity in relation to all tendencies towards being changed from below.

Here the difference between fluidity under the sign of the supernatural and the mere natural disposition of fluidity becomes clear. Some people, owing merely to their natural temperament are like soft wax, prone to any change whatever. These impressionable persons who yield to all kinds of influences lack solidity and continuity.

The fluidity which goes with aliveness to the supernatural, on the contrary, has nothing to do with spineless malleability as such. Rather it involves a firm standing in the face of all mundane influences, a character of impermeability in regard to them, and an unshakable solidity on the new base with which Christ supplies us. Even at this early stage we discern that strange *coincidentia oppositorum* which will again and again strike our eyes in the course of our inquiry: that union between attitudes seemingly irreconcilable with each other on the natural level, which is the sign of all supernatural mode of being.

Also, that fluidity in our relationship with Christ is anything but a state characterized by a continuous flow of change, in the sense that the *change as such* be credited with a value of its own. What the readiness to be transformed by Christ really implies is rather the utter negation both of the worship of being in a state of movement as exhibited by the Youth Movement and of the Goethean ideal of an abundance of life based on the concept of continual change. We are far, then, from preaching fluidity in general, be it in the sense of a glorification of movement as such, or in the sense of the celebrated verses of Goethe, beautiful though they may be: *Denn solang du das nicht hast, dieses Stirb und Werde, bist du nur ein trüber Gast auf der dunkeln Erde* ("Unless thou follow the call of dying and becoming, thou art but a sad guest on this dark earth").

Man is called to the unchangeableness of God

It does not behoove us to cherish variability as such; for, as Christians we give our worship not to change but to the Unchangeable: God, Who in all eternity remains Himself: "They shall perish, but Thou remainest" (Ps. 101:26-28). Thus, as Christians we direct our lives towards that moment in which there will be change no longer, and rejoice in the hope of sharing in the unchangeableness of God. We deny our love to the heaving rhythm of life. And the ideal of vitality, seductive to those who see the ultimate reality in Nature, has no attraction for us. Nor can we be intoxicated by any communion with Nature in a pantheistic sense. For we do not believe ourselves to be a part of Nature: we conceive of man as a spiritual person endowed with an immortal soul. We feel that he does not belong as a whole to the natural realm. It is only in respect to our terrestrial situation that we are subject to the rhythm of ebb and flow, the fluctuation of dying and becoming, the law of perishableness. *Non omnis moriar* (I shall not wholly die), says Horace, having in mind earthly fame. But we say it in awareness of our ultimate, our innermost essence. It is part of the blissful message of the Gospel that we are called to participate in the eternal unchangeableness of God.

Yet our life will acquire immutability in the degree in which we are transformed in Christ. So long as we evade being thus transformed, and insist on maintaining ourselves, this remaining fixed in our own nature cannot but deliver us up to the world of flux and reflux, and the forces of change. Such a solidification would actually mean an imprisonment within the precincts of our own changeable selves: it would prevent us from transcending our limitations as vital beings and from being drawn into the sphere of divine unchangeableness. In the measure only in which we yield like soft wax to the formative action of Christ, shall we attain genuine firmness, and grow into a likeness of divine immutability. In that measure, too, shall we rise above the terror which — seeing our status as rational persons distinct from physical nature — the rhythm of death and life's law of transiency portend for us.

Natural readiness to change diminishes with age

A glance at the normal course of human life, considered from a purely natural point of view, will show that a character of comparative fluidity, in intellectual as in other respects is proper to youth.

By that we mean not only a love of change for its own sake, but an aspiration towards higher values: an eagerness for education, for enriching and ennobling oneself. Such a disposition is the natural gift of youth.

Examine a person enlivened by the vital rhythm of youth, and you will find in him a certain forcefulness and daring which facilitate that aspiration towards higher things. But when men become older and, within the framework of natural tendencies their characters and peculiarities undergo a process of solidification, the natural mobility and urge for change will tend to disappear.

Such persons will then become much less accessible to elevating influences, less receptive to fresh stimuli (we are still speaking on purely natural presuppositions). We can no longer expect them to revise their mentality and to re-educate themselves, for they are already cast in a rigid mold.

This description does not refer merely to an inveterate habit, owing to the lengthy accumulation of similar experiences, of looking at things in a certain way. What is meant is a general condition different from that which youth implies. The natural readiness to change is gone; its place is taken by the attitude of a person conscious of his maturity, who considers himself to have achieved his period of formation and arrogates to himself the right, as it were, to endure and to settle down in his peculiarities such as they are.

These psychic peculiarities — which may not infrequently be eccentricities — are never so marked during youth. Only at a later period do certain natural tendencies assume such a character of rigidity. From the mere succession of the phases of life one seems to derive the right to be no longer a pupil or an apprentice but a master.

Supernatural readiness to change should grow with age

But if we envisage the vital phases of youth and old age from a supernatural point of view, the picture will be different. Here, in fact, an inverse law will appear. The readiness to change, the waxlike receptiveness towards Christ will tend not to vanish but to increase as man grows into a state of maturity. Accidental concerns and complications recede into the background; the pattern of life wins through to simplicity; the great decisive aspects of life become more clearly accentuated. The unrest incident to youth, the vacillating response to disparate appeals, the insatiable hunger for whatever appears attractive or beautiful will subside, and a steady orientation towards the essential and decisive become dominant.

This progress towards simplicity, which is part of the spiritual significance of advancing in age, is linked to a consolidation in Christ. A number of vital tendencies, longings of all kinds, and a certain ubiquitous unrest fostered by expectations of earthly happiness, recede before that supernatural unrest which attends the supreme yearning for Christ. A liberation from one's own nature becomes apparent. The scriptural words, "Being made perfect in a short space, he fulfilled a long time" (Wisd. of Sol. 4:13-14), refer to this true meaning and value of maturity.

Yet this attainment of full maturity also implies eternal youth in a supernatural sense. It implies that the readiness to change, the determination to become a new man, and the unconditional willingness to crucify the old self should increase; that the impatience for Christ should not abate. As he draws nearer to the gates of eternity, such a person will direct his attention to "the one thing necessary" with ever increasing concentration. It is this supernatural youth which is referred to in the Gradual of the Mass, by the words *qui laetificat juventutem meam* ("who giveth joy to my youth"). Here is, paradoxically speaking, a spiritual intactness increasing with age, inasmuch as throughout the *status viae* we continually enhance our alert readiness to change towards greater proximity to God, so that His features may be engraved upon our souls. And this is equivalent to becoming more and more free from ourselves: ridding ourselves of everything which, though it be rooted in our own nature, stands between our souls and Christ. It may be said without exaggeration that the degree of our inner fluidity in relation to Christ, our readiness to put off our own nature in order to put on Christ, constitutes the standard criterion of our religious progress.

Whenever at some moments we have the specific feeling of being privileged by God and drawn nearer to Him, we must ask ourselves: do we possess this readiness to change? — and how far do we possess it? Unless we can answer that question favorably, we are not in the right religious condition. Yet if, in the moments of inward elevation, we really possess that readiness, our being touched by God will mean more than merely receiving a gift: we are then capable of the cooperation God requires. By the degree of a man's inner readiness to change, his religious level may be decisively judged.

In the unconditional readiness to change, a salutary distrust of one's own self-knowledge is also implied. If I am really intent on becoming *another man* I will not claim the right to determine the limits between what can, and what cannot, be justified in my nature if confronted with Christ. It is He who is to determine them through religious authority. The readiness must be present, on our part, to be changed and shaped to an indefinite degree at the hands of God, wherever He chooses to intervene by the agency of our spiritual director or of our religious superior. *We are not ourselves able or entitled to determine the measure of our transformation.* This is a true sign of the ultimate relevancy, and of the radical newness by which a life devoted to the true imitation of Christ is characterized. God will be merciful with those also who possess only a limited readiness to change; but he alone whose readiness to change and whose spiritual plasticity are unlimited can attain to sanctity.

Spiritual continuity is consistent with readiness to change

It must be emphasized that there is no contradiction between the Christian's readiness to change and the principle of moral continuity. Our mental attitude reveals the trait of continuity insofar as we remain aware of the ultimate unity of all truth and all values in God. We must keep in view and continue to recognize whatever valid truth we have seized, whatever genuine value experienced; none of these must sink into oblivion once it is no longer actually present to our eyes. The man who is a prey to discontinuity accords an illegitimate priority to what happens to be present in his consciousness. He neglects more important and more valid impressions for the sake of present ones. He fails to preserve his contact with basic general truths and values beyond the range of mere present interest. He is, therefore, unable to confront the concrete situation of the moment with those truths and values, and to experience it in their light. Because he is submerged in the situation of the moment, he lacks the standard by which to measure and to judge all new impressions. Moreover, the impressions succeed one another in a disconnected flight; one replaces the other as though they were mutually equivalent, with no proportionate attention given to those of greater weight; and thus the valid content of former impressions is trampled under foot, as it were, by the dynamism of what is actually present.

Suppose, for instance, that we happen to have gained a deep insight into someone's personality. Meeting him later on a more superficial occasion, our impression is different: we see him this time *from the outside*, rather like a casual acquaintance. If we have the *habitus* of continuity we shall not let ourselves be confused by this new impression but keep aware of the former impression, which has been deeper and of greater validity. Whereas, if we lack continuity, the new impression will confuse our judgment and, because of its mere recentness, obscure and displace the older but more relevant one.

Continuity, then, consists in the twofold capacity to maintain our comprehension of basic truths, experiencing all things against a background of these truths, and to maintain particular aspects of great validity as against new ones which happen to be less substantial. Both these aptitudes are in close harmony with the quality of receptiveness towards new truths and values. Legitimate faithfulness to things established does not spring from mere inertia and formal conservatism; it represents rather an adequate response to the immutability of unalloyed truth and genuine value, which is past obsolescence. The selfsame motive which impels the person with continuity to cling imperturbably to truth will equally commit him to be ready to accept every new truth. He will be ready even to renounce what he has held to be a truth, should a new and deeper insight actually disprove it. The rectification of a former opinion, in the proper sense of the term, is not opposed to, but on the contrary definitely presupposes, continuity.

For what is operative here is by no means the merely psychological advantage of the more recent impression but the subordination of all particular convictions, whether they be formed at an earlier or a later period of time, to eternal truths and objective standards of judgment. Thus, continuity is a condition, not only for stable orientation but also for intellectual progress itself. It is on the basis of continuity that we are able to preserve established truths and at the same time to supplement them with new ones, both in the sense of an extension of the breadth of knowledge, and of a reinterpretation of old truths in the light of insights newly acquired.

It is by the attitude of continuity that we conform to the invariability and the mutual consistency — the intrinsic unity —

of all values. It implies, therefore, that the higher value should take precedence of the lower one. In granting priority to a higher value, once it presents itself, we give proof of continuity. For, in following the higher value we implicitly continue to cherish what was the object of our response in the lower value to which we hitherto adhered unreservedly. Our supreme fidelity is not due to a partial value or good, taken by itself, but to value as such — and ultimately, to God, who is the *summum bonum* (highest good). Our fidelity to that highest good requires that the objectively higher value should rise above the lower one also in regard to our experience and our conduct.

Continuity actually presupposes readiness to change

It is important to avoid all equivocation on this point: that continuity is a prime condition of spiritual growth, and even more, of a transformation in Christ; and that it stands in no opposition to the will to become another man. Without continuity, on the contrary, there could be no genuine responsiveness to the formative claim of Christ. For, with each step achieved the coinage received from Christ must be preserved and be made into a durable and inherent stamp on our nature. Only we must always remain changeable in the sense of remaining, upon each level securely attained, susceptible of ascent towards yet higher levels along the path of transformation in Christ. But every such act of remodelling refers back to the previous level, and thus has its place in the solid framework of continuity. The previous phase will not be buried or obliterated: its essential content will reappear on the higher level, although deepened, amplified and transfigured in the context of that higher grade of perfection. Thus shall we keep fidelity to Christ, when we follow His call to penetrate into Him ever deeper, and without reserve. It is one and the same Christ who by successive degrees reveals to us His face more and more fully, and who owns us more and more completely as we become more deeply transformed in Him.

But this requires our capacity to discern whether the new impression is really a more valid and relevant one. On the basis of continuity alone shall we be able wisely and fruitfully to confront the new thing with the old so as to avoid falling back from a higher level to a lower one or yielding to a new impression when it belongs to a level inferior to the one we have already reached.

Is there not, however, also a duty of fidelity towards our own God-created individuality? Is it right for us to ignore — in our unlimited readiness for transformation — what we feel to be the particular talents which God has entrusted to us, that ineffable essence which we feel to be our ultimate core?

Readiness to change preserves true individuality

Certainly, the radical readiness to change in the sense used here does not entail renunciation of the particularity of our personality as willed by God. But this concept, the particular individuality of a person, has a dual meaning. On the one hand, it may designate the character of a person as an empirical whole, including also whatever vices, defects, imperfections, eccentricities, and accidental features his personality may contain. Or else, we mean by *individuality* the particular, unique, and inimitable thought in the mind of God which every human being embodies. It is only in a saint that individuality thus conceived can fully display itself. For it contains, on the one hand, the particular natural character of the person which, however, never implies defects and imperfections as such; and on the other hand, a supernatural transfiguration and elevation of that particular nature. Now the readiness to change, as discussed here, refers in the first place to all the negative and ultimately spurious tendencies in our nature which oppose a barrier to our control by Christ. But it also refers, further, to all that is naturally good in us; for the latter is not destined to remain natural but to become enhanced and transfigured by the re-creative action of the supernatural.

No renunciation of the specific value attaching to individuality, no denial of the person's particular nature as willed by God is implied in this transformation. This is best illustrated by the example of the saints. Though it can be said of each of them alike that "he no longer lives but Christ lives in him," they are individualities with marked contours. Let us only think of St. Francis of Assisi and St. Catherine of Siena — to mention only two of the most obvious examples. It is as legitimate to preserve our individuality in the sense of the particular call of God which it enshrines as it is illegitimate to stick to what we commonly regard as our nature. The maintenance of our divinely sanctioned particular individuality can never conflict with our transformation by Christ. It cannot involve us in resisting the uplifting force and in shielding any part of our nature from Christ. For, so long as we keep immured in our nature, that divinely sanctioned individuality is not yet achieved; it is only when "we live no longer but Christ lives in us" that it can unfold integrally.

The great mystery of our metaphysical situation, that God is nearer to us than we are ourselves, is manifest in the fact that we cannot even be wholly ourselves — in the sense of individuality as a unique divine thought — until we are reborn in Christ. Undoubtedly, the preservation of divinely sanctioned individuality may mean that certain forms or modes of religious life are not appropriate to a given person. Every method is not suitable for everyone. There are several equally valid ways towards God, such as the Benedictine, the Franciscan, the Dominican, and so forth. The specific word of God that has been spoken in every soul; the name by which God has called us; the unique design of God underlying every personality — these must not be forcibly denied or suppressed.

True vs. false individuality

Yet, as we have already seen, the uniqueness of every person is something to be carefully distinguished from what is commonly subsumed under the term *individuality* and what most of us are apt to cherish as our particular nature. This so-called individuality originates from various factors, such as the experiences a man has undergone, the wounds that have been inflicted upon him, the false responses that have become ingrained in his mind, the environment in which he has lived, the education he has received, the conventions which surround him, and so forth. Only think how many rash generalizations, built upon a single and perhaps accidental experience, survive in our mind. All these things are incorporated in a person's character; but they need not by any means be consonant with the very essence and ultimate meaning of his individuality. All these forces cannot have worked out so favorably as not to have distorted in a certain way and a certain measure the true individuality as willed by God. What we generally feel to be our individual nature is far remote from the inward word by which God has called us. By our own force alone we cannot even truly discern that word. "Every man lies," says the Psalmist.

What should be relinquished without reserve, therefore, are such elements of personality as do not belong to its proper essence. And yet precisely in regard to these does the tendency to fixation persist. Most men are reluctant to sacrifice those manifold features of their personality which are no part of its inmost essence but derivatives of the various factors we have listed above. They attempt tenaciously to maintain themselves in these very features. This tendency to self-affirmation and petrification, as contrasted to the readiness for being transformed in all these points and for receiving the imprint of the face of Christ instead of the old features, is the antithesis to what we have meant here in speaking of fluidity.

To sum up — the postulate of a readiness to change does not refer to individuality in the ultimate sense, which is according to divine ordination. Individuality in this sense will be transfigured and sanctified, but by no means foregone or supplanted by another individuality. For the essence of every human person supposes a unique and incommensurable task; it is destined to unfold and to operate in a direction inalienably proper to it.

False self-appraisals hinder readiness to change

At this stage, let us signal two dangers which are naturally apt to arise and which should be avoided.

Sometimes we encounter people of a certain type characterized by a proclivity towards spiritual depression and sloth. Such a man will yield to a mood of inward barrenness. Though possessing a certain modesty, he lacks vigor and eagerness for spiritual elevation. He is unresponsive to what is best in him, and demurs at believing in it. The example of the saints, far from inciting him to emulation, only confirms him in his resignation: "I am a wretched man." In his pusillanimity, such a person leaves unused the talents of which he should make the most; he irresponsibly declines being committed by God's call. People of this kind, when speaking of themselves, even are wont to deny the virtues they naturally possess; such is their lack of confidence. They are bent on lowering their stature as much as possible. Their lack of courage and activity, which causes them to desert their higher potentialities, is most deplorable. On the other hand, their care in avoiding false pretensions deserves a certain credit.

The inverse type of deviation is exemplified by the man who, while not lacking a certain *élan*, refuses to take account of his limitations and is thus driven to magnify his stature artificially. Suppose he is present at some discussion of spiritually relevant topics: he will take part in the debate as though he were fully equipped to do so; he will claim impressions as deep as the others; he will not yield to any other man as regards intellectual proficiency or even religious stature. Thus he works himself up, as it were, to a level which he has not reached in reality — and which he may not even be able to reach, so far as it is a matter of natural capacities.

He is not without zeal; but that zeal is nourished at heart by pride. He misjudges the limitations of the natural talents which God has lent him, and consequently lapses into pretense. He is fond of speaking of things which far transcend the limits of his understanding; he behaves as though a mere mental or verbal reference to such subjects (however poorly implemented with actual knowledge and penetration) would by itself amount to their intellectual possession. This cramped attitude of sham spirituality is mostly underlain by an inferiority complex, or by a kind of infantile unconsciousness. Stupidity in its really oppressive form is traceable to this pretension to appear something different from what one is in fact, and by no means to a mere deficiency of intellectual gifts. A person who knows his position and confines himself to themes he does understand will, for all his lack of acumen, never really produce the impression of stupidity, that is to say, his fellow men will not feel embarrassed and exasperated by his intellectual weakness.

Both these attitudes — that of undue depression, and that of forced zeal, to put it briefly — are reprehensible. The supernatural readiness to change steers clear of both these dangers. The man whom it governs is cognizant, at the same time, of his natural limits and of the specific call which God has implanted in his soul. He refuses to flag, and to rest content with the lowest potentialities in his individual nature; but neither does he strain to answer a false idealized concept of himself. While he is conscious of his wretchedness, he will not sink into resignation; for he possesses a *supernatural* zeal for perfection, expecting the supreme fructification of the talents which God has in reality entrusted to him from his transformation in Christ, rather than from his own effort alone. Man must be sufficiently spirited to be ready to don his festive garment. Whatever his nature be like, he will know that it is possible for him to become another man if he is rightly disposed for being created anew by Christ — mindful of the words which the king in the parable addresses to his guest: "Friend, how camest thou in hither not having on a wedding garment?" (Matt. 22:12). The state of fluidity in relation to Christ, and the readiness to leave behind everything, particularly one's own self — such is the tissue of which the festive garment is woven.

Fidelity to error is not a virtue

There are few things more obstructive to that state of fluidity than a certain misconstrued ideal of fidelity often to be met with. Some people attribute value to the attitude of stubborn adherence as such (adherence to an idea, or to an intellectual milieu, in particular). Yet in reality it is adherence to truth and to genuine values only which is good; adherence to errors is a bad thing. What claims our faithfulness is the presence of genuine values. Fidelity is but a manifestation of that continuity by virtue of which we pay consideration to the immutability and the eternal significance of truth and of the world of values.

To abide by a thing inflexibly, merely because we have once believed in it and have come to love it, is not in itself a praiseworthy attitude. It is only in reference to truth and to genuine value that unswerving loyalty is an obligation, and a virtue. In regard to all errors and negative values (that is, evils in the widest sense of the term, but particularly in a morally relevant sense) we have, on the contrary, the duty to break with what we formerly cherished and to withdraw our allegiance from them, once we know them to be false and negative in value. Indeed, the obligation of fidelity in a formal and automatic sense must not hamper our readiness to separate ourselves from such ideals or convictions, once we have serious reasons to doubt their validity. There is only one fidelity to which we are absolutely committed: that is, fidelity towards God, the epitome of all values, and towards everything that represents God and is instrumental to us in approaching Him.

Fidelity to persons vs. fidelity to ideas

This truth is frequently obscured by considerations of this order: "I should, after all, remain faithful to a person whom I have loved, even though I cannot help discovering many negative values in him." By analogy, it is inferred that an obligation of fidelity exists also in regard to ideas, intellectual milieus, and cultural atmospheres which have formerly meant a great deal to us and have become traditional with us. In reality, however, the situation is quite different in regard to ideological entities than it is in regard to persons. A person, *in statu viae*, is never something as definitively and univocally fixed (concerning his significance and value) as is an idea or an ideal. A person may grow and unfold, he may reform and perfect himself along lines essentially unlimited in their design. Every human being incarnates a divine thought, and it is to this that my love for him in its decisive spiritual aspect is directed. Hence, I may keep in communion with him even though there be revealed to me an entirely new and higher world: for the latter may make a more basic objective appeal to him also, and that appeal may yet be carried to him actually.

Moreover, all relationships between persons involve a kind of immanent promise which, however tacit, generates a binding mutual claim; whereas in our relationships with nonpersonal entities that specific note is naturally absent. All interpersonal relations are fraught with a kind of immanent obligation; the specific character of obligation differs according to the essential quality and the objective meaning of the relationship in question; but in any such relationship a claim to fidelity remains. It is not so with our relations to ideal entities and other nonpersonal things.

Nevertheless, true fidelity towards a person may on occasion impose on us the duty to withdraw altogether from contact with him. In the case where he would constitute a threat to our fidelity to God, and when we on the other hand feel powerless to help him, our breaking off relations with him is still consistent with our true fidelity towards him: it is destined to promote his spiritual good as well as our own, and is therefore involved in our very love for him so far as love in a higher and ultimate sense implies, above all, responsibility.

Frequently, however, the concept of fidelity towards persons is transferred uncritically to the world of ideas. The unfortunate figure of speech, *the Faith of our fathers*, is misleading as to the motive for our fidelity towards the Faith; for what can be decisive in this case is only the *truth* of the Faith, and not the accident that *our fathers* already happened to believe in it. If this were not so, paganism in its turn could or should never have been supplanted by Christianity. Fidelity to ideas as such is neutral in value only so long as we abstract from the question *what* ideas are at stake. In reality, there is only one fidelity which is a strict duty: fidelity to truth, fidelity towards Christ.

Dangers of fidelity to false ideals

Not only is fidelity towards errors and false ideals a mistaken attitude; we are also bound to dissolve the bonds that unite us with such cultural or human milieus as cannot withstand the test of confrontation with Christ. Often we cherish certain old and familiar things, ensconcing ourselves in them as in a kind of home, merely because we have lived so long with them, and particularly because they are connected with many memories of our childhood.

27

Thus, we suffer the world of Christ to penetrate us with its light only so far as it does not interfere with our safe residence in that *putative* "home." There is also the danger of attempting so to redraw and to humanize the face of Christ that it may fit into the features of that home.

Many such humanizations and sentimental falsifications are to be found in so-called popular piety, and are expressed even in certain hymns. We must have the readiness to relinquish such all-too-human substitutes, however comfortable we may feel them. We must be filled with the desire to look into the unfalsified countenance of Christ as shown by the Church in her liturgy. We must long to be lifted by Christ into His world, not try to drag Him down into ours. Whatever is of genuine value and appropriate to His world we shall receive back from Him transfigured and resplendent with a new light.

Readiness to change is the core of our response to God

On the measure of our readiness to change depends the measure of our transformation in Christ. Unreserved readiness is an indispensable precondition of the *conception* of Christ in our souls and it must endure with undiminished vigor all along the path of our transformation. Beyond that, however, as we have seen, it constitutes a central response to Revelation, to God's epiphany in Christ, and to the call He has issued to us; and therefore, a high virtue by itself.

The significance and the value of such an attitude also appear from the fact that the better a man's inward condition and the more he feels touched by God the wider the doors of his heart will be opened and the readier he will show himself for being changed. Whenever, on the contrary, some baser impulse gets the upper hand in a man's soul, he will shut himself up, and the doors will close again. He will harden and attempt to maintain himself.

There is a deep nexus between a kind, unrestrained attitude in general, and the state of fluidity, openness, and receptivity to formative action from above. Still more is the act of free inward surrender to God inseparable from that state of fluidity and receptivity; whereas, by bolting ourselves up and entrenching ourselves in our nature we stifle in our souls the growth of the germs implanted by God, and an opposition to higher appeals will consequently arise in all domains.

The readiness to change is an essential aspect of the Christian's basic relation with God; it forms the core of our response to the merciful love of God which bends down upon us: "With eternal charity hath God loved us; so He hath drawn us, lifted from the earth, to His merciful heart" (Antiphon of Praise, Feast of the Sacred Heart). To us all has the inexorable yet beatifying call of Christ been addressed: *Sequere me* ("Follow Me"). Nor do we follow it unless, relinquishing everything, we say with St. Paul: "Lord, what wilt Thou have me to do?" (Acts 9:6).

2

Contrition

THE initial step of the soul's meeting with God bears the mark of contrition. The man whose heart is smitten by the word of Christ, whom Jesus' face has brought to his knees, will at first say with St. Peter: "Depart from me, for I am a sinful man, O Lord" (Luke 5:8). Confrontation of our own selves with God renders us conscious of our unworthiness and sinfulness.

That consciousness of sin fills us with pain: the guilt we have incurred burns our souls. Thus, with a contrite heart we fall on our knees before God, exclaiming: "To Thee only have I sinned, and have done evil before Thee."

It is in repenting our sins that we expressly repudiate evil, and revert to God. By the same token we also experience our sin turning in enmity against us: "My sin is always against me" (Ps. 50:5). Without this basic revocation of our offenses against God there can be no genuine surrender to Him; without a radical breach with our past sins we can evince no readiness to be transformed by God, nor obey Christ's call, *sequere me.* It is true penitence, it is contrition alone which thus melts the encrusted heart so that that fluidity of which we have spoken becomes possible — and with it, reformation by Christ.

What is the essence, however, of true penitence?

Bad conscience is not the same as contrition

There exists a kind of bad conscience which must be sharply distinguished from penitence. We can well imagine a sinner who, without being really penitent, suffers from a guilty conscience. He is oppressed with pangs of conscience: he is aware of acting badly, and that awareness disturbs his peace and deprives him of inner harmony. Yet, he still refuses to capitulate; he seeks to benumb his conscience, and clings to solidarity with his sins. This kind of sinner is typified by Macbeth, while sinners like Richard III or Don Giovanni are not bothered by remorse at all. But remorse as such may involve no *metanoia*, no change of heart. In spite of his bad conscience, a man may refuse to shift his position: he may persevere in deliberate identity with himself as the author of his sins and, much though they oppress him, heap new sins upon the old ones. He may harden his heart against remorse, being loath to reverse his path.

Contrition requires a repudiation of our past sins

In contradistinction to that attitude of soul, true penitence means a definite revulsion from one's sins, and active repudiation of them. It means a disavowal of the past, a relinquishment of one's former position with its implication of sinning. He who is seized by contrition repudiates his former self, and abandons his former position completely. He quits the fortress of self-assertion, and casts off his armor. He humiliates himself, and submits to the voice of his conscience. The very disharmony which reigns in his soul will be changed in its quality when he experiences contrition. The dull, passive feeling of depression, poisoned with the note of inner discord and disintegration that results essentially from sin as such, will yield its place to the vivid pain with which the person now reacts to his sin. His heart is transpierced by that pain; but at the same time it is already illuminated by a ray of yearning toward the Good.

Contrition implies that we not only deplore the sin we have committed but condemn it expressly, denouncing, as it were, our allegiance to it. We would revoke the wrong we have perpetrated. But immediately the consciousness of our impotence to do so will dawn upon us: for we are not at liberty to undo the guilt engendered by our deed. We feel clearly that our change of heart and our new orientation are unable to dissolve the sin and to erase the guilt. Therefore, unless it implies hope for God's mercy, contrition must lead to despair. Judas' contrition was of this kind.

Contrition involves our surrender to God's mercy

In true Christian penitence, there is always present a positive relation to God, grafted on the negation of sin. It forms in us an attitude of self-effacement before God, and of surrender to Him. We are willing to do penance and to make atonement for our sins; we offer ourselves to God so as to receive our just punishment, whatever it be, from His hands. Moreover, we seize, as it were, the spear of atonement that is to transfix us, and cooperate with the gesture that represents God's reaction to our sins. Yet, confiding in God's mercy which will open to us the path of reconciliation with Him, and believing in His power to erase all guilt of sin, we also ask in penitence for His forgiveness.

True penitence makes appeal to God's mercy, and solicits from Him the forgiveness of sin. While the Christian knows that penitence by itself is unable to abolish the guilt, he also knows that "the Lamb of God hath taken away all sins"; and that for Christ's sake a merciful and almighty God, Who alone has the power of absolving from guilt, will pardon all who with a contrite heart confess their guilt unto Him. That turning away from sin which is implicit in penitence also means, therefore, a *return* toward God: a flight

33

toward the refuge which is God's mercy. Though we are conscious of having no claim to pardon — as was the Prodigal Son, saying: "Father, I have sinned against heaven, and before thee: I am not worthy to be called thy son" (Luke 15:18-19) — at the same time we put our trust in the incomprehensible forbearance and mercifulness of God. Such was the penitence of David after his sin with Uriah's wife (as contrasted to Adam's consciousness of guilt, who after his fall, hid himself from God, and sought to flee from Him). Such, again, was the penitence of St. Peter after his denial of Christ, when the loving glance of Jesus transpierced his heart.

Christian contrition yearns for reconciliation with God

While the hope of reconciliation with God and His forgiveness of our guilt is not, properly speaking, an element of contrition as such, it is essentially formative of the *Christian's* contrition distinguishing it sharply from genuine repentance of the purely natural order. The pain inherent in the consciousness of sin will not decrease thereby: on the contrary, in facing the infinite charity and mercy of God it cannot but be greatly intensified. The pain, though deeper, will be more lightly colored, as it were, and assume a quality of limpidity: it becomes a liberating pain of love. It is **this** kind of contrition only which calls forth tears: to the dull contrition of despair, the gift of liberation which lies in weeping is denied; it may excite, at most, tears of rage against oneself. We may contrast the tears with which St. Mary Magdalene washed the feet of the Lord with that dry, despairing, dull contrition of a Judas which does not make the heart bleed but petrifies it.

Besides the pain aroused by contemplation of past sins, true penitence also implies a longing for reconciliation with God, and a desire to walk once more in His paths. Thus, it contains not merely a reference to the past but a direction to the future as well. That deep desire no more to separate ourselves from God is

34

immanent to the change of heart which underlies penitence. True, the concrete decision with God is not yet effected; nor is man able to obtain that reconciliation by his own force: it can be achieved by God alone.

Contrition also renounces future sins

Nevertheless, penitence implies more than the condemnation of sins committed, and the gesture of their renunciation. It implies more than the desire, ineffective by itself, to undo them. In addition to the inherent silent words, "How could I do this?" true penitence also implies these further words, "I will never do this again" — that is to say, the renunciation of sin even in regard to the future. Certainly this element is not present in full actuality; the reference to the past is formally predominant. Still, inasmuch as it involves an essential renunciation of sin, penitence is also implicitly directed towards the future.

Repudiation of past sins is the very essence of contrition

This must not delude us, however, into undervaluing that repudiation of the past which is the prime characteristic of contrition, and which renders it a *sine qua non* of true inner conversion. People who believe it sufficient to do no wrong henceforth, while simply passing over their record of wrongdoings, will not truly reform. The amended conduct they may display for the time being has something accidental about it. Being blind to the necessity of accepting responsibility for their past misdeeds, and claiming as it were a right of prescription in regard to moral wrongs, they cannot have attained to a conscious relationship with the world of moral values nor grasped the inexorable demand which emanates from that world. Such persons have not yet reached the stage of moral adulthood. They have not yet seized the basic truth that man is not responsible for his present behavior alone; that, according to the continuity which is essential to him, he remains in solidarity with everything he has done until he disavows it *expressly*. When such people say, "Why should we bother about past things, since we can no longer alter them?," they merely prove that the call embodied in the world of moral values, which also requires a disavowal of things that can no longer be undone, is still past their understanding. A genuine moral awakening and a genuine movement toward God necessarily involve an active position toward wrongs perpetrated at a former period. True contrition is impossible without arousing pain by the memory of each sin taken singly, together with one's former attitude in general, and without an express repudiation of past deeds.

Contrition requires us to seek God's pardon

Nor is this all. A real change of heart also demands our consciousness of the fact that we cannot obtain a reconciliation with God until the wrong is forgiven by Him, and atoned for by us. He who is really converted to God, and in His sight suddenly understands his former position, also understands that his guilt *separates* him from God. He is unreconciled with God so long as that guilt subsists, and lacks the power to conjure it away by himself. He knows that his repentance and remorse by themselves, his disavowal of transgressions committed, his breach with his former life and his search for a new orientation are insufficient to pull down the partition wall erected by his guilt which separates him from God. He knows that the guilt cannot be abolished except by divine forgiveness, and that it is Christ Who "taketh away the sins of the world" and, finally, that Christ spoke to St. Peter the words: "Whatsoever thou shalt loose on earth, it shall be loosed also in heaven" (Matt. 16:19). The Christian knows that God has granted him the great gift of grace which is the sacrament of Penance. He has the certainty that, if he penitently confesses his sins to the minister of God, Christ will erase his guilt, and will bridge the chasm that separates him, as a sinner, from God. He knows that absolution by the priest clears away the obstacle to the unfolding of supernatural life in his soul, thus raising him once more to the state of grace.

Objectively, even, contrition as such involves a radical inward change (and a change that cannot be accomplished without contrition). The painful evocation and condemnation of past sins, the groping for a new basis of orientation, the movement of reconversion to God — these aspects by themselves testify to an essential inward change. But all this is far from being equivalent to an abolition of the *guilt* incurred. The disuniting effect of the latter persists, and continues to lie in the path of a reconciliation with God. That guilt can only be eliminated by God's act of pardon, and be compensated for by the blood of Christ, of which it is said in the hymn of St. Thomas: "Of which a single drop, for sinners spilt, can purge the entire world from all its guilt."

The sacrament of Penance, strictly speaking, is not indispensable for redeeming man from his guilt. In regard to a venial sin, the act of repentance itself may be an adequate substitute for the sacrament; in regard to a grave sin, an act of perfect contrition may similarly suffice, provided that confession is impracticable — just as in the baptism of desire and the baptism of blood, an inner act and a heroic action, respectively, may stand for the sacrament of Baptism. But even in such cases it is not the indwelling force of the human act of penitence as such which abolishes the guilt: this is done, always and solely, by Christ through His death on the Cross. The change of heart, as implied in contrition, merely opens the path for the influx of the redeeming blood of Christ. Penitence reestablishes the link with Christ, by virtue of which the fruits of Christ's deed of redemption may be applied to us.

Even the penitence of the Prophets, and of all those who lived before Christ, did not achieve the removal of guilt on its own strength: here, too, the forgiveness of guilt was due to the redeeming sacrifice of Christ.

Contrition contributes to a deeper change of heart

Yet, while penitence as such is incapable of actually *securing absolution from sin*, it does possess (as we have seen) an *objective* efficacy for inward change, which is specific to it and which has no substitute. *Subjectively*, however — concerning the penitent's own state of consciousness, that is to say — he must be dominated by the feeling that without the abolition of his guilt even his change of heart as such would lack reality, and that all his desire for becoming *another man* would remain ineffectual unless his guilt be taken away first by the blood of Christ. It should be clearly understood that it is precisely this subjective consciousness which conditions the *objective* reality of the change of heart implied in penitence. We encounter here one of those mysterious paradoxes of the spiritual life to which Revelation alone provides us with the key, and to which the eyes of the world will ever remain blind. They are all intimately related to these words of Jesus: "Every one that exalteth himself, shall be humbled: and he that humbleth himself, shall be exalted" (Luke 18:14).

Contrition involves the yearning for sanctification

True penitence involves, furthermore, a burning desire not only for forgiveness of the guilt of sin but for purification and sanctification, as well as the belief in their accomplishment by the grace of God. The prayer for pardon and for purification, and the *resolve* never again to separate ourselves from God in the future proceed therefrom. There also exists a passive form of penitence which includes hope for God's mercy and pardon, but not for purification and sanctification. In his false humility, this kind of penitent considers himself so hopelessly sinful that he dismisses the belief in his emendation as presumptuous. It would seem to him that he can do no better than commend himself, in all his sinfulness, to the mercy of God, and endure all the misery of sin with patience. In its Lutheran version, the dogmatic concept of justification appears to foster such a purely passive repentance. For Luther knows no purification and sanctification but merely a non-imputation of our sins for the sake of Christ. This purely passive repentance — the contrary extreme, as it were, to that other error of considering a good resolution for the future sufficient, and contrition superfluous — generates no resolution to begin a new life in Christ.

Yet, he who is filled with true penitence will not only say to God: "Turn away Thy face from my sins, and blot out all my iniquities," but continue thus: "Create a clean heart in me, O God: and renew a right spirit within my bowels....Restore unto me the joy of Thy salvation, and strengthen me with a perfect spirit." The true Christian, though mindful of the fact that left to himself he would fall again and again, also knows that in Baptism he has received from Christ a supernatural principle of holy life, and that through God's grace he shall — and can — become a new man. He knows that God wills his cooperation in this process of transformation: "He Who hath created thee without thee, will not justify thee without thee" (St. Augustine, *Sermo* 169.13).

Contrition does not paralyze the Christian, nor does it deprive him of fortitude. In his act of penitence he will contemplate, not so much his own weakness as the merciful arms of God that are extended to receive him into His holiness, and the force that rises in him once he throws himself into the arms of God. He knows contrition to be the necessary *precondition* to any purification and sanctification, seeing that any resolve not born of the pain of contrition is condemned to shallowness and sterility because it is not rooted in the ultimate depths of the soul nor conceived out of an ultimate surrender to God. Contrition alone may thus melt our hearts so as to enable us to receive and preserve the imprint of a basic new orientation towards God.

The true Christian says with David, "A sacrifice to God is an afflicted spirit: a contrite and humbled heart, O God, Thou wilt not despise" (Ps. 50:19). From contrition thus experienced there will arise in him the genuine and heroic determination to become a new man. That kind of contrition alone enables him again to anchor himself in God. It is against the background of his weakness and wretchedness that he forms the resolution, cleansed of all illusions and conceived in holy sobriety, never again to separate himself from God, that he assumes the holy courage to *put off*, with God's help, *the old man*, and to *put on the new man in Christ*.

"Lord God, King of heaven and earth: deign to guide and to sanctify, to direct and to govern today our hearts and our bodies, our thoughts, our words and our works according to Thy law and in fulfillment of Thy mandates: so that with Thy help we become saved and free, here and in eternity, Savior of the world" (Prayer from the Prime of the Breviary).

Contrition is a form of radical self-surrender

The aspect which is entirely specific to true penitence is that of radical self-surrender. Pride and obduracy melt away. The natural tendency to self-assertion which is otherwise so firmly fixed in our nature — and which makes us reluctant to admit a wrong we have done or to ask a person whom we have wronged to forgive us — is renounced by the penitent. He surrenders himself in humble charity. The tight impermeability of his soul toward God and his fellow creatures disappears. The spasm of dogmatic obstinacy, forcing him always to defend his position, is relaxed. He assumes a state of mind receptive to the Good in all its forms; he divests himself of all self-preservation to the point of full defenselessness.

Contrition awakens our soul in its depths

But to that moral process in breadth, as it were, corresponds a no less decisive one in depth. Contrition arouses us from the sleep of unspiritual existence, from what might be called a mere *living away*. It awakens us to a keen consciousness of the things that ultimately matter: the metaphysical situation of man, considered in its full gravity; our status under God's law, and our character as confronted with Him; the task and the responsibility imposed on us by God; the importance of our earthly life for our eternal destiny. Contrition causes us to withdraw from our peripheral interests and to concentrate on the depths. It is in contrition that we respond to the infinite *holiness* of our absolute Lord, the eternal Judge, whose judgment we cannot evade; and on the other hand, to our own *sinfulness*.

Contrition imparts moral beauty to the soul

That is why contrition embodies the primal word of fallen man addressing God. Not only is it indispensable for our transformation in Christ and our acquisition of that fluid quality which renders us susceptible of such a transformation; it also imparts to the soul of man a unique character of beauty. For it is in contrition that the new fundamental attitude of a humble and reverent charity becomes dominant and manifest, that man abandons the fortress of pride and self-sovereignty, and leaves the dreamland of levity and complacency, repairing to the place where he faces God *in reality*.

Therefore did Our Lord speak the words: "Even so there shall be joy in heaven upon one sinner that doeth penance, more than upon ninety-nine just who need not penance" (Luke 15:7). By *the just* are meant neither the saints on the one hand nor the Pharisees on the other, but persons who, while leading a correct life and avoiding all transgressions in the strict sense of the term, never come to achieve that full surrender to God which (in a humanity tainted with original sin) is possible in contrition alone. Such persons are anxious to keep God's commandments but they never discover the immense, unbridgeable abyss that separates the holiness of God from our sinfulness. Full self-surrender and the renunciation of all self-assertion (however hidden); the spiritual position of standing *naked* before God and throwing oneself altogether upon His mercy — these are things beyond their range of experience. They fail to become entirely conscious of the metaphysical situation of man; they never so radically relinquish their own selves as does man in the throes of contrition; they never open themselves so unreservedly in humility and charity, nor do they ever assess the full gravity of our destiny before the face of God. They never descend so low as to be lifted up by God.

With this type of *just* persons, we may contrast the image of Mary Magdalene the public sinner, as she, stricken to her knees by the sight of Jesus, washes His feet with her tears. We perceive the new life nascent in her contrite soul. We sense the response of her heart, softened by the melting fire of humility and charity. It is to her, the repentant sinner, and not to Simon who sat beside Him in the consciousness of not having offended God, that Jesus spoke: "Thy faith hath made thee safe, go in peace" (Luke 7:50). And *she* it was who before all others was found worthy to announce to the Apostles the Resurrection of the Lord.

3

Self-Knowledge

IF unconditional readiness to change and true penitence constitute the first foundations of our progress towards the goal which God's mercy has assigned to us — our transformation in Christ — the next decisive step along that road is the acquisition of self-knowledge.

Self-knowledge is prerequisite to our inner reformation

So long as a man is ignorant of his defects and of their real nature, all his endeavor (be it ever so laudable) to overcome those defects will end in failure. Not infrequently we meet persons who, while sincerely bent on reforming, direct all their attention to merely imaginary faults of theirs, thus fighting against windmills and leaving their real defects untouched. In monastic life this danger is prevented by the discipline specific to a religious order. By his superior to whom he owes obedience, the monk's attention is directed to his real shortcomings and imperfections (including potential dangers) even before he is clearly aware of them himself. The monk or nun begins the struggle with his or her nature in a spirit of obedience, fighting this or that defect according to the superior's instructions, though perhaps at first unaware of its actual presence. Herein lies one of the great means for the process of transformation with which monastic life provides the individual. Nevertheless, the final accomplishment of our transformation — the total uprooting of our vices, the levelling of hills and filling up of valleys — requires a thorough knowledge of our defects. We must beware of neglecting the basic part played by intelligence in our psychic life. For all volitional acts are conditioned by cognitive apprehension. The radical extirpation of a defect of character requires an interior knowledge of that defect. To be sure, we are not likely to attain true self-knowledge unless we are already engaged in combatting our bad qualities, though it be from obedience only to extrinsic authority. Still, in order to bring that fight to a successful close, from a certain stage onwards we must be equipped with an interior knowledge of our faults: for not otherwise can we overcome them in a radical and comprehensive sense.

Neutral self-knowledge does not help moral progress

However, the term *self-knowledge* may refer to rather different things. While true self-knowledge is an important instrument of sanctification, there is also such a thing as a spurious and sterile kind of self-knowledge which is apt to ensnare us into an attitude of egotism far worse than the natural one.

Whenever we take a purely psychological interest in ourselves and thus analyze our character in the manner of mere spectators, we pursue a false and sterile self-knowledge. We then envisage our character not by any standard of good and evil, but in entire neutrality as though we were analyzing some phenomenon of exterior nature. We leave our solidarity with our character to one side, and look upon ourselves as though we were observing some odd stranger. The fact that the person in question happens to be ourselves merely intensifies our curiosity, without changing its quality. We experience ourselves as we would a character in a novel, without in any way feeling responsible for his defects. Nay, as it will presently be shown, such an attitude prevents us altogether from comprehending those defects in their specific moral meaning and import. For, given an essentially amoral frame of reference (as implied by the pursuit of neutral self-knowledge), we are of necessity precluded from consideration of the true significance of our person. First, we are denied the capacity to understand completely a person as such. So far as a person is concerned — that is, a free being capable of rational behavior for which its relationship with God and the world of values is basic and constitutive — appropriate presentation itself is inseparable from appreciation. Secondly, we are even less able to take an adequate view of our own person in regard to the fact that it is our own, since our method of analysis debars us from experiencing responsibility for that person's conduct. This method involves a fundamental falsification of the perspective in which to place our object of research. It is an arbitrary mutilation of our pattern of comprehension which is sure to warp our vision and to distort our picture.

This type of self-knowledge is not rooted in any willingness to change, and so it is completely sterile from the standpoint of moral progress. People who are wont to diagnose their blemishes in this neutral and purely psychological mood will draw from such discoveries no increased power to overcome their defects. On the contrary, such an indolently neutral self-knowledge will make them even more inclined to resign themselves to those defects as a matter of course. They are more remote from the chance of curing those ills than they would be if they knew nothing about them. They are often disposed to admit their faults overtly, without restraint or reticence: not however from the motive of humility, nor under the impulse of guilt-consciousness, but because they pique themselves on presenting their vices, a psychologically absorbing sight.

Psychoanalysis reveals a similarly sterile and destructive conception of self-knowledge. Its adherents believe themselves to possess a particular capacity for objective self-knowledge, thanks to their elimination of all value viewpoints and their methodic principle of treating matters of intimate human psychology as objects of pure science. The truth is that such a neutrality of outlook, being completely out of tune with the subject treated, precludes the exploration of the depths of personality, and makes adequate self-knowledge impossible. The real nature of a person's attitudes and decisions and of their spiritual origins can only be comprehended by us if we take our departure from the dialogic situation between subject and object: interpreting his object-references as *acts of response*. And that remains true, of course, if the person in question is ourselves. Once we disregard the content of meaning and value of the object to which our attitudes are directed, the very meaning of the attitude itself will become impenetrable to our gaze and all our hypotheses as to its origins will be mere arbitrary guesswork devoid of reality.

Thus, any scientific approach in the sense of a purely immanent psychology (built on a disregard of that constitutive trait of object-reference) must fail. It is doomed to fall short of achieving anything like an adequate self-knowledge. Unless we take account of the object that affects us and elicits a response on our part, we are essentially incapable of a pertinent analysis of our experiences. The obsession with a neutral approach brings in its train a general disfigurement of what we pretend to describe faithfully. Everything is flattened out and deprived of its dimension of depth; our deliberate blindness to the inherent meaning of a psychic act compels us to interpret it in terms of mechanical causation, thus dismissing the essential and holding onto the accidental, if not the imaginary.

The inadequacy of this kind of self-knowledge is confirmed by the test of its application to psychotherapy, which has proved highly unsuccessful. If diagnosis itself is dependent on a consideration of the intentional relation to the object, the same is even truer with respect to the overcoming of faults even if they be envisaged from a medical rather than from a moral point of view. What matters most, however, is the complete inability of this method of approach to provide us with any knowledge of a really decisive kind concerning the question as to whether or not a quality, a disposition, or an attitude is positive in value and can stand the test of confrontation with God. That neutral way of looking on things presents to us a shadowy counterpart of the real situation, devoid of the latter's inherent gravity. The awful problem, with its immense burden of responsibility, as to whether our conduct offends God or conforms to the divine order, is degraded to a psychologically interesting affair. Such a sterilized self-knowledge, empty of repentance and guilt-consciousness, is absolutely unfit for invigorating our endeavor to weed out our vices and debilities.

Fruitful self-knowledge calls us to a confrontation with God

The only fruitful self-knowledge, and the only true one, is that which grows out of man's self-confrontation with God. We must first look at God and His immeasurable glory, and then put the question: "Who art Thou, and who am I?" We must speak with St. Augustine: "Could I but know Thee, I should know myself." It is only in recognition of our metaphysical situation, only in awareness of our destiny and our vocation that we can become truly cognizant of ourselves. Only the light of God and His challenge to us can open our eyes to all our shortcomings and deficiencies, impressing upon us the discrepancy between what we ought to be and what we are. Contemplation of one's own self in this light is animated by a profound earnestness; it is vastly different from all species of a neutral and purely psychological self-analysis.

He who seeks for self-knowledge in that true sense of the word regards his own nature, not as an unchangeable datum or a curiosity to be studied without any implication of responsibility, but as a thing which demands to be changed, and for whose qualities and manifestations he is accountable. Self-knowledge in this sense presupposes the readiness to change. We take an interest in what we are *because* we are determined to become new men in Christ. Here is no place for idle curiosity, nor for the egoistic fixation on oneself as a paramount theme. It is *for the sake of God* that we would become better men; and because we would become so we inquire about our present state and condition. That basic attitude of a solemn confrontation with God — the motif which in a unique way pervades the Liturgy of the Church — is fitted, better than any other, to make us sensitive to values and to present us with a picture of our defects stripped of any illusions. It is an attitude which we cannot maintain while playing, at the same time, the part of unconcerned spectators. It presupposes a penitent disposition; and, in its turn, necessarily gives birth to contrition: in the *Confiteor* it finds its supreme expression.

Readiness to change renders self-knowledge fruitful

Self-knowledge thus understood, as contrasted with its false counterpart, is not destructive but fruitful. Because it is founded in our readiness to change, it implies the discovery of any defect of ours to be the first step towards its elimination. However painfully the revelation of the patches of darkness in our soul may affect us, it will always lack the discouraging and depressing effect which in the context of mere natural self-knowledge would attend disagreeable revelations. For, referring all truth to God Who is the prime source and the epitome of Truth as such, we shall derive happiness from the knowledge of any important truth, however painful its content may be, since by the very fact of its possession we progress one step nearer towards God. Our illusions about ourselves are dispelled. We no longer deceive ourselves with fanciful beliefs concerning our character; we master our proud reluctance to take account of this or that unpleasant feature in our souls, and this means a great gain secured, a new level of freedom attained. This emancipation from our pride, which is always busy imposing upon us, cannot but prove a source of bliss and elevation.

Again, if we are inspired by that unconditional readiness to change, we certainly shall be happy to know where there is work to be done. We shall then experience self-knowledge as a first step towards the goal of our transformation, in that it indicates the foe we must fight most urgently. Many sincere efforts are squandered, many energies are wasted, much time is lost because we fight against windmills, and look for our defects where they do not exist. Many of us suspect that the chief danger threatens from a direction which in fact harbors no such danger, whereas we fail to discern what really is our besetting sin.

We must appreciate it as a great gift of grace from God when He opens our eyes to the actual danger, and shows us where the battle has to be fought. We ought to feel a boundless gratitude to those who rudely destroy our illusions concerning our person. It is good to be enlightened about the fact, for instance, that enthusiasm felt for a virtue is by no means tantamount to the possession of that virtue. Thus, viewed from a distance, obedience appears to us as a great and glorious thing: hence, we may believe ourselves in possession of the real willingness to obey, while in fact we still have to cover a long and laborious road to get there.

Or again, we feel our heart aflame with the splendid and touching beauty of humility, and so we indulge in the fictitious belief that we are actually humble. We mistake our enthusiasm for a virtue for its real presence in us. Undoubtedly, the enthusiasm we have spoken of is good in itself and may mean a beginning of participation in the virtue to which it refers, but it is far remote from the actual possession of that virtue. The shattering of such illusions obviously pains our nature. Yet at the same time, it must fill our hearts with holy joy, for it means that God has freed us from the obnoxious fetters of error, and we have achieved a real step towards the acquisition of those virtues.

Faith protects us from the despair that self-knowledge can sometimes bring

Still, can we avoid becoming a prey to despondency, when we peer into the dark abysses of our failures? Will not our zeal abate, our vigor be paralyzed, when we see how remote we still are from our goal, and how much lower we rank than we have supposed? Can anyone acquire a clear insight into his inner wounds and weaknesses without becoming discouraged? Certainly, self-knowledge — be it even conceived *in conspectu Dei* — may result in discouragement and despondency, on the supposition that our general attitude still remains a purely natural one.

The true Christian, however, who lives by the Faith, will not be driven to such utter despair by self-knowledge, nor collapse under the weight of his own sins when sensing their import and magnitude. For he knows that God wills his sanctification; that Christ, "in whom we have redemption through His blood, the remission of sins" (Col. 1:14), has called him, and laid His hand upon him.

In defiance of all his sins and all the darkness in him, he will say with St. Thomas Aquinas: "O Loving Pelican, Lord Jesus, wash me clean in Thy blood." He knows that he can accomplish nothing through his own power but *everything* in Christ.

Not by his own force shall he span the abyss that yawns between him and God: Christ shall carry him over, if he is willing to follow Him without reserve. By His light, there is no darkness that cannot be dispelled, nay, even changed into radiating brightness. "Darkness shall not be dark to Thee, and night shall be light as the day" (Ps. 138:12).

We must strive continually for self-knowledge

True self-knowledge is an ineluctable necessity for him who desires to be transformed in Christ. He must be filled with a real thirst for securing, *in conspectu Dei*, an accurate notion of himself, such as he is; he must endeavor to get rid of all illusions of complacency, and to detect his particular vices and weaknesses. He must conform to the summons of St. Catherine of Siena, "Let us enter into the cell of our self-knowledge." But he must not believe that self-knowledge is easy of attainment, nor that — once he forms the desire for self-knowledge — all his defects will reveal themselves to him in due course. With a healthy distrust of himself, he should continue supposing that he is still entangled in a mesh of illusions, and pray: "Cleanse me of my hidden weaknesses."

Obedience to his spiritual director or his religious superior, above all, is destined to guide him towards the acquisition of genuine self-knowledge and the freedom implied therein. He must be aware of the fact that in order to obtain a faithful portrait of himself he needs the help of others. He must remember the words of the Lord about the mote in our brother's eye and the beam in our own; and admit that, trusting his own lights without proper guidance, he will remain a thrall to this blindness of fallen man concerning himself. That is why he cannot dispense with the more objective vision of a spiritual director, of a religious superior, of any friend of great wisdom and piety. Yet, much as he depends — in order to attain a true knowledge of his character — on the help of God and on that of his fellow men, one thing he must contribute *himself*: the unreserved determination of dying unto himself and becoming a new man in Christ, and the strong desire, proceeding therefrom, to see himself as he really is. That desire will impel him to pray: "Lord, that I may see" (Luke 18:41).

4

True Consciousness

THE inward progress in the Christian's life is linked to a process of awakening to an ever increasing degree of consciousness. Conversion itself is comparable to an emergence from a state of somnolence. In rising from self-contained worldliness towards the reality of God, in experiencing the metaphysical situation in which God has placed him and the new light in which all things and his own self are now appearing, the person attains to a new level of consciousness. The convert, in Cardinal Newman's words, is like a man ascending from a mine to behold daylight for the first time. He looks back upon his former life as a state of somnolence, a twilight of semiconsciousness.

Types of false consciousness

Again, with our unreserved decision to imitate Christ, a new brand of consciousness will necessarily permeate our life. However, there are many kinds of consciousness, only one of which will constitute the proper mark of our process of transformation in Christ. There also exists a false kind of consciousness which tends to corrode our interior life, and which is definitely opposed to true consciousness. Before discussing this true Christian consciousness, which indeed marks the "measure of the age of the fullness of Christ" (Eph. 4:13), we must first identify and discard that false way of being conscious.

Its prime characteristic is this. The man who is falsely conscious is no longer capable of full response to an object or situation. His mind is no longer able to sense the substance of things or of situations, nor the appeal which emanates from them; the normal contact between subject and object appears severed. We may distinguish two basic forms of this false type of consciousness.

First, there is the mental perversion which consists in the fact that we destroy the attitude of genuine absorption in the object by an excess of reflective self-observation.

Secondly, there is the tendency to over-intellectualism, implying that even in a situation which calls upon us to decide or to act rather than merely to know, we persevere in a purely cognitive attitude.

Excessive self-observation

We begin with the description of the first form of false consciousness. There is a type of person whose glance is always turned back upon his own self, and who is therefore incapable of any genuine conforming to the spirit of an object. If, for instance, he is listening to some beautiful music, he at once develops an awareness of his own reaction, and thus loses the possibility of a genuine response to that beautiful music. It is implicit in the normal manifestations of the human mind, so far as they are directed to the object, that we should do full justice to the given object and should in experiencing joy and sorrow, enthusiasm and indignation, love and hatred, not glance back upon our own attitude but solely upon the object towards which an attitude is directed. Once this normal rhythm is broken and we squint back at our own behavior, we shall be out of touch with the object; it will cease to address us really and hence our response to it will itself become destroyed. A dramatic work will necessarily fail to move us if we are watching ourselves sitting in the theater or if we consider the actors on the scene as actors, not as the characters they impersonate.

By the same token, we cannot experience real joy if, instead of abandoning ourselves to the joyful event, we are absorbed by our interest in our own psychic state of joyfulness. When we are thus falsely conscious, we are permanently condemned to be our own spectators. We see ourselves from outside and thereby poison all genuine life within us. For all genuine entering into an object requires that in a sense we forget ourselves. Only then do we achieve a real contact with things and with their inherent meaning.

The way in which we become conscious of a mental act is intrinsically different from the way in which we become conscious of an object; to the latter only does the phrase *conscious of something* properly apply. Our mental movements unfold along two fundamental dimensions: one is the intentional direction to an object, an object we grasp meaningfully, an object which confronts us and reveals its character and qualities to us. This is had when we look at a house, for example. On the other hand, there is the consciousness of a cognitive or emotional act which is in no way our object but which takes place inside us or in which we manifest ourselves — for instance, the act of rejoicing in something.

To be sure, our own attitude can itself be made an object subsequently; it can be apprehended in reflection. Yet, while we are performing a mental act we cannot but destroy that act if we withdraw our attention from the object which has elicited it and make our own attitude an object instead.

Our attitudes depend on their being kindled by the values of the object. These acts are essentially *intentional*, that is to say, directed to the object and we must genuinely respond without turning back on ourselves. That is the reason why no one who, instead of being fully absorbed in the beloved person and that person's beauty, is always busied with himself and his own emotion, will ever love in the true sense of the word.

This false consciousness of self will cause us to remain *outside* of all situations in which we are involved, excluded from participation in their meaning and content. On occasion this anomaly may attain a pathological degree. This omnipresence of reflection results in a nipping in the bud of all genuine contact with objects. This is particularly true of the hysterical, who are incapable of all genuine object-relationship, because they are continually engrossed in their own attitude.

Psychoanalysis is not only unfit to cure this morbid self-consciousness; it is even apt to increase the evil. For it incites its victims continually to dig for the supposedly hidden motives of their thoughts instead of singly attending to the object. It is most important to note that psychoanalysis does not content itself with resorting to that method in the face of abnormal mental reactions but insists on applying it to completely reasonable, well-motivated attitudes, too. Men are thus trained to pry about in their psychic entrails and to divest themselves of all receptiveness to the appeal of the object.

This false super-consciousness has a deadly effect on true inward life. It denatures all response to values and nourishes our pride. For, also in performing a good deed, the person who is in this sense conscious will watch himself; he plays the spectator to his entire conduct. He sees himself, from the outside, in his goodness. Here is a source of many temptations to pride.

So far as this kind of consciousness is concerned, Christians should be unconscious. In holy self-forgetfulness we should surrender ourselves to the values and the command that issues from them, according to the words of Christ: "Let not thy left hand know what thy right hand doeth."

Excessive rational analysis

The second form of false consciousness arises from a hypertrophy, an excessive predominance, of the cognitive attitude. It is found in persons who, in a situation which requires them to take sides emotionally or to intervene actively, remain confined within the bounds of rational analysis. A man, for instance, is listening to the Ninth Symphony of Beethoven. Instead of allowing his soul to absorb the beauty of the music and to give free rein to its delight, instead of allowing himself to be seized and elevated by that beauty, he dissects the object present to his senses and examines the reasons why it is beautiful.

Now, whenever we are concerned with the elucidation of aesthetic problems the rational analysis of the object is fully justified: but if the experience of the beauty of that music is at stake, this attitude is entirely inadequate. Or again, take someone who, in a developing love-relationship, at a moment when he and his beloved should naturally be dominated by the experience of their mutual awareness, turns instead the beloved person into an object of psychological research, observing his behavior and with great interest registering the results of his observation. Such an attitude, again, is fitting for an experimental psychologist confronted with his subject but is entirely out of place in a lover. Another example — suppose a man sees someone in immediate danger of life, and, instead of rushing to his rescue, studies his facial expressions.

In all these cases the cognitive attitude predominates in a person so exclusively as to prevent him from giving his attention to the objective theme of a situation and the demand which that situation sends forth. This means a destruction of the true contact with the object, and means, in spite of a seemingly prevalent objectivity, an attitude which is actually *nonobjective*, since it is based on a refusal to realize and to conform to the inherent meaning and appeal — the objective *logos*.

As in the first-described form of false consciousness, here, too, we remain outside the intrinsic context of a situation, and restrict ourselves to the status of a mere spectator incapable of being moved by the inner sublimity of values.

The proper function of rational knowledge

Rational knowledge has a twofold function in human life. On the one hand, it is a purpose by itself, a theme in its own right; on the other, it provides a foundation for all our emotions and volitions. It is one of the basic qualities of man as a spiritual person that, alone among terrestrial beings, he is able to participate in the existence of the surrounding world, not merely in the sense of exerting causality on that world but in the sense of an intentional relationship, of intellectual apprehension. Whereas the material things and the merely vital beings are interconnected only through the links of causation, man is equipped to penetrate the essence and qualities of things by the light of knowledge. By virtue of acquiring a knowledge of things, he possesses them, as it were, from above.

In this unique, ordered, resplendent consciousness of all the rest of creation, the sovereign status of man as an image of God and a lord of created things is specifically manifested. Whoever denies that knowledge by itself is part of man's destiny, that he is invited to penetrate the cosmos intellectually and to propose to himself as a self-subsistent theme the nature and qualities of existing things, cannot but fail to understand the nature of man.

To our intellect is entrusted the further function, however, of supplying a base for all our emotions, volitions, and conduct. But for our underlying knowledge of being, of *what is*, we could not be affected and enriched by the values inherent in objects. We could not give forth an affective response, nor actively influence our environment.

Yet, while by our intellect we participate in existence in a uniquely dignified way, this is not the only, not even the supreme, form of our participation. Thus, we are not only called to know God, to form a concept of Him, and in the life to come, to contemplate Him eye to eye; we are also called to adore Him; we are called to love Him and to immerse ourselves in His Love, and thus the streams of love are interpenetrating. The intimate union, the true wedlock with being, is ultimately achieved in the act of *frui*, the embrace of full awareness, in the possession through self-surrender and in the abandonment implied in the response to value. But knowledge is the indispensable basis of this union.

The spiritual deformation rooted in excessive rational analysis

The type of man whose touch with being is and remains an exclusively intellectual one, who loses interest in everything once he has mastered it intellectually, reveals a special kind of spiritual deformation. He is not filled with a genuine longing for participation in being. Knowledge is not for him a road to such participation but a mere submission to the immanent logic of an unlimited process divorced from the goal of possessing the truth. Hence, such a man cannot even truly understand the *primary* function of the intellect, with the participation in being which it embodies by itself. To such a man the process of acquiring knowledge has become a self-sufficient purpose.

What really matters, however, is always the objective theme present in a given situation. Should a profound significance and a high value attach to the contents of such an object or situation, then we are summoned by these to proceed beyond the merely intellectual contact, and beyond and above knowledge, to approach the stage of *frui*, and to evince an emotional and volitional response itself based on knowledge. Certain situations require us to intervene actively. He who is affected with a hypertrophy of the intellect is unable to appreciate the objective theme of a given situation and the demands involved in it. He cannot find his way out of the self-contained process of knowledge, and continues endlessly to dissect the object. Thus, he loses hold of the sense of that specific participation in being which is implicit in knowledge as such. Lacking a genuine touch with reality, he perseveres in asking "Why?" — and the object escapes him more and more. He falls short of that intuition of the essential which evokes a new, a secondary, an emotional and volitional attention to the aspects of a situation. He, too, remains an eternal spectator, without ever being admitted into the full presence, the intimate atmosphere of objects.

This corrosive and pseudo-objective intellectualism, then, is the second form of false super-consciousness. It deprives man of genuine surrender to value, of true union with anything that is. A man of this type, we might say, is forever loitering around all sorts of objects, asking questions unceasingly. Also, he is apt to distrust his every impression; and if anything begins to take hold of him he withdraws from direct contact to watch everything again from the outside. Nor, in so doing, is he unlikely to yield to the temptation of self-analysis. He will thus lapse into the first category of false self-consciousness.

True consciousness sees the valid aspect of things

True consciousness has nothing to do with either of these two states. It means, first, that the rational intentional relation to being takes precedence over all mere associations of images and physiologically conditioned reactions. The nonconscious are at the mercy of all kinds of fortuitous impressions. If they had a bad night, for instance, they will consequently see the world in drab and depressing colors. They fail to surmount that purely arbitrary impression, void of all validity; no, they give it credence, and behave accordingly. They are incapable of putting themselves at a proper objective distance from a physiologically conditioned, empty mood; they hand themselves over to the latter, and are disappointed with the surrounding world. That world suddenly appears to them in an entirely changed light, owing to the unreasoned trust they place in that deceptive mood.

Or again, a certain situation happens to remind them of some former experience of an unpleasant character; and, in this case they do not heed the fact that in its objective contents the new situation has no kinship whatever with that former one. These people develop a hopeless uneasiness and aversion on the ground of sheer association of images.

Accordingly their attitudes lack objectivity and conformity with reality. A person who is conscious in the more proper sense of the term will, on the contrary, orient his essential behavior so as to answer the objective meaning — the relevant content — of the situation. He is not so fully submerged in himself, not so completely a servant of his nature, as to seriously consider invalid, illegitimate, and incidental aspects. He can distinguish valid impressions from invalid ones. Here the mental form of meaningful *intentional* object-reference has asserted itself successfully against psycho-physical impulses or purely associative prejudices.

It is, indeed, the prime characteristic of intellectual maturity ("majority") that in our mental life the structural trait of intentional reference comes to prevail over the power of mere associations of ideas, and states of mind. In infantile thought, associations and body-conditioned states of mind still play a very great part; more important still, impressions thus gleaned are not then clearly distinguished from impressions legitimately founded in the things themselves. Also, mere images of fantasy freely fuse with, and are more or less assimilated into, the concepts of reality. There is as yet no clear-cut distinction between imagination and fact.

To be mentally grown up is to have one's reactions adjusted to the immanent logic, the proper meaning of things; to have established intentional object-reference in a ruling position in our mental lives. In this sense, an adult is more conscious than a child. To advance in that consciousness and to overcome all infantilism is a necessary condition for attaining the "measure of the age of the fullness of Christ," and thus imperative for the Christian. A consideration of all things *in conspectu Dei*, and a response to them conceived according to the spirit of Christ necessarily presupposes the supremacy of *intentional* object-reference, of a mode of response directed to the central meaning of things, over all merely associative and physiologically conditioned reactions; in particular, it presupposes the capacity of discrimination between valid and invalid aspects.

True consciousness responds appropriately to values

Another characteristic of true consciousness is closely connected therewith. It is the awakening to full moral majority, the discovery of the capacity of sanctioning. The behavior of *unconscious* persons is dictated by their nature. They tacitly identify themselves with whatever response their nature suggests to them. They have not yet discovered the possibility of emancipating themselves, by virtue of their free personal center, from their nature; they make no use as yet of this primordial capacity inherent in the personal mode of being. Hence their responses to values, even when they happen to be adequate, will always have something accidental about them. Their attitudes lack that character of explicitness and full consciousness which is a prerequisite of meeting in a really apposite way the demand embodied in the values. For what the values claim of us is not assent pure and simple, an assent which might as well be a fortuitous efflux of our natural dispositions; it is a fully conscious, rational, and explicit assent, given by the free center of our personality. By such an answer alone does a personal being adequately honor the values and their call, which is addressed to each of us in sovereign majesty, irrespective of his individual dispositions.

A truly conscious person has so far advanced over his nature that he no longer agrees implicitly to all its suggestions. Should an impulse of malice or envy surge up in his mind, he, actuated by his free personal center, will seclude himself from that impulse, and disavow it. Instead of endorsing it as a free personality, he expressly renounces all solidarity with it. True, such an act of disavowal is not by itself sufficient to render the impulse in question nonexistent or to eradicate it; yet that impulse is invalidated, as it were, and, in a sense, decapitated and deprived of its malignant potency. On the other hand, when faced with a genuine value the conscious person will not content himself with a contingent response to it, due to its fortuitous consonance with his nature: he also will respond with his free personal center; his response will bear the *sanction* of this free personal center.

Obviously enough, it is only such sanctioned responses to value which attain to a full degree of freedom and spiritual reality. It is through that actualization of the free and conscious center of his soul that a person comes of age morally and acquires the ability to utter that "yes" in the face of God which He demands of us. Not otherwise can our life obtain that inner unity and that establishment in God which elevates it above the accidents of our nature. In this sense, the Christian can never be conscious enough.

True consciousness serves continuity

With this aspect of true consciousness, a further one is closely associated: that of continuity — a subject which has already aroused our attention in Chapter 1. *Unconscious* man gives himself entirely over to the moment's experience. He allows the present impression (which, of course, is conditioned, in an extra-conscious sense, by many anterior experiences) to capture him. The truths he has previously gotten hold of, and the values he has sensed, are not preserved by him as an imperishable possession; they are swamped under the impact of the present impression; nor is the latter confronted with them. The life of a certain type of *unconscious* man never ceases to change with every change in his milieu. Or again, we have the conservative type: this kind of *unconscious* man remains attached to certain strong impressions of his past and is unreceptive toward new ones, yet he clings to those old impressions not by reason of their ascertained importance and validity but because they have been the first to affect him or because he has grown accustomed to them. True continuity however has nothing to do with a mere natural disposition toward conservatism (as predicated, sometimes, of a peasantry) and much less with being a slave to the force of habit.

A person who really has continuity persists in his affirmation of all truths and genuine values once they have become manifest to him. While open to every new truth and every new value, he confronts them (in a self-evident and organic way of procedure) with all those he is already familiar with. He knows that no contradictions exist in the world of being nor between values; and he longs to see all things in their proper interconnection, that is, ultimately in the light of God. Thus alone can man establish that inward order in his life which makes it possible for him to distinguish between valid and invalid impressions. It is only by virtue of continuity that man can be objective in his judgments and his behavior, for continuity preserves him from attributing to the present an illegitimate priority over the past and thus makes his decision dependent on the objective content and the relevancy of an experience alone.

Above all, the person with continuity is fixed in awareness of the ultimate truths, never sacrificing them to the self-contained dialectic of a transient situation which happens to arrest his attention. He views every event of life in the perspective of man's metaphysical situation and against the background of eternity. He alone is able in every situation to hang on to the basic truth and thus to see everything in the light of God.

Without continuity, no transformation in Christ is possible. For that transformation requires that the light of Christ should pervade all our life and that concerning everything we should ask whether it can stand the test before His face. *By confronting all things with Christ we also confront them with one another.* Continuity, too, vouches for the possibility of true penitence. By virtue of continuity, we understand that a human action loses nothing of its relevance merely because it belongs to the past; that the evil inherent in a sin is not decreased by the fact of its chronological remoteness.

Wakefulness enhances true consciousness and continuity

Consciousness and continuity are also linked to wakefulness, or alertness — to what we might call an attitude of being awake. *Unconscious* man entrusts himself to the flow of events, without setting them at a distance; therefore he is incapable of surveying them. Though he may have single impressions of great intensity, no single fact will reveal itself to him in its full significance and purport, for each lacks connection with the other, and above all, with the primal cause of being and the ultimate meaning of the world. His life is wrapped in a cloud of obscurity. Perhaps such a person will receive, time and again, a strong religious impression, and in its consequence grasp, for a moment, the metaphysical situation of man; but he fails to awaken once for all, and no sooner is his mind distracted by some other impressions than the sphere of ultimate reality has again vanished from his sight. Yet, he who is awake maintains that sphere present, over and above the concerns of the business of the moment. He always takes a synoptic view of things. He does not erect into an absolute the small accidental section of reality which just happens to occupy his mind, but views it against the background of integral reality.

This is what wakefulness means: to live *in conspectu Dei*; to interpret everything in the context of our eternal destiny, in its nexus with all our previous valid experiences, and most of all, in its function as a token and a representation of God.

Wakefulness in this sense and true consciousness are closely interrelated. *Conscious man, and he alone, avoids being submerged beneath things or living among them in the interstices of reality, as it were: he incorporates everything in the objectively valid order of ultimate reality.* Only the Christian can be truly conscious in the full sense of the term. For he alone has a true vision of reality proper and a true conception of God and the supernatural realm, from which everything derives its ultimate meaning. All those who have not yet risen to the brightness of the *lumen Christi* are (in this higher and qualified use of the term) still *unconscious*; they are still asleep. The measure in which someone lives in the light of the Christian revelation, maintains it continually present, and keeps in continuous awareness of it at all moments, determines the degree of his real consciousness.

Wakefulness perfects man as a person

The wakefulness of the truly conscious person also determines a more real and more significant mode of living. He alone, as we have seen, has a genuine comprehension of values; he recognizes their essential demand, and meets it with an explicit response. That eminently personal (and, as it were, sanctioned) form of response not only guarantees a conduct more deeply conceived from the moral point of view; in a direct sense also, it represents a reaction more adequately aimed, more bright with meaning, than is possible on the part of such a lack consciousness proper.

The conscious person's contact with the objects is not deformed by an overestimation of accidental features; and an integral, explicit comprehension of values is equally his privilege. In his sanctioned, express, and integrally shaped response to values, and in such a response only, *the whole person is present*. We might almost say that the greater the wakefulness which presides over a man's life the more he exists *as a person*.

We are now in a position to appreciate the vast difference between the false and the true kind of consciousness. Whereas the former precludes a real contact with the objects, and condemns its bearer always to watch himself without ever being touched by the *logos* of things that are, true consciousness postulates and establishes that genuine object-relationship. Here, man communes, he conspires, as it were, with the proper and valid meaning of what is: here, the true dialogue between subject and object takes place. All befogging twilight, all blind yielding to accidental impulses, all forms of determination by things taken as forces of nature instead of as *intentional* objects have disappeared: the response to values becomes clear and explicit, yet all the more intense and charged with experience.

True consciousness implies a recognition of our defects

Finally, true consciousness implies an intimate recognition of our defects (*cf.*, Chapter 3). A person who is thus conscious, who has emancipated himself from his nature and no longer agrees automatically to its suggestions, who is awakened to a sense of his free personal center and of the essential, express, and lasting response which God demands of him, has also cast off his illusions concerning himself. His own being, too, is illumined by the light of God and he allows that light to penetrate into all corners of his soul. He spreads out his whole life before the face of Christ and suffers no hidden currents of life which have escaped a clear recognition by him and a confrontation with Christ, to be active in him. The spiritual vision, illumined by Christ, of his central personality clears up all recesses of his being and sees through all illusions. Hence, he leads a unified life — in contrast to *unconscious* man in whom disparate currents of life can exist side by side without his seeing their essential inconsistency with one another.

True consciousness unifies the soul

Frequently we come across people who reveal entirely disparate aspects of character, of which now one and then another prevails, so that on different occasions such a man or woman may almost strike us as a different person. According to the varying elements of his environment, with their fluctuating appeal to this or that strain in his mental composition, a person of this kind may seem again and again to change his identity. Not so the person with genuine consciousness. He always remains himself; his life is integrated, because he has brought everything to one denominator, with no hidden particle of his self escaping the formative effect of his basic direction towards Christ. In the highest sense of the term, he has become *simple*.

A classic example of true consciousness is St. Augustine in his *Confessions*, confronting all things with God and discussing them with fearless clarity before His face, and thus also attaining full consciousness of them himself.

It must be the purpose of a true Christian that his entire life be suffused by that light of truth, the *lumen Christi*. He must endeavor to become fully capable of personal sanction, to rise to a wakeful conduct of life, to acquire complete continuity. The more we are awake and in possession of continuity, the more we are able to light up even our present life with a ray from that wealth of splendor that shall brighten us in the life to come: "We see now through a glass in a dark manner; but then face to face" (1 Cor. 13:12).

True consciousness is the foundation of our free response to God

By virtue of consciousness alone can we give the answer which God demands of us. For it is that unconditional and explicit assent on our part, sanctioned by our central personality, which He demands of us; and for the sake of that assent He has endowed man with freedom of will, entailing the enormous risk that man, misusing his freedom, may sin. Thus, in the fact of our consciousness our entire earthly task is, as it were, condensed. For that task consists ultimately in our express assenting to be apprehended and transformed by God. It possesses this "yes" which God, when He awarded us His highest gift of inconceivable sublimity, the incarnation of the Eternal Word, also required to hear from Mary the Blessed Virgin: "Behold the handmaid of the Lord; be it done to me according to thy word" (Luke 1:38).

This is the primal word, which God has called upon mankind to utter. God expects each of us individually, and man as the highest and most lavishly endowed of His creatures, to say this word. It is the constitutive core of consciousness; and it cannot be spoken too clearly, too wakefully, too explicitly. It is, therefore, one of the basic tasks imposed on every Christian to rise to a state of true consciousness, thus infusing an integral meaning into his life. Based on that primal word, life attains great simplicity, and with that word alone can we "live in that great secret of the adoration of God which is Christ."

5

True Simplicity

THE Gospel intends us to attain to true simplicity: simplicity in the sense of an inward unity of life.

Simplicity contrasts with disunity

Such a simplicity contrasts, in the first place, with the disunity in the soul of those whose lives are filled, now by one thing, now by another; who lose themselves in the motley variegation of life, who do not seek for an integration of their actions and conduct by *one* dominant principle. A similar disunity is manifest in lives controlled by diverse and mutually contradictory currents, which develop side by side, each according to its immanent law, without being coordinated or confronted with the other. A person of this kind is said to be split; his life lacks inward unity. Such a deficiency often occurs in those who also lack consciousness and continuity.

Simplicity contrasts with psychological convolutedness

Secondly, true simplicity is opposed to complexity taken in a specific sense. Certain people are prevented by their various psychic complexes and tensions, from giving a plain response to the

71

logos of a situation. Hence, instead of keeping on the straight road that points to the object, they are always compelled to choose bypaths and detours. Everywhere they come to grips with artificial problems and complications. Their inferiority complex, for instance, makes them feel embarrassed by a complaisance which would rejoice a healthier type of person, or makes them reciprocate it with some objectively incongruous act.

They are deformed by their inhibitions and are continually delayed in their reactions by many unnecessary sentiments. Everything becomes thus over-complicated: a huge amount of time is wasted on the simplest things and the most unequivocal tasks are denatured into portentous problems. Their false way of being conscious, in the sense of an ever-present reflectiveness, is often responsible for such people's lack of simplicity. They are, as Shakespeare says in *Hamlet*, "sicklied o'er with the pale cast of thought."

Simplicity does not mistake complexity for profundity

Or again, a man may develop a predilection for complicating as many things as possible because he mistakes complexity for profundity. This species of complexity, unlike the aforementioned one, is more or less an appanage of the intellectual. Its lover prefers obscurity to clarity; he is liable to credit oracular stammerings with profundity and to dismiss whatever is unequivocally and tersely enounced as trivial. He thus tends to make everything appear more complicated than it really is and consequently falls short of an adequate knowledge of reality.

For such people are blind to the trait of simplicity associated with the metaphysical wealth and height of being; they overlook the metaphysical law that the higher a thing is the simpler it is, in a sense — in the sense of inner unity, as expressed by the dictum, "simplicity is the seal of verity." They are insensitive to the value of true simplicity.

Simplicity avoids the cult of the abstruse

This kind of complexity, too, is connected with the false type of consciousness, particularly its second form: what we have called the overdevelopment of the cognitive attitude, and the cult of cognition as a self-contained process. The category of the intellectually interesting takes precedence over the category of truth. The protean vastness of untruth, the maze of arbitrary and extravagant but witty errors and sophistries are considered with great interest — if only because they divert the intellect from platitude and simplicity. The mere fact of their complexity (and often enough, of their abstruseness) confers on these errors — in the eyes of such people — a claim to be taken seriously, indeed, even a glamor outshining the simple dignity of plain truth.

Obviously the realm of concepts in which these minds roam about is a highly complicated and disharmonious world, for the possibilities of error are innumerable, whereas truth is one.

Those infatuated with complexity also enjoy the involved aspects of their own psychic life; more, they purposely complicate it by the reflective attention they pay to their feeling or impulse, no matter whether in the given case there is any legitimate need for self-observation. A person of this type takes pleasure in his emotional detours and blind-alleys which provide him with a sense of being deep and interesting. Jacobsen, the Danish novelist, has succeeded in presenting such states of mind (from which he was not free himself) in a remarkably plastic way; Dostoyevsky has depicted them with superior mastery.

This perverted spirituality hides an inherent impotence to penetrate the world of being, directly and essentially. The mind that wallows in complexity is unable to grasp the *logos* of what is in a straightforward way, to establish a vital contact therewith. It rambles around objects, without ever communicating with them intimately; its ideas are not inspired by the *logos* of the reality in question and are therefore devoid of intrinsic necessity. A sterile missing of the mark is the invariable fate of such minds: they are forever a prey to the infinitude of possibilities instead of coming close to the *one* reality. All intoxication with complexity betrays the hunger of those who feed on stones in place of bread.

Simplicity of primitivity vs. simplicity of inner unity

Before, however, we turn to the subject of true Christian simplicity, the antithesis to all forms of disunity and complexity, we must first treat of a certain type of simplicity which is scarcely less remote from true simplicity than are the attitudes we have just been discussing.

The cosmos of beings reveals a vast hierarchy of degrees in regard to their contents of meaning. In the sphere of lifeless matter, a comparative poverty of meaning seems to predominate. Lifeless matter presents a certain simplicity in the sense of a low measure of metaphysical perfection and depth of meaning — shown by the supremacy, in this province, of mechanical patterns of happening. Everywhere in matter we find a mere contiguity and combination of things rather than creative interpenetration. This sphere, too, is destined to represent symbolically the metaphysical abundance of God; but to fulfill that function it needs the category of quantity, both in the sense of a multiplicity of single units and in the sense of extensive manifoldness. A single material thing taken as such represents the wealth of being, proper to the material sphere as a whole, in a fragmentary and indirect manner only.

It is different with the sphere of organic life. In any single organism much more is "said," as it were, than in a piece of lifeless matter; at the same time, it manifests a far greater simplicity in that it is all subordinated to *one* principle. The various component functions in an organism are not merely contiguous to, and combined with, one another; they are coupled together in a kind of mutual *interpenetration*. All single aspects are united and ruled by a basic principle, as is never the case with any unit or accumulation of lifeless matter. Over and above mere contiguity and multiplicity, there appears a structural trait of mutual penetration and communion. We shall find that quality vastly increased, however, and charged with an entirely new meaning in the superior realm of *spiritual personality*.

How immensely much is said in a single human being! How much is contained in a being that possesses consciousness and is pervaded by the light of reason, that is endowed with a capacity for love and for knowledge, that is free, and a bearer of moral values; a being which, in contradistinction to all others, is not merely a *vestige* but an *image* of God. All multiplicity and grandeur of the material realm, the quantitative vastness of the material cosmos, the immense variety of the objects composing it, the solar systems, even the ineffable manifoldness of living things, fail to represent God in so high a sense as does a single spiritual person.

In the degree in which a thing represents God, by so much does it participate in the divine abundance of being, and so much greater is also the significance of a single unit thereof. In the spiritual person, the principle of mutual interpenetration is far more predominant even than in the living organism as such. And, while the spiritual person has far more substantiality and depth than has the living organism, let alone lifeless matter, by the same token it also possesses much more simplicity. Here, the category of quantity decreases in meaning and is no longer applicable in exactly the same sense. For personal essence is not resolvable into isolated, extensive, measurable, and mechanical components or aspects. Metaphysically speaking, the higher an entity is, the greater its simplicity. The *soul* is so simple as no longer to admit of a disjunction of form and matter.

Simplicity, thus interpreted, is not akin but antithetical to primitivity and poverty of meaning. The simplicity of an entity increases with its height: it implies, as it were, the expression of a great meaning in *one* word, the condensation of a great wealth of being in one individual, in one quality, in one act or manifestation.

This character of simplicity (in the sense of a condensation of being) grows along the ascending hierarchy of the cosmos until it culminates in the *one eternal Word of God, in quo est omnis plenitudo divinitatis* ("in whom is all plenitude of divinity") that illumines the face of Christ. The absolute simplicity of God precludes the distinction, not only between form and matter but between existence and essence, between *actus* and *potentia*. Yet, God is the infinite plenitude of being.

Simplicity of cognition: science compared to philosophy as a form of knowledge

In regard to the modes of cognition, too, we may visualize the increase of simplicity in proportion to the degree of height. Thus, philosophical cognition, intent on grasping the essence of things (*intima rei intus legere*), is in a fundamental sense simpler than scientific cognition, whose methods of observation and deduction are linked to an outward approach to the object.

The natural sciences depend on quantity, on an extensive accumulation of data by means of repeated experiments; the knowledge they procure covers its field in breadth. Philosophy, on the contrary, is not essentially dependent on the multitude of single observations, as it may in principle seize the essence of the object by means of one relevant example; nor is it intent on elaborating a knowledge in breadth.

The dimension in which it seeks to unfold is that of depth; moreover, it aims to comprehend the unity of the entire cosmos, and its crowning act is an advance to the ultimate principle of being: being infinite and absolutely simple, in which all abundance of being is contained *per eminentiam*.

Inner spiritual poverty is not true spiritual simplicity

Analogously to this cosmic hierarchy in reference to the inner plenitude of being, and according to the two opposite kinds of simplicity in general — the simplicity of *primitivity and crudity* on the one hand, the metaphysical *simplicity of inward unity on the other* — we also must distinguish between two extremely different types of human simplicity.

In describing people of primitive minds as *simple*, we refer to their inner poverty and their incapacity to respond to the depth and the qualitative manifoldness of the cosmos.

The attention of such people may be monopolized by elementary concerns, poor in meaning: for instance, the external necessities of life. Thus, a peasant's thoughts and worries will sometimes be strictly confined to his chattel and his parcel of land. His life is deployed within the boundaries of a low sphere, impoverished in meaning and devoid of spirituality; in fact, a small section of that sphere, his household economy, may swallow up his life.

Moreover, that tiny microcosm itself may bear no interest for him except from certain pragmatically restricted points of view. He is hardly interested in a domestic animal as a living being, in the deep mystery embodied in a living organism as such. With all that he has no concern: he is absorbed by concerns of economic usefulness. The same applies to the objects of his agricultural activities.

Thus, his world is a shrunken one, both in depth and width, and his conception of the world is simple in the sense of lacking content and differentiation. It is uncomplicated; but that freedom from complication is obtained at the cost of a renunciation of metaphysical depth and abundance. Frequently, again, his inner life will reflect that conception of the world. In such a case, he will be simple in the sense of being coarse. A few primitive motifs, always the same, occupy his mental scene in a monotonous rhythm. This type of simplicity, no less than the aberration we have labeled *complexity*, forms an antithesis to the true Christian simplicity which is always joined to spirituality and depth of meaning.

Stupidity is not spiritual simplicity

Or again, we may call a person *simple* because he is so poorly equipped intellectually as to be incapable of understanding things of any notable degree of spiritual depth or structural differentiation. As soon as he turns his mind to any higher sphere or even to the manifoldness of contents proper to a more trivial sphere, he seems to lose all faculty of comprehension: everything perplexes him. His mind is only able to grasp quite simple situations or relations, that is to say, such as enclose a very modest content of meaning. His mind is marred by a similar incapacity with regard to values. The motivation of his behavior is equally primitive and undifferentiated. Every task requiring a somewhat deeper insight or more careful discrimination will baffle him. His intellectual deficiency renders him awkward; his clumsy hands are unable, so to speak, to touch anything complicated, differentiated, or refined, without crushing it. His life will rarely be tainted with morbid complexity but that danger is prevented at the expense of depth and wealth of meaning. This organic primitivity again has nothing to do with true simplicity.

There are, furthermore, people whom we call *simple* owing to their habit of an illegitimate simplification of all things. Here again we must distinguish two varieties.

Reductionist simplicity of platitude is not spiritual simplicity

First, there are those who interpret the entire cosmos after the pattern of its lowest sphere. Without considering the specific *logos* of the object they are faced with, they apply the categories of mechanism to the province of organic life and even to the realm of spiritual personality and culture. Far from attuning themselves to the element of reality that confronts them or attempting to plumb its depth, they drag down everything into the sphere in which they feel themselves at home. Facility is their watchword; and their complacent pride impels them to treat all things in a cavalier fashion. This type of person is not awkward or clumsy but completely uninitiated. A great many popular philosophies are marked with this shallow simplicity.

But the latter is by no means confined to the theoretical domain of popular philosophizing. There are people thus addicted to illegitimate simplification concerning their private lives, too. In their candid complacency, they will (for instance) lavishly offer advice that is in no wise appropriate to the depth or the intricacy of a given situation; they imagine themselves to be able to solve every problem and to arrange everything according to some simple prescription. Their own lives run smoothly without friction, conflicts or complications because they contrive to master all its aspects by dint of a few schematic notions.

In contradistinction to the forms of false simplicity cited above, these simplifiers really occupy themselves with the higher spheres of being; but in their imaginary superiority, they denature the object of their attention and with a kind of glib dexterity doctor it, as it were, until the problem appears to be solved or, rather, enchanted away. They do not treat things adequately but merely tamper with them, though often with a show of success. They walk through life with a boastful smile, proud of being past all obscure problems and grave difficulties. They believe they see through all things and know everything; nor is there anything for which they would not promptly supply an obvious explanation.

This simplicity of platitude, which would strip the cosmos of all depth and all metaphysical stratification, is perhaps even more radically opposed to true Christian simplicity than is the disease of complexity. For he who denies the dimensions of being, its depth and width, and pretends to flatten out the entire universe, is even farther remote from truth than he who ignores the supreme value of inward unity.

Affected childlikeness is not true simplicity

The second variety of illegitimate simplification consists in passing by all problems in a falsely childlike manner, a kind of deliberate innocence — *frisch, froh, fromm, frei* ("in a brisk, joyous, candid, free way") as the Germans sometimes put it. Such a person fails to take account of the distance he must travel in order to rise from a lower mode of being to a higher one; he would skip the indispensable phases of maturing and growth; his life, if we may put it thus, is full of short circuits. He sets much store by his childlike innocence, an attitude in which he is fully at his ease, and mistakes it for true simplicity.

He thus goads himself into a simplified and debased conception of the road to eternal salvation, which in fact is a steep and narrow one. He approaches God without a properly discriminating reverence for the mysterious majesty in which He resides concealed. Misinterpreting the evangelical words, "Unless ye become as children," he enjoys his pose of being childlike and construes his petty and simplifying conception of the metaphysical situation of man, of the mysteries of salvation, and of our transformation in Christ, as a specifically direct relationship with God.

Frequently, too, he escapes from the difficulties of life into that consciousness of being childlike. He thus hopes to pass over with nimble feet the abysmal rifts in human nature. Whenever he should carry his cross he somehow evades it, mistaking Christ's transfiguration of all suffering for an elimination of all suffering, and equating his own natural, vitalistic optimism with a blissful consideration of all things *in conspectu Dei*. He is blind to the mysterious differentiation of aspects in the universe; to the presence of stages which have to be climbed and surpassed not without effort, pain, and distress. He does not suspect that true simplicity refers back to the all-comprehensive height in which those degrees are incorporated, and that for this reason only it encompasses an abundance of things and experiences.

It is not a simple thing to attain true simplicity

All these forms of false simplicity, much as they differ from one another, have this in common: that with them, the advantage derived from the avoidance of complexity is outweighed by a grave defect or aberration. It is purchased at the price, either of a self-confinement to a diminutive section of some inferior sphere of being (viewed from a unilateral angle, at that) or of a distorted vision of the universe according to a pattern taken from an inferior sphere.

The deliberate pose of simplicity (which is present in the last-named case) springs from the illusory belief that simplicity can be promptly attained *from below upwards*, whereas, in fact it results from the establishment of communion with Him who, by virtue of His incommensurable highness, condenses all in one *per eminentiam*.

While truth, as contrasted to error, bears the sign of a certain clear simplicity and directness, on the other hand it also implies greater differentiation and profundity; and it is *harder* to reach than are the varieties of error. Just as in art it is easier to accomplish an impressive work by a motley diversity of details than by sublime classic simplicity (as for instance the Parthenon), so also in general the true simplicity which encloses an abundance of meaning is more difficult to attain than is complexity.

The basic error of all false simplicity lies in the assumption that it is a simple thing to have true simplicity. It may be said, on the contrary, that we can in no way attain to full simplicity by merely natural means; that the key to it is given us by Revelation only.

True simplicity comes only from single-hearted devotion to God

Certainly, in experiencing and responding to the *logos* of the various sections of reality, we are to take cognizance of the aspect of simplicity that goes with metaphysical height. But, within the limits of the purely natural sphere, we cannot — and must not — aspire to an all-pervasive inward simplicity. Only to God, only to the living God who manifests Himself in Revelation, may we so deliver our whole life as to keep our regard fixed on one thing exclusively: the *unum necessarium*. He alone (of whom St. Paul says, "For of Him, and by Him, and in Him, are all things; to Him be glory for ever") may impart to our whole life that ultimate unity and simplicity which, far from diminishing its wealth of substance, permeates it with a new and incomparable abundance of being.

Therefore, all forms of false simplicity, except the one based on a deficiency of intellectual gifts, constitute an insuperable obstacle to the attainment of true simplicity. For they keep us bogged down in the flat regions of our nature, devoid of the heroic readiness to die unto ourselves and to be lifted towards the heights where alone we might receive the gift of true simplicity.

It is not so with those who are primitive owing to their intellectual limitations. In their case, false simplicity is not rooted in a deliberate, guilty attitude; thus, by fully surrendering themselves to Christ they may retrieve abundance and depth of being *per eminentiam* by virtue of their genuine and direct contact with supreme value, which compensates for their natural shortcomings. No deficiency of natural dispositions can prevent us from transformation in Christ. He, too, who is simple out of helplessness and is undifferentiated because of his lack of gifts, may attain to true simplicity if transformed by Christ. In confirmation of this statement we may point to certain types of saints, such as a Brother Juniper or the holy Curé d'Ars. In them we see examples, not of *false* but of *true* simplicity, which however is not an expression of their lack of intellectual differentiation but a fruit of the full dedication of their lives to Christ. Intellectual plainness as such does not facilitate our progress towards that true simplicity, which was quite compatible with the genius of a St. Paul or a St. Augustine; but neither is it an invincible impediment to such simplicity.

The simplicity proper to the Christian pertains to that order of simplicity which increases with the grade of metaphysical height and is concomitant with a richer content of meaning and differentiation. It is, as we have seen, only possible as the fruit of a life directed towards God, who is the epitome of total simplicity. The more our life is permeated by God, the simpler it becomes. This simplicity is defined by the inward unity which our life assumes because we no longer seek for any but one end: God.

No longer do we judge things from different points of view, from that of our temporal interests, for example, or of the interests of others, or of our consideration for public opinion, and *in addition* to these, from that of our consideration for God's will, as though all these points of view were on a level with each other. One supreme point of view governs our entire life and in subordination to that point of view all else is judged and settled. It is the principle of conduct enjoined by these words of the Lord: "Seek ye first the kingdom of God, and his justice, and all these things shall be added unto you" (Matt. 6:33).

The life of a man who, after having found Christ, gives all he has for the one costly pearl (as did the merchant in the Gospel) becomes simple in the highest and most proper sense of the word. It becomes unified instead of being divided in the sense in which St. Paul says of a man who marries, *divisus est*. Nor, because of that, will his life decrease in its depth of meaning or wealth of substance;

rather it will become deep, substantial, and differentiated in a measure inaccessible to those who are lost in the multicolored variety of terrestrial goods, and who, like Faust, again and again engage in fresh pursuits.

This is immediately evident as regards the aspect of depth. For the height of the value we are genuinely experiencing (be it in a direct sense or by implication, as a background to our primary object) determines the depth of our response. A life entirely consecrated to God, the *summum bonum*, is necessarily deeper than one given over to earthly goods.

True simplicity engenders abundance

But the consonance between simplicity and abundance, too, will become intelligible if we remind ourselves that by simplicity is meant the unity of a life anchored in God, who encloses all plenitude of being. Even within the limits of the natural sphere, a life filled by *one* high vocation is richer and more differentiated than the life of a person whose energies are frittered away on many peripheral things. A great love not only informs a person's life in greater depth but lends it a far greater abundance than a multitude of superficial love relationships.

The old wisdom still holds which sets *multum* (much) higher than *multa* (many things). How much truer is this of unity centered on God, who not only contains *per eminentiam* all fullness of being but is the Cause and the End of all created things.

The light of Christ simplifies all things

Yet, in order to establish such an enriching relationship to God a mere formal reference to God as the epitome and fountainhead of being (*ens a se*) is not by itself sufficient. Such an end requires the integral consecration of our life to *that* God who reveals Himself to us in Christ, whose living word addresses us from above, and to whom we cannot ascend by our own forces.

More, we must actually throw ourselves open to the radiance of the *lumen Christi*, without attempting to adapt it to our own nature or to falsify it by our natural categories. We must not humanize and interpret in an easy oversimplified manner that One in whom is all plenitude of divinity (*in quo est omnis plenitudo divinitatis*), lest we succumb to the pitfall of false simplicity. We must envision *that* face of Christ which the Liturgy of the Holy Church proposes to our eyes, that is, the true, undistorted, authentic face of Christ, which *per eminentiam* enfolds all wealth and universality of being and before which all natural measuring rods lose their validity.

If we consider all things *in conspectu Dei*, every genuine good finds its right place in the cosmic order and discloses its specific value more splendidly than if we attend to it in arbitrary isolation, merely for its own sake. In that light of God, all spurious goods will be inexorably laid bare, while all true goods that convey a message from God will be discerned and appreciated in their deepest, their most proper meaning.

Thus, our exclusive direction towards God should not be confused with that extrinsic and unilateral method of looking upon things which we adopt when we place some created being in the center of our perspective.

On the contrary, by being so directed towards God we shall interpret all things from a legitimately central and comprehensive point of view, which — and which alone — equips us with a key to the proper and particular meaning of every entity or aspect of creation.

We only take true account of a genuine good if we see it in the place where it properly stands in the thought of God. Nor do we fully honor or love a created good of genuine value unless we honor and love God *more* than that good.

Christ is the principle of true simplicity

In other words, true simplicity ensues from our bringing all things to one denominator which, far from distorting or limiting them as does an approach alien to their essence, leads to the elucidation of their innermost meaning and mystery. We can never decipher them so long as we abandon ourselves exclusively to the specific immanent *logos* of each of those things as such. That one denominator to which we should bring all things is *Christ*.

Thus will our life receive its inward unity. We shall no longer be divided owing to our fixation on many equivalent but disparate goods. We are no longer a function of several mutually unconnected currents of life. By the light of true consciousness, all things in our mind and our life are confronted with Christ, and consequently, with one another. Unlike those who are a prey to complexity, we are not hampered by all kinds of irrelevant sentiments nor is our inner freedom disturbed by a multitude of petty or imaginary problems. The lure of what seems *interesting* can no longer beguile us into wasting our time on the protean pageant of falsehood; there is no longer anything that could divert us to bypaths which lead away from the one supreme Goal. For we have acquired that holy sobriety which renders us unable to bear any but sound doctrine, unlike those who "will not endure sound doctrine; but, according to their own desires, they will heap to themselves teachers, having itching ears: and will indeed turn away their hearing from the truth, but will be turned unto fables" (2 Tim. 4:3-4). On the contrary, all our desire is directed to the "unleavened bread of sincerity and truth" (1 Cor. 5:8).

Plain honesty contributes to true simplicity

In their common antithesis to the egoistic attitude of complexity, we perceive the close interrelation between true simplicity and a certain trait of plain honesty, which contains at least a rudiment of Christian humility. All complexity, on the other hand, stems from a root of evil pride. The man of pride uses the manifoldness of his interests and problems, so to speak, as a retinue subservient to his luxury. He surrounds himself with a court of multiple things. For he has lost the center of all comprehensive unity, God; nor does he take it upon himself to find his way back to that center again. He glories in his unsolved complications and attributes a preposterous emphasis to many unimportant things about him because he fails to give its due weight to the one really important thing, the *unum necessarium*.

The man of plain honesty and simplicity, on the other hand, abhors that pageant of complications, not because he enjoys his own sweet primitivity (this pose of false simplicity is no less a work of pride than is the attitude of complexity), but because he is entirely concentrated on the *unum necessarium*. He does not leer around him; still less is he watching himself: his eyes are directed straight to the *logos* of truth, which he follows without restraint.

Continuity in aspiring to God engenders simplicity

Above all, he never quits his basic attitude: an attitude essentially aspiring towards God, receptive, and steeped in charity. Though he must answer the infinite variety of specific situations with a vast compass of outward reactions and emotional tones, he yet never abandons that one central attitude which is defined and shaped by Christ. He is not at the mercy of disparate principles of behavior, assuming control according to the mood of the moment. Manifestly, simplicity corresponds with continuity. The truly simple man always preserves his basic identity: though his *register of tones* be designed to meet a vast diversity in types of situations, that register itself always remains the same and is always governed by one unchanging central attitude.

As a rule, we are only too ready, under the impact of everyday life, to slide from the God-seeking central attitude we have adopted in prayer. We are quick to slip out of our festive garment and to relapse into a purely natural, dull, unloving attitude from which to react to the diverse situations of life. There is even a type of people, markedly discontinuous and wanting in consciousness, who show changes so abrupt and radical as to create the impression of a change of personal identity. Such people are apt suddenly to apply standards entirely different from their previous ones; they unexpectedly lose their taste for what fascinated them but a moment before; they show themselves insensitive to an appeal that has until now seemed to carry much weight with them. It might indeed be said of such a person that *two souls* (or more) *live in his breast.*

To this type of behavior true simplicity forms a glaring contrast. It implies a basic identity with oneself, meaning, not only a solid preservation of the essential direction towards Christ, once acquired, but a structural trait of continuity. So far as we possess this virtue, we always keep in contact with what we have formerly recognized to be valid. We do not alter our essential attitude even in relation to single persons and things or to single values and truths, unless an objective change should actually arise which may legitimately account for such a modification.

Continuity exclusively toward one natural good may threaten simplicity

A person confined within his natural attitude may not squander his interests on a multitude of trivial irrelevancies: he may concentrate upon an important cause, consecrate himself to a noble vocation, or be overwhelmed with a great love. However, he will then be exhausted, as it were, by that one thing, valuable, maybe, but yet only one among many human concerns. Everything else is obscured, and he cannot afford to pay adequate attention even to a genuine good if it be unconnected with the thing which now engrosses his interest.

True simplicity empowers man

It is not so with true simplicity, involving an exclusive devotion to the *unum necessarium* alone. With this, new forces spring up in man; an abundance of spiritual intensity arises from his participation in the life of Christ. New torrents are released, of which he knew nothing before; he is now enabled to react adequately, in a far greater measure than in his former life, to human individualities and the manifoldness of situations. It is a state of mind entirely different from the obsession of blind zeal which compels one to talk always about the one thing one is absorbed in, without regard to the situation and without applying the necessary discretion. Rather we become able, in the attitude of true simplicity, patiently to penetrate every situation, lend ear to every person, and attend to every task.

How inexhaustible becomes thereby the capacity for devoting ourselves to our fellow creatures and to their legitimate cares. Only think of the saints: St. Paul, for example, when he says, "Who is weak, and I am not weak? Who is scandalized, and I am not on fire?" (2 Cor. 11:29). This is a measure of love which transcends all natural categories. Or again, what a never relaxing intensity in attending to a variety of high tasks do we find in St. Albert the Great, adding the immensity of his scientific work to his monastic duties and his episcopal functions! With a similar intent we may point to the life of a St. Bernard of Clairvaux.

From the natural standpoint, such a simultaneity of nobly performed duties might well seem impossible. But the saints could achieve such an abundance of life precisely because they were simple and by reason of their simplicity participated in the life of Christ.

God alone must have primacy

Having examined the essence of true simplicity and distinguished it from its false counterpart, we are now faced with the question as to how it can be attained. The answer is: not by pursuing simplicity itself as a supreme goal, but by striving for a just and adequate response to the divine truth. The methods which lead us towards true simplicity, and which we are about to expose, must be looked upon not as devices for the acquisition of true simplicity but as attitudes intrinsically precious and in conformity to the will of God, and thus productive — among other good results — of true simplicity.

In the first place, we shall be on the road towards true simplicity by investing the *unum necessarium* with an unconditional primacy in our life. We must have the inmost readiness to relinquish anything if God wills it. No creaturely good must possess our heart to the point of setting a limit, of whatever kind, to our total devotion to Christ, in the sense that we should say, as it were, "I would willingly renounce anything else, but not this one thing." Everything else must be ready to vanish before the call of Christ, *sequere me*; we must follow Him, *relictis omnibus*. Nothing must limit our devotion to God, nor make it dependent on certain conditions.

Our full self-donation to Christ, the *surrender* as Cardinal Newman has called it, the heroic relinquishment of the natural basis and of our natural selves: such is the primal act conducive to simplicity. At this point we become aware of the great task of ridding ourselves of all inordinate attachment to creaturely goods: a task which is the chief object of all ascetical training. Throughout the Gospels, the Lord admonishes us thereto. "He that loveth father or mother more than me…and he that loveth son or daughter more than me, is not worthy of me" (Matt. 10:37). Christ does not withhold from our eyes the consequences of our failure so to detach ourselves from all goods, our failure to acquire freedom for the *unum necessarium* and hence for true simplicity: "And they began all at once to make excuse. The first said to him: I have bought a farm and I must go out and see it: I pray thee, hold me excused. And another said: I have bought five yoke of oxen and I go to try them: I pray thee, hold me excused. And another said: I have married a wife and therefore I cannot come" (Luke 14:18-20).

Yet we must live in the world

Yet, is it not the will of God that we should apply ourselves to the *manifold* tasks which are inherent in life and which every day carries with it? Even a hermit in the desert cannot wholly eschew a modest diversity of daily tasks; how could we, who are certainly not all elected to live as recluses? Surely, the primacy of the *unum necessarium* cannot dispense us from our several duties concerning our fellow men, our profession, our daily bread, and so forth? Much as we may recognize that preeminence of the *unum necessarium*, is not our life essentially subject to the multiform system of great and small agenda, compelling us to divide our attention and our interests?

We must shun sinful or frivolous activities

Certainly, full simplicity will only be possible in eternity, when God will be *all in everything,* and when we shall behold, condensed *in one moment,* "what shall be in the end without end" (St. Augustine, *De civ. Dei* 22.30). Still, even our life *in statu viae* will glow with a character of simplicity if we put the *unum necessarium* first, and more, bring everything to the one denominator which is Christ. In view of the fact that all things are controlled and ordered by one principle, and that this principle of unity is objectively identical with the Word ultimately addressed to all being, the manifold concerns and tasks will no longer be apt to despoil our life of simplicity and inward unity.

But how may this process, which we have termed *bringing everything to one denominator*, be *in concreto* accomplished? First, by considering and judging all things in the light of their relation to God and to our transformation in Christ. By confronting all things with Christ and keeping in communion with such only as we can cling to before His holy face, we bring into our life a qualitative harmony.

As a first step, we part with everything that is sinful and opposed to God. Beyond that, however, we also discriminate against everything that, without being actually sinful, is out of accord with the world of Christ or apt to divert us from God. Certain things carry about them an unlovely savor of worldliness, although one may deal with them without necessarily lapsing into sin. Such are, for instance, certain illustrated magazines, fashionable beaches, music halls, shows, many cinema pictures, etc.

If we confront these things with Christ, we shall feel them to be incompatible in quality with His world. Owing to the impudent, frivolous, and trivial quality which is rarely absent from them, they (at their best) shrill into the holy world of Christ as a discordant tone; their atmosphere is destined to entice us into levity and irreverence, thus undermining the dikes which we have erected against sin.

Apart from these, there is a further class of things which, though not qualitatively incompatible with Christ and hardly deserving the epithets *frivolous* and *worldly*, are yet superficial and ephemeral, and thus calculated to distract our eyes from God, our eternal Goal. Certain shallow pleasures which are meant to gratify our craving for sensations or to bewitch our fantasy belong to this class: thrilling novels, for example, which cannot be qualified as real works of art; or again, certain social gatherings in which there is much idle talk done and much food supplied for wanton (though, perhaps, harmless) curiosity. These things draw us away towards the periphery of being; they make recollection and aliveness to God and eternity, more difficult. They dishabituate the mind from the *unum necessarium* and so interfere with the progress towards simplicity. The Christian who insists on confronting everything with God will keep away from these things also. He will only take an interest in things which can stand the test before the face of Christ and which do not lead him away from God even in a merely formal sense, by fettering him to peripheral concerns.

We must not even fully abandon ourselves to natural goods

However, even as regards goods or tasks which, being objectively valuable or at worst neutral, can stand the test before the face of Christ, we must never abandon ourselves unqualifiedly to their immanent logic. In spite of the natural value of such objectively good things (such as, for instance, a noble friendship, a work of art, scholarly pursuits, the nursing of the sick, etc.), we are not justified in unconditionally abandoning ourselves to the immanent logic of these goods. Our direct relationship to Christ, and, through Him, to God, should radically inform our relationship to all goods and tasks.

It is not sufficient to confront everything with Christ, and, having decided that a given thing does not contradict Christ, to abandon oneself to that thing without any further qualification. The Christian's relation to what is naturally valuable, too, is a different one from that of the non-Christian. Our primary devotion and self-consecration to Christ should manifest itself in every phase of our service to some genuine good or in dealing with some noble task, enriching the immanent logic of the theme with a new aspect. That one great theme, Christ, must have the last word, as it were, sounding through all others as a dominant tone. We must accomplish everything on the basis of our relation to Jesus, taking our departure from Him, thus substituting Christ for our original, unbaptized nature as a basic principle of our responses and our actions.

Everything in our life will then receive a sacral character; all our feelings and doings will be hallowed at least in a vicarious sense, and, whatever be our avocations or concerns, we will remain in the world of Christ.

We must "baptize" all of our actions

Therefore, we must also guard against being submerged in the morally indifferent but necessary functions of ordinary life. While we eat, wash, or dress; while we put our things in order or examine our accounts, etc., we must never allow any of these functions to occupy our mind entirely with its brute specificity. We must, on the contrary, expressly *baptize* all these things in the sense of not being possessed by them but rather we must dominate them by reason of our conscious, direct, and permanent contact with Christ. In constant awareness of our determination to belong to Christ and to perform all our activities as His servants, we must incorporate even the trivial details of our daily routine into the essential meaning and direction of our life. Thus shall we live if we keep in mind the words of St. Paul: "For none of us liveth to himself; and no man dieth to himself. For whether we live, we live unto the Lord; or whether we die, we die unto the Lord. Therefore, whether we live or whether we die, we are the Lord's" (Rom. 14:7-8).

That the goods and tasks with which the texture of our life is interwoven should not contrast with Christ is not enough. Neither is it sufficient for us to avoid being absorbed by the immanent teleology of indifferent concerns and to consider everything in a *general* perspective centered on Christ. We must advance beyond that minimum and place everything in a direct relationship to Christ, so as to be guided back toward the Alpha and Omega by even the specific meaning of every single thing to which we devote our attention.

This may be achieved in various ways. The institutional and corporate aspects of such a sanctification of life, all-important as they are, do not enter into our present scope and may be referred to in brief. Certainly human things are given a specific connection with God, inasmuch as the Church, by a particular act of consecration or benediction, assigns to them a place in the sacral sphere, as is the case with the sacramentals. That specific connection is restricted, here, to definite provinces of being (notably, material objects), and within these limits, again, to definite exemplars consecrated by a particular act. There is, further, the entirely different and unique case of marriage, a high creaturely good which Christ has erected, generically, into a Sacrament. What we in these pages are concerned with, however, is that connection of creaturely things with God which every Christian, individually, is able — and called upon — to establish; and which applies to all classes of things in creation.

We must offer everything to God

First, we may expressly offer as a sacrifice to God all our works, our joys and sufferings, whatever goods we are blessed with and whatever evils we have to endure. Everything is thus brought into a direct relationship with God and our mind is again and again reoriented to God. Yet, this relationship is a highly formal one; it is established, so to speak, above the head of the thing in question. It may be of great value, but it cannot actually fill our lives with a truly sacral atmosphere. The good intention which underlies that general sacrifice of our actions and sufferings on the one hand, and our specific contact with the object on the other, are not deeply interrelated. If one prevails, the other must decline and in both cases our life falls short of a full impregnation with the atmosphere of Christ. The good intention by itself is insufficient to baptize all things and to connect their very essence with Christ, to consecrate the world intrinsically. It does not pervade the things which are placed under its sign, but merely directs them externally towards God.

We must thank God for all things

A more profound connection between the genuine goods of the world and God will arise from our consciousness of possessing every such good as a gift from God, of the fact that everything we have is bestowed upon us by His *charity*. Thus, in a spirit of gratitude, through the medium of creaturely things we again and again hark back to the "Father of all lights"; and by all gifts we are reminded of the Giver: "In all things give thanks" (1 Thess. 5:18). For all the multiformity of our pursuits and cares, we are yet governed by the one great absolute Theme, and our life assumes the *habitus* of true simplicity.

We must see God reflected in created goods

There is, finally, a third way of instituting a connection between God and all goods, tasks, and activities. It consists in a comprehension of the profound analogies that inhere in the universe of things. In a sense, according to a certain gradation of the modes of being, all that is, is somehow representative of God. In this rich hierarchy of levels, the sharpest distinction is that between *vestigium* and *imago*. The created person alone is an image of God; every other created thing is merely a vestige of Him. We may propose to divine the analogy contained in every being, advancing up to the focal point where the inward relation between that thing and the *causa exemplaris* — the primal idea or exemplar — becomes discernible. Not that we ought to search, in a schematic fashion, after the specific analogy proper to each entity or type of being, taken individually; nor is such a strict allegorical interpretation possible. What we have in mind is rather a general vision of creation as something which has not only been *made* by God but which somehow reflects God.

The Christian is to discover God in the cosmos, not only as its author (*causa prima*) but as its primal exemplar or paragon (*causa exemplaris*). Once he is touched by the *lumen Christi*, man will see the world with new eyes.

A new light falls on everything, disclosing the secret ties of all reality to the divine essence. Now, against the background of this general vision, as a next phase the analogy of being, in the concrete, will reveal its broad lineaments. So far as the inferior (the material, the vital) spheres are concerned, a differential manifestation of analogy according to special objects will scarcely be present except in a vague and accidental manner. In higher spheres of being, marked by a more condensed substantiality, the analogy will tend to take on more characteristic forms in a closer coordination to concrete types or even individual entities. With man, in particular, an entirely new plane of representation is introduced. In this new vision, created being becomes transparent, as it were: reaching beyond its own limits, it points towards God and speaks of Him directly.

However, we can derive that vision not from an empirical contemplation of the universe but from Revelation alone. For the analogy that is meant here is not confined to a representation by concrete reality of absolute being as such, the *ens a se* in the sense of rational metaphysics, which we might approach *from below upwards* by the natural light of reason; it is conceived as representing the nexus of created things with God as He reveals Himself to us in the features of Christ.

Guided by analogy so interpreted, we shall be able to sense a reflection of the *lumen Christi* in the beauty of sunlight and to discern a likeness of God in every eternal, though merely natural, truth.

Thus shall we also grasp the coordination of natural to super-natural concepts and entities, and discern the many images and exemplars in the tissue of natural objects and relationships which refer to the world of the supernatural. The cleansing effect of water will evoke in our minds the redemptive power of Baptism. The deep union of two human beings in marriage will acquire a new meaning in the light of the bond between Christ and His Church, and of the mysterious union, transcending all conceptual understanding, of the three Divine Persons in one Substance.

We must view all things with eyes of Faith

Only when our entire vision of the cosmos is thus intrinsically imbued with the mystery of Faith, can we properly apply the phrase about our consecration of the cosmos to God. Here, unlike the above-discussed case of a mere formal consecration achieved by the good intention, there is question of an objectively preexistent connection.

Certainly that connection is not visible except to the eyes of Faith. Vision illumined by the Faith is alone able to fathom these depths, which remain inaccessible to the natural light of reason.

Further, this connection with God is not something superim-posed on the object; rather it leads us through its innermost core to God. Therefore, it becomes possible for us to entertain a full contact with the object, to accord an ample response to its specific meaning, and yet at the same time to continue dwelling in the sacral atmosphere. This comprehension of analogy alone, by virtue of which whatever thing we envisage may lift us towards God, will confer on our life a character of perfect simplicity, safeguarding our inward qualitative unity amidst the manifoldness of mundane objects and tasks.

Faith enables us to see the hierarchy of values more clearly

In this perspective, however, we shall also become aware of the vast hierarchy of values in regard to their respective connection with God. With a new clarity and certitude we shall understand that eternal truths — for example, that man is endowed with free will, or that all finite beings require a cause — reflect God more directly than do empirical and accidental truths, such as the true statement that on a certain day it was raining or that hydrogen and oxygen combine into water. By the same token, we will grasp that the sublime beauty of a landscape like the Roman Campagna or a work of art like the Ninth Symphony of Beethoven, conveys to us more from God and draws us more powerfully into His world than does the beauty of a magnificent garb or a jewel. We shall no less clearly grasp the hierarchic distinction that moral values like charity, faithfulness, or veracity, refer to God in a much deeper and much more specific sense than do a man's vital values, such as healthiness, a lively temperament, etc.

We must conform our life to that hierarchy

This gradation of values is not indifferent, either, from the standpoint of the part we intend to assign to them in our lives. To be sure, we cannot select arbitrarily the goods with which we shall or shall not occupy ourselves. Our profession, for instance, is likely to compel us to divert a great deal of attention to many objects which have comparatively little direct connection with God. Yet, so far as our free preference, our general receptivity, and our basic interests are concerned, we may well adjust these to the hierarchy of objects as determined by their measure of representing God. By keeping in mind the ideal order of values conceived from this point of view, we achieve a step in making our life simpler and bringing it to the one great denominator which is Christ.

The encounter with genuine values simplifies the soul

Every genuine value as such, however, operates towards true simplicity in him who experiences it; and it does so in proportion to its place in the hierarchy of values. Our state of mind always reveals greater simplicity when a genuine value is possessing and shaping us than when we are engrossed with neutral concerns, as are mostly the requirements of workaday life. Certainly, *any* dealing with creaturely goods, notwithstanding the formal simplifying power of values as such, *may* interfere with our disposition for simplicity; it will do so with certainty whenever we, in attending to these goods, isolate them from the world of higher values and detach them from their function of a representation of God.

Yet, however real this danger may be, considering the natural proneness of our fallen natures to let outward influences distract them from God, the created goods are also capable, on the other hand, of elevating us towards God in various ways and of apprising us of His charity and His glory. Only if we receive every good (by the methods just described) in mindfulness of God and *qua* gifts and tokens of God — if in all values we are anxious to discern and to meet God — then the formal simplifying power of every value as such will become operative and conducive to true simplicity.

Values elevate us above a multiplicity of interests

As regards the relation between value and simplicity of soul, the following aspects should be noted. To begin with, every value by reason of its wealth of meaning elevates us above the extensive multiplicity of the interests belonging to lower planes. The higher that value is, the more we find (in a comparative sense) *all in one*. In our response to that value, our interest will expand in depth rather than in breadth. Yet, depth as such, even apart from the specific height of the value concerned, acts in favor of simplicity, inasmuch as it implies a recollected state of mind and a withdrawal from peripheral interests.

Values unify communities and individuals

Moreover values are characterized by a certain *vis unitiva*: a faculty of coordination and unification, both in an interpersonal and an intrapersonal sense. Definite values may integrate a number of persons into a community; and again, within a person they tend to effect an integration of divergent emotions and impulses. Counteracting the dispersion and dissipation of energies in our soul, they tend to make us recollected and simple. This effect increases with the height of the value. It is only in our surrender to God, our loving adoration of Him, that we are wholly collected and our whole essence is actualized in one all-comprehensive attitude.

It is our duty, therefore, to recognize the elevating action of the great goods of creation, their mission to liberate us from lower attachments and to guide us towards God, and accordingly to lay ourselves open to their operation. A great enemy of true simplicity is our dependence on peripheral considerations — such as human respect, the pleasure derived from being spoiled, a comfortable life, freedom from cares, this or that cherished habit, and so forth. The more we are captivated by peripheral interests, the less simple our life will be. Some people are so anxious to have the proper utensil, instrument, or contrivance on hand at every occasion and in every possible emergency (nor will that object do unless it is their personal property) that they never have time or energy left for attending to really great and relevant things. They are completely enchained by their concern about a multitude of superficial affairs to which they are fettered by many small ties. The slightest disturbance in their accustomed comfort deprives them of peace.

But imagine our heart being touched and lit up by some high value — the chain is burst; all the marginal preoccupations are swept out of sight and are no longer able to tie us down. Whenever some high good in our life appears threatened — a beloved person, for instance, has fallen gravely ill or our own life is in danger — we at once become aware of the pettiness and futility of all those paltry things to which we have formerly attached so great importance. How willingly would we renounce all of them, if only we could thereby save that one precious good! Or again, suppose that we are initiated into a new realm of beauty, or gain insight into a great central truth — then, too, we rise above all shallow things; we increase in freedom, and so also in simplicity.

This liberating power of a high value or a deep experience is most strikingly manifested whenever a person's heart is inflamed with a noble passion of love. At one blow, what has been his habitual world breaks down. It is this which finds its plastic expression in the first act of Richard Wagner's *Tristan und Isolde*, when, having drunk the philter, Tristan cries out of his "dream ill-omened of Tristan's honor." All the world of outward honor and renown suddenly appears so sunk into immateriality that he is no longer able even to recall its meaning. In this sense, again, he refers in the second act to himself and Isolde as being "enveloped by night."

With the surge of this great love, which lifts them both into a new and higher world, a new principle of value has entered into their lives, in the sight of which all things that peopled their former "day-worlds" are condemned to evanescence. These things do not fit into their new "night-world." As lovers they have acquired a new simplicity.

We must consciously yield to the elevating power of values

Of such deep experiences we must make the most so as to detach ourselves from transient goods. We must seize the offer of God contained in that gift-like descent upon us of a high value, and, yielding to its attraction, ascend to a new point of vantage, where we shall be past many things which have previously confined us within the zone of the petty. We must not resist this shattering of a more trivial world where we have found a snug and cozy home for our everyday existence. We must evince a perpetual and alert willingness to follow this upward pull instead of fearfully and slothfully barricading our hearts against it. "Today if you shall hea᛫ his voice, harden not your hearts" (Ps. 94:8).

It does not suffice to accept that detachment from lower and more irrelevant things as a gift; we must actively cooperate with it, and assent to it once for all. Otherwise, the effect of that deep experience towards making us free and simple will be confined to its actual duration, as of a psychic episode. Above all, whenever a high human good exercises its releasing effect upon us, we must consciously evoke and experience its manifold relations to God, in order that it may lead us before the face of God. That elevation above petty terrestrial goods must take root in our soul as a permanent attitude of *sursum corda*, of eagerness to let ourselves be borne aloft to God.

If, invoking Jesus' assistance and imitating His example, we undergo these experiences in a spirit that enables us to penetrate not merely into the specific content of the high goods in question but into the very presence of the "Father of all lights" (a condition for fully comprehending that specific content itself), then all these experiences will become milestones along our path to true simplicity. Every such gift placed in our lives by God entails an obligation for us to change, to soar upwards, to extricate ourselves from certain meshes, and to acquire greater freedom for God.

Heroism is impossible without true simplicity of soul

Without the possession of true simplicity, no true heroism is possible. Such heroism implies that we are ready to sacrifice, without reserve, all lower goods to a higher one; that we gladly sell all we possess in order to buy the land where the treasure is buried. Heroism in a man means that he does not glance sidewards but straight ahead; not hesitating to cast away, with one gesture, all the scrap heap of trifles, amenities, dependencies, and considerations that hamper him whenever he hears the call of a high value, and the more so, when the *unum necessarium* challenges him with its high demand.

The heroic man is simple, and in his heroic act becomes the simpler. Every heroic act is the victory of a dominant aim over a multitude of petty ties and distractions. All experiences which enlarge our hearts, which expand and embolden our souls, and which render us able to sacrifice inferior things heroically — as does, above all, a great love under Jesus — contribute to our achieving true simplicity. What we must seek is a general readiness to give away lower things for the sake of higher ones, according to the divinely sanctioned legitimate order of values, and in this sense, ultimately, even to abandon any and every high good for the sake of the highest one — that is, Christ.

This pursuit of simplicity makes it imperative for us to lead a collected life. Certainly, recollection — the process of *collecting ourselves* — is not only a corollary of true simplicity but, more generally, one of the most important elements in our transformation in Christ. Therefore, a more extensive study of this subject follows. But even at first glance its close relationship to simplicity must be perceptible. Like simplicity, recollection implies a process of integration and unification, as contrasted to dispersion and dissipation. The very same words of Our Lord that stress the primacy of contemplation also contain an admonition to true simplicity, which must ever sound in the Christian's ears: "Martha, Martha, thou art careful, and art troubled about many things; but one thing alone is necessary" (Luke 10:41-42).

6

Recollection and Contemplation

IN recollection and contemplation — kindred but not identical attitudes — we encounter two more basic constituents of religious life. Recollection is a condition of all truly wakeful and deep modes of living, and hence indispensable for our transformation in Christ. Contemplation, again, is the *source* that feeds all life in Christ, and at the same time, the *end* in which that life finds its fulfillment.

Distraction as the inability to concentrate

What, then, is recollection? It is primarily an antithesis to *distraction*. We say sometimes we are not able to recollect ourselves in prayer: we are distracted. We then mean that we are unable to concentrate our attention on one point; we are controlled by the automatism of our associations; our mind is flying from one object to another; the images of our fantasy fitfully displace one another. This state of mind, in which we do not attend fully to any object and fail to penetrate the *logos* of any part of being but are at the mercy of our mechanism of associations, is properly termed *distraction* — a state of being dragged along from one object to another, never touching any of them but superficially. That distraction is the exact antithesis to recollection.

Distraction as the inability to determine the object of our concentration

On other occasions, however, when speaking of distraction we mean that our attention is too much captivated by a certain object to allow us to concentrate voluntarily on any other object. This is distraction in a relative sense only. In this case we are not unable to concentrate at all but merely unable to control our attention at will; unable to detach it from the object that happens to hold it and to direct it to that other object which at the moment possesses thematic importance. Suppose the object which thus captivates our interest is more peripheral, less essential and less relevant than the other one which constitutes the theme of a situation and to which we vainly attempt to direct our attention; then, too, we have a state of mind opposed to recollection.

Recollection is the antithesis to concern with the superficial

For recollection proper always means an awakening to the essential, a recourse to the absolute which never ceases to be all-important and in whose light alone everything else discloses its true meaning.

Thus, recollection is more than the absence of distraction in the narrower sense of the term. It is more than the inner coordination resulting from our concentration on any given object. It also embodies an antithesis to all superficial diversion as such. Every attitude contrasting with distraction proper does not necessarily imply recollection. A man driving a motorcar through a busy street, who is keenly concentrated on the business of steering, is not therefore recollected.

Recollection is not merely the antithesis of reverie, of loose flights of fancy, and of the state of being swayed by the play of associations, but also of all submersion in trivial activities or interests. It is not merely a formal integration of our mind (as implied by concentrating our attention upon an object, no matter what); rather, it means an integration of the entire person; a realization of its true self out of the depths of its being. "Recollection is the accomplishment of unity in the ground of the soul," says Ernest Hello.

A person who exhausts himself in the moment's concern, who passes without a breathing space from one concentrated work to another, who always gives his unreserved attention to the task of the hour without ever pausing to recollect himself — such a person is as little recollected as one who dissipates his life in dreaming, playing, and empty chatter. The latter way of life is certainly more reprehensible; but both are alike opposed to true recollection.

In recollection, we recover our deepest orientation toward God

True recollection contains both an aspect of tension and another of relaxation. It implies a release from all tension of surface interests, but at the same time an enhanced consciousness of our central direction. In the attitude of recollection, we place ourselves at a distance from things so we can survey them all from a point of vantage, without ever being swamped in any special concerns or interests.

Yet, every kind of withdrawal from the peripheries towards the depths may not amount to recollecting ourselves. Concentration on a philosophical or artistic work necessarily implies a direction towards the depth, but it need not imply a state of being recollected. One may even be deeply touched by the beauty of nature or of great works of art, without positing an act of true recollection.

We may better understand this by visualizing some moment in which we are attempting to recollect ourselves. An important decision or a task of great dignity is ahead of us. We do not feel equal to it, as things are; we say we must first recollect ourselves. Withdrawing from all direct contact with the concern that occupies us, we try to forget whatever is on our hands, to escape the pressure of what is incumbent upon us, and to recover ourselves. To that end, we should remember the last things; and, from the whirlpool of the great and the small things of life, emerge towards God, the Cause and the Goal of all being. We return to what is truly and unchangingly omnipresent: the ultimate meaning of our life, our eternal destiny, our supreme goal.

Then only, when all else fades away for a moment, when we recover our deepest, unique direction towards God, when we stand before Christ, saying: "Behold the handmaid of the Lord" (Luke 1:38), do we actually recover ourselves and resume identity with our innermost selves. Thus alone can man attain to a real *habitare secum* (dwelling with oneself), as the Rule of St. Benedict calls it. For, as we have already seen, God is nearer to us than we are to ourselves. In His perspective alone can we see every finite object in its proper place in creation, revealing, in the light of the supreme truth, its particular meaning and value.

And thus alone do we secure the necessary distance which guards us from being submerged in the immanent logic of a task or a situation; a distance not calculated to destroy our living contact with the object of our vision, but on the contrary, enabling us to penetrate its essence more truly than would exclusive attention to that object.

We must proceed to the depth in order to gain a full and adequate awareness of things, hearkening to God's call from the depths of our being, and bringing our most intimate selves to full actuality. Until we meet the demands of life on a plane provided by such a primarily unpragmatic and nonfunctional attitude (that is, ultimately, by our relationship to God), we are unable to actualize ourselves except in a partial and distorted way. Our experience of things is otherwise still affected with incidental admixtures; it lacks the full sanction of personality.

Recollection may be voluntary or involuntary

However, recollection is not always a result of a voluntary act of recollecting oneself. Without a deliberate act in this sense, a high value that seizes our heart may lead us into the presence of God and so render us recollected. This process (which, to be sure, is not provoked by every value experience, however genuine) even constitutes a deeper and more organic form of recollection than the method of recollecting ourselves by a voluntary act.

Nevertheless, it would be an error merely to wait for the gift of such a recollecting influence to guide us towards awareness of God and of the true meaning of our life. Again and again we should voluntarily relinquish the turmoil of our current occupations, the pursuit of this or that concrete aim, and return to the essential that is proper to our inmost self.

Thus, the Divine Office is preceded by the prayer *Aperi*, which represents not only a prayer for the grace of true piety but an express act of recollection. In fact, the Office itself, besides its primary meaning which is to praise God, also represents an act of emergence from the welter of life towards God, a recovery of the essential — an attitude of recollection.

Only the recollected man is fully alive

In recollecting ourselves, we empty our soul of all current concerns, and are no longer possessed by the things which fill our life; we escape from the network of those autonomous systems of particular aims into which life's single situations and tasks erect themselves. We face God directly, and take a new departure from the Alpha and Omega of our being.

Through finding our way to God, we find our way home to ourselves. Thus (and not otherwise), we establish that inward order of our life which makes it possible for us to attend to its details without yielding to the illegitimate pretension of the present as present. So our care for the various concerns and details of life will become legitimate before the face of God. From the center thus secured, everything can be brought to a common denominator, so that we may achieve unity in our life and our personality.

For, mostly, our life implies a continual desertion from the *habitare secum*. As a rule we incline to lose ourselves in the present situation and to accept the exclusive sovereignty of its immanent logic; to forget the proper and ultimate meaning of our existence. In this dispersed attitude, we are not really and truly alive. We actualize our peripheral being only or fragments of our deeper self at most.

Notwithstanding our intense concentration upon some object, our keen attention to one task or another, in the depth of our being we are asleep; we are not wholly existent, as it were. He only who is recollected is really awake; he alone, therefore, is alive in the full sense of the word.

Recollection is essential to transformation in Christ

The importance of recollection for the process of a transformation in Christ need hardly be pointed out. Without it, there is no full and valid life rooted in the depths and consequently, there can be no genuine, essential, and deeply penetrating transformation.

Without recollection, all good resolutions — all honest endeavors to overcome a defect or to achieve a supernatural transfiguration of natural virtues — are bound to remain impotent and sterile. Without that mobilization of our depths which the act of recollecting ourselves implies, we cannot become marked with the seal of Christ.

Recollecting ourselves vs. being recollected

Obviously, we must distinguish two phases of the attitude of recollection: these are, to put them briefly, the act of *recollecting ourselves* and the permanent state of *being recollected*.

The first is the act of *recollecting ourselves*, of rising towards God and recovering ourselves; of setting ourselves at a distance from all present concerns; of ordering all things before the face of God, and referring everything to the great common denominator, Christ.

And the second phase is the state of being and remaining recollected. This state will have to endure, while we are attending to a concrete task, engaged in a serious conversation or some meaningful work, or performing any other activity. To be sure, we are then no longer empty of all present details or cares; we again divert our vision from God to some concrete creaturely thing, and actualize a partial aspect of our being. Yet, we do not separate ourselves from God; we do not sever connection with the profound and ultimate center of our being. We keep within the divine context; we accord to the theme on hand that place only which it can rightfully claim in the eyes of God; we envisage it from that ultimate point of view; and we remain wakeful and alive in the depth of our being. According to the specific nature of the activity we are engaged in, this attitude can be realized in different ways.

Recollecting ourselves for higher tasks

Suppose we are dealing with some essential task of high rank, which we cannot even approach in an adequate manner unless we are recollected. In this case, it is recollection alone which will render possible a deep devotion to this task. From the depth of our being we should give ourselves to the task in question *in conspectu Dei*, on the very basis of our devotion to God. The temptation to lose ourselves or to be dispersed does not arise. Our present interest is incorporated into the integral order of a recollected mental life; an uninterrupted current leads from God, and our soul's depth, to that significant concrete thing.

Recollecting ourselves for necessary, but relatively superficial tasks

Or else, we are faced with a neutral theme which does not require — and is not even compatible with — devotion arising from the depth, but which holds a legitimate place in the outward order of our daily life or is legitimately proposed to us by circumstances. Then, again, we shall remain recollected by maintaining an essential, a *superactual*, connection with God and with the real center of our being. Far from exhausting ourselves in that peripheral concern and in spite of concentrating on it in the required measure, with our integral personality we dwell in another region. While we are attending, technically and intellectually, to the task in question, our awareness of God continues to resound in our soul like an unending melody.

This phenomenon of a superior motif resounding in the background, while the foreground is filled by peripheral interests, also occurs within the context of purely creaturely things. A great love, for instance, which inspires our heart and lends wings to our whole existence, is likely to resound with its melody throughout our external occupations; it never allows our soul to be dulled by the wear and tear of our daily routine, nor silences the voice of our deeper personality.

However conscientiously we may be attending to an outward task, we remain *in the world of* the beloved one. Our love of that person, not the activity of the moment, colors the atmosphere in which our soul is moving. At every moment it is present to our mind (however discreetly) that what we are just *doing* is not the real thing that fills and guides us; that we are not centered in this petty, peripheral section of our life but continue dwelling in the depth.

The same is true of the recollected person with reference to God and to the ultimate meaning of his life. He always keeps on the superactual level of wakefulness; amidst the welter of his outward activities he dwells in the world of God. His momentary concentration on a peripheral object never results in a submersion of the essential and valid thing.

Still, this second mode of being recollected while dealing with the concrete situations of life, meaningful or superficial, requires an intermittent renewal of the express act of recollecting ourselves. From time to time, we must bring ourselves to a full and exclusive awareness of God and of our essential goal, emptying our minds entirely of pragmatic interests and considerations. For the latter invariably expose man, in his fallen state, to lose hold of the *habitare secum* and to surrender all reserve in adapting himself to the immanent logic of the present particular situation. In order to remain recollected in the broader sense of the term, we must (aside from particular cases of extraordinary grace) lead an unceasing struggle, regaining unity with our true self again and again by an express act of recollection. The creaturely things that surround us involve, in varying degrees, a constant danger to our recollection in the real and ultimate truth; a danger inherent, above all, in many peripheral interests which appeal to our lust for sensation.

Contemplation is superior to action

Deliberate recollection is closely related to a further basic element of all true Christian life — *contemplation*. The words of Our Lord, "Mary hath chosen the best part" (Luke 10:42), clearly indicate the primacy of contemplation above action in our life. That primacy means not that we all should spend more time on contemplation than on action, but that we are to acknowledge and to experience contemplation as the higher of the two, as the more ultimately significant attribute of our nature.

Antiquity itself discerned the preeminence of the contemplative as against the active attitude. The magnificent words of Aristotle regarding the dianoetic (cognitional) virtues in the conclusion of his *Nicomachean Ethics* sufficiently testify to this. But ancient thought erroneously limited contemplation to the cognitional sphere. This identification contains a twofold error. In the first place, every search for knowledge does not imply contemplation. The scientist who is tensely working for definite results, who strides from fact to fact in order to solve a given problem, is not doing his researches with a contemplative intent. Only the intuitive penetration of the essence of a thing and the conscious dwelling in a truth already established, are truly contemplative attitudes. Secondly, contemplation embraces not only *cognition* but also the conscious state of *being affected* by a value; dwelling in the bliss derived from the light of beauty and goodness. The *frui*,[1] the enjoyment of value, the absorption in beauty — these are attitudes purely contemplative in nature. Many of our emotional acts have a contemplative character. Responses of joy, love, and adoration are typical embodiments of contemplation. Thus, Mary Magdalene not only listened to the words of Our Lord but in loving adoration immersed herself in the beatific presence of Jesus.

We contemplate ends, not means

In order to describe the characteristics of contemplation, we may start from its contrast with the position we take towards the *means* when engaged in a purposive activity. In all such activities our inward appreciation of the *end* is strictly differentiated from our

[1]St. Augustine distinguished *uti* (the use of a thing) and *frui* (the blissful penetration of a thing, the happy communing therewith) as two basic forms of our attitude toward the good. (Cf., the first book of *De doctrina christiana*, and *De civitate Dei* 19.10.)

relation to the *means*. Suppose we wish to meet someone, and for that purpose betake ourselves to a certain place. Meeting that person, or the performance of a definite task in this connection, constitutes our end. Walking to the place in question — or taking a train for that destination, buying tickets, etc. — are means pure and simple. It is the end that directs our steps, governs our activity, coordinates our thoughts and movements; it represents the *telos* and the thematic meaning of our enterprise. The means are mere points of passage as it were; they are merely used; none of them becomes thematic except in the context of its usefulness for the end. We are not intent on them as such, nor do we take any one of them seriously as a whole, in its essence; we are only interested in them according to their serviceableness for our purpose.

The structural difference between our attitude towards the end and towards the means is obvious. The strict attitude of *uti*, of using something, as applied to the means within a system of action, is the exact opposite of the contemplative attitude. It embodies the specifically pragmatic way of treating an object, characterized by the fact that our proper attention belongs to something other than the object with which we are now dealing, namely, to our *object* in the sense of our end or *purpose*. The immediate objects of our activity, with which we deal in terms of *uti*, play a merely instrumental (and transitory) role. On the other hand, full attention to an object as such, or an interest taken in its essential character as a whole, constitutes a first mark of contemplation.

Certainly, as a formal principle of our attitude, the difference between our relation to the end and to the means is always present. Yet, when the end itself is subordinated to a greater whole, which in its turn is governed by another supreme end, that difference becomes a merely relative one. Such is the case, for instance, when our meeting a certain person or our execution of a certain task — for which purpose we are to betake ourselves to a specified place — is again meant to subserve some other purpose.

But even if there is no such successive subordination of aims — if, that is to say, our given purpose is not incorporated into a superior teleology but represents a relatively *final end*, the conclusion of a chain of meaning — even then, with the *formal* difference between end and means being clearly present, the *material* difference between our attitude towards the end and towards the means may not necessarily be great. Thus, for example, when we wash or eat, the momentary aim we are pursuing is not, strictly speaking, experienced as a means towards some other superior aim, but rather as a conclusive end in itself; but neither is it a substantial or important purpose, whose attainment could possess anything like the dignity of a self-contained theme. Most activities in our life are of this kind; they subserve some purpose which is not a sovereign theme by itself and which cannot, on the strength of its own substance, become the object of a *frui* proper — of contemplative or self-immersing enjoyment.

The object of contemplation must be seen as having great value

In all these ordinary cases, not only our attitude towards means but also our attitude towards ends (though, in a formal sense, the latter implies an essentially higher appreciation) are characteristically *non*-contemplative. For a second mark of contemplation consists precisely in this: that the object faces us as a thing *of great dignity and importance in itself*, which by virtue of its own substance may appreciably enrich our souls. Whenever we approach an object in the mode of contemplation, it is not only that we esteem it as such in a *formal* sense; materially, too — that is, on the ground of its specific content and quality — it must belong to the class of such entities as are able to affect our heart and mind by virtue of their own intrinsic significance. That it may be desirable, necessary, or indispensable, is insufficient; it must be important in itself.

An active attitude is future-oriented; a contemplative attitude dwells in the present

An active attitude, even though it be directed to the attainment of a purpose important in itself, is always typically distinct from a contemplative one. Thus, if we undertake a journey in order to see a beloved person again, or if we perform a lofty moral action, our intent is not contemplative. For first, it is filled by a tension towards the future: the thought of something which does not yet exist and which is to be brought about. And, secondly, in contemplating an aim we do not accord to the good we intend to realize that broad, undivided attention which is implicit in contemplation proper.

Our attention to the object conceived as an end for action, express and emphatic as it may be, always retains a certain narrow and functional quality (akin, in some measure, to a technical attitude of abstraction and formalization), which also manifests itself in the fact of our advancing towards our end through a succession of means.

The contemplative attitude, on the other hand — such as the contemplation of an object of great beauty and the pure, restful joy it yields — is free from that dynamic tension towards the future; it implies, not a hastening forward but a dwelling in the present. Further, the attention we accord to the object is direct, unqualified, broad (as it were); it is undivided, instead of being limited by attention given to other objects as well, as is necessarily the case when we intend an object purposely in action, which we cannot do without also devoting ourselves to the means.

Accomplished ends are not true objects of contemplation

In order to grasp this difference in its whole extent, we must even go a third step further. Let us visualize the moment when an aim of great value and importance is actually reached — when, say, a moral action like the saving of a human life or the frustration of an injustice is on the point of being accomplished. The stages destined to lead up to the realization of the good are now behind us; the distance that separated us from our goal appears covered; our action now bears directly upon the final good, and the concluding *fiat* is at last being pronounced.

Even this phase of our active contact with a good reveals a characteristic difference from the contemplative attitude. For the good is still embedded there, in the thematic context of *realization through my action*; whereas, in contemplation, the thematic quality of the object's inner goodness unfolds in unalloyed purity. So long as the *realization of a good through my action* is still part of my *theme*, the prevalence of the good as such cannot fully express itself in all dimensions attached to that good. Nor do I, in that case, experience the good by my striving. In contemplation, I abandon myself to an object as a majestic entity which reposes in itself and does not *require me* in order to exist.

Contemplation is unconcerned with means or agents

Fourthly, our attention to the object — unlike the linear direction towards a purpose — can unfold in its full breadth without being altered by our concern with means; it is undivided attention.

In the fifth place, the contemplative attitude — as contrasted to action in all its stages, including that which precedes the final fulfillment of the end — is ruled entirely by the thematicity of the object as such. The aspect of a *realization through my action* is absent; the object acquires full thematic value.

Contemplation is reposeful attention to an object

Further, contemplation implies an inward penetration of the object, a communing therewith in awareness of everything it means, as though the object turned its full face to us. Whereas, in action, including even its final phase, we only touch the object from the outside intent on accomplishing it rather than facing it in all its plenitude.

Again, contemplation represents a specifically *restful* attitude, in which we, free from the circumscribing function of acting as agent, actualize our entire *being*. Finally, contemplation contrasts with action owing to its basic trait of receptivity.

Contemplation differs radically from relaxation

We have just described contemplation as a *reposeful attention to an object fully present*; this must not be construed in the sense of crediting every reposeful or relaxed state of mind with a contemplative character. Relaxation as such need not have anything to do with contemplation. I may dream, muse, or take a walk free from all particular purpose, without the slightest trace of contemplation proper. Nor is the relaxed state which denotes recreation — a state of mere rest, without any actual direction towards an aim — in any sense in the nature of contemplation. For all these forms of relaxation involve a temporary extinction of wakeful, alert spiritual life; they entirely lack intensity and are not far distant from a cessation of all intellectual activity. Nor are they consonant with the express attitude of *intentional* reference to an object. In these forms of relaxation, the dialogic situation between subject and object which is constitutive for all higher mental life cannot possibly thrive.

Contemplation, on the other hand — as has been explained by Jacques Maritain in his study on "Action and Contemplation" (*Revue Thomiste*) — represents spiritual *activity* in the most eminent sense of the word; only it is an *immanent* (in contraposition to a *transitive*) activity. All activity which in some way intervenes in the events happening outside its subject, all work in the broadest sense of the term, we call *transitive*. In contrast, an act of loving adoration, for example, is a purely immanent form of spiritual activity. Here, the actualization of the mind and the intense realization of a mental attitude take place within the person himself, devoid of any operation beyond the range of his own being — be it a fact brought about by action, an object produced, or a change effected in some object already existing. Yet, for being thus limited in range, immanent activity is by no means a less noble or intense form of activity.

Contemplation involves intense spiritual activity

It would be a gross error indeed to confuse contemplation with trivial or recreative relaxation as described above. On the contrary, it embodies activity of the highest degree, the fullest actualization of the person, and the most wakeful, genuine, and intense form of spiritual life. True, it is distinguished from action not only by the fact of its being immanent instead of transitive, but (as we have seen) apart from other aspects by the fact of its being unrelated to any purposeful, teleological coordination of behavior. Yet, contrary to the dull forms of relaxation, it reveals an eminently intentional structure; it implies *attention* to an object in the strictest sense of the term; and once more in contrast to ordinary relaxation, it manifests a quality of specific *depth* and significance.

But we cannot properly understand the nature of contemplation without putting the question as to its possible objects.

Nothing considered as purely instrumental can be an object of contemplation

To begin with, nothing purely instrumental in character is eligible for becoming an object of contemplation. One cannot, properly speaking, contemplate what is *par excellence* an article of use — a bicycle, for instance. To be sure, objects of this kind also can be envisaged in themselves, in their essence, instead of being merely utilized regardless of any aspect of them besides the abstract, functional one which is their availableness for a definite purpose. In the face of such objects, too, one element of contemplation — that of a purely cognitive, non-purposeful attitude — can be actualized. But their metaphysical content is too poor and insignificant to qualify them as possible objects for contemplation proper. They cannot deeply affect us, nor elicit the attitude of *frui*; attention based on a response to value in which our total personality is present would clearly be out of proportion here. We cannot immerse ourselves in the essence of such objects, nor can our soul rest in their embrace. The same is true of all other entities which do not possess a deep and noble content or a high value of their own.

Contemplation demands an object of value and depth

Contemplation proper demands, as its object, either a deep general truth or an entity of high rank and value. We may visualize, in contemplation, the contingency of all created beings or the essence of the spiritual person; we may be absorbed in the contemplation of the virtue of purity or of charity. The beauty of a work of art, too, may become an object for contemplation whenever we drink in that beauty, free from all preoccupations, and let our souls be elevated by its magic. Again, we may penetrate contemplatively the soul of a beloved person, becoming aware of its full splendor and, remote from all pragmatic concerns, in the devotion of love surrendering ourselves to its presence.

The object of contemplation determines the character of contemplation

But the *quality* of our attitude of contemplation is itself essentially determined, in part, by the nature of the object. Above all, an important difference must be noted according to whether the object of our contemplation is of a personal or a non-personal nature. In relation to a person, a form of contemplation is possible in which the fact that the contemplated object is also endowed with subjectivity is itself experienced in a certain definite manner.

We might describe this, if such a technical term be allowed, as *I-thou contemplation*. It is sharply distinct from all contemplation directed to a non-personal object which, correspondingly, might be termed *it-contemplation*.

The fact, however, that what we are contemplating is a personal being, does not of necessity qualify our contemplation as *I-thou contemplation*. (This requires the further condition that a mutual relationship of loving awareness should underlie our contemplation of the beloved person.) The *thou-contemplation* which may be present in such a case will, in a certain sense, be less perfect than our solitary contemplation, uncomplicated by the element of mutuality, of a person to whom we are devoted; the latter type of contemplation is likely to be of a more restful, a more static character, more timeless and more purely contemplative in quality.

The perfections in *I-thou contemplation*

But on the other hand, in the type we call *I-thou contemplation* the dialogic character of the relationship and the enrichment we receive from the contemplated person (who, in this case, actively reciprocates our love) acquire a new and higher degree of reality. The fact that the person we are contemplating by virtue of his love for us *actually* enters our own personality and pervades our own soul, confers a new dimension on the aspect of communing inherent in contemplation.

Most important of all, our loving approach is caught up, as it were; our response is directed to an object which is itself responsive to our love, our awareness of this aspect, again, coloring our very experience of the object in question. Thus, the object not merely happens to be a person but formally confronts us *qua* person, which renders possible a far greater intensity of contact. In this case alone will the fact that our object is of a personal nature manifest itself fully in our mode of approaching it. Thus, in *I-thou* contemplation the contemplative attitude acquires new, specific features of metaphysical perfection; a greater actualization of the receptive aspect of contemplation; and — something entirely new — the counter-response of the object, with the enhanced personalization of the contemplative relationship which results therefrom.

The perfections in *It-contemplation*

On the other hand, there is also (as has already been hinted) a metaphysical perfection specific to what we called *it-contemplation*, an exclusive privilege of this form insofar as we confine ourselves to objects of contemplation belonging to the realm of created things. In *it-contemplation*, which presents the object strictly *qua* object (even though it be a person), a broader, a more serene, a more purely contemplative attitude of spiritual immersion is realized than is possible in *I-thou contemplation*.

With this point reached, a further important division of contemplative attitudes becomes discernible.

Sometimes contemplation intensifies our experience of a particular moment

On the one hand, contemplation may mean a halt at a real moment in the flow of time, a "now" in which we are fully present and concentrated on a concrete object likewise present to us. Here, the normally latent — or, superactual — depth of our personal essence undergoes an *actualization*. When in the mutual spiritual interpenetration we drink, as it were, the being of the beloved, the rest of the world fades away around us. Dismissing all preoccupation about aims, I am then only directed towards the beloved, entirely immersed in his being and I nevertheless do not withdraw from the framework of temporal actuality but experience a more condensed, a *fully valid actuality*. I realize a unique and express *now*; I am aware — if the phrase be permissible — of a particularly momentous moment. The world of true and ultimate reality, the world of what soars above all transient aims and objects — a world to which I am only related, as a rule, in a superactual manner — enters my life, here, in the form of such a contemplative presence; it actualizes itself in the real stream of my life.

Sometimes contemplation seems to lift us out of time

It is quite different with those more frequent instances of the contemplative attitude when I visualize and experience a great truth, a high value, or even the essence of a beloved person, from an *extra-temporal* level of vision. Then I withdraw, as far as the center of my consciousness is concerned, from my actual life, emerging towards the world of genuine and ultimate things which I now see ordered in the perspective of eternity, located as it were in their *topos uranios* ("celestial place").

I do not, in this case, realize an express *moment* which is only raised above the rest of life by virtue of its specific *quality* of inward wealth and depth; rather I ascend, so to speak, a high peak soaring above my actual life and beyond the level of time experience. From that point of vision I perceive all things in their remoteness and their timeless being, independent of their real presence, penetrating their essence entirely at rest, in a specifically contemplative mode of consciousness. Let us think of the words of St. Augustine, in the liturgy of the Matins of Maundy Thursday. His voice there seems to reach us from a region beyond time; we sense his mind absorbed in contemplation, in the mystery of the Psalm text, immersed in the *logos* of that truth, unyoked, as it were, from the functional processes of life. In this form of the contemplative attitude the aspects of tranquillity and timelessness, of a pure and undisturbed intellectual devotion to the inward *logos* of the object, are particularly preeminent.

Contemplation brings us into contact with ultimate reality

In the first type of contemplation, then, it is the world of true and ultimate reality which enters our life; whereas, in the second, it is we who emerge from our actual life into that world. This renders a further important characteristic of contemplation easier to understand. It does not suffice in any form of contemplation that we should abandon ourselves to the object — to "rest" therein, to be "filled" by it — in an attitude however devoid of pragmatism.

In order that contemplation may bring out its full meaning and attain its perfection, another feature must be present. The object must affect us not only with its isolated specific content, it must elevate us into the world of valid and ultimate reality. We must, in contemplation, meet that world as such, so as to acquire suddenly a comprehensive new attitude towards all things.

Who of us does not know the supreme moments when a great truth, a glorious beauty of art or of nature, or the soul of a beloved person manifests itself to our soul with a lightning-like splendor, gracing our eyes with a vision of ultimate reality and prompting us to exclaim, "O Lord, how admirable is Thy name in the whole earth!" (Ps. 8:10)?

It is not as though the specific content of what has thus manifested itself to us were presently to vanish again, after having fulfilled a transitory role. On the contrary, we continue to envision that object in its deep and unique proper essence, situating it, as it were, in its abode in the *cœlum empyreum* ("the highest heavens") of that valid and ultimate reality into which it elevates us.

In other words, not until an object which by virtue of its specific content admits of contemplative attention so affects us that we at last face God Himself, encountering that object in the world of God and seeing it in the light of God — not until then will our attitude be that of contemplation proper. Then only, with our awakening to a sense of true and eternal reality, will our state of consciousness outgrow the limits of time. The halt we make will no longer mean a mere interruption of the stream of purposeful actuality but a triumphant soaring above it, an essential liberation from its fetters. So long as we are merely contemplating an object as such, not following it up to its abode in the *cœlum empyreum* and not being led by it into the presence of the "Father of all lights," we may at most actualize certain formal features of the contemplative attitude; we will not rise in triumphant freedom and sweep above the neutral, pragmatic process of life with its succession of conative tensions and its inherent unrest.

Perfect contemplation always implies at least an indirect reference to God

Thus, all perfect contemplation implies an indirect reference to God. Unless it helps us to establish a contact with God, the contemplative attitude cannot attain a complete unfolding of its specific character. This does not mean that God must be its formal object; that all true contemplation must be religious contemplation proper. The contemplation we have now discussed is directed to some created entity as its formal object. Yet, even here, a reference to God is necessarily implied.

For first, contemplation is more than the intellectual analysis of an object or even the enjoyment of disinterested knowledge. It requires that the object should help us to approach the world of valid and noble reality, which again involves, as a background at least, our awareness of the presence of God.

And, secondly, no thing discloses *its own* deepest meaning and unique value until it is seen *in conspectu Dei*: "And in Thy light we shall see light" (Ps. 35:10). Finally, it is only through our contact with God that the depths of our own being will be fully actualized and that we awaken to our full selfhood, thus becoming able to realize our contemplative attention to the given object with complete consciousness and receptiveness.

Religious contemplation simultaneously actualizes all the perfections of contemplation

Let us turn now to contemplation in the strictest sense of the term — to religious contemplation proper. The characteristics previously established, naturally, hold good here. When we face God in adoration and surrender, we again realize that relinquishment of the world of purposeful processes, that halt in our vital activities, and that restful immersion which are the marks of contemplation in general; only all this happens in a more perfect way.

But another important difference must be noted. Whereas in the contemplation of the created good, the different perfections of contemplation cannot be actualized simultaneously, they can be and are united in one in the contemplation of God. In our contemplative surrender to the absolute Person, we experience the light of His loving glance penetrating our soul and are conscious of His personal response to our loving surrender.

Thus, on the one hand, what we have called "I-thou contemplation" is fully present. And yet, on the other hand, that more particularly "contemplative" attitude of timeless tranquillity which we called "it-contemplation" appears in equal splendor. We may dwell in God with that absolute, changeless tranquillity which is alien to the precious, condensed supreme moments in the spiritual relationship between finite personal beings joined in mutual awareness of one another. God the omnipresent, who pervades all presentness, is also the eternal Being, towering above time in its entirety. He unites the concentrated actuality of the supreme moment to the timelessness of unaltered superactuality; He incarnates the abundance of all being and possesses all perfections of being. In Him the two specific aspects of contemplation which are mutually incompatible within the range of creaturely objects, here converge and become one.

Full surrender is possible only in religious contemplation

Moreover, religious *I-thou contemplation* differs essentially from the one which is possible towards a created person. Even in a purely formal sense, surrender to God is more properly possible than surrender to any created person. God alone can be an object of loving *adoration*. A unique form of subordination is implied therein — the only possible case of an absolute subordination, different from all relative surrender in kind and not merely in degree. There is further implied, however, an unconditional *delivery of self*: "Into Thy hands I commend my spirit" (Ps. 30:6). In religious contemplation alone — which, whatever be the special mystery we are viewing, is always in essence subsidiary to the worship of God — is it possible for us to fling ourselves, so to speak, into the object of our contemplation with our entire being. Here alone can the consciousness be given us that not merely our love but our entire being is received; that we rest encompassed by our absolute Lord from whose hands we have issued forth, in whom our being rests, and who in holy Baptism has communicated to us a new supernatural life.

Religious contemplation presupposes a personal God

As a result, genuine religious contemplation is unimaginable in relation to a deity impersonally, pantheistically conceived. Not only would the idea of an *I-thou contemplation* be meaningless; there would be no place either for the experience of resting securely in God's arms — an experience that can be granted to us by an infinitely superior absolute Person only, never by the phantom of an impersonal force. Incidentally, the very concept of an impersonal absolute contains a self-contradiction, for any personal being is in essence superior to everything impersonal.

The encounter with ultimate reality is preeminent in religious contemplation

The aspect of immersion, though it belongs to the formal structure of the contemplative attitude in general, acquires a more preeminent and literal meaning in religious contemplation. "Lo, to Thee surrendered, my whole heart is bowed, tranced as it beholds Thee, shrined within the cloud" (Hymn of St. Thomas Aquinas). To religious contemplation, the character of a bursting through towards valid and ultimate reality is specifically proper. Its clear presence in our consciousness may vary according to our disposition at the given moment and to the measure of grace which God imparts to us; but, as a formal aspect at least, the intentional reference to rising up towards the *coelum empyreum* is never absent from religious contemplation.

The latter must necessarily fulfill the function of drawing us before the face of God and rendering us aware of His reality, for God Himself is here, the proper object of our contemplation. It is not needful therefore that we should in each case actually *experience* the beatifying gift of being thus touched by the world of ultimate reality; whereas, when creaturely essences are the object of our contemplation, such an actual experience is a condition for bursting through: past the formal object of our attention and toward ultimate reality as seen in God's perspective. Yet, in religious contemplation, an express reference to the world of ultimate reality is necessarily present; and if a full joy-giving, blissful experience of that world is also granted us, we do not thereby enter an altogether new sphere, but merely intensify our experience of what has already been the object of our *intentional* direction. As regards the actualization of the experience proper, a variety of degrees is possible.

In discussing the contemplation of creaturely objects, we pointed out that there were two classic cases: in one form of contemplation, the higher world *enters* our life, embodying itself, as it were, in a supreme, condensed "now"; in the other, we *emerge*, we are transported, in a sense, from our life towards that higher world.

On the level of religious contemplation, the division reappears. The moment of the consecration of the Host (which eminently appeals to a basic contemplative attitude in the faithful) is the supreme archetype of such a "now," representing the influx of the world of valid reality into our life. In a similar, though not an identical sense, the act of holy Communion also contains such a "now." The other pole is exemplified by interior prayer, and the so-called *prayer of quiet* — contemplation in the very strictest sense of the term. This constitutes the supreme archetype, not of a paramount "now," but of our withdrawal from vital actuality (a plastic expression of that withdrawal is furnished by the word *ecstasy*, whose literal meaning is "stepping out"), our elevation into a region beyond time, our ascent to the plane of eternal validity.

Religious contemplation is possible only after we renounce sin

Our loving absorption in God, foreshadowing the beatific vision we are to be granted in Heaven, is the most perfect contemplation. In moments of reposing in God and experiencing His all-pervasive presence, of our loving adoration of God, we achieve *in statu viae* something like an anticipation of our status in eternity. Every created being, however, though in very different ways according to its metaphysical rank and value, can become a point of departure for religious contemplation as described above.

In order to find our way to religious contemplation, we must, before all else, have renounced everything that cannot be upheld before the face of Christ. We must be firmly resolved to part with "the world and its pomp," and to shut out whatever offends God. "Who shall ascend into the mountain of the Lord: or who shall stand in his holy place? The innocent in hands, and clean of heart" (Ps. 23:3-4).

We must abandon preoccupation with creaturely goods

Next, to find our way to religious contemplation, we must rid ourselves of all preoccupation about any creaturely good. We must begin by becoming entirely empty. Not only must all conative tension, directed to some pragmatic purpose, disappear; for a moment we must forget everything, pronounce a *nescivi* ("I have forgotten"), and achieve a total inward silence, dimming all desires and longings in our soul.

More, we must possess an essential readiness to renounce any legitimate good, if that be God's will. We must deliver back everything into the hands of God, so as to receive it again from Him according to His holy will. Not before we have thus waxed inwardly empty can we be completely filled by God, face the full reality of His presence, and belong to Him wholly.

Nowhere has the very tissue of contemplation been depicted in more tangible terms than in the conclusion of St. Augustine's great work, *De civitate Dei (22.30)*, which treats of eternal life: "There we shall rest and we shall see; we shall see and we shall love; we shall love and we shall praise. Behold what shall be in the end without end!"

Contemplation is the proper form of our spiritual life

In life eternal, all our being will be contemplation. That bears evident witness to the truth that contemplation as against action represents the higher, more final, and more proper form of our spiritual life. That which "shall be in the end without end," which embodies the crowning perfection of our being, which constitutes our eternal goal, the object of our longing and the content of our eternal happiness — that must be the higher, the ultimate good.

Undoubtedly, *in statu viae* it is not for us to abandon ourselves exclusively to contemplation. Even in the lives of men and women who, in answer to a specific call, have vowed themselves to a life of contemplation — the Carmelite Sisters, for example — a certain measure of action is indispensable. The outward process of life itself demands, to a degree, a rhythm of pragmatic activities. Beyond that, however, work proper must not be wholly foregone even in contemplative orders — a principle expressed in the monastic device *ora et labora* ("pray and work"). Our nature *in statu viae* is so ordained for action that the latter cannot be wholly eschewed without spiritual injury. But to mankind in general, God has entrusted a more definite task of activity. "Subdue the earth," the Lord said to Adam and Eve. Even in Paradise, man was destined for activity; only, in that state, it would have been toilless activity. It lies in the divine plan that *in statu viae* (a state of unfolding and actualization), man should intervene creatively in the processes of nature and should build up a culture. We are thus called on to acquire an increasing knowledge of the world; to create material and spiritual goods; to elaborate and order a life in common.

Action has both dignity and necessity in our lives

Action, too, possesses a high dignity of its own; it embodies a specific mode of representing God. That man is an effigy of God is also manifest in the fact that of all earthly creatures he alone is able to change and to shape his environment by a free and conscious choice of purposes; that the right has been conferred on him to perfect outward nature and to share in the creative rulership of God. This is implicit in all action as such; in a specifically high and pure form it is expressed in moral conduct on the one hand, in creative art on the other.

The *status viae* as a whole is characterized by a realization of things not yet real, a production of new things, a tension inherent in tasks awaiting their fulfillment and aims claiming to be accomplished. Moreover, for man in his fallen state, the process of sanctification — of a transformation in Christ — is dependent on a systematic effort towards a moral formation of self and is thus inseparable from a set of ends and means. Consequently, that process is by no means free from that tension towards a purpose to be realized which we have seen to be specifically opposed to contemplation. This aspect of purposefulness attaches both to our effort towards self-perfection and to the works of charity organically issuing from that peerless virtue. We are, *in statu viae*, not merely *being* but *becoming*, subject to the law of change; wherefore, even in our innermost selves we are tied to the world of action and the tension that goes with action.

Yet our primary attitude must be receptive

Nevertheless, in spite of the high metaphysical dignity of action, in spite of man's specific mission of activity *in statu viae*, in spite of the requisiteness of action, even for the attainment of our *eternal* goal, the contemplative attitude ranks higher than any transient activity, however noble.

The primary attitude of man, as a creature, is a receptive one. To let ourselves be apprehended by God, to lay our soul open to the influx of God's eternal Word, to expose ourselves to the sword of the love of Christ — therein lies what is most proper to our essence. Our transformation in Christ, again, means primarily our *undergoing* a process of transformation by Him; He is to engrave the seal of His countenance upon our soul. Our basic attitude remains a receptive one. Thus, too, it is our emptying ourselves before the face of God, our abandoning ourselves to His operation to be filled by His presence, the *vacare et videre* ("to rest and to see") that effects a regeneration of our souls, enabling us to realize the further elements of contemplation, the *amare et laudare* ("to love and to praise") in full completeness and depth. Unless we again and again drink of the water "springing up into life everlasting" (John 4:14), the source of true and valid life in us is bound to dry up.

All deep activities are nourished by contemplation

Even as regards our contemplative attitude in relation to creaturely objects, the law of our primary receptiveness holds good. Think, first, of the predominant part in our soul's life played by cognition, through which the universe of being discloses itself to our mind. Furthermore, all realization of values on our part, in the active sense of the term *realization*, presupposes our realization of values in the passive sense of that term. The inward wealth of a personality depends closely on the comprehensiveness of its vision of values. Unless it be supplemented by contemplation, an action directed to high and relevant aims is liable to become a hollow, cramped pursuit, lacking genuine fruitfulness.

Of this we shall easily convince ourselves if we consider the fact that all moral action has its basic root in charity, which is contemplative in essence. For, while charity as such is contemplative, in the situation of the *status viae* it necessarily generates action, according to the words of St. Paul: "For the charity of Christ presseth us" (2 Cor. 5:14). As soon as moral action is not nourished and animated by love (thus steeped on one side in a medium of contemplation), it becomes shallow, and comparable to a "tinkling cymbal" (1 Cor. 13:1).

However, all other activities of a deeper meaning, such as artistic creation or scientific work, equally need the regenerating effect of contemplation. Without this, everything is apt to lose its centrality and to end in shallowness. Efforts devoted to perfecting oneself, in particular, are doomed to such a fate if divorced from contemplation. St. Bernard justly says: "Thus, if thou art wise, thou shalt make thyself a well, not a canal. For whatever a canal takes in, it again pours out almost in the next moment, whereas a well holds back until it be filled; it so communicates from its superfluity without suffering damage, knowing well that whoever has chosen the worst part for himself is doomed."

The peripheral activities, in their turn, require no contemplative substructure in order to be well performed according to the meaning of their immanent teleology. But, were it not for the counterbalancing effect of contemplative elements in our mental texture, such surface activity is apt to overgrow our life and to draw us entirely into the peripheral sphere, superseding all higher aspirations in us by the set of interests it represents. Not unless we again and again pause to take breath, abandoning ourselves to contemplation, can we escape the danger of losing ourselves in the peripheral and of allowing the deeper meaning of our life to be swamped.

Summary of the superiority of contemplation over action

To sum up: it is for three reasons that the contemplative attitude, including that which is related to creaturely objects, excels in rank the attitude of action. First, as against all purposeful activity, it constitutes the deeper and more final form of our mental life. Secondly, it represents the superior form of contact with the object, the only one which — by contrast to all *uti* — is consonant with an adequate appreciation of the object. Thirdly, it is the source of all spiritual fruitfulness and inward wealth, the necessary *precondition* to all truly valuable activity and the most proper attribute of human nature which, as we have seen, is primarily receptive. Above all, however, it is contemplation alone in which the central theme of our whole being — our union with God — is realized. Though action is necessarily implied by our advance towards that union, its accomplishment takes place in pure contemplation.

Contemplation must not, of course, be considered exclusively or even primarily because it constitutes an indispensable base for fruitful and valid action. It is never a mere means but is in very truth the end. For apart from its regenerating and enriching influence on personality in action, it represents by itself the higher and more enduring part in the soul's life, the one that is to subsist alone in eternal life. Even on earth, the contemplative moments are the highest and most condensed. That is why the Lord said, "Mary hath chosen the best part."

The preceding enquiry has demonstrated, then, the privileged position of contemplation as against action, and the specific dignity of religious contemplation proper. Notwithstanding the high specific perfection inherent in action, the moments of contemplative attention, even on a creaturely level of objects, embody a more fully valid actualization of our deeper being than do even the highest forms of action on the same level. In the moral domain — the most central of all for every human being — charity is supreme, and charity is contemplative in its inmost nature, although *in statu viae*, if it be genuine, it cannot but generate deeds.

The excellence of contemplation is also revealed by the fact that it does not, in essence, presuppose an unfinished situation. All creaturely action, on the other hand, is conditioned by the incompleteness characteristic of the *status viae*, the empty space to be filled, the thing that remains to be accomplished. Contemplation, not being thus tied to imperfection, will subsist even where "God shall be all in all" (1 Cor. 15:28). All creaturely action is necessarily transient; yet, the contemplative mode of existence is to maintain itself in eternity. Contemplation, therefore, is the "final word" of all creaturely being.

Recollection is the preamble to contemplation

How are recollection and contemplation related to each other? They have many features in common, but they are not mutually equivalent. All true contemplation implies a state of being recollected; again, the act of recollecting oneself requires a rudiment of contemplation. Both attitudes contain a turning towards the depth and a withdrawal from the welter of the temporal, the immanent mechanism of the functional. Yet, while in recollection we *become* or *make ourselves* empty of pragmatical concerns, directing ourselves to the absolute; in contemplation we *are* thus empty, *resting* in the absolute. In this respect, recollection is a preamble to contemplation. Furthermore, while the basic characteristic of recollection is integration in depth as opposed to dispersion, that of contemplation is the restful immersion of self as opposed to purposeful tension.

Hence, recollection is not limited to the moments of contemplation. It may continue to be present while we are active, if not as an express act of recollecting ourselves, at least as a general attitude of being recollected. Whereas our earthly life could not be purely *contemplative*, it should always remain *recollected*. That *habitare secum*, that dwelling with oneself, ought never to be forsaken.

Yet contemplation nourishes recollection

On the other hand, we cannot recover that general attitude of being recollected unless from time to time we pause in our active life to seek refuge in contemplation — particularly, in religious contemplation. In a formal sense, recollection as a rule precedes contemplation, but it cannot be developed into a full recovery of self except in contemplation. The withdrawal from outward pre-occupations, and the rest of what is meant by "recollecting our-selves," are introductory to contemplation; but again, the latter, putting us in the presence of God and in contact with the world of ultimate reality, prepares the way for our confronting everything — including relevant impending tasks — with God, and thus lead-ing a recollected life.

We may say that a recollected mode of life is only possible if contemplation is given its due place as the focal element of life and its spiritual center of gravity.

Regular religious contemplation helps us grow recollected

Recollection being as decisive for our transformation in Christ as it is, how are we to achieve it?

In the first place, by the practice of religious contemplation. The true Christian must at any cost conquer a place in his life for contemplation. He must firmly refuse to let himself be dragged into a whirlpool of activities in which he is driven incessantly from one task to another, purpose succeeding purpose, without a pause. The present period of perpetual unrest, in which the machine has come to be the model, the *causa exemplaris*, of well-nigh all things, in which everything is caught in a process of instrumentalization, in which *Leistung* ("achievement") with the emphasis on quantity and mere technical perfection, has assumed priority over *being* in a substantial and meaningful sense — this period of shallow hyper-activity is only too apt to drag us into that whirlpool of outward preoccupations.

All our actions, even those with a religious or moral impor-tance, which therefore essentially appeal to the contemplative attitude, we tend to perform in the manner of discharging a duty or of acquitting ourselves of a task — not to say, of turning out the required output. We live in uninterrupted tension, never ceasing to be concerned about what has next to be settled; and many of us no longer know any alternative to work except recreation and amusement.

Fully aware of the obstacles which, today more than ever, threaten to prevent us from recollecting ourselves and from practicing contemplation, we must endeavor to overcome them by different methods.

To achieve recollection, we must daily spend time in inner prayer

First, we should consecrate every day a certain space of time to inward prayer. There must be such a fraction of the day, in which we drop all our topical or habitual concerns before God, facing Him in complete emptiness, so as to be filled by the holy presence of Christ alone.

Yet, we must guard from performing the inner prayer as though we were dispatching a business among others, assimilating it to the rhythm of current tasks. We must really loose the spasm of activity and be dominated by the consciousness of departing in our inward prayer towards the superior realm of ultimate being, in radical transcendence of the aims and concerns which habitually rule the course of our thoughts.

All these we must leave behind, pronouncing a *nescivi* ("I have forgotten"): *I will forget everything that was, and is to come; nor think of what lies ahead of me. Whatever I am wont to carry and to hold in my arms I will let fall before Jesus. It will not fall into the void: standing before Jesus, I deliver it all up to Him. Everything belongs to Him: all burdening worries and all great concerns, both mine and those of the souls I love. I am not abandoning them as I would abandon them in seeking diversion: I know that in Jesus they are truly in a safe harbor.*

When at His call I relinquish and abandon all things, I am not casting them away; on the contrary, I am assigning everything to its proper place.

Inward prayer is the utmost antithesis to all tense activity: we cannot practice it fruitfully unless we succeed in extricating ourselves from the rhythm of affairs to be settled. To preserve that pragmatic attitude during our inward prayer is to falsify the latter's essence to the point of absurdity.

We must integrate prayer into the events of our day

Also, we must interpolate free moments in the course of our day; moments in which we raise our eyes to God, forgetting everything for a second and experiencing His presence. In the midst of our occupations we should halt from time to time, and turn towards God for a moment, emerging from the world of *causae secundae* to God, the *causa prima* — the primary and supreme Reality and Truth, by whom and in whom alone everything unfolds its meaning and realizes its value.

We must remain always conscious of God

Above all, we must resist being swallowed up by the immanent logic of our activities and of the diverse situations in which life places us. Here lies the chief threat to our leading a recollected life. Certainly, we are obliged to respond to the immanent logic of the diverse situations and tasks that face us; but we must never deliver ourselves to them unreservedly.

We must not be possessed by them but remain firmly anchored in God, thus preserving a perspective which enables us to accord every created thing as much only as is due to it *in conspectu Dei*. This means a permanent struggle which we must renew again and again, in the spirit of St. Peter's words: "Brethren: be sober and watch" (1 Pet. 5:8).

We must avoid superficial diversions

Yet, the purposeful tension involved by our tasks and concerns is not the only great obstacle to recollection. Another is the attitude of peripheral diversion.

Therefore, in order to recollect ourselves, we must shun everything that appeals to our craving for sensation. We must guard against yielding to our idle curiosity, against cramming our mind with wanton things. We must keep out of situations that pander to our appetite for the sensational. We should also leave books unread which, devoid of artistic value, are meant to captivate our interest by their exciting contents or technique — "thrillers," for instance. For all these things are apt to drag us into the peripheral sphere and to hinder us from recollection, be it only for the reason that they encumber and dissipate our imagination.

Likewise, we should avoid meaningless conversations and irrelevant social gatherings as far as it can be done without offending charity. It has been pointed out on an earlier occasion that these trivial things enclose a danger to us, inasmuch as they hamper us in attaining true simplicity. It is not without good reason that we have that hollow feeling — that we feel *washed out*, as it were — after a long run of empty and superficial conversations. It is because we have strayed far from reality proper and the sphere of valid meaning; from God; and, by the same token, from our own true selves.

We must cultivate silence and inner stillness

Nay, prolonged talks as such, be they even of a less irrelevant nature, tend to interfere with our concentration. Silence is of great help in recollecting ourselves; that is why it plays such an eminent part in monastic life. Conversation (in the sense of mere chatter) obviously allures us towards the ephemeral; but even if it is devoted to more important topics, it implies a certain exhaustion, a tendency to dispersion. It is, therefore, a form of activity which needs to be compensated by not too rare intervals of silence. Silence fulfills an important function in mental regeneration. It is only in the passivity of silence that the things which have deeply impressed us may resound and grow in our soul, and strike root in our being. Silence alone evokes that inward calm which is a prerequisite of recollection.

To be sure, by *silence* we do not mean here a mere outward abstaining from speech, coupled with its mental continuance. We must also cultivate an inward stillness. At any rate, however, outward silence is a condition for recollection.

Far be it from us to contest the dignity and weight of a noble word; the nobility and importance of man's high gift of objectifying and communicating his knowledge by words charged with meaning; and least of all, the greatness and depth inherent in his capacity to embody his love in a word and to pour it thus into the soul of the beloved. Yet, we shall fail of the deepest actualization of the gift of speech itself unless we intermittently undergo periods of silence so as to recollect ourselves. In most cases, unhappily, talking is but a form of letting oneself go, a misuse of the high gift of speech, a perversion of its proper meaning. Talk of this kind is always an antagonist of concentration, stultifying that high mission of human speech which the Psalmist had put into these words: "I have believed, therefore have I spoken" (Ps. 115:10).

We must find time for solitude

From time to time, not only silence but solitude is requisite for concentration. The presence of a person we know forms an interpersonal situation, which by itself involves a certain tension. That tension varies according to the character of the person in question, and of our relation with him, but in no case is it compatible with full inward relaxation. Should someone even exercise a specifically recollecting influence upon us, should a noble attraction emanate from his nature, drawing us nearer to God, the necessity for solitude will not thereby be eliminated but rather confirmed. For it will be in moments of solitude that the intensity of this spiritual contact will build itself up and bud in the depths of our soul. A moment saturated with meaning, a valid "now" requires a period of calm relaxation for taking effect. Nor is this function of solitude disturbed by the fact that, while being alone, we are engaged in some kind of activity, for the relaxation inherent in solitude has a character of its own, different from that of the relaxation due to the absence of activity.

We must get sufficient rest to remain mentally alert

Lastly, a certain measure of mental alertness, too, is necessary for recollection. In an exhausted condition we can hardly recollect ourselves; and often enough, we cease to be recollected because we are tired. Psycho-physical exhaustion tends to warp the *intentional* structure of our mental life, to abolish the predominance of objectivity and logical orientation. We then become more or less a puppet of our mechanism of associations, losing control over our thoughts and the images of fantasy. In a specific fashion, this condition manifests itself in dreaming. So also does a state of distraction, owing to a deficiency of psycho-physical vigor, interfere with recollection, with that recollected state of mind which is meant by the term *habitare secum* ("dwelling with oneself"). We then react too impulsively; we are more than usually inclined to be irritated; we lose control over our reactions. Thus, exhaustion may cause us to fall a prey to the immanent mechanism of any situation in which we happen to be placed, and particularly, to our own specific defects. All things are likely to possess us at will; and we tend to react impulsively on the basis of our natural dispositions, instead of freely taking our stand, with the full sanction of our personality.

We must balance intensity with relaxation

Therefore, a certain quantity of sleep and a modicum of simple recreation also belong to the preconditions for a recollected life. Since we are psycho-physical beings, we cannot invariably live with the same spiritual intensity. Nor can our life be filled exclusively with activities devoted to the higher good, with the pursuit of important aims, with the reception of deep impressions. Even for the sake of recollection itself, there must be intervals of pure relaxation, of a mere absence of tension, with no aspect of intensity.

If the periods of purposeful tension and relevant action require the balance of intervals of relaxation and recreation, the contemplative attention to high values, again — with the intense spiritual experience and elevation it implies — must be followed by pauses without any kind of intensity, during which the impressions received may thrive in stillness and strike root in our soul. Such a pause might, for example, take the form of a solitary walk during which we meditate, but without any effort or any express act of concentration, on what we have received, not intending, as we do in contemplation proper, to evoke a full response. Humble moments of this kind will contribute, in a unique and necessary sense, to the very completion of a deep and genuine spiritual experience. Or again, the pause we speak of may be represented by some external, neutral activities which we perform in solitude.

Thus, on the one hand, receptive contemplation will regenerate us so as to render us better able to accomplish valid and meaningful actions; but on the other hand, there is also a regenerative function proper to simple, neutral activities, which in its turn conditions our full capacity for realizing the contemplative attitude itself. It need hardly be said that regeneration is of a very different kind in the one and in the other case. The need for recreation in the broader and in the closer sense of the term is a specific stigma of our metaphysical insufficiency as fallen men *in statu viae*. The fact that we cannot maintain our life invariably on a level of high intensity but are obliged to intersperse it with nondescript, neutral moments, should evoke in us a humble awareness of our insufficiency. In contradistinction to the natural idealist, whose attitude was touched upon in Chapter 1, the Christian essentially accepts this limitation inherent in his human status. Avoiding the pitfalls of strained ambitiousness and exaltation, he is familiar with the reality of the limits imposed on us *in statu viae*. Yet, he envisions wistfully the *status termini* — the final state of man in our celestial home — in which he will never have to quit the highest intensity of being that fills the deep all-comprehensive "now" of eternity. "There we shall rest and we shall see; we shall see and we shall love; we shall love and we shall praise. Behold what shall be in the end without end!" (St. Augustine, *De civitate Dei*, 22.30).

Recollection nourishes simplicity

We perceive the profound relationship between recollection and simplicity. By virtue of recollection alone can we reduce everything to the common denominator that is Christ. In the attitude of *habitare secum* alone do we gain the stronghold where we are safe from all division by the multiformity of life. Recollection alone makes it possible for us to keep awake in ourselves the basic attitude of charity, elicited by the melting fire of Jesus' love, and — notwithstanding the manifoldness of the different keys of emotional attention required by the changing situations — always to preserve our essential identity, to remain *semper idem*. Recollection provides the groundwork for that wakefulness thanks to which no mutually disparate currents of life can flow side by side in our soul without being confronted with one another.

Recollection and contemplation are goals for us to attain

No less clearly do we perceive the central importance of recollection and contemplation for our transformation in Christ as a whole. Unless we cultivate a recollected mode of life and recognize the primacy of contemplation, we remain essentially unfit for receiving the holy imprint of Christ.

Still more, it can be said that the attitude of *habitare secum*, as well as a primarily contemplative rhythm of life, are no mere conditions but actual elements of the process of transformation in Christ; they form part of the goal which Christ has called us to attain. For our very being in eternity will consist in an ultimate, wholly concentrated, and purely contemplative surrender to God "that, beholding Thee with eyes unveiled, I shall be made happy by the sight of Thy glory" — as heavenly bliss is described in the words of St. Thomas Aquinas.

May the true Christian, always seeking and yearning for Christ, sit at the Master's feet listening to Him and responding in words such as these: *O Jesus, I know that it is my supreme task to let myself be shaped anew by Thy love; to empty my soul so that Thou shalt rule and unfold therein; and melted by Thy love, to see all things in Thy light, to experience and to do everything in Thy spirit. I know that this reforming of my soul can only come to pass if I lay myself open to Thee, and listen to Thy holy voice. Therefore, at whatever cost, I will be intent above all on providing room in myself for the gentle irradiation of Thy light, and on exposing my heart to the sword of Thy inconceivable love. Thou hast called on me to accomplish the ultimate breach with the world. The spirit that fills the prayers of the holy Church, the prayers in which Thou forever adorest and exaltest the Father shall expand my soul, fill it with Thy holy light, and draw it to Thy most holy Heart in which dwells all plenitude of divinity; and this holy life which fills our souls shall mirror and proclaim Thy brightness, "that you may declare his virtues, who hath called you out of darkness into his marvelous light"* (1 Peter 2:9).

I cannot become transformed in Thee unless that holy stillness spread out in me; unless Thy gifts of grace and the calls of Thy love slowly expand and mature in my soul. Therefore, wherever Thy will has placed me, it will always be my chief task to face Thee, free from all haste of earthly activities; to drink in Thy love, and to live in Thee, loving and adoring. Then only can the prayer of Thy Church become a love song of my soul.

Permit not, O Jesus, that my daily obligations make me forget my chief task, that my life be exhausted in the individual works which it is my duty to perform. Thou, Lord, who once said to Martha, "thou art troubled about many things: but one thing alone is necessary," grace my soul with holy simplicity, so that it be filled with yearning love of Thee; so that I await Thee with burning torches and girt loins; so that I stand awake before Thee; and let all else be merely a fruit of this holy life, a superabundance from this inexhaustible source. Set the stamp of greatness and breadth, of holy freedom and wakefulness, upon my soul. Let my ear never miss Thy voice in the symphony of Thy gifts. Let me never pass over Thy graces with ingratitude, preventing them from bearing ample fruit in my soul. Grant me the fulfillment in my soul of Thy holy word: "Mary hath chosen the best part, which shall not be taken away from her" (Luke 10:42).

7

Humility

Everyone that exalteth himself, shall be humbled;
and he that humbleth himself, shall be exalted. (Luke 14:11)

HUMILITY, as St. Francis of Sales has said, is the highest of all *human* virtues; for *love* — the consummation of all virtues, on which "dependeth the whole law and the prophets" — is a *divine* virtue. What is true of love — that without it, all other virtues and good works are valueless — is again, in another respect, true of humility. For, just as love embodies the life of all virtues and expresses the inmost substance of all holiness, humility is the *precondition* and basic presupposition for the genuineness, the beauty, and the truth of all virtue. It is *mater* and *caput* ("mother and fountainhead") of all specifically human virtues; for, inversely, pride (*superbia*) is not only by itself our primal sin, it also inwardly contaminates all intrinsically good dispositions, and robs every virtue of its value before God.

Pride is worse than concupiscence

We have two great enemies to combat within us: pride and concupiscence. The two are mostly intertwined in some definite manner. Men tainted by pride alone are seldom to be met with. It is these two enemies that render us blind to value. But they are not of equal importance: it is not concupiscence but pride that constitutes the primal evil in our souls. Satan's original gesture is the act of absolute pride that rebels against God, the embodiment of all values, in an impotent attempt to appropriate His power and dominion. True, in the sinfulness of many men (indeed, of most men) concupiscence plays a more conspicuous part; but, nevertheless, it falls short of being the primal evil. That is why in the Gospels even the sin of impurity, however grave, is less severely judged than that of pride. Christ denounced pride and obduracy in far more incisive terms than the sins of the flesh. Thus, pride is the deepest root of the malignancy within ourselves, which is entirely consonant with the fact that Adam's sin, too, consisted in an act of disobedience inspired not by concupiscence, which was only to be a consequence of the Fall, but by pride.

The fact alone that pride is the primal source of all moral evil clearly demonstrates the paramount importance of humility. What is most essential in the process of dying to ourselves is the conquest of pride and that liberation from one's self, whose name is *humility*. On the degree of our humility depends the measure in which we shall achieve freedom to participate in God's life and make it possible for the supernatural life received in holy Baptism to unfold in our souls. "God resisteth the proud and giveth grace to the humble" (James 4:6). On the other hand, every virtue and every good deed turns worthless if pride creeps into it — which happens whenever in some fashion we glory in our goodness. This is clearly set forth by the parable of the publican and the Pharisee in the Gospels.

There exist formally and materially distinct forms of pride. As humility represents an antithesis to every form of pride, a consideration of the various forms and degrees of pride will help us become aware of the various aspects of humility, each of which expresses a negation of pride in one or the other of its manifestations.

Satanic pride hates goodness

Let us begin this survey of the types of pride with the worst, and most characteristic one, which we may call satanic pride. He who is afflicted with this knows one kind of satisfaction only: the glorification of his self. For him, the entire world is devoid of interest except insofar as it offers him an opportunity to experience his own superiority, power, and splendor. Subject to this spasm of the ego, enslaved to his exclusive interest in the excellence of his self as such, he is unable to grasp the inherent beauty and nobility of objective values.

Satanic pride blinds

He is, then, blind to value; but his kind of value-blindness is not that dull insensibility to values which marks the slave of concupiscence. On the contrary, he does in a sense grasp the metaphysical force that resides in value, the majestic sovereignty proper to it.

However, he grasps it in a way that implies, at the same time, its profound misconception. For — and herein precisely consists his value-blindness — while he is aware of that character of compelling sovereignty inherent in values, he fails to see its essential nexus with their self-contained beauty, their objective significance independent of any utilitarian or decorative use in the service of an ego.

Hence, it happens that *his* value-blindness bears a tinge, not of dull indifference but of hostility. Values, to him, are a scandal; he fatally endeavors to alienate their sovereignty and transfer it to his own self. He fears them as a menace to his supreme glory derived from his autonomous selfhood; the claim to submission which emanates from them he meets with resentment and rebellion. He does not, as does the concupiscent man, content himself with ignoring values and turning a deaf ear to their call. He would, as it were, *dethrone* them; again and again he performs the impotent gesture aimed at depriving them of their metaphysical power.

Frequently enough his endeavor takes the form of an attempt at enthroning some false value in the place of the true ones. In certain typical cases, it is this mechanism of disguised pride which underlies the cult of idols.

This attitude appears most clearly in the rebellion of Lucifer, who would fain be "like God." He shuts his eyes to the goodness and holiness of God; he fails to perceive the indissoluble union between all-powerfulness and all-goodness; he would separate omnipotence from all-goodness and attribute the former to himself. All his thoughts are centered in the one overwhelming consciousness of "counting for much."

This yearning for self-supremacy is not satisfied by terrestrial power, by actual physical power as such; he also hungers for the possession of that metaphysical grandeur which is implicit in all possession of value.

Yet, to be sure, it is not for the sake of the value *qua* value that he covets it; what preoccupies him is that mysterious power without which he may not attain the plenitude of power, and which therefore irritates him as an irksome limitation imposed on his pleasure in "counting for much."

Thus original pride engenders a hatred of values, a combative opposition to whatever irradiates light, to all self-contained glory; ultimately, to God. Clearly, this attitude is tantamount to ethical evil in an eminent sense; it constitutes the utmost antithesis to the harmony of values and the extreme negation by a creature of his creaturely status. It represents the most express refusal to honor value by an adequate response to its appeal.

Satanic pride isolates and divides

By taking this position, man cuts himself off from the world of values in its entirety. He will be incapable of all response to value, not so much owing to his value-blindness as because he lacks the readiness for submission that underlies all response to value. His value-blindness will be the consequence, not the cause, of his pride. It is, therefore, a blindness that involves a high degree of guilt. Also, pride determines a specifically grave form of obduracy. Its effects diametrically oppose those of love (which opens and melts the soul) and contrast dramatically to the specific qualities of responsive kindness and luminous harmony which love connotes. The proud personality is lacerated by a deep disharmony; a corrosive venom pervades his entire life; and all the gratification he derives from whatever flatters his pride is unable to provide him with any genuine inner happiness, any blissful peace.

Satanic pride turns freedom into license

Another formal characteristic of satanic pride consists in the abuse of liberty. The gift of free decision, conferred upon man as a mark of his likeness to God, is granted him by the divine Will so as to empower him to respond to values and to surrender to God in a way that carries the full sanction of his personality. Under the sway of pride, that gift is perverted into a stimulus for his orgy of self-glorification and nourishment for his consciousness of counting for much.

The basic fact of freedom — the dimension of our being where we most possess ourselves and actualize ourselves — disjoined from its ordination to God and from its correlation with the world of values, becomes the source of an illusion of absolute power and of a primary claim to dominion. Freedom is degraded into arbitrary license.

In certain conditions, the man governed by pride will commit this or that action, not because it satisfies his cupidity — or even his pride, so far as its material import goes — but as a mere confirmation and exercise of his independence, a test of the position of power he derives from his gift of *liberum arbitrium*. This is the horrible sin of Kirilov, the lonesome atheist in Dostoyevsky's *Possessed*, who according to a deliberate plan shoots himself at a moment convenient for the purposes of a gang of nihilist scoundrels, not in order to promote their revolutionary designs, but just to prove his absolute liberty unrelated to any concrete aim or value, the meaninglessness of death, and the nonexistence of God. Here is a key to many an evil deed which apparently lacks motivation, since by virtue of its contents it cannot possibly offer its perpetrator any subjective satisfaction, even a wholly illicit one.

Satanic pride refuses all submission as such

Apart from his antagonism toward the world of values and its serene harmony, the maniac of pride repudiates all submission as such; his *non serviam* is meant to challenge any kind of authority; he would bow neither to man nor to God. This specific mode of pride, with its quality of supreme malice, may of course appear in various degrees. It may take hold of a person completely, so that he is no longer able to evoke any response to value and becomes a prey to total value-blindness. Lucifer is the prototype of this absolute pride. By analogy, we may class with him Cain, as well as the figure of Rakitin in Dostoyevsky's *Brothers Karamazov*.

There is also a category of men who are filled with this form of pride in part only. Their pride is similar in nature, but restricted in extension. These would recognize and esteem certain sets of values — such as justice or faithfulness, for instance, and others not explicitly impinging on their ego-worship or their sense of grandeur — but refuse to take cognizance of, and respond to, values like humility, meekness, or mercy. Such men are but partially afflicted with value-blindness, nor do they lack a *conditional* readiness to submission. What shocks them is not the intrinsic importance of value as such, but only the claim inherent in certain high values which, by virtue of their particular nature, imply a specific negation of pride and invite man to relinquish it altogether. Values of this order, and not the others, evoke such men's antagonism. Of course, whenever men of this type do display a response to values, it always remains a conditional one, and therefore mutilated and impaired in its quality.

Response to value is fundamental to humility

Humility is, first, an antithesis to all metaphysical pride of the kind just described. In the humble man, the basic attitude of responsiveness to value has the whole field; he is not dominated at all by the desire of absolute power or of counting for much. He grasps the objective meaning of values in its independence from the pursuits of the subject, and honors them with an unhampered and adequate response. The readiness to posit that submission and surrender which belongs to every response to value is present in him. He is concerned with the glory, not of his own ego, but of the objectively important, of that which pleases God. The inward nobility of good, its intrinsic beauty, touches his heart and delights him. In his devotion to the good he participates in the harmony of values; his soul is bright and serene, free from the corrosive poison that eats the heart of the proud.

True, all this he has in common with every one in whom the fundamental attitude of response to value has acquired prevalence; that is to say, with everyone who has awakened to a life in the light of moral consciousness. Not humility alone, but also every response to value and every virtue forms an antithesis to metaphysical pride, which is the stem of moral evil. Opposition to this original pride equally underlies justice, veracity, faithfulness, and even purity, although the opposition specific to the latter is directed towards concupiscence. For all these virtues derive from a value-responsive central attitude; they all presuppose awareness of value, and the readiness to surrender to value and to submit to its demands.

Hence, the antithesis to pride in this sense only reveals to us that element of humility which is alive in all virtue, which constitutes an aspect of the value-response pure and simple. It manifests humility insofar as humility is the basis of all virtues. It does not, however, enable us to grasp the nature of humility in its narrower and specific sense. In the latter, more elements are required than have been described above. We shall see this presently, having considered further types of pride.

Some forms of pride reject the sovereignty of God

From satanic pride and the hatred of God it implies, we must distinguish a much milder form of pride — associated with a less fearful variety of rebellion against God — which, nevertheless, still shares the metaphysical character of satanic pride.

We find it in persons who are by no means blind to value, and are capable of a positive response to it. With them, the desire to count for much plays no decisive part; nor do they exhibit the specific obduracy of the victims of satanic pride. Their life is not spoiled through and through by disharmony; theirs is not the scorching hatred of light as personified by Alberic in Wagner's *Ring of the Nibelungen*. On the contrary, they are capable of an honest moral effort; in their lives, the problem of good and evil may rank paramount; they may well show great receptiveness to all kinds of beauty. But they shun confrontation with a personal God; they evade the full avowal of their creaturely status; they balk at that ultimate act of subordination which goes far beyond what is implied in every response to value.

So long as they are only concerned with the realm of values — which, after all, they may in a sense face as *equal partners* — they are ready to submit to the call of the object. Nay, they would even surrender to an Impersonal Absolute, to which they would be as parts to the whole. For, so long as there is no question of their relation with an absolute Person, they may still keep a last remnant of ego-sovereignty; moreover, as parts of the whole, they may, after a fashion, rejoice in their identity with the absolute.

It is only in our confrontation with a personal God that we become fully aware of our condition as creatures, and fling from us the last particle of self-glory. The idealists who cherish ethical autonomy, the pantheists, the theosophists: these all are bent on escaping from subordination to an almighty Lord, and consequently, from relinquishing a certain minimum sovereignty which flatters their pride.

Humility acknowledges our creaturely status

By contrasting it with *this* type of pride, we are better able to grasp the specific nature of humility. Humility involves the full knowledge of our status as creatures, a clear consciousness of having received everything we have from God. "Or what hast thou that thou hast not received? And if thou hast received, why dost thou glory, as if thou hadst not received it?" (1 Cor. 4:7).

It is in humility that we attain to an exact consideration of the metaphysical situation of man. Humility presents in specifically sharp relief that general aspect of all Christian morality — the unreserved recognition of the metaphysical situation of man, the attitude of throwing all illusions overboard and granting to the whole of reality the response that is due to it. Thus, it has been said justly: "Humility is Truth." Correspondingly, the soul of pride is falsehood, for pride means a refusal to realize our metaphysical situation.

True knowledge of our status as creatures, however, implies a confrontation of the creature with its Creator: it is not possible except in reference to a personal God. For awareness of our creaturely status is more than a mere awareness of our debility and limitation. It amounts to experiencing not only our relative imperfection and the restrictions to which we are subject, but the infinite distance between us and absolute Being; it requires a full understanding of the fact that we have received "all that we have and are" — except sin — from God.

So long as he fights shy of a confrontation of the infinite Person with his finite person, so long as he clings to an atheist or pantheist conception of the world, howsoever flexibly formulated, man can never attain to a fully weighted awareness of his status as a creature. Either he will confine himself to an awareness of his dependence on his body and on the surrounding nature or else he will see himself in terms of his participation in an absolute Whole. To the atheist, who knows no absolute being, no more than an awareness of our relative limitation and impotence is possible.

Again, in the pantheist's view we are parts of the Absolute, be it even so small and unimportant parts as to be negligible when taken individually.

Here the distance between us and the Absolute is transposed to the level of quantity. We still imagine ourselves to be of the stuff of the Absolute, as it were, and sharers in its glory. A hidden playground is still reserved for the antics of a certain refined species of pride; the nerve of pride has not been cut; the idol of self-glory has not been thoroughly uprooted. This becomes even clearer when we further consider the distinction between a mere avowal of our weakness and true humility. It is only the overwhelming contrast between creature and personal Creator that discloses to us, in all its depth, the principal fact about ourselves: that we receive all our being *from* God; that He is That Which Is, whereas we are "as though we *were not*."

Humility joyfully assents to creatureliness

Furthermore, humility also implies blissful *assent* to this our creatureliness and *non-being*. What it demands is not a reluctant or resigned admission of our nothingness: it is, primarily, a joyous response to the infinite glory of God, similar to what is meant by the words of St. Catherine of Siena: *Che tu sia ed io non sia* ("That Thou shalt be, and that I shall not be). The humble man does not want to be anything by his own resources; he is free from all ambition to be something by his own power and to have to recognize no master over himself. He *wills* to receive everything from God alone. The glory of God makes him happy; he is thus so centered in his love of adoration for God that the idea of being something by his own force — aside from its unreality — would not tempt him at all; nor does the concern about keeping his sovereignty intact carry the slightest meaning to him. Such an attitude, however, is only possible in reference to a personal God; moreover, as Pascal says, "not to the God of the philosophers, but to the God of Abraham, Isaac and Jacob"; above all, to the living God who approaches and addresses us in the Person of Jesus Christ, His only-begotten Son.

Humility delights in the existence and glory of God

In true humility, then, we may discern three elements. First, *awareness of, and responsiveness to, the glory of God.* God in His infinite holiness having revealed Himself to our minds, it is for us to respond with holy joy and loving adoration. Prior to everything else, we must be filled with the blissful consciousness that the infinitely perfect Person — God who is omnipotent, omniscient, and all good — is the Prime Cause of all being. We must give, in reference to God, the pure response to value, our joy being elicited *by His glory alone* — that is, we must say with the holy Church:

"We thank Thee for Thy great glory." Touched by the ray of God's supernatural holiness that transcends all our concepts, we must exclaim with the Psalmist: "For better is one day in Thy courts above thousands."

Even in perceiving a human value we may evince this wholly disinterested, pure joy, which refers to the existence of value as such. We rejoice in considering that truth exists; that a certain good and noble person dwells on earth; that there are such beautiful things as the starred sky or a great work of art.

But what we have now in mind is our joy related to the fact that the absolute Being is infinitely perfect and that this infinitely glorious Being is a Person. What an immense augmentation of the reality of good is implied in this — that the *summum bonum* ("the highest good") should not be a mute impersonal something, an idea or a principle, but a Person speaking to us: *Ego sum qui sum* ("I am who am"); the absolute Person in whom all values converge at their highest, who has created us and keeps us in being, who embraces us and owns us as only a person can.

Humility calls upon us to allow our hearts to be wounded by the glory of God, to fall on our knees in loving adoration, and to deliver ourselves over to God entirely. We must display that pure response in which our center of gravity is thus transferred from ourselves to God, that His glory taken in itself, without any reference to His benevolence towards us, becomes for us a source of precious joy: *Deus meus et omnia* ("My God and my all"), said St. Francis of Assisi.

Humility acknowledges our debt to God

Yet, no less essential to true humility is a second step: *the confrontation of our own person with the infinite Person* who is God. In the face of God we become aware of our sinfulness and our weakness. We say with St. Francis, "Who art Thou, and who am

I." We discern our nothingness and our obscurity and join in the words of the Psalmist, "But I am a worm, and no man" (Ps. 21:7). We come to understand that we are utterly in the debt of God and completely dependent upon Him. "Know ye that the Lord is God: he made us, and not we ourselves" (Ps. 99:3).

In humility, our knowledge of God's glory takes precedence over our recognition of our creatureliness

As has been shown above, it is only in our confrontation with God that we gain sight of the measure of our debility and our nothingness. However, the knowledge of our relative imperfection and finiteness would by itself suffice to cast us down and to fill us with despair, unless preceded by a contemplation of the glory of God. The revelation of divine glory is the *objective* condition for the realization of that essential postulate of humility: that the knowledge of our nothingness, far from casting us down or even persuading us into a resigned acceptance of our misery, shall evoke in us a blissful assent to our creaturely status.

Again, the *subjective* condition lies in our assumption of that attitude of responsiveness which enables us to fully understand a value and to take joy in that value in itself. If we are immersed in the prideful, value-blind attitude which seeks satisfaction in the sovereignty of the ego alone and in impotent resentment, and which challenges the majesty of objective value, then the revelation of the glory of God will itself be of no avail to us. In place of blissful self-surrender, it will only provoke on our part Lucifer's proud gesture of defiance to God. Nay, given this negative attitude to value as such, it will be true to say that the greater the glory which confronts us, the deeper will be the resentment which it arouses.

In other words, a certain state of mind is requisite on our part so that the objective condition of humility may operate in our soul.

We must possess the fundamental attitude of respect which renders value visible for us, as well as the aliveness to values which enables us to honor their glory, once we are aware of it, with a response of love and joy. And, in order that the value-response of loving veneration and pure joy may blossom out in us, it is not sufficient for us to be rid of proud contempt and resentment. The craving for self-sovereignty, the desire to preserve a remnant of the ego's impregnability, must dominate us no longer. On the other hand, even though we did possess this fundamental attitude which is a predisposition of humility, the knowledge of our creatureliness and sinfulness could not but produce a fearsome feeling of despondency along with some form of the consciousness of inferiority — unless we had already found God, and caught the light of His glory.

He who has true humility is not oppressed and cast down by the knowledge that God is everything and he nothing; no, his awareness of the glory of God carries him in a state of bliss over the precipice of his nothingness and his obscurity. He *wills* that God shall be everything and he nothing; past all oppression and despair, he is filled with a holy longing for God. He lifts his hands to God, exclaiming: "One thing I have asked of the Lord, this will I seek after: that I may dwell in the house of the Lord all the days of my life" (Ps. 26:4).

Humility experiences dependence on God as a "being sheltered" by Him

He who possesses humility derives from his confrontation with God not only an awareness of his nothingness and obscurity but a keen experience of his *dependence* as well. He realizes the truth that he is wholly at the mercy of the all-powerful Lord of life and death, that whatever thought he might have of escaping or eluding God could not but be a pure illusion. "Whither shall I go from Thy spirit? Or whither shall I flee from Thy face?" (Ps. 138:7). However, for the Christian this sense of dependence takes on the aspect of being sheltered in God. The thought of his total impotence in relation to God does not arouse anguish or depression in him; he does not attempt to keep up an illusion of sovereignty and to arrange his life as though he were his own master.

Rather, he flings himself into the arms of the Almighty; he deliberately assents to his status of dependence, and prays with the holy Church: "Into Thy hands, O Lord, I commend my spirit" (Compline). Humility, then, contains not merely the knowledge of our dependence on God but the active conformance of our will to it; our blissful surrender to God. The humble one feels sheltered in God, indeed, as a possession of God: "We are his people and the sheep of his pasture" (Ps. 99:3).

Humility recognizes the ontological dignity of man

For humility demands that we not only take account of the personality of God but at the same time remain fully conscious of our own. Our awareness of "being naught" must not by any means entail on our part a tendency to depersonalization, a kind of a drab submersion in impersonal nature. That blissful assent to our creatureliness and our nothingness, our entire dependence on God, must be given freely and expressly: it must be, precisely, a *personal* act *par excellence*. Humility does not command a rejection of one's own self, pure and simple.

Though we be nothing by ourselves, though *everything* we have is received — still, we have received *a great deal* from God. In the first place, humility certainly is our response to the infinite distance that separates absolute from creaturely being. Secondly, it is a response to the fact that whatever we have, we have received from God rather than brought about by ourselves. We grow aware, in humility, of our impotence and our total dependence on God. Finally, we fathom the depths of our wretchedness, our sinfulness, and our pitifulness; we are struck by the divine plenitude of light and our own obscurity.

Yet, by the same token we also realize what God has granted to us. First of all, humility must not cause us to forget the fact that God has created us *in His likeness*, that we are spiritual persons. It is not lack of humility which makes the Psalmist say: "Thou hast made [man] a little less than the angels" (Ps. 8:6). Any form of the negation of our nature as a spiritual person (be it, say, materialism or the worship of vital force) — any idea of levelling down the incomparable ontological superiority of man to all mere vital being, let alone to mere matter — is hopelessly remote from the attitude of true humility. For a denial of that ontological dignity which God has conferred on us forcibly involves a disregard for the glory and all-powerfulness of God; yet humility is above all a *recognition of the glory of God*, and in a secondary sense only, a recognition of our own unimportance.

Over and above the natural dignity that God has conferred on man, Christian humility will remember that far higher and ineffable gift of divine mercy; its call upon man to participate in divine life; the imparting of supernatural life through Baptism.

Pantheism simultaneously depersonalizes man and exalts him, rendering humility impossible

The humble Christian, therefore, will be the last to emulate the pantheist in minimizing human personality or regarding man as a *quantité négligeable*. He will not become a victim of that infatuation for size which, in view of the colossal dimensions of material nature or the immensity of the solar systems, suggests a notion of man as a mere drop in the world's great ocean. In this case man's actions could never, of course, mean more than a sequence of irrelevant details in the process of nature. Behind this suicidal nihilism — as we have already hinted — a kind of sinister pride is hidden; for howsoever its teachers may emphasize the irrelevance of man, from their conception of being constituent parts of this vast and divinized cosmos they again snatch a vertiginous sense of bigness; at bottom, that vast cosmos is nothing but an ego inflated beyond measure with which one may identify oneself. The individual's alleged function of being a *part of the great whole* holds out a compensation for pride; for the significance one may yet have as part of the whole is at any rate inherent in what is ultimately the same thing as oneself, not a gift from above, from an absolute Being radically different in kind.

Inasmuch as it denies a personal Godhead — creating out of nothing a world distinct from itself, through a free act of its will — pantheism, of necessity, blurs the concept of man as a finite being. The bond between Creator and creature is superseded by a relation between the whole and the part.

This has the double implication, on the one hand, of raising man to the level of absolute being, thus making his finiteness ambiguous; and on the other hand, of depriving him of the character of a distinct being and consequently of his peculiar dignity by contrast to the rest of nature. Regardless of the contradiction implicit in such a conception, an impersonal absolute is posited (though it cannot be but something metaphysically inferior to the persons who are supposed to be parts of it) and man is subordinated to that impersonal absolute. Man, a spiritual person, rests with his being in the non-personal absolute that engulfs him — an interpretation which is clearly intended to divest him of his character as a person.

This implies a tragic misconception of man's metaphysical situation. Viewed as a drop in the world's vast ocean, man is cheated of his specific dignity and his central importance; he is thus appreciated far below what is due to him. Again, being made part and parcel of the absolute — though it be in fact a sham absolute, beneath the level of personality and hence bare of dignity — he is on the other hand enormously overestimated. This is the aspect that panders to his pride.

Further, *the depersonalization of God points unmistakably to a depersonalization of man as well.* By assimilating man — as part of an impersonal deity — to the absolute, we at the same time displace his center of gravity from the sphere of personality within him into the impersonal lower regions of his nature. The rash attempt to elevate him to a level of absoluteness operates, actually, towards his degradation.

Classical polytheism trivializes God as well as man's encounter with the Divine

In the conception of ancient *polytheism*, man, it is true, is created by a personal god; but this god, Jupiter, is himself finite. There can be no question, therefore, of a confrontation of man as a finite being with the *absolute*, the uncreated, the infinite. By virtue of the anthropomorphic conception of the gods, the pattern of earthly existence is projected upon the level of eternity; it is not human life which, in the *conspectus* of the absolute, acquires a universal and indelible meaning, but inversely, the world of the gods which becomes tinged with the flighty irrelevance of terrestrial life. Hence, the trait of playfulness which, in Homeric antiquity, seems invariably to cling to the image of man, as though he were irrevocably confined in his finiteness.

Here the transcendental *glance* of man which seeks for something absolute and simple — something that surpasses all manifoldness *per eminentiam* — is directed towards a mere magnified finiteness charged with all the motley plurality of earthly things. Man allows his ties with true Divinity to wither; he casts himself before the idols of which the Psalmist says, "They have eyes and see not: they have ears and hear not...they have hands and feel not" (Ps. 113:5-6).

True, man does not fall a victim to depersonalization; but he is deprived of his ordination to the absolute and the possibility of confrontation with God. And this, too, portends a fundamental loss of the deepest significance and nobility of man, chiefly because it conjures away the gravity and depth inherent in man's metaphysical situation. Whereas in the Old Testament, which again clearly conceives of man as a creature and person facing his personal Creator in full distinctness, man's whole life is dominated by the great dialogue between him, the created person, and God, the living, knowing, and loving God, Creator of heaven and earth.

Humility allows us to see our true moral and metaphysical condition

He who has the virtue of humility knows that the infinite love and mercy of God "spared not even his own Son, but delivered him up for us all" (Rom. 8:32). He is aware of the importance of each immortal soul before God: "Precious in the sight of God is the death of his saints" (Ps. 115:15). Against the background of what he has received from God, in the light of the gratuitous gifts of God and the high call addressed to him, he comes to understand that he is nothing by his own force, that he has made inadequate use of the natural endowments as well as of the supernatural gifts of grace he owes to God, that he is but an "unprofitable servant."

Humility is closely connected with that holy freedom in which we acquire the proper perspective in relation to our own person, regarding ourselves no longer with our own eyes but in the light of God. The humble man no longer presumes to determine where he stands; he leaves it to God. The consciousness that God attributes importance to him does not evoke in him a sense of self-importance or a pretension to sovereign autonomy. On the contrary, it makes him see all the more clearly his weakness, and the darkness he represents without God and outside God.

Humility leads us to acknowledge God's personal call

Finally, a third implication of true humility: our *awareness of God's personal appeal* addressed to each of us as to *this* specified individual. In the Prophet Isaiah's words: "I have called thee by thy name — thou art mine." There are those who, while they recognize the glory of God as well as the importance of man and the call addressed to him in general, believe, in false humility, that the call is meant for all others but not for their own person. They deem their own person too wretched to dare assume that they may refer the divine call to themselves. They would hide in a corner and play the part of mere onlookers. The sight of their wretchedness impels them to exclude themselves from the great dialogue between God and man.

This ostensible excess of humility, for all the diffidence it involves, is not free of an element of pride. For here, once more, man presumes to decide himself where he stands, instead of leaving that decision to God. Yet, this is precisely the test of true humility, that one no longer presumes to judge whether or not one is too miserable to be included in the call to sanctity but simply answers the merciful love of God by sinking down in adoration.

The question whether I feel worthy to be called is beside the point; that God *has* called me is the one thing that matters. Having abandoned all pride and all craving for being something of my own resources, I shall not doubt that God, from whom I receive everything, also has the power to lift me up and to transform any darkness into light: "Thou shalt wash me and I shall be made whiter than snow."

I give up the wish to enlighten God as to the degree of my worthiness, knowing that by myself I am worth nothing; but if He wills to draw me to Him, if He calls me by my name, my duty is to say the one word, *Adsum* ("Here I am"). Thus did the most humble Virgin answer the highest call merely by the words: "Behold the handmaid of the Lord: be it done to me according to thy word" (Luke 1:38).

The fact that he has been called to a communion with God, that Christ has addressed his *sequere me* also to him, that he is one of those to whom He speaks thus, "Be you therefore perfect, as also your heavenly Father is perfect" — this fact, to be sure, must again and again strike man as a manifestation of the inscrutable mercy of God.

He must never take the place which God has assigned him as though it were something evidently due to him; rather he should, on every occasion, begin by saying with St. Peter: "Thou shalt never wash my feet" (John 13:8). With trembling heart, like Zacchaeus, he should stand before the Lord in surprise, as it were, and speak with the tongue of the holy Church: "Lord, I am not worthy." Nevertheless, in all humility, he must *accept* the grace of God. Even though preserving an attitude of wonder and experiencing that grace as something inexplicable, he must yet receive, adding to his *non sum dignus*, "But say the word and my soul will be healed."

Humility contains an element of holy audacity

For to the core of humility belongs a gesture of holy audacity. As faith, hope, and charity cannot be without an element of boldness, so also does true humility demand it. Our jubilant assent to our own insignificance, our heroic abandonment of all self-glorification, the relinquishment of self in following Christ — all this is incompatible with tepid mediocrity and cautious smugness. Humility is the opposite, not only of all *malicious* pride but of all forms of self-centered mediocrity, such as emphasis on petty pleasures or honors, any kind of slavery to conventions, any attachment of importance to unimportant concerns, any cowardice, any bourgeois complacency.

Humility, which springs from our confrontation with God, necessarily bursts the bonds of all *mundane immanence*, of the peripheral, terrestrial, everyday aspect of all things, based on a vision of the world which would forever bar our access to God. Whereas the virtue of modesty, operating on the level of earthly relationships, is linked to an attitude of quiet reserve or even resignation in which there is no place for boldness, humility implies a heavenward aspiration that carries with it a breath of greatness and holy audacity. The total relinquishment of self, the blissful dying away of the ego — this means an ultimate jubilant freedom; an unthwarted subsistence in truth.

Humility is the antithesis to all forms of pride — above all, to the two types described above which, for all their distinctness, are both characterized by an act of rebellion against God. But there are other kinds of pride: *self-complacency* and what we may call *haughtiness* or *social pride*. To these, too, humility stands opposed.

Prideful self-complacency uses values to enhance its own position

A person who is merely self-complacent is not blighted with resentment against value as such; nor does he reach out to dethrone the values or God, the exemplar of all values. Rather, in order to nourish his consciousness of *counting for much* and his cult of self, he would possess all values. He does not feel insulted by their existence and splendor; he may not even find it difficult to recognize God as the supreme Lord. Rather he would insinuate himself with God and bask in the sunshine of his dignity before God.

At heart, he too is afflicted with value-blindness. For it is not the intrinsic importance of the good and the beautiful that moves him; he is interested in values merely as an ornament for his own self. He accepts them as one accepts a convention, out of his desire to stand confirmed and glorious in the face of his fellow men, of himself, and even of God. His pretensions are not so great as those implied in satanic pride. He does not consider challenging values or defying God; his presumption is to use the metaphysical power of values, and the respect they compel, to gratify his pride.

The complacent man does not expressly deny that he has received his grandeur from God; but like the Pharisee of the parable in the Gospel, he boasts of whatever excellence he may possess as though he had it of himself. In his heart of hearts, he fails to take account of the fact that he has received everything from God. The Pharisee, in particular, though not expressly bent on dethroning God, is anxious lest God, as it were, should dethrone *him*; hence, he only tolerates God at a remote distance, a majestic looking and not very troublesome God whom he may use for the confirmation of his own glory. Against the incarnate God-Man, however, who spells a threat of direct confrontation with God, who is Himself humble and demands humility of others, the Pharisee conceives a mortal hatred.

The quality of self-complacency varies according to the values it abuses

Next, the specific quality of self-complacency varies considerably according to the *class of values* which the subject would abuse for self-decoration. Here we are faced with an apparent paradox. The higher the values of which one boasts, the worse his immorality in doing so. The more the values in question determine an objective elevation and nobility of man, the more reprehensible it is to flaunt them.

Pharisaism

The gravest case, therefore, is that of the Pharisee, who boasts of his piety and of his being "a just man" before the Lord. He would feed his self-infatuation with the highest values, and pass for glorious not merely in the judgment of his fellow men and of himself but in that of God. His motto is, "O God, I give Thee thanks that I am not as the rest of men" (Luke 18:11). This type of pride, again, is a specifically malignant one, though not in the same degree as satanic pride. The Pharisee, too, is hardened, and incapable of loving kindness and self-surrender.

Self-righteousness

Compared with him, a person who is merely self-righteous in the narrower sense of the term seems less vicious. Though equal to the Pharisee in that he, too, advertises his moral accomplishments, he at least does not abuse the very highest values — sanctity and justness (in the Old Testament sense) — but contents himself with the values of natural morality. He rejoices not in his stature before God, but in his self-respect and in the social figure he cuts: the respect he supposes others pay him. Men of this kind also take pleasure in contemplating the defects of others, against which their own superiority stands out more glowingly. In them, too, there lives an evil resentment, not against value as such, to be sure, but against the virtues of others, which they experience as a threat to their self-glory. Although, as has been said, the merely self-righteous person is by one degree less execrable than the Pharisee, his attitude is still one of the prototypes of all morally damnable conduct and it insults God. Although Satanism as well as Pharisaism proper remain excluded, self-righteousness makes a person obdurate and void of love to the extent that it takes hold of him.

Lesser forms of self-complacency

Self-complacency centered on intellectual values, however, is incomparably more harmless. A man who glories in his erudition, his acumen, or his genius, a man whose ambition it is to be deemed *remarkable*, presents at any rate a much milder case of moral aberration.

Again, he whose pride is related to his wealth, his title of nobility, or the public honors awarded to him, is tainted with even less malice. The lower a value, the more stupid it is to be conceited on its account and to derive from it a consciousness of counting for much or a feeling of self-glory — the more stupid, but at the same time the less evil.

This ostensible paradox finds its explanation in the law of ethics stating that the moral evil inherent in the *abuse* of values is directly proportionate to the height of the value.

Why some forms of self-complacency are more harmless than others

Similarly, the less we may claim a value as representing a merit on our part — in other words, the less we, as free beings, are responsible for its possession — the more stupid it will be on our part to exhibit conceit on its score; yet, the more harmless from a moral point of view will be the pride involved in that conceit. The more we are proud of a value which (as is true of moral values) requires our active participation and effort to be realized, the more reprehensible our pride will be.

This second paradox is accounted for by the fact that our attribution of value to ourselves means a glorification of self in a much stricter and deeper sense whenever the values in question presuppose our free and active — as it were, creative — participation.

Here God has called on us to cooperate with Him; here He has elevated us to the uppermost plane. To abuse this high gift and requite it with a warped response is what makes our pride guilty of a more particular degree of malice.

It must be considered, in addition, that by his pride the Pharisee actually destroys all merit attached to his good works; that is, to put it more explicitly, he lacks the capacity of realizing any moral value so long as he perseveres in his proud attitude. On the other hand, whereas self-complacency does not annihilate intellectual values, it certainly casts an unfavorable light on them insofar as it implies a specific aspect of stupidity. Vital values are still less affected by the fact that they are boasted of, and outward goods — such as wealth or a high social position — least of all.

There is another side to self-complacency which requires mention. This vice involves not merely a self-satisfaction derived from the putative possession of values, but a gnawing ambition to possess them, a restless eagerness to secure them. A kind of dim, smouldering fire seems to consume the souls of such people; they are hardened, shuttered, empty of love; the fury of climbing higher never ceases tormenting them.

Vanity is less harmful than ambitious self-complacency

An attitude widely different from this is *vanity* in the strict sense of the term: the placid, self-sufficient rejoicing in values one presumes oneself to possess. The addict of vanity (in this sense) is not fired by that sinister ambition; he is satisfied with what he has, which he believes to be no small thing. He is not hardened like the self-complacent type previously depicted; rather he displays a trait of pleasure-loving softness.

As contrasted to ambitious self-complacency, vanity represents a comparatively harmless form of pride. A vain person can be good-natured; the ambitiously complacent one, never. Moreover, vanity as a rule is referred to intellectual, vital, and exterior assets rather than to religious or moral virtues. What occupies the center of attention here is one's social figure. Nor is it repugnant to the victim of vanity to recognize other people's virtues, if only the particular point to which his vanity refers is not interfered with. Values other than those abused by his vanity do not interest him; he neglects or minimizes them without any note of resentment.

The humble man attributes nothing to himself

Now humility embodies a specific antithesis, not only to metaphysical pride, but to all varieties of self-complacency and vanity as well. The humble man is not interested in values as an instrument of decorating his own self and enhancing his dignity; he understands and responds to their importance in themselves. He is interested in the good for its own sake.

He finds the cause of his joy in the *magnalia Dei*, the glory of God as mirrored and signified by the cosmos and its wealth of values, including, in particular, the values he discerns in human beings other than himself.

Not subject, as we have seen, to the urge of counting for much, he neither boasts of his virtues nor takes pleasure in their contemplation. He knows that he has received whatever good there is in him from God, and attributes nothing to himself. He says with St. Paul: "But God forbid that I should glory, save in the cross of our Lord Jesus Christ" (Gal. 6:14). He does not feel in any way superior to others; even, say, in regard to criminals his first thought will be, "Who knows what might have become of me, had the grace of God not protected me or had I been exposed to the same temptations." He considers himself the least among his fellow men, more sinful and unworthy than everyone else.

This does not mean that he should falsify facts and be blind to the defects of others. He need not deny the gifts which God has granted to him, nor the fact that he may possess certain advantages in a higher measure than his fellow men. But his attitude in considering his own advantages differs in principle from the one he takes in reference to other people's perfections.

Degrees of awareness of our own perfections

In our awareness of our own perfections, three degrees can be distinguished. First, our mere consciousness or knowledge of them, registering them as plain facts. Next — and here begins perversion — the pleasure we take in them. Finally, which is worst, the attitude of glorying in them. This implies a behavior on man's part as though he possessed those virtues by himself and in his own right, even though theoretically he may not deny that he owes them to God. He anticipates a favorable judgment, a confirmation of his worth, which is ultimately reserved to God alone, and in an analogical sense to his fellow men, but on no account to himself.

While glorying in or boasting of one's advantages is *a fortiori* incompatible with humility, their pleasurable contemplation — as has been shown — is also an offspring of pride; for what vanity delights in is not the value as such but its ornamental function in the service of the ego. Accordingly, a vain person is indifferent to values exhibited by others, and only interested in those which he deems to be distinctive of himself. But — so one might object — why should it be wrong of man to delight in his own values, even in the sense of taking delight in objective value? Why should he be encouraged to discover, to recognize, and to rejoice in the values of others, and at the same time bidden to forego any such rejoicing in his own virtues, nay, to suppress in his mind any emphatic awareness of them?

Humility proscribes all contemplation of one's own virtues

It is here that we reach the core of humility, its innermost secret as it were. In addition to banning all desire to count for much, all proud glorying and all vain delighting in one's own self, humility, indeed, proscribes all contemplation of one's own values, nor does it even tolerate any keen consciousness of them. The reason is, first, that humility implies our consciousness of our own frailty and of the constant danger of sin in which we live, and above all, a trembling anxiety lest we should lapse into pride. No one is truly humble unless he is imbued with the sense of the permanent menace which pride represents to fallen man. As the Psalmist says, "Set a watch, O Lord, before my mouth: and a door round about my lips. Incline not my heart to evil words: to make excuses in sins" (Ps. 140:3-4).

Because the terrible sin of pride, which he repudiates with all his heart, is always present to his eyes, the humble man will never direct his glance to any one of his virtues, lest he should lapse into pride and (in however disguised a fashion) attribute that virtue to a primary goodness of his own self. In holy modesty he will extend a veil over any values discernible in him and never seek to reveal the ultimate value hidden in the depth of his being. To be sure, he has to know about the abilities with which God has equipped him, if only to be aware of the responsibility they entail. Yet, these abilities must appear to him in the light of the tasks they impose on him, rather than as values which he owns; having regard to the responsibility he is charged with, linked to his consciousness of being an *unprofitable servant*, he will not abandon himself to the enjoyment of "his" values. Nor will he, lastly, yield to the suasion of that false sense of security which suggests that he might, without lapsing into pride, consider his advantages and enjoy them in a pure response to value as though they were the virtues of another. For *the false sense of security is itself an offspring of pride*.

Contemplation of our own virtues eviscerates them

Moreover, the ethical and religious values of the person himself, as constituted by and founded upon *his response to the value* (of a good), are essentially outside his field of vision. Because they are built up *by* the person's response to value, they do not themselves enter his consciousness in his experience of the values which elicit his response. The self-values thus displayed remain, as it were, on the margin of his consciousness; their presence is but indirectly signalized by the interior peace and luminous harmony that brighten his soul in the act of responding to the values whose call he experiences. As soon as our glance alights upon the ethical value of our moral action or value-response *itself*, we lose contact with the value (of the good) *referred to* in that act or response; and with that contact disappears the ethical value of our attitude: the more we admire it the more thoroughly it disappears.

Hence, it is strictly impossible in the same act to refer our value-response to the value of our own response in a given case. Even with respect to our own attitudes in the past, it is not possible to look at their value and to take delight in them. It is not impossible to display an ethically valuable behavior and later to reflect upon it with satisfaction; yet even this is destructive of value and inconsistent with humility. For it still severs our contact with the value to which our original moral attitude, the object of our subsequent contemplation, was referred and devoted; it therefore undermines our moral continuity with the subject of our past action, reducing the memory of our accomplishment to an empty shell whose content of value has evaporated.

The humble man remains ever conscious of his own imperfections

More than that, far from relishing or even pondering over his own values, the truly humble person is likely to look upon himself, after the example of many saints, as the greatest sinner. For he is most keenly aware of the gratuitousness of the grace he has received; and the higher he has risen objectively, the more clearly he sees the abyss that separates him from the infinite holiness of God.

He measures his station, not by what he represents absolutely but by the distance between what he has received from God and what he has actually accomplished. Nay, it is inherent in ethical perfection to be constantly advancing towards Christ and never to attribute to one's moral status a completeness which would give one the feeling of being the possessor of a value. Humility does not prevent a person from seeing that, with God's help, he has been making progress in some direction; but he must never lose sight of the essential relativity of that progress. The determination never to cease advancing — a process that has no term *in statu viae* — is one of the basic conditions of holiness.

To sum up: we must not, *in statu viae*, indulge in a contemplation of our own values; much less can we enjoy them even in the sense of a response to value. Our position in relation to ourselves is intrinsically different from what it is in relation to others. Accordingly, too, love of self is not love in the full and proper sense of the term, as is the one typified by our love for another person. Self-love is confined to our concern for our own happiness and salvation, together with our assent to the divine idea of a fully deployed value-response and of a genuine *frui* which we are ordained to realize; it lacks those aspects of delight in the beauty and in the splendor of values which are proper to our love of other persons.

This fundamental difference between our position towards ourselves and towards other persons is also revealed in humility. We are to lift our eyes to the majestic splendor of God and to God's reflection in our fellow men. As regards our relation with ourselves, however, we are to look at our defects and the vastness which separates us from the glory of God; the talents and the gifts of grace which God has given to us we are to consider only insofar as is necessary in order to examine what use we have made of them. Walking in the paths of God, a life pleasing to God will suffuse our consciousness, as said above, with the inward happiness and peace evoked by the soul's concord with the world of values; whereas it would but undo its own meaning and disprove its own truth, were it to seduce us into an appreciative contemplation of "our" values. Others may do that, never we, ourselves.

Haughtiness prizes independence and self-assertion

We have, lastly, to speak of a further and distinct form of pride, which may be described as haughtiness or social pride. (The French term is *fierté*, in contradistinction to *orgueil*, meaning pride in the general and theological sense; the German terms *Stolz* and *Hochmut* are respectively equivalent to these, notwithstanding the etymological kinship between *Hochmut* and *haughty*.) Haughtiness refers, not to a perverse attitude to value, but to a repugnance against submission to other persons. It may not hinder a man from giving a positive response to impersonal values or from complying with a demand of morality. But the haughty man will find it intolerable to feel dependent on other persons, to serve others, to subordinate himself to an alien will, and above all, to suffer ever so slight a humiliation. He is unable to admit before others of having been in the wrong, even if he knows it in his heart; much less could he prevail on himself to ask anybody's forgiveness. He is stricken with a crabbed anxiousness about preserving his dignity, which mostly takes the form of preoccupation concerning his rights and his honor. In his relations with others, he lays great stress on occupying the stronger position. He frequently declines the voluntary help of others, lest its acceptance should be construed as an avowal of weakness. He is loath to engage in any partnership where his would not be the senior position. He is eminently hard; and inclined to despise compassion as a sign of feebleness.

Haughty men are for the most part fanatics of the idol of "manliness." Neither a resentment against value as such nor the abuse of values as an ornament for the ego belongs to their characteristic defects. All their interests subserve their urge for *self-assertion.* They may not grudge recognition of another's merits, but are highly reluctant to perform any act of obedience, to endure any kind of slight, to yield or to surrender in any fashion. That is why the haughty man, even though admitting in his conscience that he has done wrong and regretting his conduct, is incapable of genuine repentance. Much less would he admit his wrong to others and make amends. Confession and the very spirit of the *Confiteor* are therefore essentially distasteful to him.

Haughtiness exists in various degrees

Haughtiness can attain various degrees. It may go so far as to interfere with man's subordination to God, whenever this demand assumes a concrete form which appears too painful to bear. There is a type of haughty person who would not bend his knees even before God. As a rule, however, the vice of haughtiness only affects man's relations with his fellow men. What the haughty person is chiefly bent upon is to avoid receiving anything as a gift from others, accepting any mercy or sympathy, being in the debt of anyone else, or owing gratitude to anyone. Every act that would imply on his part a recognition of any kind of dependence on others is connected, in his feeling, with an unbearable loss of dignity. For instance, though he may not find it difficult to acknowledge other people's merits of his own accord, he would at once feel it incompatible with his dignity to do so, were he to suspect that his homage was counted upon as an obligatory tribute.

Again, while he may be willing to respect official prerogatives or codified laws, he will meticulously refuse every gesture of submission to any authority not strictly official or legal in character. The haughty person, in a word, is hard, cramped, and morally close-fisted. His behavior constitutes an express antithesis to charity, loving kindness, and readiness to serve; it forms the utmost contrast to a soul penetrated and opened up by the light of Jesus.

This form of pride, too, is evil and entirely incompatible with our transformation in Christ. The pride of the stoic or the cynic is of this kind. And it is this pride which is erected into an ideal at war with charity and humility, in the famous lines of Horace: *Si fractus illabatur orbis, impavidum ferient ruinae* ("If the world should collapse in ruins about him, struck by its fragments he would remain fearless"). It is the same pride which is at the basis of many a form of fearlessness and *natural virility*. There is nothing the haughty soul dreads so much as fear. Yet, it is precisely he who so often becomes a slave to the basest kind of fear — the fear of other people's judgment, which is also called *human respect*. (This mad pursuer of independence is very dependent on the admiration others give to his independence.)

This type of man, then, loath to ask for anything; convinced that he is above the need of redemption; abhorring any situation in which the goodwill of others (or its absence) would affect him; infatuated with the idol of his "upright" self-sufficiency; ashamed of any movement of love or compassion, indeed of any kind of sentiment; in a word, an epitome of cramped tension, is, again, a type of which humility embodies an integral negation.

Humility does not fear legitimate subordination to others

He in whom humility is present does not have to overcome any inner resistance in order to subordinate himself to others. In his supple freedom of soul, he always keeps aware of basic realities and is past seeking freedom in the immature illusion of self-sufficiency. As long as it does not interfere with his devotion and obedience to God, his dependence on other men by no means evokes in him a sense of oppression. He receives the breath of mercy with gratitude. The consciousness of being in someone's debt does not distress him at all; the thought of being the weaker partner in relation to another does not disturb the peace of his soul. Nor does it embarrass him to have to ask someone's pardon or to confess a wrong he has done. For he is free of all spasm of autarchy and of all allegiance to the idol of stoic virility. Even at the social level he preserves the Christian indifference to self; he wills to be nothing and to count for nothing. All this, however, derives its character of true humility from the subject's *attitude toward* God.

Humility is neither spinelessness nor servility

For humility proper is not the only possible antithesis to social pride: there are others of a purely natural (and some of them of a morally negative) character. Such is, for example, the spineless, pliant type of man, whom one may treat as one likes, who suffers any insult or humiliation without defending himself, not because in his freedom of soul he has rid himself of all pride and egotism, but because he is too spiritless and feeble to think of resistance or too cowardly to risk any conflict.

Another form of the absence of social pride that must not be confused with humility is the one which denotes the specifically servile nature. This type of man cannot live except as a hanger-on, a subordinate to some strong and powerful personality. Dependence on others means to him no discomfort at all; the position of a lackey or flunky is what suits his inclinations. Being a satellite is natural to him and the sole condition in which he feels happy. At the same time, he is by no means necessarily free from pride. In given circumstances, he may ride roughshod over weaker ones or social inferiors. He is very sensitive to honors and greedy of praise for his services; his natural submissiveness, the expression of his constitutional need of leaning on a stronger personality, has nothing to do with that relinquishment of self which issues from our confrontation with God.

Apart from these morally negative contrasts to haughtiness, there are yet even further natural varieties of the capacity for self-subordination, which may impress us favorably rather than otherwise, but which must still be distinguished from humility. Thus, the disposition we find in many women to center their lives in full self-surrender to serving a man and supplementing his personality, to seek support in him in a way comparable to the ivy clinging to a tree; or again, the modesty prompting a man to keep demurely to an inferior station, instead of affecting the first place in the manner of the haughty. These attitudes, too, are the fruits of a natural need or a certain reasonable sobriety — they are not humility.

Humility originates in the right response to God

For, even in the perspective of our relations with our fellow men, true humility has its origin in our *right response to God*, which implies not only our awareness of the glory and omnipotence of God, and of our own creaturely finiteness, but a total emancipation from our spasm of self-centeredness in the presence of Christ. He is humble in whose heart the infinite merciful love of God, which bends down to us in the person of Christ — the descent of God, who longs to gather the lost sheep, and who solicits our love — has dissolved all pride, even the hidden and the limited one, and reduced all self-assertion: that is what places him in an entirely new position even in regard to his fellow men.

In its full and specific unfolding, humility calls forth what we shall later describe as the virtue of meekness. The humble one has divested himself of all hardness; he faces his fellow men, not mailed and armored, but in the luminous attire of invincible charity. Even his foes — and this is the test of meekness — he confronts unarmed.

In specific contradistinction to the haughty character, the humble man is not hampered by any inhibitions in subordinating himself to others; he is past all self-assertion and therefore ready to obey all authority that has its place in the divine plan. He sets himself at a distance from his own arbitrary will and does not seek satisfaction in the consciousness of unbridled freedom. Whereas a haughty person (apart from the question of the particular objects for which he strives) resents and feels any curb placed on his arbitrary good pleasure to be intolerable, the person imbued with humility adopts as his maxim — in conformity with the seventh chapter of St. Benedict's Rule — the words of Our Lord: "I am not come to do my will, but the will of Him who hath sent me." Likewise St. Benedict says, concerning the third stage of humility: "Out of his love of God, the monk submits himself to his superior in perfect obedience." *Holy obedience*, the expression of a complete breach with self-will and self-assertion, is that actualization of humility which is most explicitly opposed to social pride.

Christian humility calls us to an act of self-humiliation

But we must go one step further. He whose soul has become a seat of consummate humility is not only able to confess his wrongs with ease, to submit himself, or to bear an offense with resignation; he actually *elects to be the last*. He yearns for the practice of obedience; he is glad to suffer slights and avid of contempt and rebuke. It is here that we reach the mysterious innermost core of Christian humility.

What the latter implies is not merely a liberation from pride in its various forms (including haughtiness); not merely a recognition of our true metaphysical situation and an emergence from all illusions; not merely the habit of seeing ourselves in blissful freedom of soul as we appear in the eyes of God and of giving our joyous assent to this truth.

Beyond that, Christian humility implies an express act of *self-humiliation*, a voluntary descent *beneath* our legitimate natural dignity, an act of reducing ourselves to naught before God. It implies the gesture of a permanent inner dying of the self, so that Christ may live in us — a gesture that has found its unique expression in the figure of St. John the Baptist and his words: "He must increase: but I must decrease" (John 3:30).

If, as has been pointed out earlier, humility is only conceivable as a response to the personal God of the Christian revelation, again this deepest fulfillment of humility is only conceivable as a response to the God-Man, Jesus Christ; to the very gesture of descent performed by Him who "emptied himself, taking the form of a servant, being made in the likeness of men and in habit found as a man; humbled himself, becoming obedient unto death, even to the death of the cross" (Phil. 2:7-8).

Let us represent to ourselves the ineffable scene, as reported by St. John in his Gospel (13:2-15): "And when supper was done (the devil having now put into the heart of Judas Iscariot, the son of Simon, to betray Him), knowing that the Father had given Him all things into His hands and that He came from God and goeth to God, He riseth from supper and, having taken a towel, girded Himself. After that, He putteth water into a basin and began to wash the feet of the disciples and to wipe them with the towel wherewith He was girded....Then after He had washed their feet and taken His garments, being set down again, He said to them: Know you what I have done to you? You call me Master and Lord. And you say well: for so I am. If then I, being your Lord and Master, have washed your feet, you also ought to wash one another's feet. For I have given you an example, that as I have done to you, so you do also."

Thus does Christ call on us to step down from the natural position in which God has installed us. Humility certainly means the habit of living in the truth; beyond that, however, it means an *active gesture of quitting the status that is our natural due*, a step towards reducing ourselves to naught. It constitutes a specific element in the imitation of Christ.

Here the deep connection between humility and charity manifests itself. In its deepest roots, humility is a fruit of charity; it is our love of Christ that makes us will to "die" so that He may live in us and again inspires our readiness to serve all men, because He has said: "What you do to the least of my brethren, you have done it to me."

Such alone as have absorbed the spirit of these words of the Lord: "Even as the Son of man is not come to be ministered unto, but to minister" (Matt. 20:28) — such hearts alone as have been wounded to the core by this descent of love "unto the end," may acquire the humility that has filled the saints; the humility that made every insult, every injustice, every humiliation taste sweet to them; that caused them permanently to undergo the process of self-surrender and self-humiliation, and stirred up in their souls the fire of an unlimited readiness to serve. Christian humility proper encloses the mystery of an inward descent down to the abyss of nothingness, so that God may be "all in all" within us.

Humility confers beauty on the souls of the humble

He who lives in humility deliberately assigns to himself a place even beneath the one which he can naturally claim. He is like the guest to whom the Lord has said, "Friend, rise higher." Humility, therefore, is not only a presupposition for the genuineness and truth of all our virtues, but is the central condition of our transformation and regeneration in Christ. Moreover, it embodies a high value in itself, conferring on man a unique kind of beauty.

Humility bursts the bonds of all narrowness; through it, even a personality insignificant by nature will acquire width and greatness. For it is only the humble soul, the soul that has emptied itself, which can be fully penetrated by the divine Life it has received in holy Baptism; and it is upon such a soul that there falls a reflection of the greatness and infinitude of God. Here is a great mystery, paradoxical yet true: precisely he who speaks the word of total assent to his finiteness and *limitation* will thereby illuminate his nature with an aura which in some way images the *unlimited* breadth of God. In him alone who *dies* inwardly, descending almost beneath the natural level of being that has been his due in the order of creation, who wills no longer to occupy any *space* at all, may the wealth of supernatural life blossom out, according to St. Paul's words: "I live, yet it is not I who live but Christ who lives in me."

Qui se exaltat — humiliabitur; qui se humiliat — exaltabitur. The exaltation of the humble is by no means merely a reward which God grants to them in life eternal; it is also an intrinsic effect of humility, accomplished even on earth. For indeed, the humble walk as if clad in the attire of a unique nobility, before which all splendor of purely natural talents and gifts wanes into insignificance. By his descent beneath his natural rank, the humble man in a mystical sense prostrates himself, at the feet of the Lord, as did St. Mary Magdalene. He is lifted up by Jesus and thus enters the celestial realm.

All height, width, and depth, all greatness and beauty of humility, with its irresistible victorious power, shine forth most luminously in the Blessed Virgin, the Queen of the angels and all saints. In humility there is mirrored the central mystery of the process of our transformation — the mystery that Our Lord has put into these words: "Unless the grain of wheat falling into the ground die, itself remaineth alone; but if it die, it bringeth forth much fruit" (John 12:24). The path that leads man to his ultimate union with Christ is not the unfolding of his natural powers and of the wealth of his gifts but his radical renunciation of self-assertion, the relinquishment and mortification of the self: "He who loses his soul shall win it."

Thus, yearning to be transformed in Christ, we must pray: *Jesus, meek and humble of heart, make our hearts like unto Thine.*

8

Confidence in God

THE knowledge of our need of redemption, as we have seen in the beginning, is the prime condition of our transformation in Christ, for it provides the only possible basis for our readiness to change.

We must have confidence in the whole message of love in the Gospels

However, that knowledge is condemned to sterility unless it is completed by another fundamental act on our part: our confidence in God. The knowledge that we are in need of redemption would merely cast us into despair unless we also knew that it is God's will to redeem us. Even under the Old Covenant, man's awareness of the necessity of redemption was qualified by his expectation of the promised Messiah.

To us, however, more is given: the faith that Christ has redeemed us, that the merciful love of God bends down to us; the faith that God *wills* to purify and to sanctify us and to fill us with His holy life; the faith that Baptism infuses a new supernatural life into us; and the faith that we are called by God, and that — though it be an incomprehensible mystery, since He, who rests in absolute beatitude, in no wise needs us — God seeks us in love and wills to be loved by us. In a word, we have been given Faith embracing the *entire* message of the holy Gospels. Confidence in God implies this living faith in the whole message of the Gospel; a faith that is no mere theoretical belief in an objective truth but a vital creed, by whose agency a superior Reality is continually at work informing our lives.

We must trust in the omnipotence of God

This creed must refer, first to the omnipotence of God. It is not enough for us to entertain a theoretical and general belief that God has the power to do everything. In every concrete situation we are faced with, the omnipotence of God must be so palpably present to us as to lessen the reality of all other facts, immutable as they may seem. Even in the face of outward dangers, which make our situation appear desperate — of a person whose state of mind robs us of all hope as to his conversion; of our own wretchedness when we see ourselves relapsing again and again; of the crushing weight of our sins committed in the past — we must always remain vitally aware of the paramount truth that the archangel Gabriel announced to the Blessed Virgin: "No word shall be impossible with God" (Luke 1:37).

Not for a moment must we forget that "God can raise up children to Abraham out of stones." We lack true faith so long as we are not constantly aware of what the Psalmist has thus put in words: "Whatsoever the Lord pleased he hath done, in heaven and on earth" (Ps. 134:6).

We must believe that God truly loves us

In the first place, we must believe in God's omnipotence as regards our own concerns. In view of our misery and debility, of the sins whose weight we vainly struggle to shake off our shoulders, we must say with David, "Thou shalt sprinkle me with hyssop, and I shall be cleansed." Yet, to be thus conscious of God's *omnipotence* is only the first step; we must next believe in His *love* for us, His inscrutable mercy that has bent down to us in Christ, and aims at redeeming us.

"God (who is rich in mercy) for His exceeding charity wherewith He loved us, even when we were dead in sins, hath quickened us together in Christ" (Eph. 2:4-5). We must firmly believe not only that God *can* save us but that, having called us to eternal communion with Himself, He *wills* to redeem us; nay, that He *has* redeemed us in Christ.

Nor does it suffice for us to believe that God is infinite Love as such, that St. John's words, *Deus caritas est* (1 John 4:8), adequately define the essence of God for our understanding; we must believe in God's love *for us* and experience the sweet inexorable compulsion of His love as it touches our person. Incomprehensible as it may seem to us that God should bestow His love upon us notwithstanding all our unworthiness, we must believe in this infinite love directed to each of us, and fall to our knees before this mystery.

We must believe in God's omniscience

Further, confidence in God implies our belief in an *omniscient* and omnipresent divine love. He who truly trusts in God knows that, as St. Augustine says, "To us is promised the sight of a living and seeing God" (*Sermo* 69.1-2); that God, while resting in Himself in infinite beatitude, is yet constantly aware of us and presiding over our destinies.

He who trusts in God never forgets the words of the Lord, "The very hairs of your head are all numbered" (Matt. 10:30). He knows that, even though we be far from Him, God is always near to us. He does not confine the operation of God to the limits that our rational thinking is wont to draw to it; rather he believes that, whether we turn our attention to God or not, we are continually in the hands of God and secure in His all-powerful and all-wise love.

Confidence in God also requires the consciousness that the glance of God penetrates everywhere and that nothing at all can escape it, should we even attempt to flee from its ken. "If I ascend into heaven, Thou art there; if I descend into hell, Thou art present" (Ps. 138:8). No matter what we do, and though we try ever so hard to hide ourselves, we are and remain the property of God and utterly impotent to elude Him: "I am the Lord, who search the heart, and prove the reins" (Jer. 17:10). Yet, no less definitely must we know that He from whom we cannot escape is infinite holiness and eternal love, "the great delight of our souls" (Laud of St. Francis of Assisi); He of whom the Psalmist says: "O taste, and see that the Lord is sweet" (Ps. 33:9).

We must believe that we are each called individually by God

Finally, confidence in God implies the belief in our being *called* — as it were, addressed — by God. "I, the Lord, have called thee in justice, have taken thee by the hand, and have preserved thee" (Isa. 42:6). That consciousness of *being called* (which we have seen to be an element of humility) is equally relevant to what may in the full sense be termed confidence in God.

And the contrary attitude — that of considering ourselves, so to speak, excluded from God's sphere of concerns; of contemplating the God of infinite love merely as onlookers; of deeming ourselves, in false modesty, too unimportant and unworthy to refer the divine call to ourselves — is not only inconsistent with humility but also indicates a deficiency in faith. For God not only *loves* us, He also wills to *be loved* by us. To each of us, too, Christ addresses the question He asked three times: "Simon, son of John, dost thou love me?" The mysterious word He pronounced on the cross — *Sitio* (I thirst) — expresses a never-ceasing call for our love.

Confidence in God, then, demands a vital faith in the integral message of the Gospels. But it demands more than that. Beyond giving credence to what the Faith proposes to us, we must relinquish the base on which we are primarily established and which provides us with our natural security, and must fully remove our center of gravity from our nature into God. We must definitively renounce the concept of attaining our goal by our own natural forces, and expect everything from the holy new life that Christ has infused into us in Baptism.

Confidence in God is essentially different from optimism

A clear distinction should be made between confidence in God and the natural sense of security that denotes the optimistic temper — the resiliency that is simply the fruit of a robust vitality. More, this sense of security must collapse and depart, so as to clear the ground for true confidence in God; for it is rooted precisely in that natural attitude of self-assertion which the true Christian is bound to abandon.

To interpret this natural sense of security, this rugged trust we place in our own nature, as confidence in God is a most deplorable error; for it cannot but taint our relation to God with a note of presumptuous platitude. "The good Lord will arrange everything somehow" — such people are wont to say. They are never roused into a full awareness of man's metaphysical situation; their vital buoyancy prompts them to skip, as it were, that all-important stage in the soul's way to God — contrition. They spare themselves the fear of God, which is "the beginning of wisdom" (Ps. 110:10); they forget "it is a fearful thing to fall into the hands of the living God," (Heb. 10:31). This pitfall of a comfortable smugness masquerading as religiosity we must studiously avoid; in full awareness of the gravity of our metaphysical situation, in penitent humility we must lift our eyes to God, and in constant effort work for our sanctification. At the same time, we must bear in mind that it is not on the basis of our nature but through Christ and in Christ alone that a real victory over our sinfulness can be obtained. Our life must be integrally reposed on our faith in the new supernatural principle we have received in holy Baptism, according to the words of St. Paul: "For when I am weak, then am I powerful" (2 Cor. 12:10).

We must establish the center of our own personality in God alone

Again and again we may observe ourselves relying and depending on our nature — now in the sense of minimizing our defects in the spirit of a natural optimism, now in that we are moved to helpless despair when our infirmities reveal themselves — a sure indication that we have not yet acquired true confidence in God, that we have not yet transported the center of our personality into the supernatural and are still clinging, as it were, to our native selfhood. Otherwise, in spite of (and linked to) our repentance of our lapses; in spite of the pain due to our awareness of being still so far removed from God, we should be filled with joy because we have come to know ourselves better and gotten rid of our illusions about our character.

For, as we have seen it earlier, the very fact of our being more deeply pervaded by the light of truth renders us more closely attached to God. Do we not know, after all, that we must expect nothing from our nature? How can we thus feel deceived and thrown off our balance, whenever we meet with a tangible sign of our imperfection? Ought we not, rather, to count with it beforehand and to be happy and grateful if we can at least detect its concrete manifestations, so as to make sure in what respects we must try to amend with God's help?

Contrition is compatible with confidence in God

The abyss of our faults, the immense distance that still separates us from the perfection which God has set before us as our goal — they may well prompt us to say: "Have mercy on us, O Lord, have mercy on us" (Tob. 8:10); yet they must never cause us to lose heart. Rather we must say, again, with David: "Thou shalt wash me, and I shall be made whiter than snow" (Ps. 50:9); and believe firmly that the mercy of God is greater than all the vastness of our weakness and infidelity.

Certainly, whenever we have offended God by any definite transgression, whenever we have betrayed Christ in any manner, we should be filled with profound contrition. Even then, however, we should not for a moment flee from God, nor yield to the temptation of doubting either His omnipotence or His mercy. What we are to do is to fall down before Him in penitence and to flee into His merciful arms. Such moments precisely are the test of our confidence in God, of the firmness of our faith in God's mercy, from which no sin can, *in statu viae*, separate us *irrevocably*.

It has been noted on an earlier occasion that what brought Judas to perdition was not his betrayal of the Savior but the fact that, shaken with remorse, he despaired of the mercy of God: in other words, that he *lacked confidence in God*. The deeper our contrition, the brighter and the more steadfast must be our faith in the all-powerfulness and all-mercifulness of God.

Habitual sin sorely tests our confidence in God

Our trust in God is exposed to a particularly hard test if we have to wrestle with a habitual sin. When we again and again relapse into the same fault, when all our moral effort seems ineffective and all our religious zeal fruitless, we shall almost inevitably feel tempted to lose patience, to get discouraged and give up the struggle, or to remonstrate with God; or again, to despair of God's help and believe ourselves abandoned by Him. The very fact that we have honestly striven to overcome our defect, that we have done so relying on God's help, that we have been eager to follow His call, and yet encountered defeat, is likely to upset our equilibrium and threatens to throw us into utter confusion.

Yet we must believe in God's inexhaustible love and mercy

It is in such situations, precisely, that our unconditional trust in God has to assert itself. We must stick unswervingly to the belief that God loves us with an infinite love and *wills* our sanctification, whatever our spiritual status may appear to our eyes. He who truly confides in God does not presume to decide himself, by experience, whether God is intent on saving him or has withdrawn from him. Once he has absorbed the message of the Gospels, his conviction of God's infinite mercy, of God's inexhaustible love which embraces him also, is so firm and unconditional as to preclude its dependence on any confirmation drawn from experience. He does not arrogate to himself a competence to ascertain from the evidence of facts whether God has turned from him and abandoned him.

On the contrary, he knows that nothing *can* come from God that is not a manifestation of His love, and that every situation must be *a priori* considered against this irremovable background. Much as his ever-recurrent backslidings may depress him, he will seek their cause in himself alone, in his own weakness and lack of zeal; and at the same time thank God for the humiliation to which he owes a clear consciousness of his weakness. How could he judge on his own authority *what* God means thereby to convey to him! Even in these disappointments, he will humbly look for the traces of God's love, and abide by the words of St. Paul: "For I know in whom I have believed" (2 Tim. 1:12). Aware of the untiring mercy of God, full of confidence he will again and again begin anew.

Our confidence comes not from our own earthly fortunes, but from "who God is"

For this exactly is the essence of trust that, instead of inferring from the symptoms — from the way we are treated in one respect or another — what a person's intentions are, we assume them to be good and then interpret the situation in the light of this prime assumption. Suppose I make the acquaintance of a person and from my various experiences concerning him derive a conception of his character and of his emotional attitude to me. Suppose, again, that I arrive at the point of forming the judgment, "I have implicit trust in this person; there is no one I should trust more."

From this moment onward, I no longer judge that person's character from his behavior; I no longer proceed, as it were, from the appreciation of his single acts to a comprehension of his nature or his essential position. Rather I proceed, henceforth, in the inverse sense: I interpret all his acts in the light of the definitive concept I have formed of his character.

This implies that, even though his forthcoming acts should seem to contradict the picture I have made of his personality or of his attitude to me, I shall keep to this central determination of his essence, telling myself that I must either be mistaken about the facts or ignorant of the particular motives which had impelled the person in question to behave in the way he did, and that they cannot be repugnant to the loftiness of character or the kind dispositions towards me which I have ascribed to him.

Let it be admitted that in our relations with a *human* being, we may again arrive at a point where — be it on the strength of many symptoms or even because of one unequivocal indication that retains its validity after having heard the person in question — the conclusion imposes itself that his central attitude has changed. For every human being may change; he may fall; his love may cease.

Yet, in relation to God, "in whom there is no shadow of alteration" (James 1:17), who is goodness and mercy, of whom the Psalmist says: "For His mercy is confirmed upon us: and the truth of the Lord remaineth for ever" (Ps. 116:2), our trust must be absolute; the possibility of its being dislodged by any kind of experience whatsoever must be precluded axiomatically.

Whereas God's merciful love speaks to us in all benefits and blessings which constantly surround us, and above all, in His eternal Word which has become flesh, of which St. Paul says, "the goodness and kindness of God our Savior appeared" (Titus 3:4), it is by no means an absence of this Divine love which manifests itself to us in our misfortunes or failures. In these we must seek the traces of our guilt on the one hand and the hidden love of God on the other, for we know that "his mercy endureth for ever."

Our consciousness of being children of God and of being secure in His all-powerful and all-wise love must provide the central presupposition from which we view everything, be it joy or misery, be it the tangible help of God or the apparent failure of our endeavors. He whose confidence in God is genuine will, whenever his failures or his relapses threaten to discourage him, flee into the arms of God with undiminished trust, entreat God's help with increased fervor, and combat his defects with greater vigilance than ever.

God answers all prayers with omniscient charity

It is said sometimes that, when in spite of all our prayers a thing we have dearly wished for falls short of realization, our prayer has not proved efficacious. There is only one good for which we know that our prayers shall be granted: our eternal salvation. To this good all other goods that we may enjoy are subordinated; they are genuine goods only so long as they are subservient to it. Whether some single good *is* subservient to that supreme end, and in what way, we can *never* determine with absolute certainty; knowledge thereof belongs to God exclusively.

Hence, we must never say that God has *rejected our prayer*; from the fact that our wish has not been fulfilled we must in no wise infer that God has turned His face from us or that our prayer has passed unheard. Rather we must assume that God knows better than we do about what furthers our salvation; that the ultimate intention of our prayer, our true happiness, *has* been realized precisely through God's refusal, in this case, to grant our concrete request.

Nor is this all: even in the context of our earthly welfare we may often observe that something we deplored as a great calamity subsequently turns out to be highly fortunate for us. Who of us cannot remember occasions when he strove with all his might to attain a certain object, begging God to grant his desire, only to thank God, a while later, for having withheld from him an apparent benefit which he now sees would have involved him in disaster.

He who has the right confidence in God knows that his prayer is never condemned by God, whose merciful glance is always turned towards us; but he also knows that God alone can judge what profits us best and that, therefore, His answer is always the answer of *omniscient charity*.

Again — and more important, perhaps — he knows that the nonfulfillment of our request, though we may feel it as a heavy blow, must in reality accord with what is objectively more valuable: in other words, that we ought not to consider the decisions of God exclusively from the narrow angle of our life and our desires. On the contrary, it is the adjustment of our wills to the objectively good that we should care about: "Grant Thy peoples that they may love what Thou commandest and desire what Thou dost promise" (Collect of the fourth Sunday after Easter).

Prayers denied are nonetheless valuable as words addressed to God

This is not to say, however, that we must not pray except for the salvation of our (or other people's) souls. We may, and should, pray for any legitimate good, and for the averting of evils, as does the holy Church: "From plague, famine, and war deliver us, O Lord." The prayer of supplication, by which we humbly solicit His aid — expecting everything from Him — is pleasing to God. In his Second Homily on Prayer, St. John Chrysostom justly says: "Consider what happiness is conceded, what honor is accorded to thee: to hold speech with God, to have colloquy with Christ in thy prayers, to ask for what thou wishest, to demand what thou desirest."

It may well be in a given case that God is willing to accord us a certain good *if* we confidently pray for it. All our entreaties, however, should be inspired by the spirit of the words of Christ on the Mount of Olives: "Nevertheless, not as I will but as Thou wilt" (Matt. 26:39).

We, on our part, *should* pray for what appears desirable to our limited vision; for it is in such prayers of supplication that our confidence in God and our vital contact with Him takes body. Whenever we believe we may without injustice desire a certain thing, we do well to actualize by praying for that thing, showing our dependence on God and our trust in His goodness and His inexhaustible mercy.

Yet, we must not assume that should God's infinite wisdom decide to withhold that good from us, our prayer has not been received or answered. For the prayer of petition is not a *means* to secure an object; it is a word addressed to the absolute Person, by which we lay our desires in His hands; and that word retains its meaning even though God answers it in a way different from what we should have preferred. Never must we flinch from believing that

God's answer, whether or not directly *favorable*, cannot but be an answer of love.

Even our afflictions reflect the infinite mercy of God

It is in a similar light that we must interpret our afflictions. Suppose that a person whom we love dies or that a grave bodily evil befalls us — for example, we lose our eyesight. It is natural and right that we should experience such an event as the misfortune it is, and suffer accordingly; and yet we must not doubt that it, too, harbors some hidden good, because God has willed it to happen; that, even in this affliction, the loving hand of God has touched us.

We must always remain aware of the immeasurable distance between our limited vision, which cannot grasp more than a tiny detail of the whole, and the all-comprehensive mind of God. "For my thoughts are not your thoughts: nor your ways my ways, saith the Lord" (Isa. 55:8). Above all, too, we must think of the entirely new meaning that all suffering has acquired through Christ's death on the cross. The suffering of Our Lord purified the world; His sorrowful love of atonement redeemed it.

Whether the suffering that has fallen to our lot is meant to provide us with an occasion to atone for our sins here on earth; to try us and detach us completely; or again — a costly privilege — to make us atone for the sins of others, or to allow us to participate in Christ's suffering on the cross, so as to become more like Him; in all suffering we are touched by the merciful hand of God, who is infinite love.

Christian confidence in God implies an integral response to Revelation and therefore an appreciation of the meaning that Christ has conferred upon suffering. Even though his heart be pierced by sorrow, even though he may see nothing but darkness around him, the Christian must still implicitly believe in the supernatural meaning of suffering illumined with the love of God. And so, though we may and should pray for the averting of future evils, to every visitation of sorrow which God *has* inflicted upon us we must respond with the words *Fiat voluntas Dei*, ("God's will be done"); more, we must also see in it the love of God, which purposes to guide us through our sorrows to eternal happiness, to the joy whereof the Lord says, "But your sorrow shall be turned into joy" (John 16:20).

Yet we must oppose evil

However, we hear the objection: "Yes, this may hold inasmuch as sorrows and sufferings alone are concerned. But what if we are to witness the frequent triumphs on earth of willful malice; the reverses not seldom suffered for the cause of God by the soldiers of Christ; the dangers that threaten so many souls owing to the successes of the foes of God? Are we still to interpret these incomprehensible, these strictly and intrinsically *bad* things as an outcome of God's love?"

Certainly these things, by contrast to whatever is sad without being evil, must not be interpreted as an expression of God's will. They are *permitted* by God; and the fact that God has permitted them to happen must not by any means induce us to doubt their intrinsic badness. Nor does it in any way relieve us of the obligation to combat the power of evil wherever it confronts us. Though God, time and again, permits a temporary triumph of evil, to infer from this that we ought to accept it with resignation would be a fatal misconception. On the contrary, we are to fight it to the best of our ability; and when we are no longer able to oppose it actively, we should sacrifice and pray that "God may humiliate the enemies of the Church": "Break, O Lord, we beseech Thee, the pride of our enemies: and with the power of Thy right hand, strike down their insolence" (Prayer against persecutors and foes).

That God sometimes permits evil to triumph does not make that evil into goodness

It would, indeed, be the climax of perversity on our part to construe the fact of the divine permission as meaning that evil triumphant, because it is triumphant, is not *merely* evil and that it is our duty to find out the good it connotes and appreciate the latter. Then we could not reasonably refuse to find something good also in the conduct of those who crucified Christ. What our confidence in God impels us to believe is merely that God's *permission* of an evil thing has its *hidden* meaning and value; a mysterious truth which does not in any degree diminish or modify the intrinsic evil of that thing — or to put it in different words, the negative value-character inherent in its content. "The Son of man indeed goeth, as it is written of him. But woe to that man by whom the Son of man shall be betrayed. It were better for him, if that man had not been born" (Matt. 26:24).

As for the positive aspect (so far as it is not essentially inaccessible to our understanding), this can reside merely in the *indirect consequences* of the permission of that evil. In particular, it may be meant as a test for the virtuous. But then this meaning as intended by God engages us precisely to meet the evil thing in question with an adequate response; that is, not to allow our inward rejection of evil or our profession of God and His holy truth to be confounded or bewildered by any success of the evil power; not to let us be bribed by any consideration into a compromise with evil; never to bow to it on account of its display of outward strength.

At the same time, we must be aware that this temporary prevailing of evil, too, carries a certain meaning and value, provided that we give the right response to that call of God which is hidden in the background; that God's permission of this victory of evil does not signify that He has turned His face from us; and lastly, that the triumph of evil is bound to be a *passing* one, seeing that we are given the word of promise: "And the gates of hell shall not prevail [against the Church]" (Matt. 16:18).

To be sure, it mostly remains an impenetrable mystery for us why God permits such a passing triumph of evil at all. So much is certain, that this mystery is related to the part God has assigned to man's freedom of will. But we must not presume to unriddle the secrets of God. Even though we feel tempted to exclaim, "Arise, why sleepest Thou, O Lord!" (Ps. 43:23), our belief in the meaning and value of all divine permissions must remain unshaken. No matter how insoluble the puzzle may appear to our human understanding, even in such moments we must feel secure in the infinite love of God. He who has true confidence in God knows that God has not become indifferent to us because He allows His foes to parade in triumph for a while; he remembers Jesus chiding His disciples when they, frightened by the tempest, awoke him, "Why are you fearful, O ye of little faith?" (Matt. 8:26).

Nor does this right confidence in God, implying the conviction that the victory of evil can never be final, lead to an attitude of quietistic resignation. On the contrary, it supplies us with imperturbable strength in our struggle for the kingdom of God, though sometimes that struggle can no longer consist in anything but prayer and sacrifice, suffering and martyrdom.

We must be confident that God will provide for our needs

As regards the outward concerns of life, in particular, the Gospels again admonish us to put our trust in God. The Lord says: "Behold the birds of the air, for they neither sow, nor do they reap, nor gather into barns: and your heavenly Father feedeth them" (Matt. 6:26). The reference is, above all, to the spirit of poverty. We are warned to preserve our inner freedom, to which our concern about our property may easily become a menace; our attention is drawn to the impossibility of serving two masters. Besides that, however, these words of Christ also exhort us to have confidence in God, to put away that cramped attitude, the anxiety to provide everything one may ever need by one's own labor and foresight; to avoid being *enslaved* by our concern and worry even about the real necessities of life: "Be not solicitous, therefore" (Matt. 6:31).

True, we must not, while living idle from sloth or levity, expect God to sustain us. Nor must we expect God to repair by a miracle the damage our unreasonableness and our omissions have inflicted upon us.

Yet, should God excite in us an earnest desire to devote ourselves to some high task, we should follow this call unhampered by any worry about the outward necessities of life and be fully confident that God will take care of what we had to pretermit for the sake of a higher object. The spendthrift who dissipates everything he has for the sake of momentary pleasures must not expect God to dispense him from the consequences of his defects. The generous character, on the other hand, who would give a beggar one half of his cloak as St. Martin did, may confidently speak: "God will provide" (Gen. 22:8). He who has vowed holy poverty shall indeed believe that God, who sent a raven to feed St. Benedict in the hermitage of Subiaco, will provide food and shelter for him.

Or again, if God — without any guilty negligence on our part — imposes the burden of poverty on us, we should not waste ourselves away with care nor feel as though the bottom of our existence had been knocked out; rather — while sparing no effort to provide for our livelihood — we should preserve a deep confidence that God will assist us. We should, in such a case, seek to comprehend the particular call of God to us that lies in this visitation, not allow ourselves to be submerged by our concern for outward necessities. The fact that we have lost the secure natural basis of our outward existence should impel us to throw ourselves entirely upon God's mercy; notwithstanding all reasonable endeavors to cope with the situation on the natural level, we should firmly resist the tendency to lose heart or to become wholly absorbed in our worries.

Above all, we must always preserve, by our trust in God, our inner freedom to care about the *one thing necessary*, mindful of the words of the Lord: "Seek ye first the kingdom of God and his justice: and all these things shall be added unto you" (Matt. 6:33).

Fear is the opposite of confidence in God

There is, further, one current attitude specifically opposed to confidence in God — fear; or, to put it more exactly, the state of the soul abandoning itself to distress and anxiety. There are many things which on the purely natural level are apt to frighten us — grave diseases, for instance, the hostility of wicked and powerful men, the turmoil of battle, the uncontrolled fury of a mob, and last but not least, death itself.

Now it is quite right that we should be aware of the helplessness and insecurity inherent in our earthly situation, rather than in-dulge — owing to a natural disposition in this sense — the thoughtless illusion of being immune against all evils. Nor should we, in stoical obtuseness, refrain from experiencing as an evil what really is an evil. He who faces death in fearless impassivity, al-though he does not see in it a gateway to eternity but a submersion beyond which there is nothing but the darkness of utter uncer-tainty, only proves his dullness or his lack of imagination. His incapacity to understand or to respond to the fact that death really and objectively is a terrible thing, is no display of confidence in God or even an attitude that is praiseworthy on natural grounds.

Confidence in God liberates us from fear

In an entirely different sense, however, does the duty to over-come fear confront the Christian. He must integrally take account of the new light that has fallen upon our earthly situation as a consequence of the Redemption. He knows that the inherent uncertainty and forlornness of our natural situation on earth have been dispelled by Christ, who says: "In the world you shall have distress. But have confidence. I have overcome the world" (John 16:33). In the face of death, he will say with St. Paul, "O death, where is thy victory? O death, where is thy sting?" (1 Cor. 15:55). No matter what dangers and menaces may face him, he is aware of their relativity and transitory character, as well as of their character of trial; he feels fully sheltered in the all-powerful love of God, a security which no outward evil can ever destroy.

What confidence in God does to us is not to make us blind either to the evils that threaten us or to the fact of their reality, but to liberate us from the perplexity, unrest, and anxiety linked to them naturally. Confidence in God arms us, then, not with a habit of blunt indifference, but with that supernatural courage which causes us to dread nothing in our struggle for the kingdom of God: that conquering intrepidity which has animated the martyrs.

He who is filled with true confidence in God clings, in the presence of all things that by themselves justly arouse his anxiety, to the supreme reality and the omnipotent love and mercy of God. He never forgets that whatever sufferings and evils he is destined to bear, everything falls beneath the towering reality and the all-wise reign of God, who is infinite love and goodness; that everything is but a phase in the road advancing towards Him; that all dire things are deprived of their venom by Christ, to whom we speak in adoration with St. Francis: "For by Thy holy cross Thou hast redeemed the whole world."

Why we sometimes succumb to fear

Nevertheless, it is a fact that even convinced Christians, who seek Christ in all sincerity, may sometimes lapse into a state of anxiety which palsies their free response to value. How does this happen?

How does it come about that our souls, even though Christian, may be numbed into a kind of spasm in which they are unable to look at anything except a certain evil, the dread of which fascinates us to the point of caring about nothing but our escape from that evil?

How can we so much fall under the domination of that fear that we stoop to considering everything from this one point of view only? What moved St. Peter to deny the Lord, though only a few hours before he had declared he would follow Him everywhere?

What makes us often, even in the face of minor evils, so preoccupied with the desire of avoiding them as to let this obsession hinder us from responding to high values, so afraid of them as to tell a falsehood or to sin gravely against charity? How is it possible that, having received the message of the Gospels and giving credence to it, we should still tremble sometimes before even comparatively puny evils?

The chief reason lies in our habit of *submitting to the sovereignty of a self-evident purpose* like that of avoiding an obvious evil, which causes us to omit confronting that evil, taken in its actual content, with God.

We no longer consider the question as to what, after all, it would mean to us if we had to endure that calamity, but formally erect its avoidance into an unequivocal and autonomous aim, to the pursuit of which we then completely subordinate ourselves. Thus, the evil in question acquires an enhanced significance which is out of proportion with its real import.

Mostly, it is a significance that exaggerates the real weight of the matter even in the natural context; always so if the object is viewed in a supernatural light. Anxieties of this kind not seldom afflict us with far heavier distress than would the thing we fear itself, were it really to happen.

We overcome fear by confronting evils with God

From this charmed circle one can only escape by concentrating oneself on God, and *confronting* the evil one apprehends *with God*; by contemplating it in the light of our eternal destiny, and repeating the words the Lord spoke: "My Father, if it be possible, let this chalice pass from me. Nevertheless, not as I will but as Thou wilt" (Matt. 26:39).

To be sure, let us then use all means that reason can provide to avert the threat; but the scope we accord this preoccupation in our minds must be kept *in proportion with the true import* of that evil. We must never simply deliver ourselves over to the autonomous mechanism of the campaign we wage for averting it. Again and again, in the course of varying situations as our action of defense develops, we must confront the evil in view with God, and renew the act of surrendering ourselves to the holy will of God. Thus only can we avoid being completely dominated by our anxiety and preserve our inner freedom.

In the presence of great tasks, again, to which we feel called by God, we should not rely on a sense of natural security but draw strength and courage from our confidence in God. If we possess all natural equipment needed for these tasks, we should in humility remember the truth that it is to God we owe our natural endowments and that without His help we may fail in spite of all our natural talents.

Moreover, any blessing that may derive from our work either for ourselves or for others depends exclusively on the help of God. And again, if we do not feel equal by nature to the tasks proposed to us, we should by no means lose heart but pray, as we should in the contrary case, too: "O God, come to my assistance, O Lord, make haste to help me" (Ps. 69:2). To God's arms we should repair, and say with the Psalmist, "Through my God I shall climb over a wall" (Ps. 17:30).

Even in inner darkness, we must trust God

The supreme test, however, of our confidence in God lies, perhaps, in those moments of complete inner darkness in which we feel as though we are forsaken by God. Our heart feels blunt; our prayers for strength and inspiration sound hollow; they seem plainly to be of no avail; wherever we look, our glance perceives but our impotence and, as it were, an impenetrable wall separating us from God. We doubt our being called; we appear to ourselves rejected and abandoned by God. It is in such moments, when we are most tempted to part with our confidence in God, that we need it most. An ardent belief in His love; a steadfast conviction that *He* is near to us even though *we* are, or imagine ourselves to be, far away from Him; an unbroken awareness that "He hath first loved us, and sent His Son to be a propitiation for our sins" (1 John 4:10) — these must carry us across the chasms of darkness and lend us strength to blindly let ourselves fall into His arms.

Our confidence in God must be independent of whether we experience His nearness, whether we sense the enlivening touch of grace, whether we feel ourselves being borne on the wings of His love. Has not God too much overwhelmed us with graces to allow us to forget them even for a moment? How could our present aridity obscure the irrevocably valid proofs of God's grace or make us doubt the primary truth that God has created us and redeemed us out of love and that there is no darkness that cannot be lit up by His light?

Confidence in God is an indispensable condition for our transformation in Christ

We have seen in this chapter that confidence in God constitutes man's adequate response to the omnipotence, the omniscience and the charity of God, as well as to the merciful word which God has addressed to every one of us. It constitutes our central response to the God of Revelation: the response we *owe* to Him, together with that of love and adoration. Further, it represents an indispensable condition of our transformation in Christ.

Without confidence in God, neither our readiness to change nor our critical self-knowledge are of any avail; without confidence in God, neither true contrition nor humility are possible.

Without that basic surrender to God which implies a cheerful reliance on Him, we could never advance along the path that leads to those goals. How could we risk that leap in the dark, the act of dying unto ourselves; how should we be ready to *lose our souls*, unless we knew that we were not to fall into the void but to be received by the mercy of God? How might we even dare to think of putting away the old man and becoming a new man, unless we relied on the message: "This is the will of God, your sanctification" (1 Thess. 4:3)? How could we bear the sight of our wretchedness and weakness, and in spite of our ever-recurrent relapses keep out discouragement, unless we were certain that God's mercy is infinite? — so that we may say with Thomas of Celano (in the *Dies Irae*): "Thou who hast absolved Mary and granted the thief's prayer, hast given hope also to me."

Confidence in God is an essential trait of holiness

Not only is confidence in God a necessary condition of our transformation in Christ; in its perfection it is itself an integrating part thereof, an essential trait of holiness. Complete, unreserved, victorious confidence in God is a *fruit* of Faith, Hope and Charity. It is a manifest sign of our being *dead unto ourselves* and living *in and from God*; a mark of him that has "put on the new man, who according to God is created in justice and holiness of truth" (Eph. 4:24). And from confidence in God, again, issue the triumphant freedom of the saint, and the peace of Christ, which the world cannot give us.

But, rudimentary as its initial act must be if compared with its final perfection, confidence in God is what we need as a supreme guide throughout the entire course of life with its turmoils and vicissitudes, its temptations and trials; what we need as a governing faith all along our path, from our first awakening up to the moment when we are summoned to the throne of the Judge Eternal. Confidence in God, directing and shaping our actions, itself growing apace with our transformation; the confidence that makes us speak with the mouth of the Psalmist, "In Thee, O Lord, have I hoped, let me never be confounded" (Ps. 30:2).

9

Striving for Perfection

THE gift of free decision — the capacity of freely choosing one's position, commonly called *freedom of will* — is one of the deepest and most characteristic marks of the *person*.

Man alone is a free creature

Alone among earthly creatures, man is not exclusively dependent on the blind causational rhythm of nature. To be sure, he also is placed in the framework of this causational rhythm; his body, together with some provinces of his psychic life, are dependent upon it. Beyond that, however, he is endowed with the capacity of entering into an entirely different kind of relationship with his environment. In his *cognitive* acts, the link of natural causation is superseded by the absolutely different and spiritual one of intentional object-reference. Based on that, his *affective* acts, too — such as joy, enthusiasm, and so forth — enclose a meaning, a reference to some object; which is to say, they have *motives* in the proper sense of the term and not simply *causes* in the manner of mere biopsychical reactions.

Nor is this all. In an even more integral sense of freedom than the one implied in his single cognitive and emotional acts as such, man — by virtue of his personal center of consciousness — can posit *free decisions* and thus call into being an entirely new sequence of causes. The *Yes* and *No* he pronounces, his free assent and dissent, are no mere effect of forces and influences, impressions and impulsions canalized or arranged by his personal center in the fashion of an agency of exchange, as it were; they are properly and actually *generated* by man's central personality.

Free will is a sublime gift

This freedom of man is a truly miraculous aspect of earthly existence, and at the same time, one of the most sublime gifts that God has conferred upon our race. Freedom is the presupposition of responsibility: it is by virtue of his freedom than man can acquire merit and fall into guilt. It is on the basis of his freedom that man can be morally good or evil; and above all, that he is capable of that response to God which glorifies him in an incomparably higher sense than any values that may also inhere in unfree beings. God *wills* us to serve Him in the mode of this free assent, which is one of the deepest expressions of man's God-likeness.

Free will introduces the possibility of sin

However, in order to endow man with this greatest of gifts — which lends him his specific dignity, provides his life with its ultimate gravity and emphasis, and underlies the importance of his behavior — what did God, so to speak, take into the bargain? Nothing less than sin: the possibility that man might offend God. For without freedom there can be no sin. Unfree nature cannot offend God; but for freedom, no disharmony would exist in the universe. And yet, God has assigned to man the gift of freedom, because, were he not free, *he* could not give God the response that is due to Him.

The individual alone has power over his own will

No power on earth, no temptation or attraction however potent, can force our assent; no pressure or influence can forcibly — in the way of a *force majeure* — provoke our decision. Much can be imposed on man's body by violence (and also on his psychic state, so far as it is linked to the physical one); he can be made to perform certain actions repugnant to him, and particularly, can be prevented from doing anything he wishes to do; but no matter what limitations are placed upon his outward sphere of action, nothing, except himself, has any power over his inward decision, over his ultimate, and irrevocably free, *Yes* or *No*.

Freedom's first dimension: sanction or disavowal

We must next distinguish two dimensions in which the freedom of man extends. The first dimension denotes man's basic capacity of assent and dissent itself — the fact that he can confirm and reject things, recognize and repudiate values and non-values, by taking up an inward position in regard to them and engaging his person in defense of that position; that he is able to stamp the spontaneous responses of his nature, as elicited by a variety of values, with the ultimate sanction of his central personality, or inversely, to invalidate these natural reactions by a disavowal issuing from this supreme center; that he has the power to decide his attitude to things out of himself as it were. This basic, inward fact of personality has been described earlier as a constitutive element of what we have called *true consciousness*.

Freedom's second dimension: the initiation of action

By the second dimension of freedom, we mean man's capacity to enact, to decree, to command certain movements or actions. He is endowed with a certain range of effectiveness; his will has power over certain outward things and can cause or prevent their happening. We may effectively decide whether to do something or to forego it; to tell something or to keep it secret, according to our will.

Limits to the second dimension of freedom

In contradistinction to the first dimension of freedom, this sphere of our power is circumscribed by limits, both essential and accidental. We could not snatch the moon from the sky (should we even wish to do so); we cannot, in general, cause other people to execute what we want them to do.

Even within ourselves, there are many things we cannot bring about by a simple command. If, for instance, our reason approves of an event and our will consequently acclaims it as something that ought to evoke joy, we may nevertheless not be able to evince actual joy at the mere command of our will; similarly, when we are ashamed of feeling a certain malicious pleasure, a mere act of will may not suffice to uproot and to dissolve that pleasure. Our loves, hopes, enthusiasms, and other emotional attitudes, are by no means so definitely subject to our will as are our actions (their outward possibility taken for granted).

Again, among the things exempt from our will we must make a distinction. Some of them are strictly outside our range of power: thus, it is impossible for us to raise a dead man to life or to transform a stupid person into an intelligent one. On the other hand, there are also things which we cannot bring about by command but to whose securing we can yet indirectly contribute a great deal. In general, our affective attitudes, as well as those of others with whom we are in contact, belong to this class.

If it is true that we cannot feel love, joy, or fervor at the command of our will, it does not follow from this that we are as little responsible for feeling or not feeling them as we are for some physiological process in our brain or for the outbreak of a tempest. In an indirect sense, we do contribute in a high measure towards the presence or absence of such emotional attitudes in ourselves. We can consciously prepare the ground (in our inner world) for the rise of the adequate affective response to values, remove the obstacles from its path, and pull down the towers of pride and concupiscence within us so that Christ may extend His realm in our souls.

Sanction and disavowal are deeper and more important than free action

The first dimension of man's freedom, his capacity for a free assent to values, is by far deeper and more important than the second. Whereas in relation to all that directly falls within his power — notably, his actions — his will plays a *master's* part, his relation to values is not that of a master but of a *partner* acting in humble self-subordination. In exercising our freedom in the sense of its second function, we *command*; in regard to its first function, we on the contrary *obey* the demand that emanates from values. Our freedom in the first sense is our fundamental and decisive moral freedom.

By the same token, it is that of which no external power can rob us. Our range of power proper can be grievously restricted — by imprisonment, for instance, or bodily diseases like a paralysis of our limbs or a loss of our power of speech. Yet, no outward force nor any bodily ailment can ever take from us our capacity for the right response to value. Also, it is on our first kind of freedom that the second one is based. It is by virtue of the former that we select the object for whose attainment we require the latter. Whether we make the right use of our first freedom essentially decides the value of the use we make of the other.

Virtue calls for the proper training of both dimensions of freedom

These two dimensions of freedom are by no means always kept apart with sufficient clarity. Hence it comes that too often an education of the will as such, aimed at enabling the pupil to overcome the inhibitions that may hinder him from translating his decisions into actions — destined, in other words, to temper his will and to make him a disciplined person — is by itself supposed to furnish him with an adequate moral training. A person thus disciplined, it is believed, will *ipso facto* be more fit to display the right response to values.

Now a cruder error than this is hard to imagine. There are many people who, while possessed of an iron will, able to pursue their aims with great energy and remarkable success, and giving proof of the utmost self-control, yet neglect their deeper spiritual freedom and refuse an adequate response to the call of value. While free from any paralysis of the will, they are yet slaves to pride and concupiscence. Many of the great evildoers in history (Richard the Third for instance) were at the same time disciplined personalities whose will power left nothing to be desired.

On the other hand, the converse type undeniably also exists: persons who do make use of their deeper freedom and respond adequately to values, whose inward decisions are not dictated by pride or concupiscence; but who labor under various inhibitions and in many cases, owing to their weakness, fail to translate their good intentions into actions.

Self-discipline is not the same as moral freedom

Certainly, to acquire a healthy will that is able to wield the power of command normally due to it is by no means immaterial for our inner development. Still, the place of that purpose in our striving for perfection is only a secondary one. The central object of our striving for perfection bears on the more essential capacity of using our freedom (in the first sense) adequately, in conformity with the will of God. In other words, the prime task of the education of personality is not to teach man how to make his innate freedom practically valid — though that may be next in importance — but to heighten his innate freedom into *moral freedom* proper. A mere preservation and exercise of our physical freedom — in the broadest sense of the term, including even the freedom of our inward response — does not by itself amount to the acquisition of that moral freedom which our freedom of will is really meant to prepare and support.

In contrast to persons who, drifting along as though unconscious, allow their freedom to droop to a point nearing extinction, those habituated to exercise their will power may be described as *free*; yet, as we have seen, they may at the same time lack the freedom of inner response and choice, being slaves to pride or concupiscence. They cannot be credited with moral freedom; nor even can those who, though enjoying a degree of inner freedom insofar as they are not simply dominated by their sensuous appetites or their instinct of self-assertion, have not used that inner freedom for an integral response to values and a subordination of self to the demands they utter, nor turned it into a basis for a free assent to God and His holy will.

He alone can be said to possess *moral freedom* who makes the right use of his inner freedom, in whom the central attitude of value-response has achieved a definitive victory over pride and concupiscence, and whose behavior in general and in its significant details is actually adapted to the *logos* of values as it appears in the various situations and aspects of life.

Moral freedom implies, not only the capacity to obey the demand of the values accidentally, but a permanent and intimate conformity to their suasion, sealed with the express sanction of the central personality. Moral freedom in this sense — which obviously belongs to what we have labelled as the first sphere of freedom — is equivalent to freedom proper, freedom in its perfection; above all, it goes incomparably deeper than the merely formal or technical freedom embodied in the controlling position of the will.

Hence, the means that conduce to this moral freedom cannot be the same as those destined merely to impose a discipline on nature, that is, to ensure a formal preponderance of the conscious will. In certain schools of ascetical training, this fact has sometimes failed to receive due appreciation. There has been a certain tendency to expect too much from the development of man's capacity to subordinate his entire nature to his will.

Yet, the mere fact that a person has achieved self-control — that whatever he decides to do he executes without inhibitions; that everything in him promptly obeys the command of his will — does not by itself indicate, let alone guarantee, that he has achieved moral freedom.

Again, this failure to distinguish between the two dimensions of freedom has worked out in a sense apt to discredit the very idea of freedom. The somewhat excessive stress laid on the education of will power — in keeping with the view that considers a formal ascendancy of the will over all spontaneous emotions as the mainstay of man's progress towards perfection — has provoked a reaction, not unjustified in itself, against the all too artificial and inorganic character of such a conception of life.

Let us trust (some have argued) organic evolution rather than a highly-strung effort of the will; let our remolding be a work of God, who alone is able to transform souls, not a specious result of our own conscious planning. It mostly happens in such cases that this reaction, though healthy to a degree, has certainly overshot the mark. The sublime central meaning of freedom proper — in the sense of the first dimension of freedom — which constitutes the deepest expression of our God-likeness, has been overlooked.

It was because they failed to distinguish clearly enough between the two dimensions of freedom that certain votaries of the liturgical movement went too far (in a direction suggestive of magic automatism and moral passivity, as it were) in their emphasis on an organic inner life informed by the *spirit of the liturgy*. True, a unilateral education of will power as a means to achieve freedom, stressing the second dimension of freedom well-nigh exclusively, does deserve the reproach that it involves a mechanistic outlook on psychic life; yet such a criticism hardly applies to a conception of freedom centered on its first dimension. For the freedom of assenting to values and of stamping this assent with a personal sanction has nothing to do with mere technique or discipline; it definitely represents an inward and organic function of the will.

Without a doubt, the mechanism of the innervations subject to the command of the will may be regarded as a comparatively artificial structure in man's moral life; without a doubt, it is characteristic of the deepest manifestations of our personality that they cannot be promptly and infallibly evoked by pressing, as it were, a button in the apparatus of our emotional dispositions.

But no grosser misconception could be thought of than to attribute this aspect of mechanical artificiality to our free and conscious assent to values, for the reason only that freedom in this sense, too, means a decisive step from out of the penumbra of a subconscious, primarily biological, mode of existence to the higher region of clear, distinct, express, and responsible acts.

Far more than any biological display of spontaneity, our free spiritual motion towards a union with values is, on the contrary, a true prototype of things *generated* (of whatever is *genitum*: that is, a manifestation in which our very being is somehow expressed and coined out) as contrasted to the mere artifact (to all things *manufactured* or *made*: *factum*). Instead of giving ear to the minimizers of freedom who would conceive of man's progress towards perfection as modeled after the growth of an apple, as it were, we must

221

understand that we cannot esteem the human capacity for a free and voluntary assent highly enough; for it constitutes the central condition of all adequate tribute to God from our part, so much so that for its sake (as has been pointed out above) God has even permitted sin to be possible.

We are called freely to assent to our transformation

And this, also, contains the answer — in its most important part, at least — to the question we are next faced with: What can, and should, be our own contribution to the process of our transformation in Christ? What is meant by the cooperation on our part to which St. Augustine refers in saying: "He who created thee without thee, shall not justify thee without thee" (*Sermo* 169.13)?

First, it is the free word of assent we are to speak to God and to our own transformation in Christ. In the free gift of ourselves that is implied in our decisive turn towards God (which finds its most tangible expression in the act of conversion); in the *Volo* uttered in the rite of Baptism as an express statement of the person's being delivered to God; in the words of the Blessed Virgin, "Behold the handmaid of the Lord: be it done to me according to thy word" — herein lies the basic actualization of our freedom in the process of our justification and sanctification. This is the *word* which God expects from us and from which we can never be dispensed.

But this alone does not suffice. We are also called upon to concur with our transformation in Christ by single acts subject to the command of our will; that is, by the operation of our freedom in the line of its second dimension.

Transformation involves both our acts and our virtues

The moral being of the person, which we envisage here in its comprehensive sense, from the point of view of his transformation in Christ, has a twofold extension: it embraces the sphere of his single concrete acts of knowing, choosing (in the widest sense of the term inclusive of affective overtones), and doing, on the one hand; and on the other hand, the superactual or habitual sphere of what are commonly called his *qualities*, such as, for example, the virtues of faithfulness, justice, humility, purity, or kindness. These permanent qualities should not be interpreted as mere dispositions for this or that single decision or action, for, say, a specified act of humble submission or of charitable forgiving. They constitute a reality *sui generis*.

Each of the two spheres — of concrete behavior and of habitual being — has its own significance; neither is merely subservient to the other. They both glorify God in their own respective manner. Thus, every just action or attitude as such represents a new value in its own right, which *adds* to the value embodied by the habitual justice of a person. And again, the possession of a virtue — humility for example — means the realization of a specific value even apart from the person's particular acts of humility.

Notwithstanding, however, the independent meaning inherent to these two spheres of personal morality, there is between them a close interconnection and interaction. On the one hand, our virtues provide the ground for our single moral acts; they facilitate the latter and underlie the special dispositions we need for their performance in the various kinds of situations that confront us. On the other hand, our single moral acts and achievements prepare our acquisition of the corresponding virtues. By repeating a good action again and again in a number of analogous cases, we shall more and more take on the habit of the virtue in question itself.

We can directly determine actions and affect our virtues

Still, our capacity to enact particular moral decisions is not *conditioned* by our possession of the respective virtues; conversely, our endeavor to acquire a virtue is not *restricted* to our performance of concrete particular decisions within its province. The center of our personality, the free agent that is the actual subject of our behavior and our decisions — as well as of our basic intention of assent to God — is by itself independent of either of the two spheres. It has the direct capacity both to evoke a moral attitude in any given particular case and to exercise in various ways a shaping and transforming influence upon our superactual moral being, our moral character as such.

Thus, the free cooperation of our central personality and our will proper is ordained to two tasks: first, that of moving us to conform to God's will and to display a response to value pleasing to God in our single *acts* according to given concrete situations; secondly, to the task of rectifying our *permanent* superactual moral being; of stamping upon it the impress of the Christian virtues. Both are implied in the process of unfolding the supernatural life which we have received in Baptism. Now the way in which our will may exercise its influence is appreciably different in the two cases.

We can affect the character of our particular acts both directly and indirectly

First, we consider our *particular moral acts*. Here we are faced, first of all, with the vast domain of *actions* in the narrower sense of the term. These lie within the range of our direct power; they can be properly and truly commanded by our will. It is within our power to assist or not to assist a certain needy person, to revile or not to revile a person who has offended us, to tell a lie or not to tell it, or to treat somebody considerately or otherwise.

But this is not all. It is not by our capacity of a direct command alone that we can influence our actions. In addition to that, we can also contribute to their determination indirectly; above all, by a daily examination of our conscience, with the taking of good resolutions as its result.

Further, we can — and should — diminish occasions of sinning by avoiding certain situations which are calculated to tempt our weakness. We may, so to speak, establish guards in advance, destined to prevent us from faltering in the crucial moments. From repeated acts of mental communion with God and of spiritual concentration, we may draw fresh strength for dealing adequately with given tasks and demands newly confronting us. In certain dangerous situations we may protect ourselves preventively, as did Ulysses in regard to the song of the Sirens; we, too, may, as it were, have ourselves tied fast, or — like his mates — have our ears plugged with wax. In periods of contemplation and moral stability, we may preventively fight the danger of being again caught in a centrifugal vortex and hopelessly enmeshed again in the autonomous mechanism of certain situations.

Finally, we may harness ourselves for this struggle against sin by a temporary renunciation of certain legitimate goods; that is, invigorate our readiness for good works, for conforming to the commandments of God, through the practice of asceticism. In sum, we are able to determine our actions not only in a direct sense, in view of their strict dependence on the command of our will, but also in an indirect sense, inasmuch as, by manifold preparatory acts which in their turn are subject to the direct command of our will, we may create favorable conditions for our doing right in certain foreseen situations in which our steadfastness is likely to be put on trial.

We cannot directly command affective responses, but can sanction or disavow them

But as we have seen, there is also a large class of inward acts that does not fall within our radius of power proper. If, for instance,

225

the news of a person's conversion leaves us in a mood of blunt indifference, our will is not at liberty to conjure up within us the mood of joy which would be adequate to the event. Similarly, we cannot force our cold and unsympathetic heart to bestow upon a person in need the full response of compassion and merciful love which would be congenial to the situation.

Certainly, by our free will we can command ourselves to perform some action destined to alleviate his trouble; yet the inward contribution of love we cannot give him just by deciding to do so. Nor is our will able to extinguish or silence, by direct command, a mood of envy or malicious satisfaction that colors our feelings in a given situation.

Against this fact, however, must be set another of no less importance. By an act of our free personal center we *can* either sanction or disavow our emotional attitude, which involves a far-reaching modification of the inmost nature of our attitudes. A mood of malicious satisfaction, for instance, which we expressly disavow in our mind, is *decapitated* as it were; it is revoked and declared invalid, and thereby deprived not only of its outward efficacy but to a large degree even of its intrinsic virulence. Still, by that alone it is not yet wholly uprooted, nor is its affective content annihilated. The will to be charitable from which may derive charitable deeds and good works, is not yet charity.

A further distinction commends itself: it makes a considerable difference whether the personal *sanction* (that is, the ultimate act of assent or disapprobation relative to our spontaneous feeling) is issued isolatedly in any random event, as it were, or whether we expressly refer it back to our permanent moral principles, our habitual basic intention. In the latter case it has far more meaning and weight.

But even so, our freely posited intention as such is a mere skeleton of the full-fledged affective attitude, be it that of love, joy, compassion or contrition.

We must avoid artificial efforts to awaken good responses

Our range of direct power, then, as far as our affective attitudes are concerned, only extends to the possibility of a free sanction or disavowal; in an indirect sense, however, much more can be done to influence them. We can consciously create space in ourselves for the right affective responses and remove such factors as are apt to thwart their unfolding. Yet, there is a certain kind of misdirected effort from which we must rigorously abstain. We should never try artificially to conjure up a noble mood as such — to emotionally implement our free intentional act by any direct effort in the deceptive hope of forcing it thereby into full affective growth. Such cramped efforts are doomed to sterility; but more disastrous is their effect in turning our glance away from the *intentional object* in question (which alone, if anything, may kindle in us an adequate emotional response) and fixing it upon our own *behavior*. An unhealthy self-reflectiveness is thus fostered which, far from any likelihood of completing the reality of our affective attitude, is almost certain to stifle it.

Above all, we should never stoop to the method of trying to lend body to the thin ghost of our *intentional* attitude by drawing on the fund of cheap general emotionalism which every one of us carries in him as a mechanical potentiality. Thus, let us never seek to awaken true compassion in our souls by setting in motion the machinery of sentimental associations, nor to flog ourselves into enthusiasm by willfully heaping up in our minds a succession of turbulent imagery, a crude artifice reminiscent of the unclean fire we see flare up in cases of mass suggestion and mental epidemics.

Genuine affective responses cannot be commanded

Our genuine and complete responses to value, with the personal uniqueness and weight proper to them, grow organically from seeds implanted in the secret depths of our personality; it is only by indirect ways that we can contribute to their arising in us. This precisely is inherent in their nobility, that they have the character of *gifts* as opposed to things that can be commanded or made to order. What should properly preoccupy us is merely our adequate attention to the *object*, not the full flowering of our attitude as such. For it is precisely the distinctive mark of a genuine attitude of response that the object alone — and by no means the attitude itself — constitutes its *theme*.

But we can, by virtue of our free will, provide (for instance) against being absorbed by the rhythm of incessant highly-strung activity or dominated by the machinery of our concrete aims: the exclusive prevalence of pursuits and efforts which is apt to stifle our deeper psychic life and with it any fully experienced response to values.

We may free ourselves from the false attitude of always asking, "What can I do in this matter? How can I change this?" — the attitude underlain by the disastrous error that it is pointless to take an interest in any object unless we can do something about it. By recollection and a contemplative approach to God, we may again and again seek to reach spiritual depths. By ascetical practice we may seek gradually to clear away the obstacles which pride and concupiscence oppose to our adequate response to values. Finally, we may beseech God in prayer to accord us love, holy joy, and deep contrition.

Transformation of our moral character is not directly under our control

Yet, the path of the indirect education of all these concrete attitudes lies along our transformation as a whole — that of our habitual being. Even though we take our departure from the problem of our single acts and attitudes, the consideration of our striving for perfection will necessarily arrive at the second great task that God has imposed on us: our contribution to the transformation of our moral *character*, or in other words, our acquisition of the Christian virtues.

Secondly, our *habitual being*, generally considered, is outside the range of our direct power. We are not able to conjure up in ourselves, merely by an act of free will, either humility or faithfulness, either confidence in God or loving kindness, either mildness or mercy. This does not mean, however, that we can do nothing relevant to the unfolding of those virtues in us. The ways in which our free central personality may exercise an influence in this sense vary, it is true, according to the single virtues.

We can influence the development of certain virtues

In some cases, such as the readiness to change, the virtue in question originates in a direct act of our free central personality, the effectiveness of which is similar, however, not to that of our will when it commands our single actions proper, but to the way in which our ultimate free assent (as discussed earlier in this chapter) determines our behavior. Only the engagement of our person as implied in our readiness to change — in an act of conversion, notably — necessarily affects the depth of our being; also, this virtue chiefly consists — the very term *readiness* indicates it — in a durable disposition of the will as such.

The essential moment here is, therefore, the free act of inner conversion, the central decision of our will to let ourselves be transformed by Christ without any reservations. The road that leads herefrom to our habitual readiness to change is marked by many single acts reviving the original one, by which we again and again actualize, as it were, the attitude of readiness once adopted. This progressive penetration of the entire personality by a definite direction of will, which has started by a basic personal decision and has unfolded in manifold single decisions or types of conduct (mostly such as come within our range of direct power), finally leads to the acquisition of a habitual readiness to change. The way in which the virtue of confidence in God may develop in us presents a similar structure.

These virtues, then, though they cannot be acquired by our will except in an indirect manner — inasmuch as, like everything habitual, they can only be brought about gradually and not at once — are yet subject to our direct power of will insofar as the free self-engagement of the person constitutes their inmost essence, and moreover, insofar as a set of concrete single acts equally subject to our direct will power will serve, not merely as an accidental means to acquire them, but as a substantial element of their unfolding and amplification.

In regard to certain other virtues, however — such as humility, charity, and kindness — we are in an entirely different position. To be sure, here, too, the act of a free and self-engaging assent to God's will, both as an initial presupposition and as a permanent element of our attitude, is of eminent importance. But our free decision as such does not suffice to generate, as it were, the living substance of these virtues (nor of the single attitudes correlative to them). The full affective reality of what we call *humility* — and the more so, that of *charity* towards God and our fellow men — implies an integral response of our personality to God and the world of values, which we are not free to command directly by our will. In an indirect sense, we can do a great deal to acquire them by removing obstacles from their path, as we shall see it more in detail later.

Again, with regard to another class of virtues such as simplicity, patience, or consciousness as described in Chapter 4, the central element of what we must do to acquire them consists in definite single acts which, in given situations, can be called forth and sustained by our free will. The man who, in the various trials and tribulations of life, again and again endures the test — expressly recognizing God as *the lord of Time* — and masters, by a free act of his will, the unruly stirrings of impatience and the un-Christian self-assertion that underlies it, will slowly but surely develop the true habitual virtue of patience.

The ways, then, in which our habitual being can be influenced by our volitive acts are in a wide measure different according to the single virtues. Let us examine now more closely those methods of a conscious striving for perfection which are the only ones to be applied in regard to such virtues like charity or kindness, which are, in a particular sense, gifts of grace, and therefore least subject to the command of our will.

Virtues develop when we devote ourselves to good things for their own sake

In this matter, there is one basic fact we must consider before all else. *It is not from what we undertake with a view to our transformation, but from the things to which we devote ourselves for their own sake, that will issue the deepest formative effect upon our habitual being.* The transformation of our character under these influences is essentially, on our part, the reception of a gift rather than a purpose attained by our will. All true values to which we attend in a contemplative attitude, with which our souls become imbued, unfold such a transforming effect in the depths of our being. The vision of the beautiful, as Plato says (*Phaedrus* 249d), causes the soul "to grow wings."

Whenever a true value affects us, whenever a ray of beauty, goodness or holiness *wounds* our heart, whenever we abandon ourselves in contemplative relaxation to a true value that comes within our presence — so that the full process of *frui*, of the creative ripening of its experience within us becomes possible, so that that value may penetrate us wholly and elevate us above

231

ourselves — a certain actual change (which is, in itself, transitory) is produced in our being, which, however, according to the height of the value that affects us and the depth of our actual response to it, will leave permanent traces far outlasting our actual experience. By this spiritual nourishment our very essence will be changed and, as it were, leavened.

God transforms us directly with His grace

An entirely new element is present, however, in the case of a similar value-experience as referred to God. The eternal beauty and absolute holiness of God, as manifested in Christ in a way particularly appropriate to evoke our love, still determine, formally speaking, a *natural* effect as do other high values; an effect which is certainly in accordance with the will of God and has its place in our spiritual progress.

Yet, over and above it there appears the aspect of our *supernatural* transformation by Him who has created us and from whom we have received the new divine life as a pure gift. Of course, God's action of grace is by no means confined to the salient moments of our contemplative experience.

But we know by Revelation that God wills us to deliver ourselves to His action of grace *expressly*, to empty and to open ourselves so as to undergo it; and that, in these moments of a specific personal contact with God, particularly favorable conditions are given for the influx of grace.

That process of being received, embraced, and assumed as it were, which in reference to value as such is present in an analogical sense only, happens actually and literally when we give ourselves to the almighty God who has the power to elevate our being to Himself and to transform it in its very roots.

Our *natural* transformation under the action of the values we experience, a primary potentiality of our intellectual constitution, prefigures and prepares in a way — and continues to assist — the *supernatural* one, which it is essentially destined to subserve.

Thus, the deepest effect on our being emanates from our contemplative surrender to God. Whenever we grow empty of all created things including our own self; whenever we offer ourselves to God in thematical awareness not of our transformation but of Christ alone; whenever we lose ourselves in the vision of His face and dispose ourselves to be permeated by His light, He stamps our essence with His seal.

Hence, apart from the purely supernatural effect, the deepest transformation in our being issues from the Holy Sacrifice of the Mass, in which we participate *per ipsum, cum ipso, et in ipso* (through Him, with Him, and in Him) in Christ's sacrifice.

We must never use values merely as a means for our transformation

An analogical power belongs to mental prayer and to the Divine Office. Mental prayer, again, should be undertaken not *primarily* for the sake of our transformation but in order to let God speak to us, to be touched by Him in our depths. This is even truer in regard to liturgical prayer, which we perform in response to the glory of God, by no means to utilize it for our transformation but because that response is *due* to God.

It is generally implicit in the character of these primordial agents of our transformation which we are here discussing that they must not be instrumentalized in the service of that transformation. The moment we enjoy a beautiful thing in order thereby to enrich our soul or love a person so as to derive therefrom an inward gain; or again, worse still, the moment we use liturgical prayer (as we might use some ascetical practice) as a means of our spiritual progress, we render these acts of response to value or surrender to God virtually invalid. And, along with their basic autonomous value, they also lose the faculty of a transforming influence upon our essence.

But notwithstanding the fact that we must never instrumentalize these attitudes of response and surrender by subordinating them to the purpose of our transformation, in their context all intentional reference to that transformation need not be so completely excluded as it has to be in the case of all moral actions in which we are directed to the realization of some concrete good — for instance, in actions which flow from love of our neighbor. In contemplation, the thematic aspect of our transformation — though it must never be accorded a primary place — may legitimately enter at several points.

Contemplation awakens in us a deep desire for transformation

First, all contemplative attention to God (and, by virtue of an analogical relationship, to all true values as such) involves a *confrontation* of one's own self with God. We become aware of the immense distance that separates us from the holiness of God, as St. Peter did when he exclaimed, "Depart from me, for I am a sinful man, O Lord" (Luke 5:8). It dawns upon us that in order to be worthy of any contact with God, we ought to become thoroughly different from what we are. "Who shall ascend into the mountain of the Lord: or who shall stand in his holy place? The innocent in hands, and clean of heart" (Ps. 23:3-4).

Thus there awakens in us a longing for our transformation into Christ as a *condition* of the *frui* of God, of our contemplative union with God, the ultimate end of our desire and the enduring theme of our endeavor. In this spirit do we then pronounce the liturgical words preceding Holy Communion: "Lord, I am not worthy that Thou shouldst enter under my roof, say but the word and my soul shall be healed."

Contemplative surrender to God is felt as a transformation

Secondly, we *experience* our contemplative surrender to God as an *incorporation* of our being in Him. Precisely in the measure in which God is the exclusive theme of our attention, we shall feel impelled to say with St. Peter, "Lord, it is good for us to be here: let us make here three tabernacles." Similarly shall we be willing to say with St. Catherine of Siena: *Che tu sia ed io non sia* ("That Thou be, and I be not").

Although our transformation in the sight of God does *not* assume the place of a primary aim, it is implied in the logic, as it were, of our elevation by God and our response to the divine attraction, and is thus inevitably woven into the fabric of our contemplative attention. It is not that we degrade the latter to a means of our transformation; but we are *aware* of its transforming effect, and in this secondary sense our transformation does play a thematic part, which is entirely legitimate.

Contemplative surrender to God keeps us aware of His call that we be transformed

Thirdly, we may (and should) also perceive and keep aware of the *call of God* that reaches us from above in our contemplative state, and that *refers to our transformation*. Our glance proceeds thus naturally from God — or from the value that has *spoken* to us — to the subject of our striving for perfection.

All true contemplation is likely to engender, in an organic and almost self-evident fashion, specific good resolutions: one such, at least — the express decision to keep faithful to our upward course — is essentially inseparable from true contemplation as such. Our discernment of what may be justified in the face of Christ is sharpened anew; and our will turns away from everything repugnant to His most holy gaze.

In this sense, again, our transformation acquires a thematic significance as an adjunct to our every act of contemplative surrender.

We remain aware that contemplation and value-responses are sources of transformation

Finally, in the fourth place, in the general framework of our transformation in Christ we may take account of the moments of contemplative attention to God and to true values as the *principal source* from which issues the gift of our transformation. The measure of this secondary reference is scaled according to the various modes of contemplative attention.

One pole is represented by the *Opus Dei* — that is, liturgical prayer — in which the thematic role of our transformation is restricted to a minimum; the other pole is represented by our communion with created values, which admits of it to a comparatively high degree.

As regards our attention to created values and their *frui* in us, our consciousness of their mission in contributing to our transformation in Christ may be accorded a significant place. We are rightly aware that our experience of the beauty of nature and of great genuine art — provided that we are fully receptive to its radiation and let its voice pervade the depths of our being — cannot but make us better.

We should similarly take cognizance of the fact that our union in holy love with another person — a love-relationship rooted in Jesus — is certain to transform us and to bring us nearer to God. True, at the moment when our response to the object is actualized the essence of that object (with the value-power emanating from it) constitutes the only theme of our attention; but that does not prejudge the question as to what part the *frui* of created values is to play in our lives as such.

Contemplative delight in values is commendable

Many religious persons erroneously believe that in reference to created things no *frui*, no joyful immersion of one's self in the essence of an object, as it were, is commendable; they hold the narrow view that no created object has any *use* for our eternal aim except in a purely instrumental sense, as a subordinate means of our pursuit irrespective of its intrinsic value. All *frui* of created values they subsume under the category of *pleasures*, and deem it less pleasing to God than any kind of neutral *work* (as the latter escapes the suspicion of being undertaken for its pleasurableness).

They take no account of the truth that the natural gifts of God, "the Father of all lights," are assigned a function in our transformation in Christ; that, therefore, their *frui* is nothing in the nature of a frivolous diversion but, on the contrary, a valid task in conformity with the will of God. So afraid are they of losing sight of the ultimate goal that they leave unused one of the most important factors of its attainment. They fail to understand that on this plane a really effective *uti* (that is, a utilization of created things as directed to our eternal aim) presupposes a *frui* free from all concern about the *uti*.

All high created values can purify and transform us

The aim of our transformation in Christ itself compels us to accord an adequate place in our lives to our contemplative attention to the high created values which put us in a kind of contact with God and exercise an irreplaceable formative effect upon our being. Hence, we should recognize that the world of created things is not merely a training ground for ascetical mortification; that, provided we give them the right response according to the will of God, the created goods are only also bearers of a *positive* mission in the service of our eternal end.

We should realize the purifying and elevating effect that emanates from all high beauty; how, by virtue of its sheer quality, it transmits to us an aspect of the Divine, and how it tends to divert our minds from everything sinful or paltry, if only we yield to its suggestion of ascent, and grow fully aware of its meaning and nobility. No less is it in the nature of a great and deep love in Christ Jesus to liberate us, to loosen the bonds of our attachment to trivial goods, and to guide us towards God. We should perceive the enduring *sursum corda* that emanates from it, and the way it makes us grow in true simplicity.

In all these marvellous goods we should discern the call of God, nor ever resist the upward drift they tend to communicate to us. We must keep alive in us a general readiness to follow every call of God as contained in these gifts, and cultivate a conscious attention to their *logos* as an essential aspect of our striving for perfection. In this respect, again, the words remain true: "Today if you shall hear his voice, harden not your hearts" (Ps. 94:8).

In moral actions, transformation cannot be our motive

Moral actions and good works, in their turn, equally exercise a transforming effect upon our habitual being. Here, however, our transformation must not be present to our minds even in the sense of a thematic overtone, as is legitimate in the case of our contemplative attitudes. Moral actions as such, including acts of abstaining from sin, great as their indirect significance is for our transformation, *must never be performed with this aim in view.*

Moral conduct issues from our general basic direction to God; in its concrete singularity, it expresses our response to some definite value or negation of value, or accordingly, to some (positive or negative) commandment of God. In our moral conduct we must concentrate entirely upon this concrete aim prescribed by God, and be guided solely by our interest in honoring the obligation it entails for us. Suppose a man is in danger of death and we hasten to succor him; obviously, in so doing, our interest must be absorbed by the peril that threatens him and we must not by any means act with a view to promoting our inner growth. We must follow the call of God that engages us to avert that evil, without any regard whatsoever to enhancing our own perfection.

Performed as a *means of our transformation*, our action would be, morally speaking, untruthful and in a sense invalid. For it derives its moral valuableness precisely from the fact of our being interested in the realization of an objective good (or, correlatively, the frustration of an objective evil). Our glance must be kept fixed on the object in question, and through the medium of that object on God, and not be diverted to the sanctification of our person. We *owe* this response to the object as such; hence, by instrumentalizing it, we deprive it of weight and validity.

Good deeds should be seen as a consequence, not a means

In the context now under discussion, the subject of our transformation cannot be thematic even in the secondary forms we have been describing above. The *good works* are *fruits* of our essential nexus with God; they must not be treated as *means* of its acquisition. It is to them that St. James refers when he says, "Religion clean and undefiled before God and the Father is this: to visit the fatherless and widows in their tribulation" (James 1:27).

Nay, good works in this adequate sense of the term themselves belong essentially to the new man in Christ, so much so that they are included (as consequences) in one's intention to become a new man. That intention must actualize itself after our daily examination of conscience, in various concrete resolutions expressing our determination to better obey the call of God according to the diverse situations that confront us and no longer to offend God by any definite action subject to our will power.

Whenever, for example, we are sorry for having told a lie, or been too hot-tempered, or again, for having turned an indifferent eye to a fellow man's suffering, or having omitted a prayer, this contrition should engender the resolution not only to overcome our habitual defects as manifested by such and similar instances of improper behavior, but to gird ourselves inwardly for acting on the next occasion in a fashion consonant to the situation — that is, to display an adequate free response to the good presented to us in the call of God. We strive for the habitual virtue out of the desire, also, to be able to abstain from any concrete offense against God, and correspondingly, to fulfill the will of God in our definite single actions.

In the moment of our *action*, then, our attention should be directed exclusively to the demand that confronts us: thus, while rescuing a man from mortal danger, we should think of the preservation of his life alone; while fighting a temptation to lie, we should have in mind nothing but the high dignity of the human word, the function — assigned to it by God — to express and communicate the truth.

On the other hand, our *resolution* to act correctly in new situations of the same type also refers to the actualization of a *habitual* right attitude in conformity with the will of God. In a thus qualified sense, the concrete resolutions we take after our examination of conscience may well be regarded, also, as a material element of our own contribution to our transformation in Christ. They are, among others, an indispensable means of our transformation, a means God has placed within our range of direct power.

Our actions performed in the spirit of Christ, our good works, are, as we now see, on the one hand, a consequence and a fruit of our transformation, and on the other a specific actualization thereof — visible stages, as it were, of our progress towards union with Christ. Yet they must never be done *with this intention*; we must not *apply* them as a means of our transformation.

For, independently of their function in our spiritual progress, they have their primary and proper meaning as a response to the concrete object proposed, and the particularized call of God that it transmits.

The factors contributory to our transformation, as discussed in the preceding pages, hold that character in a more or less gratuitous fashion only; in the sense, that is, of a *surplus* over the proper and autonomous meaning of our attitudes. It is now time to raise the question as to the possibilities at the disposal of our freedom of working towards our transformation with an express intention.

Transformation calls us to see all things *in conspectu Dei*

In the first place, we should again and again extricate ourselves from the fabric of unilateral aspects in which the concrete situations of life inevitably plunge us and rise to a total vision of Truth, ascending again and again to an awareness of God, of the message of the Gospel, and of our eternal destiny. Our prayer, our daily examination of conscience, as well as frequent moments of reflection and contemplation must help us to keep alive in ourselves a vision of all things *in conspectu Dei*.

Various aspects of our daily life should serve to remind us, for example, of the greatness and nobility proper to every human being as a person created in the likeness of God, loved by Christ with an infinite love, and redeemed by His most holy Blood. An express and frequent realization of this truth is important, because many people allow their spiritual life to be submerged in a certain trivial atmosphere which deforms their character. By acquiescing, as it were, in this attitude, by contenting ourselves with an outside picture of men and taking them simply in the guise in which they present themselves, we impose on our own minds a flattening perspective that does not extend beyond the peripheral sphere of single situations.

We should, again and again, see through the unessentialness of this distorted perspective, and realize the greatness and beauty of the metaphysical situation in which (whether or not he is aware of it) man is objectively placed, the dialogical situation in which his soul faces God. We should never lose sight of the greatness there is about being called and addressed by God, being responsible before God, being — as is every man — called to account by that eternal question of God: "Adam, where art thou?" We should never look at a person without there being present before our eyes the entire gravity and solemnity of the things that are the *objective* theme of every human soul.

Against this background the defects of any person will appear not as so many trivial irritants or repellent traits, but in their character as sins or consequences of sin, possibly as something terrible and monstrous, but at any rate as something that betokens the wretchedness of human nature *in its universality*, and above all, something that causes us to think of both *the justice and the mercy of God*. Moreover, even against the background of sin, the greatness of the spiritual person as an image of God, the fact of the Incarnation uniting and elevating — in an ineffable way — human nature to the Divine one, as well as the sublime beauty of a human soul in the state of grace, must remain present to our vision. Thus do we establish a decisive condition for charity and spontaneous kindliness to rise in our souls. How should love blossom in us, unless we penetrate the ultimate reality and grasp the beauty attached to every human soul? — a beauty that can never be definitively destroyed before the *status viae* is terminated.

The same consideration applies to all virtues. In regard to all of them, we must begin by liberating ourselves, again and again, from the unessential aspects inherent to the natural plane of vision, by rising to the truth of God, by endeavoring to see all things in their creational meaning and in the transfiguring light which Christ has spread above them. All virtues consist in a habit of the right response to God and the world of values: to place ourselves in the perspective of Truth complete is the prime condition for our acquiring them.

Transformation calls us continually to renew our surrender to God

The second thing we may do by our own will for the transformation of our nature is to renew from time to time our express act of *surrender to God* — an act leading to a prayer of petition. Again and again we must come to realize that we can do nothing by ourselves but may expect everything from God, and entrust our souls to His hands, saying with the Psalmist, "I am Thine" (Ps. 118:94). In the same breath, we must realize the insufficiency of this our act itself; our impotence, that is to say, to anchor ourselves in God once for all, by one act of devotion or surrender. Hence, that act itself will move us on to ask God for His freely granted help, continuing to speak with the Psalmist: "Save Thou me."

Transformation calls us to ascetical practices

In the third place, we may contribute directly to our transformation by single *salutary practices*, particularly of asceticism. Renunciation of certain permissible pleasures will help us in dying unto ourselves and becoming empty so that God may enter in us.

By a kind of minute daily work we may thus loosen the innumerable bonds that fetter us to the earth. It would be false to assume that ascetical renunciations are relevant to a virtue inasmuch only as they imply a material reference to that particular virtue. The practices of fasting, of silence, of restraining the delight of the eyes, and others like them — they all have no direct nexus, for instance, with the virtue of charity, but yet they create space in our souls for charity. For our slavery to the interests of the body, as well as our concupiscence from which we are to free ourselves by fasting, thwarts the path of charity within us.

Again, the practice of silence serves to prevent us from lapsing into a certain kind of irrelevancy, an absorption by peripheral concerns. For supernatural love cannot thrive in us unless we are composed, that is, concentrated in a dimension of depth. All easygoing and dispersive states of mind draw us away from the fountainhead of charity. Complacency, sloth, and love of comfort are so many forms of egoism which make our lives unfree and narrow, an arid soil for charity; it is to rid us of these impediments that the mortification of the flesh is largely intended.

However, we must never consider ascetical practice as a means effective by itself, nor use it, so to speak, as a medicine which in a purely causal sense is certain to produce the desired effect. No asceticism can make us free for God and for transformation in Christ unless it is permanently animated and directed by our longing for God and our firmly settled determination to become a new man in Christ.

While applying these means we must well keep it in mind that they cannot do more than clear the path for more direct and positive operations in the framework of our striving for perfection; that their effectiveness, far from being automatically given, always depends on our inward dedication to God, and above all, on the help accorded us by God. That is why the Church prays in the time of fasting (Collect of Tuesday after the first Sunday in Lent) in these terms: "Look down upon Thy household, O Lord, and grant that our minds which have been chastened by the tormenting of our bodies may be made to glow with desire of Thee." (In the next chapter, we shall have more to say about the close relationship between true freedom and charity, and, accordingly, the function of ascetical practices — which are directed to our liberation from the manifold shackles of inordinate attachment to created goods — in clearing the ground for charity and also for other virtues.)

Transformation calls us to shun the shallow and trivial

Another indirect means in the service of our striving for perfection consists in the endeavor to keep our minds away from everything that is apt to deflect them from God. To avoid certain unnecessary conversations, to do without the entertainment provided by shallow readings (which cannot but focus our attention on matters peripheral), to shun everything that panders to our delight in sensations; in general, to steer clear of whatever is calculated to draw us away from God and impale our minds on worldly concerns, thus interfering with simplicity and a collected attitude of mind — here, again, is an important means at the disposal of our will, of contributing to our transformation.

Nay, so far as possible we must avoid contact with everything that has an air of triviality. Not that we should shrink from intercourse with trivial people or a trivial milieu in all circumstances: considerations of charity or apostolic tasks may well make it a duty for us to frequent them.

But we must never, as it were, set up our quarters in such an atmosphere, nor even rest at ease in its midst. While dwelling there we must remain a stranger to it, keeping ourselves impermeable to its infiltration, nor ever cease to experience our sojourn in such a medium as a sacrifice.

An orderly life aids our transformation

To ordain our daily lives according to some definite rule constitutes a further method in the service of our inner transformation. Apart from the specific importance which the single provisions of that rule may possess for our progress in virtue, a certain wholesome effect proceeds from order as such. It pervades life with a certain rhythm of composure and continuity, which makes it easier for us to collect ourselves; it protects us from being absorbed by the succession of varying events and impressions, so apt to interfere with our concentration upon essentials.

An orderly regulation of our lives relieves us from the temptation to let our attention to prayer, contemplation, and work, our avoidance of peripheral concerns, depend on chance and circumstance; it enables us to provide systematically for the meaningfulness and depth of our existence. It makes it possible for us to acquire constancy without which all good endeavors are condemned to sterility.

Finally, an established outward order also raises us above our dependence on our own arbitrary whims and momentary dispositions; it commits us from the outset, and enduringly, to our direction towards God. The last-named advantage is more perfectly attained, of course, in the case of a rule followed — as in monastic life — from holy obedience, as contrasted to merely self-devised and self-imposed regulations.

In any event, however, we must keep aware of the fact that all technical regulation of life is but a means, not an end in itself; its observance must not be allowed to become a matter of rigid mechanical routine. We should not erect the rule into an absolute, nor abandon ourselves to its automatism as to a supreme law. Otherwise it may easily blunt, rather than sharpen, our perception of the call of God, and harden our hearts rather than open them to Christ.

Work promotes virtue

An indispensable function in our lives is assigned, furthermore, to work as such. Idleness — the absence of regular activity and effort — cannot but demoralize us and hamper our inward progress. Human nature is ordained to a regulated display of its active energies; to the habitual performance of activities subservient to some objective and rational purpose.

No matter how humble that purpose may be, in order to impart to the activities it governs any moral relevancy it must possess some rational meaning and usefulness; mere activity for the sake of activity, or activity of a merely playful character, falls short of that function of moral training and strengthening. No such function can attach to activity unless it implies an element of service, which, in however indirect a fashion, has some place in the hierarchy of services in reference to the kingdom of God. To despise work because of its character of subservient usefulness would be, therefore, a gross mistake.

Man in his fallen condition is by no means capable of permanently maintaining, *in statu viae*, that intensity and actuality of spiritual experience which is proper to the purely contemplative attitude. That aspect of *vacare* in eternal life of which St. Augustine speaks, that freedom of *rest* and, as it were, *emptiness* which we shall obtain in eternity, cannot, even in an analogical sense, be anticipated on earth except in comparatively rare moments. A large portion of our lives will be spent, accordingly, in an unhealthy way unless it is devoted to some kind of work subservient to a rational purpose.

Such leisure as lacks the note of true contemplation — that is, mere recreation or amusement — must not occupy more than a small fraction of our time, lest it should impart to our lives a tinge of frivolousness and effeminacy; nay, by evoking a sense of boredom produce in us a specific aptness to sin. Work, on the other hand, also fulfills the function of being a strong curb on the overactivity of the instincts and on the poisoning of illicit appetites of all kinds, to whose pressure idleness makes us far more liable to succumb.

Certain moments magnify the range of our freedom

Beyond, however, all of the opportunities offered by the tissue of our daily lives, our freedom has the power to promote the transformation of our being in a much deeper sense so far as *certain particular moments* are concerned. Time and again, certain specific situations may occur — situations, to be sure, that we cannot conjure up at will — in which our free center of personality is given the capacity to bring about, by a single and definite act, a durable transformation of our inmost being. For example, there may be a moment when our renunciation of a cherished good of high intrinsic value will usher in, beyond the limits of our relation to that good, a process of detachment from terrestrial goods in general.

There may be cases, again, when our forgiving a person whom we have long held in scorn takes on the form of a softening of heart in a general and in an enduring sense as well. Or again, a deep humiliation may, in given circumstances, start off our wholesale emancipation from our slavery to pride.

These are moments in which, thanks to a gift of God, our range of direct power is suddenly extended, so that the effectiveness of our free decision may advance into the depths of our being. In such cases, the concrete object to which our act refers has the function, as it were, of a *pars pro toto*, an exemplar representing a whole sphere of objects.

Thus, in the act of detaching ourselves from that object we change our attitude towards a vast province or the entire domain of created goods. In the act of bursting our bonds in this one case, we lift in principle a general state of bondage to which we were hitherto subjected. Such was the victory St. Francis achieved when he embraced the leper and kissed his sores. He then not only broke the specific shackle imposed on his love by his natural repugnance to ugly and disgusting things but made an essential breach with his dependence on his natural dispositions as such. In cases like this, the outward deed means at the same time an effective interior act, by which a new situation is created in the soul itself. This is most explicitly the case, it need hardly be emphasized, in regard to an act of conversion.

It is not, as has been observed above, in our power to conjure up such situations. These moments, when the operativeness of our freedom is increased and the range of our power expanded to a degree far beyond normal, bear an unmistakable character of gratuitous gifts. Whereas ordinarily we can only posit such free actions as may be supposed to exercise an indirect effect in favor of our transformation, in these supreme moments we may make a decisive step forward concerning our permanent state of soul. It is to these moments that St. Paul refers when he says: "Behold, now is the acceptable time...now is the day of salvation" (2 Cor. 6:2). Nor must we allow these decisive moments to pass unused: "Today if you shall hear his voice, harden not your hearts" (Ps. 94:8).

Receptivity to grace in the sacraments transforms us

Yet, the ultimate and all-important source of our transformation in Christ lies not in what *we* do or what we *can* do by our free will, but in what God accords to us in the Sacraments: above all, our participation in the Holy Sacrifice of the Mass and the reception of Holy Communion. The Lord Himself alone, who has redeemed and regenerated us by His most holy Blood, can receive us and transform us in His nature. Indeed, He cries to us: "If any man thirst, let him come to me and drink" (John 7:37). What *we* can contribute is that we *do* thirst — and drink. It is reserved for our freedom to receive the grace of God, the supernatural life He bestows upon us, and to open wide the gates of our souls so that the divine Life may penetrate us. This communication of grace is not given us in a way extraneous to our freedom of overriding it, but in that we go to Christ, and *drink*. Nevertheless, what we receive far surpasses everything we may intend or desire, indeed anything accessible to our power of experience. In the full objective sense of the term, we thus receive a new life which is to transform our very being — we may well say our ontological nature.

We should pray that we be transformed

Finally, it is certainly also within our power to *pray* for our transformation in Christ; to continue imploring God that He shall grant us the grace of that transformation and bless our own contribution to it. Mindful of the words of the Lord, "Without me you can do nothing" (John 15:5), and again, "Ask, and you shall receive" (John 16:24), we must pray with the holy Church: "O God of virtues, to whom belongeth every excellent thing, implant in our hearts the love of Thy name, and bestow upon us the increase of religion, fostering what things are good, and, by Thy loving care, guarding what Thou hast fostered" (Collect of the sixth Sunday after Pentecost).

Transformation calls us freely to cooperate with God's action in our soul

Such, then, are the manifold ways in which man is called to cooperate by his striving for perfection in the process of his transformation, and such is the part God has assigned to his freedom as a basis for that cooperation. As for the roads that lead to the single virtues — fruits of the Holy Spirit, in which the divine Life as received in Baptism, unfolds and manifests itself — we treat of these more specifically in the appropriate chapters. Here our emphasis has lain on the general conspectus.

Before all else, it should be stressed that the new supernatural life that Christ imparts to us in Baptism is a purely gratuitous gift of divine Mercy. Man is not the author even of his natural life; he is not able, as the Lord says, to increase his stature by so much as an inch. How much less is he capable of attaining supernatural life by his own forces. Yet, the complete *unfolding* of this life of holiness — that is, his transformation in Christ — does require his free cooperation. Even the initial reception of that holy life in Baptism

250

supposes, in an adult at any rate, not only the Faith but a certain determination of the will. This is clearly expressed in the baptismal rite, which prescribes a thrice-repeated *Volo* to be pronounced by the catechumen.

The call of the Lord, *sequere me*, refers both to the primal surrender to God that precedes Baptism and to the striving for perfection that is to pervade the whole of life up to the last breath. Small as our contribution is if compared to the operation of God, we cannot help feeling overawed with the magnitude, the manifoldness, and the difficulty of the work it requires on our part.

For the success of that work, the Holy Church prays in almost all Collects of the ecclesiastical year; thus, in the Collect of the thirteenth Sunday after Pentecost: *Almighty, eternal God, grant us the increase of faith, hope, and charity; and, that we may deserve to attain what Thou dost promise, make us to love what Thou dost command*; or again, in the Collect of the third Sunday after Easter: *O God, who dost show the light of Thy truth to them that go astray, that they may be able to return to the path of justice, grant unto all who profess themselves and are reckoned Christians, both to reject the things that are opposed to that name and to follow after the things that befit it.*

10

True Freedom

BY *true freedom*, as it will be discussed in this chapter, we mean
that ultimate and blissful freedom which Christ — and He alone
— can give us, if we give ourselves to Him without reserve. Nega-
tively speaking, it consists in the dissolution of all spasms of
egotism, in getting rid of all inhibitions. It must not be confused,
of course, with the freedom of man, in general, including the two
dimensions of which we spoke in the preceding chapter; nor must
it be confused with the potentiality, not always actualized, of moral
freedom.

True freedom is a consequence of our transformation
   in Christ

As distinct from these, we are now concerned with that freedom
which one cannot possess except as an element of Christian
perfection: in other words, which constitutes a goal which is
reached in our transformation in Christ.

Possessing this freedom, we participate in a higher life. We are
lifted by Christ above our nature, including all factors that tend to
weigh us down. We no longer live, as it were, on the natural plane
but in the perspective of Christ, released, in a sense, from all the

weight of our nature. In this freedom, we experience the truth of St. Paul's words: "Who then shall separate us from the love of Christ?" (Rom. 8:35). Nothing but a complete and unreserved surrender to Christ — meaning that we fling ourselves in His arms without any thought of a natural security or stronghold, that we burn the bridges behind us, that we answer the call *sequere me* unconditionally — can give us this freedom of the children of God.

Let us now examine the chief obstacles that hinder us from achieving this ultimate freedom; the bonds we have to break so that we may attain to it. (The sequence followed in our enumeration of the obstacles to freedom is not meant to express their order of importance.)

Egotism hinders attainment of true freedom

Most obvious is the hampering effect of our various *egocentric preoccupations*. A certain type of man feels, on every conceivable occasion, that his *rights* are threatened or trespassed upon. He always keeps on his guard lest some impairment of his rights should escape his attention. Dominated by his fear of such an injury or encroachment, he seldom stops to consider whether a thing is valuable in itself or not, whether it glorifies God or offends Him. Hence, his vision of various situations is obscured, his capacity of adequate judgment is blunted. He is incapable of a free, unwarped response to values.

In his mind, the theme of his rights overshadows the question of the objective value involved; thus, instead of a disinterested love of truth and of right he is likely to develop a bitter and cantankerous attitude. Indeed, *summum jus, summa injuria*, his inordinate insistence on his rights may sometimes tempt him to ride rough-shod over the rights of others. Such people, in their *cramped* egotism, are as far removed from true freedom as it is possible to be.

In others, morbid egocentrism takes the form of over-susceptibility. Every now and then they feel slighted, offended, treated with disregard or, at any rate, unkindly. They are always on the lookout for slights inflicted upon them. Their capacity for objective judgment is also gravely impaired. An elaborate set of inhibitions prevents them from displaying an adequate response to values. They are crushed under a heavy burden; they are continually moving in a circle around their ego. They never raise themselves above a situation in which the consideration due to their person seems to be involved, and must in their turn be qualified as specifically *unfree*.

Disgust about unsavory things can hinder freedom

An entirely different but scarcely less important form of unfreedom is that which proceeds from the attitude of *disgust*. In various situations, certain people labor under grave inhibitions owing to the fact that they feel disgusted at the thought of any closer contact with others. The theme of the situation escapes them because of their preoccupation lest they should have to touch something that inspires them with disgust. They would shudder, for instance, at the idea of drinking from a glass from which someone else has drunk.

Of course we must distinguish between the different types of disgust. The disgust evoked by really and obviously unsavory things — such as dirt, purulent sores, and so on — is in itself perfectly legitimate; a complete indifference in this respect betrays a coarseness and crude lack of sensibility, which is anything but a virtue. Even this normal reaction of nausea, however, must not reach the point of hampering us in the practice of charity. It must never keep us from helping a person in need; furthermore, while tending a sick person we must so repress it so that it is unnoticeable to the patient. Certainly it is not a duty to emulate those saints who kissed the fetid sores of lepers; that was in response to a particular vocation. Yet, whenever the situation objectively requires us to undergo contact with such things — whenever, that is to say, it does become a duty of charity — we must silence the voice of disgust in us, and subordinate everything to the imperative of love. Our failure to do so proves our deficiency of inner freedom.

Disgust at naturally private things may hinder freedom

Another type of disgust refers to a too intimate bodily contact with other persons. Certain things that are not really disgusting by themselves may, as possible vehicles or symbols of such an intimate contact, become vicarious objects of disgust. Here, again, sensibility as such is by no means a defect: it is right to be aware of the fact that things of this order belong to man's corporeal sphere of privacy, and to shrink from penetrating into that sphere.

Take, for instance, the case of conjugal love. Here the *intentio unionis* is a predominant theme and can legitimately unfold itself; accordingly, the bodily sphere of privacy is itself translucent with the precious radiance that pervades and represents the being (in its totality, comprising also the outward aspects) of the beloved person. The feeling of embarrassment otherwise evoked by all intimate proximity with a strange body yields its place here, normally, to a feeling of joy — not devoid of, but on the contrary, based upon reverence — at being allowed to participate, in a sense, in the other person's corporeal privacy. It is as though the negative note otherwise attached to this whole sphere were transformed, here, into a positive one.

Whoever is so imprisoned by his general disgust at contacts that, even though united to another person by such a bond of love, he still feels repelled by the nearness of that person's bodily sphere of intimacy, gives proof of a kind of *cramped* egocentrism in his character. More explicitly, he gives proof of the exaggerated stress he lays on his distinctness from others, owing to his overvaluation of his own self. This attitude of a too anxious isolation of self from strange humanity, an overemphasis of one's inviolable particularity and distance from others, obstructs the free circulation of love. It is incompatible with that bold self-surrender without which no genuine love is possible.

With an important modification, similar considerations apply to the other great classic type of love (as distinct from the conjugal one, which, anyhow, is *a priori* restricted to the relations between man and woman): the deep love that animates true friendship, particularly such as is embedded in a common allegiance to Christ. Here, to be sure, the other person's corporeal intimacy cannot become a source of attraction; but here, too, it must cease to have anything deterrent about it.

Whenever the logic of a situation (we are not maintaining that such situations should expressly be sought for) engages one to undergo a contact with that sphere of corporeal privacy, one should not recoil from it nor be so preoccupied about it as to let one's inner freedom fall a prey to self-consciousness.

Our love of the other person must span the abyss of his bodily *strangeness*. Then the contact with his sphere of privacy, as typified, for instance, by our having to drink from the same glass, will acquire a trait of neutrality. If viewed against the background of my spiritual communion with him and of the beauty I see in his soul, the other person's sphere of bodily privacy will gradually become something familiar to me. My contact with that sphere I shall experience as an obvious consequence of my close solidarity with his personal life, inherent in all genuine relations of love — as is, also, a certain community of possessions; that is to say, one's spontaneous readiness to share what one has with a friend in need.

A man who lives in Jesus will deem it inconsistent with his true freedom to experience the distance between another person's bodily privacy and his own as an unbridgeable gulf, especially when his relation with that person is such that they may address to each other the words, "The love of Christ has gathered us together" (Antiphon in the Liturgy of Holy Thursday, Washing of Feet). He who is so far dominated by his reactions of disgust as to live in a continuous solicitude about the protection of his bodily privacy, not allowing either the duty of charity (whenever it presents itself in a way requiring the breaking down of those barriers) or a close personal friendship in Christo to interfere with his anxious self-isolation, is most certainly wanting in true freedom. He is imprisoned in an unessential concern. By yielding to this tendency of his nature, he will in time slide into a kind of spinster-like fussiness about his jealously guarded intangibility — an attitude of prim egotism entirely unworthy of a Christian and certain to make its victim more and more incapable of love.

What true freedom implies in this context is not, in a word, a natural lack of sensitivity to disgusting impressions, nor a primary absence of the sense of distance and privacy, as it occurs in rude and primitive people. The right freedom concerning the sphere here referred to consists not in a natural antithesis to the state of feeling disgusted as such, but in the capacity, originating in a supernatural basic attitude, of responding to the call of God as transmitted by a given situation without being inhibited, in so doing, by the trammels of disgust: or, to put it differently, in the habit of a prompt and quasi-automatic control of disgust whenever an objective situation arises with which it appears incongruous, and which demands its exclusion.

True freedom means, to sum up, the primacy of love: its victory over all feeling of strangeness and all seclusion of self; an openness of the soul by virtue of its ultimate and unreserved dedication to Christ.

Disgust is sometimes associated with a certain vague fear of contagion, of infectious diseases one might catch from other people. In these cases of squeamishness, the stranger makes us shrink back as a possible carrier of germs. Of course, in dealing with persons who really suffer from some contagious disease, it is our duty to protect ourselves against infection as far as possible; for our health, too, is a *talent* given by God, of which we must make the most. But whenever a duty of charity requires that preoccupation to yield, it is charity that ranks supreme.

Apart from this obvious principle, what concerns us here is our duty of controlling the tendency to suspect all possible diseases in others, a suspicion which, with little or no basis in reality, serves unconsciously to encourage our inclinations towards fastidiousness and disgust. As long as there is no solid reason for it, we must not look upon our fellow man as a possible carrier of diseases, for this is a bad mental habit which hampers the free flux of love and fosters our tendency to egocentric self-isolation.

Fear of illness hinders freedom

In an even more general sense, the exaggerated *fear of illness* constitutes a notorious form of unfreedom. There is no merit in neglecting our health, but our preoccupation with it should be kept in bounds by our confidence in God, and in this respect as in others we should fear above all the danger of self-centeredness. The hypochondriac with his imaginary diseases also presents an example of egocentric unfreedom. So long as there is no manifest ground for anxiety we should not waste our time with apprehensions concerning a possible deterioration of our health.

Nor should we allow ourselves to slip into that perspective of generalized fear in which one regards the ambient world primarily as a source of possible dangers to one's health — the expression of a cramped anxiety about the safety of the ego, which strikes at the very root of freedom. To overcome this vicious evil, we must keep well aware of the truth that our lives rest in the hands of God: "My days are in Thine hands" (Ps. 30:16).

Feelings of inferiority diminish freedom

Let us take now another type of unfreedom, different in character but equally an expression of the ego-spasm, and one very frequently to be met with. It is that which consists in being dominated by an *inferiority* complex. Feelings of inferiority must not be confused with humility: on the contrary, they proceed from a basic attitude essentially, though not completely or overtly, controlled by pride and egocentrism. He who is afflicted with them is primarily anxious to represent something and count for something; but he is bothered by fears that the account he really gives of himself does not answer his wishful picture of his own person.

In most cases, inferiority feelings refer to defects that are either imaginary or real but devoid of culpability. One such person regards himself as inferior because he is of humble birth; another, because he is poor; another, again, because he has no academic degree. Their fear lest the "disgraceful" fact that worries them should become public knowledge oppresses the hearts of such persons like a coat of mail and prevents them from reacting adequately to most of the situations in which they are engaged.

With others, again, the "disgraceful blot" whose possible revelation they dread is of a morally relevant (or at any rate, more unusual) character, but still no fault of theirs: that one's father has gone bankrupt or drinks; that one is an illegitimate child or the issue of an unhappy marriage; or, that one is afflicted with some crippling bodily defect.

Yet, even in cases where one tries to hide a shortcoming for which one is actually responsible, so that its becoming manifest would justifiedly evoke in one a sense of painful humiliation, the desire to keep that guilt secret at all costs betrays a certain inner unfreedom. A true Christian will accept even this highly unpleasant kind of penance should his consideration for some important value demand it. But, above all, he will never allow his dread of shame to become the paramount factor dominating his inner life. For he knows that the wrong he may have committed is an evil merely for the reason that it offends God, and in comparison to that, the "disgrace" means nothing — it may constitute a well-deserved and salutary punishment.

Ultimate freedom removes all things into the public medium of Heaven, in whose perspective earthly publicity with its standards dwindles into irrelevancy. That is why, in primitive Christianity, confessions were public — or why, in later times, a St. Margaret of Cortona publicly accused herself of her sins from the top of her house.

The true Christian must see everything *in conspectu Dei* and lift himself above all terrestrial standards to the point of no longer according his dread of disgrace any part in his life. He must habitually remember that "one thing only is needful": his *obsession* with Christ must be so powerful as to deprive such mundane concerns of all power over him.

Fear, in general, is one of the greatest enemies of our freedom — be it the fear of physical danger, the fear of poverty, the fear of incurring somebody's hatred, the fear of becoming an object of people's talk, or, above all, the fear of being doomed to sin in spite of all moral efforts. Of this last-named important variety of fear which is commonly referred to as scrupulousness, we need not treat here especially, as it has been discussed in Chapter 8 on "Confidence in God."

Concern for human respect diminishes freedom

We shall pass now to a further type of unfreedom, closely akin to the one engendered by fear — the unfreedom due to what is currently termed *human respect*. This means, in particular, that we make our judgment of ourselves, and with it, largely, our mood, dependent on the impression we seem likely to produce on others, on the social image we believe we present. Two forms of human respect may conveniently be distinguished.

The first form is that which deserves a more severe censure. Here, it is a combination of pride and a sense of insecurity that causes the subject to base his appraisal of self on the image other people may have of him rather than on the picture of himself he may derive from his confrontation with God.

In the first place, therefore, he will be anxious not to appear stupid, crack-brained, backward, and in general, ridiculous in the eyes of others. Hence, in many cases, he will shrink from professing his faith before others, dread being seen in church, refrain from crossing himself at table in the presence of unbelievers, and so forth. This type of unfreedom is particularly obnoxious in a Christian. Of course, it will hardly ever occur in such blatant forms in the case of a person who *has* determined to follow Christ unreservedly; but in a more mitigated form, at least, it easily steals into anyone's mental constitution.

Yet, the true Christian should be *completely free* from this pitiable dependence on the world. Knowing that Christ must be a "scandal to the world," he should serenely endure being deemed by the world a fool, ridiculous, or narrow-minded. He ought never to forget these words of Christ: "If you had been of the world, the world would love its own: but because you are not of the world, but I have chosen you out of the world, therefore, the world hateth you" (John 15:19).

It is often easier to profess Christ in big things and even to accept heavy sacrifices for Christ's sake, than to put up with disdain or derision in the humdrum situations of daily life. And yet we should at every moment be ready — and gladly so — to pass for a *fool for Christ's sake.*

This is not to deny that we do well to avoid in our outward bearing all unnecessary demonstrativeness; to observe certain canons of discretion too often neglected by zealous converts; and to

take account of the circumstances, including the degree of susceptibility of those who happen to be present. But this must proceed
from a state of inner freedom; from a sovereign attitude of mind
rising above the situation. Far from allowing our human respect to
make us dependent on the unbelievers' appreciation or letting our
behavior be determined by their taste and their measures, we must
— in joyful readiness to appear, if need be, as *fools for Christ's sake*
— be able to decide before God what, with regard to the salvation
of the souls of our fellow men, we should do and what we had better
omit.

Indifference to human opinion may have good or bad roots

To be unconcerned from natural motives about our social image
is not always a virtue. In some cases, it is an outcome of haughty
conceit; a defect that deprives one of every sense of the impression
one is likely to make on others.

This attitude is not, at bottom, so very different from that of
human respect; for both are derivatives of pride. Only, the unconcerned man differs from the other in that *he* feels secure (he is
usually conceited); whereas the slave of human respect, in addition
to his pride, labors under a sense of insecurity.

However, there also exists another type of natural indifference
concerning one's social image, which is by no means objectionable.
We mean the attitude of the sober kind of person who is always so
much absorbed by the objective theme of the situation that it never
even occurs to him to examine what others may think of him. The
ingenuous kind of people who simply and spontaneously do what
seems right to them, without stopping to consider how others may
judge it, belong to the same category. Now the sort of people we
have here in mind are undoubtedly very much freer than those
afflicted with the ill of human respect. They are healthier and more
independent of the tyranny of outward agents.

True freedom judges by the standard of Christ

But they, too, do not possess true freedom in the full sense of the term, which implies a supernatural basis and direction. This true freedom requires us to seek and yearn for nothing but Christ; to be dead unto the spirit of the world; to submit willingly to any humiliation and endure any shame for the sake of Christ; in a word, to live up to the principle: *To contemn the world: to contemn contempt.*

True freedom means that we see nothing either with the eyes of the world or with the eyes of our nature, but in the light of Christ, and with the eyes of the Faith. He who is truly free is not, then, simply unaware of the effect his behavior may produce on others, but essentially independent of it and superior to the plane of considerations to which it belongs. His conduct will be decided by Christ and His holy word, and not determined, for instance, by an inordinate zeal which, spurning the virtue of discretion, gives vent indiscriminately to one's natural enthusiasm rather than translating into action a true and unreserved surrender to Christ.

A spectator view of ourselves limits our freedom

Besides the first form of human respect, as discussed above, there is a second one, less reprehensible but still an expression of inner unfreedom. We find it in people who so much attune themselves mentally to their environment that they grow accustomed to see their own behavior with the eyes of others, thus becoming unable to behave in company with any degree of spontaneity.

The image of their own person which they attribute to the spectator warps their attention to the given thematic object. In the end they come to observe themselves from the outside constantly and habitually, in a fashion apt to prevent them from taking up a genuine and independent position in any matter at all. Thus, for instance, they would feel it to be a profanation of their prayer if it were said in the proximity of others, whom it might impress as fanatical, in bad taste, or excessively pious.

Not that pride impels them to attach an undue importance to their social image; it is merely that they are to such a degree swayed by the (real or imaginary) impression they produce on others that their genuine experiences and spontaneous impulses are crushed beneath the weight of that all-comprehensive dependence.

The perspective in which they suppose others to see things destroys their contact with the objects that solicit their response. Hence, their behavior becomes the function of whatever, at the moment, happens to be their environment. In the company of people whom they know or suspect to be irreligious, for instance, they will be ashamed to cross themselves at table or to say their Breviary in the train.

Love may sometimes call us to moderate the display of our convictions

Of course, it is not a good thing either to lack all faculty of empathy — of sensing and being in tune with other people's emotions — and, confining oneself entirely to the thematic object of one's attitude, to be wholly unconcerned with the effect it is bound to produce. As has been hinted above, both natural ingenuousness and a primary emphasis on being in harmony with other people's states of mind are inadequate.

True freedom means, not either of these, but the habit of seeing everything *in conspectu Dei*, and *hence* giving heed to the state of mind prevailing in one's environment.

Thus, there are situations in which charity requires me to exercise particular discretion lest I should perplex or repel others; in which, that is to say, the emphatic profession of my faith might act as an irritant to such persons around me as are neither firm believers nor perhaps very decided unbelievers, and embitter their opposition.

Love, then, may secondarily compel us to ponder the impression our behavior is likely to produce; but on no account must the thought of that impression substitute itself for the free unfolding of our own experience and thus automatically govern our conduct. We must never, from natural weakness, become dependent on the anticipated and often, in fact, merely imagined impression on others. This secondary, shadowy, and false aspect must not come to dominate objective reality to the point of making us unable to give adequate response to God or values because others might misconstrue it.

This automatic deformation of our own experience, this illegitimate dependence on the errors and delusions of others, has nothing in common with a conscious and superior consideration — sanctioned by our free personality — for our *brethren of an infirm faith*, which causes us to omit certain manifestations of our religious allegiance in the sense of an express sacrifice.

As we have said, this second form of human respect is an offspring not of pride but of a general weakness and an excessive receptivity to impressions. We can overcome it, too, however, by the spirit of a basic surrender to God. It depends on our free will whether we simply deliver ourselves to its compulsion or withstand it. By yielding to this tendency in our nature, we become more and more slaves.

On the other hand, if we combat it resolutely — if, again and again, we follow the spontaneous impetus of our experience, for the sake of God and in conscious disregard of our environment — we shall not fail gradually to free ourselves from the tyranny of that extraneous domination.

Only let its magic circle be pierced frequently (and *with conscious design*, not merely by accident owing to the intensity of our emotion) and it will ultimately fade away.

Pliability of views may hinder freedom

Close to this second form of human respect, we find a further type of unfreedom: that which results from too great a receptivity to outside influences as such. Certain people are inclined to become dependent in their inner lives on others simply because these are possessed of a more dynamic personality. A man typifying this kind of unfreedom will, for instance, rally to another's opinion, not as a result of his having been convinced of its objective truth, but just because it has been set forth with an impressive vigor.

After a time, it is true, when his contact with the person superior in dynamism has ceased, he will very probably dismiss that opinion again. But, for a while, another's view of the subject in question has overlain, in his mind, his own; and the same thing will continue to happen, in regard to other alien opinions and under the impact of other vigorous personalities.

The mental dependence of persons thus generally subject to alien influences is more far-reaching even than the one inherent in human respect. For not merely does it stifle the outward manifestation — nay, not merely interfere with the inward unfolding — of one's own genuine attitude in the presence of others; worse than that, a person of so malleable disposition goes to the length of subordinating his concrete decisions to the dictate of a stronger will confronting him and for no other reason than that it *is* a stronger will; or even, frequently, of adopting slavishly the opinions and attitudes of others with the force of a more aggressive temperament behind them.

In most cases, it is true, this mental dependence will not bear upon one's ultimate principles or fundamental convictions and positions but rather, only, on one's judgment of concrete situations or newly arising matters. That judgment will be inspired, illegitimately, by the suggestions of others taking the place of a consistent application of the principles one really holds.

Ways to combat pliability of views

This grave danger to one's freedom must be combatted with the utmost energy. If we are aware of having such a pliable disposition, we must, in the first place, avoid contact — as far as possible — with persons who excel us in dynamism and who, at the same time, represent a false outlook. It would be unjust to despise such a withdrawal as cowardice; it is, in fact, the wholesome fruit of a humble self-knowledge — of a correct estimate of our forces.

Secondly, so far as we cannot evade contact with persons of this kind, we must expressly gird ourselves beforehand against their influence. In a healthy distrust of our weakness we must first collect ourselves in God, and, as it were, barricade ourselves inwardly against the influence which we know is going to impinge upon us.

Not for a moment should we allow ourselves, in the presence of such people, to relax mentally, nor to assume the attitude — though it is otherwise the right and indeed self-evident one — of being open and permeable to the radiation of a fellow soul. Here, we must sternly deny ourselves the natural enjoyment of concord and sympathy. We must learn how to distinguish the situations in which it is well for us to fling the gates of our souls wide open from those which require us to bolt them fast; so also do we breathe deeply in pure mountain air but hold our breath when traversing a locality where the air is foul. A true Christian who inclines towards this weakness must, before he enters into a situation that is dangerous in the sense here indicated, prepare for it adequately in obedience to the advice of his spiritual directors.

Pliability in conduct diminishes freedom

There is, also, another form of pliability affecting the soul less deeply but still a source of unfreedom: namely, false compliance. Some people, in whom good-naturedness degenerates to weakness, are unable to offer any resistance to the desires and requests of others. While they do not adopt slavishly the opinions or positions of other persons, in their outward conduct they allow themselves to be persuaded by the representations, entreaties, and objurgations of anybody who needs their cooperation for some purpose of his own.

To be sure, if their consent is solicited for things which they look upon as definitely wrong — things against which their conscience would vehemently revolt — they will resist. Not so, however, if it is a question of neutral things, or such as they deem merely useless or irrelevant. All of us have known such helpless persons whose kindness is presumed on by everybody and who squander their time and their energies because they are not able to refuse any request of others. Perhaps it is that, at a given moment, they would think it discourteous to refuse what is asked of them; or that they are moved to compassion; or they feel that they cannot face the ill humor their refusal would evoke — anyhow, they yield and thus easily lapse into servility. In more extreme cases, compassion can even seduce them into conniving at some definite wrong or at least tolerating it passively.

Ways to combat pliability of conduct

Obviously, this pliancy, too, endangers freedom, and should be fought if present in one's character. Holy obedience — a strict conforming to spiritual advice — is eminently helpful in such cases. Here, again, the subject should consciously develop moral armor and put it on before he enters a situation that is likely to test his firmness of will. Even to become well aware of being afflicted with this defect of excessive pliability will by itself mark a first step towards his cure.

He must recollect himself *in conspectu Dei*, and engage in a systematic campaign against his weakness. Having regard to his particular case, he must train himself to mistrust the suasions of compassion in general. Also, he must learn how to refuse a request firmly from the outset and how to cut short an interview immediately when he feels his resistance to be wavering. He may resort to specific ascetical practices calculated to increase his firmness of character.

Above all, he must see to it that he fulfills punctually all his actual obligations towards others, lest he should develop a guilty conscience, which would further aggravate his natural proneness to yield. As far as possible, he should avoid being in the debt of others. If, nevertheless, such a situation emerges, he should consider it soberly in its true proportions — again *in conspectu Dei*, that is — endeavoring to conceive of his indebtedness as the concrete and limited thing it is rather than derive from it a generalized guilty conscience tinging his relations with his fellow men indiscriminately. He should also, of course, hasten to acquit himself of that debt — taking care, however, not to magnify its dimensions.

Compulsive independence as a limiter of freedom

A certain contrast to the defects we have now discussed is offered by another type of unfreedom, which we might call the *complex of independence*. There is a category of people who feel irked by being in any way obliged to others. They think their freedom curtailed by any debt of gratitude. The truth is that their state of mind — the delusion that being obliged to others takes away from their freedom — is itself a manifestation of their lack of inner freedom. He who is truly free enjoys the gratitude he may owe to his fellow men.

The stickler for independence sees his ideal in being able to go through life in a state of splendid indifference to others, avoiding all obligation towards them. At heart (we may refer, in this context, to Chapter 7) it is a certain kind of pride that makes him feel the consciousness of owing anything to others as an intolerable burden. The true Christian will abhor this *complex of independence* in all its varieties. To him it must be clear, not only that he owes everything to God — that he is, and shall be, a beggar before God — but that he is dependent on the help of other men. He will receive a benefit he is accorded with happy gratitude. The consciousness of being obliged to others will not weigh him down, since he looks upon the duty of gratitude as self-evident and since the ill-conceived ideal of outward independence has no appeal to his mind.

Of course, we are not referring here to the case of benefits accorded with the intention of securing thereby some kind of unjustified influence. It is entirely right to avoid becoming indebted to people whose purpose it is thus to secure a hold on us so as to wring from us this or that illegitimate concession. In such cases it is our downright duty to refuse the benefits we are offered.

Compulsive intellectual or spiritual independence diminishes freedom

If this independence complex — taken in its general and material sense — is a bad enough thing, a similar attitude in regard to one's intellectual or spiritual possessions is even more to be warned against. It is utterly unreasonable to shy at the idea of receiving any intellectual help or guidance from others, to insist on working out one's ideas all by oneself and to remain uninfluenced throughout.

Certainly, again, we do well to endeavor to keep our minds shut to all illegitimate influences — the suasions of suggestion, the techniques aimed at producing an impression, etc. — but nothing could be falser than to extend this wholesome caution into resenting the intellectual help of others communicating genuine new values to us, and lifting us to a higher level, as an encroachment upon our spiritual independence.

The desire to elaborate one's outlook all by oneself is a typical offspring of pride, and entirely at variance with the mind's true attention to its object. For if we are really concentrated, as we should be, on the purpose (the only justified one as far as our intellectual pursuits are concerned) of enriching our vision of the values and of widening our access to the truth, we shall care little about whether we achieve this through our own forces or with the help of strangers — a question of no objective relevancy at all.

But, generally speaking, the true Christian is aware of the great extent to which he is dependent on the help of others and sees in this inescapable dependence — which is as necessary for the nourishment of a spontaneous inner life as the servile, illegitimate kind of dependence is detrimental to it — a realization of community in which he has every reason to delight.

He is aware of the heritage he receives through tradition, of all that he owes to the Liturgy and the great Doctors of the Church whose words they hand down to him. Animated by his zealous wish to be transformed in Christ, he will joyously grasp the helping hands of all those who have advanced nearer to God than he has. He desires to learn from others; nor does the consciousness of having acquired a knowledge alone, without the cooperation of anyone, fill him with particular satisfaction. For he seeks after nothing but a closer union with Christ, and is wholly unconcerned about the part played by his own forces in securing that aim.

Public opinion may limit freedom

Separate consideration, again, must be given to that form of essential unfreedom which consists in our dependence on public opinion. The views currently professed beyond the limits of a particular milieu, in the public sphere as a whole — the ideas which, at a given time, permeate the entire intellectual medium of a nation, or even of a wider zone of culture — often influence to a high degree the mental cast of such persons even as can by no means be called weaklings. Many people adopt opinions of this kind as a matter of self-evidence without probing into the question of their truth; without, indeed, confronting them with the basic principles they themselves hold. They come to share those views simply because they cannot resist the dynamism of the dominant atmosphere of their age.

In branding this as a form of illegitimate suasion, we are anxious to avoid a possible misconception. We do not mean to deny that public opinion may also act as a vehicle for men's contact with true values, thus paving the way for their genuine and spontaneous experience of such values or value-realities as would otherwise have remained inaccessible to them.

The Christian who has received the gratuitous gift of absolute truth must beware of all illegitimate and imperceptible influences. He must not let anything pass before he has confronted it with God and His holy truth; nothing that is out of accord with the doctrine of the holy Church must be accepted. He must grant no influence to any dynamic pressure in his life. It is this conclusive confrontation that St. Paul has in mind when he says, "But prove all things: hold fast that which is good" (1 Thess. 5:21).

Ways to combat illegitimate influences of public opinion

Public opinion as such should have no hold whatsoever on a true Christian. With his vision enlightened by the divine Truth, he must not attach any weight to the fact that a certain opinion is held by a great number of people or that a certain point of view is modern or fashionable.

His life is lived in the sight of Him in whose eyes "a thousand years...are as yesterday, which is past" (Ps. 89:4). He says with the Psalmist: "They shall perish but Thou remainest: and all of them shall grow old like a garment. And as a vesture Thou shalt change them, and they shall be changed. But Thou art always the selfsame: and Thy years shall not fail." (Ps. 101:27-28).

He should regard public opinion with a healthy distrust, for it is only a work of man and a nursling of the spirit of the world. In order to make himself impermeable to all mere currents of the age, he must look for a support in the doctrine of the Church. He must turn his eyes away from the garish pageant of the idols of the day and shut his ears to the noise of ephemeral appeals.

Above all, the Christian must be on guard against the subtle poison of public opinion which is ever trying imperceptibly to seep in through his pores. He must not for a moment forget this danger of contagion and must systematically immunize himself against it by absorbing the right spiritual counter-poisons.

Again and again, he should represent to himself, together with all their implications, the eternal truths of God; again and again, he should open his mind to the radiation of the light of Christ, and in that light examine with unbending sternness whatever the spirit of the age offers and suggests. He must never breathe the air of a profane environment in the attitude of naïve trustfulness. Let him be always conscious of his own frailty and of Christ's warning: "Beware of false prophets."

For he will not have attained to true freedom until public opinion no longer has any hold on his spirit; until he no longer knows any dependence but one — an unconditional dependence on Christ, to whom he has given himself, for all times, by a free and full decision which involves his whole personality.

There are, however, two distinct forms of dependence on public opinion. The one we have just discussed consists in being fascinated by that which is topical: the salient ideas of the age. The mind of such a person is captivated by the mere fact that a thing is *vital* in this external sense of publicity and topicality; he disregards its particular meaning and content. He delights at being in tune with things *coming* and new, with whatever is in the air, with the great forces of the future. He is intoxicated with the dynamic impetus of an intense movement.

Conventionalism diminishes freedom

The other form of dependence on public opinion lies in the opposite direction. It is present in those who feel secure and comfortable in their unreserved adherence to a stable public opinion hallowed by tradition, the attitude of *conventionalism*. The first form of dependence on public opinion is the great danger to characters eager for novelty and sensation, discontinuous, over-susceptible to the charms of dynamism; the second form is likely to occur in the narrow-minded, habit-ridden type of man.

The conventionalist is more or less immune to the seduction of the changing ideas and fashions that dominate public opinion, so impressed by its spirit of the new. All the more however, is he anxious to conform to a medium of ideas upon which tradition and long custom have placed a stamp of valid public authority. He cleaves to *what has always been held*; what his fathers and forefathers have deemed right. By contrast to the worshipper of the moment's idols, who succumbs to the impact of current opinions and newly surging enthusiasms, owing to his conservatism the conventionalist falls short of an objective vision of things unobjective.

To him, a thing is valid for the sole reason that it has long been recognized as such. Accordingly, he inclines not so much to excess and indiscretion (as do those who serve the idols of the day) as to mediocrity. He would not dare to think or do anything that is not sanctioned by the milieu which to him incarnates authority — anything in which he does not feel supported by that public opinion to which he adheres.

Yet, that authority is not defined as such by any objective test, but merely by the fact of its constituting the environment in which he has grown up and whose ideological traits he has come to regard as self-evident. The conventionalist cannot do without the support of such a terrestrial public opinion where he may rest comfortably. Hence, he lacks objectivity and freedom in much the same way as does his progressive counterpart; for he, too, is incapable of an adequate response to values. The views the conventionalist borrows from his system of conventions prevent him from understanding such values as have no place in that set of conventions.

Moreover, even his response to the values that do have a conventional standing is incomplete and falsified inasmuch as his appreciation is primarily conditioned, not by their value-significance as such but by the fact that the values in question happen to be endorsed by convention. If, for instance, the conventionalist is a Catholic, he is that because his parents and his ancestors also were Catholics; because it is *the thing* to comply with one's duties towards the Church — *not* because the Church is the surviving Christ and the depositary of infallible doctrinal authority. Or again, he will practice continence because it is looked upon as indecent to have affairs.

Everywhere an objectively unimportant motivation is substituted for the genuine, the objectively valid one. In his stuffy narrowness, the conventionalist in a sense degrades whatever good he may do to a lower plane than the plane to which it intrinsically belongs. He lacks the sense of distinction between things essential and nonessential. He places any conventional taboos that happen to thrive in his milieu on a level with the commandments of God.

Both conventionalism and bohemianism are incompatible with true freedom

The incompatibility between the conventional attitude and true freedom needs no elaboration. The true Christian is of necessity unconventional. The mere fact that something "has always been done that way," that it is part of a public tradition, is no motive force with him. He accepts unconditionally only what has been willed by God and is pleasing to God. Great and glorious is the tradition of the Church, without doubt; but that tradition is merely a fruit of her continuity, by virtue of which she preserves through all the whirlpools of the times all that is of true value and of divine origin. It is not, by any means, the automatic product of pure conservatism.

Nothing could be falser, however, than the inference that the anti-conventionalism of the so-called *bohemian* indicates, therefore, the road to true freedom. The bohemian — the sort of person, that is, who dislikes all fixed rules and loyalties whatsoever, who makes an idol of informality and of the unbridled sovereignty of subjective urges, is as unfree as any conventional bourgeois. For he rejects conventions not inasmuch as they embody illegitimate restraints, but inasmuch as they embody restraints as such.

He fails, exactly as does the bourgeois, to distinguish the essential from the inessential. The conventionalist sets mere accidental human statutes on a level with the divine commandments and with the demands of the true values; so also does the bohemian. Only, while the former assents to all these with the selfsame emphasis, the latter repudiates them all. The conventionalist accepts the divine commandments insofar as they fit in with his system of conventions, and in so doing, he is actuated by the objectively invalid motive that those commandments are sanctioned by a traditional public opinion.

The bohemian, in his turn, also takes the divine commandments and the demands implied in true values for mere human statutes, deriving their claims from the stamp of tradition; hence, he rejects them along with what are in fact mere conventions. For he would have nothing of rules or restraints whatsoever. He is just as ignorant of the true nature of divine commandments and genuine values as is the conventionalist. He is not a whit less unfree nor more capable of an adequate response to the object.

True freedom clearly distinguishes between human statutes and divine commandments

True freedom, on the other hand, consists precisely in establishing a clear distinction between mere human statutes and divine commandments, and adjusting one's orientation in all things to the will of God. It requires of us that we not allow our position to be determined by any natural preference for, or by any natural aversion to, accepted standards; by any love or by any hatred of custom and usage.

We must base our position exclusively on what is important in itself and pleasing to God.

He who is truly free will joyfully assent to every rule that in some sense is of divine origin, *because* it expresses an aspect of the divine order and makes evident an act of the divine will. He will disregard any mere traditional human rule whenever a superior value demands it.

He is untrammeled by any prejudice. Yet, for the sake of his fellows, he will respect all conventions so far as they contain nothing that infringes the commandments of God or bears a note of petty triviality which can have no place in the world of God. Within such limits he will appreciate and loyally observe all customs and conventions prevailing in his environment. Insofar as they were once invested with a deeper meaning but have in time become mere conventions, he will seek to restore them to their original content.

But he will always keenly distinguish them from the eternal laws. He will not cherish them to the point of refusing to disregard them even when his love of God or his neighbor, or some higher value of another order, demands that he should do so.

On the other hand, the mania for challenging all conventions — so as to prove oneself a superior person — is nothing but another variety of unfreedom.

Propriety differs from holy reserve

Above all, we should take care not to confuse the sacral reserve that marks those who bear "the yoke of Christ" with the attitude of reserve displayed by the conventionalist, which issues from considerations of mere propriety. To be sure, the saints always avoid behaving in a loose or free and easy way. On every occasion their bearing reveals them to be a *property of Christ,* shaped and contained by His holy law. Nor is the monk allowed to indulge in any kind of free and easy behavior. In various situations his state imposes on him a duty of holy reserve. This holy reserve is an expression of his inward poise, his spiritual governance of self, his *habitare secum;* first and foremost, of the fact that he is a *property of Christ.* His reserve exhales an atmosphere, not of social decorum but of mystic consecration. Nor is it at all inconsistent with the boldness of a heroic love or of losing one's self in Christ. That holy reserve was not alien to a St. Francis of Assisi, although he was a *fool for Christ's sake,* a soul *drunk with Jesus,* who — the son of a wealthy merchant, leading the life of an errant beggar — trampled under foot all purely earthly conventions. Again, it is one thing to shun indecent or ambiguous themes out of a mere conventional sense of propriety and another to shun them because they cannot bear confrontation with Christ.

Sacral reserve is an offspring of true freedom, for it flows from our free and unconditional dedication to Christ. It is based on our response to value, and constitutes an entirely legitimate restraint. It means setting ourselves at a distance from the world: the opposite of all facile sociableness and easygoing automatism. Hence, it can never impede our integral obedience to the call of Christ, *sequere me.* Sacral reserve grows, after all, from the same root as the fervent Christian's characteristic indifference to conventional decorum. He who possesses it is by the same token able to disregard all outward considerations whenever a superior value requires it. That is why this holy reserve is realized most perfectly in the saints, who at the same time are the most unconventional of men.

Prejudices can enslave us

Akin to the conventionalist's type of unfreedom is another one, which consists in the subject's enslavement to *prejudices*. In one class of instances, the prejudices are themselves conventional in origin; in other cases, however, they are traceable to purely personal experiences. Thus, some men are woman-haters because they have had one or several unpleasant experiences with women. Some people abhor all animals because they have once been bitten by a dog. Others are forever angry at Italy because they have once been cheated there. Others, again, are confirmed anti-Semites because they have come across a number of unattractive Jews. There are even people who, owing to some distasteful memories that cling to their school days, refuse to appreciate ancient culture.

Briefly, although many prejudices are rooted in conventional traditions, many others have their source in rash generalizations. Now prejudice always means unfreedom, seeing that it means the obscuring of objective judgment by mere accidental impressions. Above all, it implies a shrinking of one's intellectual horizon. Prejudiced people are in an eminent sense narrow-minded.

Our lack of true consciousness, too, can be held accountable for our prejudices. We allow our judgment to be guided by mere associations which interpose themselves between the object and our vision, and so falsify our impression. Instead of letting the thing itself, with its true content, speak to us, we suffer our position to be determined by some association which in our mind, from purely subjective causes, happens to adhere to that thing.

For instance, we find a place unlovely and depressing because on some earlier occasion we were ill there. A melody seems to us devoid of beauty because it reminds us of a gloomy period of our life. We feel repelled by a person because he was present at some painful, humiliating episode of our past; or again, we close our mind to a certain truth because it was a person we dislike who first drew our attention to it.

The true Christian must be entirely free from prejudices. In him, all prejudices must be uprooted, so that unhampered by any conventions and any fortuitous experiences and associations, he may accord to every good the response that is objectively due to it *in conspectu Dei*. And, conversely, the more one has made one's home in Christ and boldly moved one's center of gravity into the supernatural realm, the more those shackles will tend to fall away.

Rancor diminishes true freedom

Rancor on account of some (real or imaginary) wrongs one has suffered, and similar experiences of resentment, are always likely — unless they have been consciously effaced in confrontation with Christ — to injure the freedom of the soul. An insult that rankles will, even though it may not engender any generalized prejudice, create a *spasm* thwarting the free flow of love.

All such inveterate grudges, which one simply leaves alone instead of dissolving them in Christ and sublimating them into a mood of calm and serene melancholy, continue eating one's heart and destroying one's peace of mind, and inevitably conjure up certain aspects of egocentrism. Our consciousness of every wrong we have suffered and have not truly forgiven before Christ forms an obstacle to the unfolding of supernatural life within us. An inward inhibition extending far beyond the sphere of our relations with the perpetrator of that wrong is created. The deeper the insult has wounded us, the stronger is the inhibition it produces.

In order to lift that paralyzing effect, a mere formal pardon on our part does not suffice. We must forgive really and truly, dissolve all bitterness and resentment of the wrong endured, and make an end to all sulking, retirement into ourselves and hardening of heart that has issued from it. All this must be expressly eradicated before the face of Christ: nothing less than our immersion in the stream of His inconceivable, all-conquering love will restore our inward peace.

Self-indulgence is a form of unfreedom

Another mainspring of unfreedom, one of a very different kind, lies in the various forms of *self-indulgence*. This is easiest to recognize when manifesting itself in the form of an inordinate attachment to this or that pleasure or urge-gratification. In one case, food and drink are the object of that excessive and tyrannical attachment; in another, it is sleep; in a further one, smoking; again, it may be certain kinds of entertainment or certain comforts.

Any one of these pleasures may, by becoming so indispensable that missing it makes us preoccupied and restless, maim our inner freedom. Such bodily ties are apt to prevent our souls from attending to all values in a free and unhampered way, according to the will of God. With this form of unfreedom we are all familiar; indeed, to free us from these inordinate attachments is an elementary task of asceticism.

However, the unfreedom implied by certain other types of self-indulgence is often less clearly recognized; or, rather, it is the presence of self-indulgence itself which in such cases escapes recognition.

Here we refer to the tendency displayed by many people to yield to certain obnoxious natural dispositions, which may be of various kinds and which are less patent to the observer's eye than the need for such concrete pleasures as those listed above. We shall examine, in particular, two antithetic types of such psychic dispositions, both fairly frequent and both fraught with dangers. One is the *cramped* character, revealing what we may call, a *spastic* disposition; the opposite type, again, is afflicted with an inordinate propensity to *relaxation*.

A "cramped" character reflects a subtle form of self-indulgence

Let us take the cramped character first. How does a person belonging to this category behave? Now he ruminates incessantly, as though he were spellbound, over some irrelevant idea, or uselessly reiterates some long-exhausted chain of considerations that can no longer yield any further result; now he overstrains his will, pressing himself to unnecessary and meaningless sacrifices, or trying to force things which by their very nature cannot be commanded, such as joy, sorrow, or enthusiasm. Or again, he flogs himself into certain kinds of eccentric attitudes that bear a note of specious sublimity: an ungenuine heroism, for instance, or an excessive contempt for the body and its needs with an oriental or gnostic flavor about it. This very crampedness he may often experience as the manifestation of an extraordinary will power and hence as a sure sign of his freedom.

Because he never relaxes, he forms the conviction that he always maintains himself on a level above the situation, that he makes no concessions to his nature, and that therefore he is eminently free. Is he not always watchful, always on his guard, always keeping out whatever might be interpreted as self-indulgence?

Yet in fact he *is* guilty of self-indulgence, inasmuch as he obeys the dictate of a spastic automatism that is prevalent in his nature. The strain he constantly displays does not spring from a vital response to values. It expresses a general tendency of his nature, which discharges itself in the way of a functional necessity, without any proportionate foundation in the respective objects. Such a person is, in truth, characteristically unfree.

The "duty complex" is a form of unfreedom

The cramped attitude may also manifest itself in reference to the fulfillment of one's duties. The duty complex is an important source of unfreedom. Some people are possessed by certain duties or are hypnotized by certain tasks they have taken upon themselves, to the point of no longer being capable of responding to any higher demands.

However, the mere fact that they bear a responsibility expressible in juridical terms, or that they have charged themselves with a task, does not confer upon the thing they are attending to a surplus of objective significance above everything else. Often, for instance in the minds of such people, vocational obligations will unduly outweigh the demands of charity; or again, kind offices or acts of charity to which they have formally committed themselves will take precedence over others which lack the motive of a formal commitment, even though the latter may imply a deeper meaning and constitute, in the ultimate sense, a higher obligation.

To this type of mind, duty is primarily defined in terms of a tangible, outward, officially sanctioned and specified obligation: one that can somehow be subsumed under the aspect of juridical obligations. They tend to overemphasize such obligations as result from ties either of kinship or of contract, and to underestimate such others as follow inherently (but less automatically, being less susceptible of a statutory formulation) from the *logos* of a deep and meaningful relation of friendship.

Obligations implicit in the *logos* of love they will at best take for granted inasmuch as they have their place in the framework of conjugal or family relationships; yet even as regards the sublime and holy obligations inherent in marriage, they will stress their legal aspects in a one-sided approach. Whatever lacks the official hallmark of obligation they would hesitate to recognize as obligatory.

In such cases, then, the consciousness of obligation does not arise organically from a true appreciation of values; it lies rooted, rather, in a general disposition to cramped and constrained states of mind. Persons of this type, as soon as they enter into a situation that implies an element of publicly recognized, formal obligations, develop a kind of interior spasm in which they stay immured, with souls deaf to other and higher demands. Subordinating themselves entirely to the autonomous mechanism of a definite set of obligations, they become unable to see either the duties in question or the hierarchy of values in general according to their true proportions.

Should they even theoretically discern the superiority of some value outside the circle of those duties or recognize the primacy of some demand of another order, in fact they will not be able to relax their taut attention to the task with which they have charged themselves and in which they are held tight as in a strait jacket. They are simply unable to break through the automatism of that self-imposed strain. Though they were ever so much attracted by some other theme, though their heart cried out after that new value — the compulsion is stronger than they. They fail to overcome the delusion that represents to them this pure dynamism of obsession under the specious guise of an objective command. If once in a while they are in some way forced to quit the charmed circle that holds them prisoners, they are tormented by pangs of conscience.

Self-indulgence means yielding to one's dispositions instead of to values

It must be clearly seen that whenever we yield to these *spastic* tendencies of our nature — even to this "duty spasm" — we in truth make ourselves guilty of a kind of self-indulgence. For the decisive mark of self-indulgence is not relaxation, but the fact of letting one's attitude be determined by one's natural dispositions rather than adjusting it to the demand of the object. What these natural dispositions are varies, of course, according to individual characters. The point at issue, however, is whether one delivers oneself over to the autonomous process of one's natural tendencies or responds to the appeal of objective values and the call of God.

True freedom overcomes self-indulgence by responding to the call of God

The true Christian never lapses into self-indulgence and therefore is past enslavement to a *cramp-mechanism*. He possesses that inward attitude of serene aliveness which implies an eager response, unhampered by any tyrannical inhibitions, to the call of God. Such a response precludes any obligation he has contracted from dominating him as a sovereign absolute. He is ready to desist from everything, give up everything, leave everything as the disciples left their boats and fishing nets at the call of the Lord. He who is truly free preserves a constant readiness to speak, as Abraham did, the *Adsum* of full self-dedication whenever the Lord calls him.

A Christian must attain to this true freedom. The virtues of true self-knowledge and true consciousness will help him to recognize all cramped attitudes he may observe in himself as a form of self-indulgence, and thus to overcome them in the spirit of holy obedience. He must install guards in himself to watch this danger; and, again and again, meditate before God the perennial truth, "But one thing is necessary" (Luke 10:42).

He must shatter the spell of obsession by relinquishing everything, from obedience, as soon as a higher value calls him. Whenever he feels in danger of succumbing to the tyranny of such a cramp, he must flee to Jesus and collect himself before His face, thus restoring his roots in the depths of his being and thereby recovering a serene detachment and an inner distance in regard to any given situation and particular concern.

Spiritual relaxation also inhibits true freedom

Now, as we said above, there are many people whose danger lies in an opposite direction: in the tendency, that is, to a false relaxation. These are characters inclined to drift along and to take easy whatever matters they have to deal with. They live in a thoughtless abandonment to the moment, and are happy if they can elude any consciousness of obligation. They are prone to disorder and an illegitimate love of comfort; they show little accuracy in redeeming their promises; they exhibit a lax and loitering behavior in general.

The unfreedom entailed by such an attitude is obvious. Persons of this type very often fall short of their chosen aim because they shun the tensions and efforts implied in its realization. They complacently submit to their natural aversions and inhibitions. They unreservedly surrender to whatever element or theme in a given situation happens to appeal to their nature. Any occasion for prattle is likely to seduce them into neglecting their duties. They waste the time assigned for work by dozing or daydreaming.

Without regard for the hierarchy of values, they obey the tendency of their nature to prefer always the easy way, to choose in any alternative what is more comfortable, less arduous, requiring less effort and involving less asperity.

Their unfreedom consists in the fact that, instead of a true response to value engaging their personality, they follow the pull of their nature and without resistance yield to its tendency towards the peripheral and the irrelevant and whatever is devoid of tension.

This glib submission to their natural tendencies many of them mistake for freedom, seeing that they always do what they like, without feeling constrained by any shackles. Others, again, rightly experience their inability to convert their resolutions into acts as a painful lack of freedom; their laxity appears to them a disgraceful sign of their decadence. Yet, they continue drifting along, without ever taking any measures to stop the rot. On the contrary, the consciousness of their profligacy renders them the more passive; they apply less and less effort to halt their downward drift. "Now," they would say to themselves, "it is too late anyway." The disorder that engulfs them grows from day to day; they are buried under a thicket of unfulfilled duties, self-reproaches, and aching fears concerning the initial effort towards order they feel to be necessary but dreadful.

We must uproot self-indulgence of every sort

This state of unfreedom is the utmost antithesis to the state of self-possession, of *habitare secum*. A Christian who has lapsed into this paralyzing form of self-indulgence must wage a relentless war against it. He must find out his particular inhibitions, and fight them by a systematic ascetical practice.

Whatever the dispositions of his nature, the law of his life must be taken not from his nature but from Christ. Above all, he must dishabituate himself from self-indulgence in general. He must take care never on any occasion to throw off the holy restraints imposed upon him by his awareness of the metaphysical situation of man and his membership in the *Mystical Body of Christ*.

In holy wakefulness he must beware not to give free rein to any impulse lacking the sanction of his conscious central personality. He must never, as it were, say, "Well, in the rough my daily work is done, so now I may let myself go." Rather he must uproot his specific inhibitions and thus break a path for himself across the underwood of his nature, so that he may at any time follow the call of God uninhibited.

Habit may constrict our freedom

A heavy curtailment of our freedom arises from our frequent subjection to the force of *habit*. The mere fact that we often do or undergo a thing, or that we are accustomed to certain conditions, fosters a tendency in us to stick to those things or to maintain those conditions, whatever their intrinsic merits. This tendency reflects a general trait in human nature, but we must not suffer it to govern our feelings and acts unchecked. The mere familiarity of a thing is not by itself a legitimate reason for our cultivating it.

Two cases may be distinguished here. On the one hand, there are things which have no primary attraction for us at all which owe their power over us to the force of habit only. To this purely formal dominance of habit as such a Christian ought never to submit. He should never allow a thing of neutral content to become indispensable to him through habituation alone. For this means a ballast thwarting his free response to the call of God; an illegitimate power gradually fettering him with invisible chains. He should combat a habit of this kind whenever it raises its head, by specific ascetical practices.

On the other hand, there is the case of habit reinforcing our allegiance to things that do attract us by virtue of their content itself. Thus, we may grow habituated to things really valuable, such as an orderly regulation of our daily life; to things merely agreeable, certain comforts for instance, or smoking and drinking; or again, to outright vices. In respect of this second case, our task is not to fight the power of habit as such but to place it at the service of our free will. We must not leave to chance which habits we contract.

Habit must play no part in value-response

We must allow this power a claim in regard to such things only as we have *chosen* according to a free response to value. In this sense asceticism, too, makes use of the force of habit. Strictly speaking, it is not so much things absolutely valuable that are meant here as, rather, means to some good purpose: a training that enables us to attain something properly valuable. The *technique* of good works alone, never the value itself, should become the object of a habit. Thus, for example, we may train ourselves for early rising by acquiring the habit; yet, in the motivation of our hearing Mass every morning the fact that it has become a habit with us must play no part whatsoever.

Even as regards the technique of good works, however, the power of habit should not extend beyond its usefulness as a means in the service of our freedom. We must preserve the freedom to discontinue without great difficulty, even a salutary habit whenever that is demanded by our obedience to the call of God.

In other words, we must remain masters even of our good habits; and much more must we guard against allowing anything that is merely pleasant or comfortable to become our master, just because we have grown accustomed to it. It is not the accident of habit that ought to determine our orientation but we who ought freely to direct the evolution of our habits.

Habit may decrease our sensibility to genuine values

There is another side to the possible danger involved by habit. It may not only enchain us to certain things which it causes us to overvalue; it may also numb our aliveness to genuine values.

This, again, may happen in various manners. First, habit as such may sometimes bring about a general decrease of our sensibility to true values. Man is so fashioned that whatever he experiences for the first time — whatever he has just discovered — is likely to evoke in him a particularly vivid and plastic impression. It need not be his first actual contact with a thing — what we mean is the moment when the true significance of that thing first dawns upon him. After a while, the impression will in many cases tend to fade; familiarity with an object is apt to breed, if not contempt, a kind of indifference. This we cannot but register as the manifestation of a specific and ineradicable human weakness.

To be sure, in regard to many things it really means a gift of divine mercy. Inasmuch as it results in a mitigation of physical pain, of the suffering caused by want, of the terror inspired by perilous situations, the blunting effect of habit deserves to be considered a happy and liberating influence in the lives of men.

Yet, in relation to true values, the power of habit takes on a negative character; because here, no blunting effect should take place. The degree of this unfavorable influence varies according to individual dispositions. The more vividly a person reacts to impressions — the greater his responsiveness to the stimulus of novelty — the more liable he is to the danger of disregarding the perennial relevancy of genuine values, the never obsolescent meaning of truth, and of developing a certain dullness in regard to such values and truths as have become familiar to him. This is especially the case with people who are eager for sensations.

We must deliberately fight this effect of habit by again and again recalling the valid first impression that the value in question produced upon us and thus evoking in our mind its timeless meaning and its never-aging splendor. At least we must always bear in mind that what has lessened our receptivity towards that value is merely deficiency on our own part. On the other hand, by adapting our intellectual judgment of a value and our affective attitude to it, to the evanescence of the vivid impression it has once created in us, we give proof of a deep lack of freedom.

Habit may diminish our gratitude

Nor is this the only form in which the dulling effect of habit can manifest itself; it may also impinge on our gratitude for the gifts of divine mercy. Thankful as we may have felt at first for those gifts accorded to us — a great love or friendship, for example, or our being allowed to live in a beautiful country or again, some special grace of God — all too soon we grow accustomed to them and cease to appreciate them in any adequate degree. We are no longer aware of their character as gifts; our gratitude for them, if not obliterated, has become dormant.

Is not our life a continuous succession of the mercies and charities of God, and at the same time, an incessant display of ingratitude on our part? How scantly disposed are we to sing again and again the litany of the mercies of God; and even though we sing it, how many particular mercies do we not forget! If we take advantage of the inconceivable gift of daily attendance at Mass, of daily Holy Communion — how sadly is blurred, through habit, our clear perception of its *being* an inconceivable gift!

This deadening effect of habit on our awakeness again means unfreedom. We permit our value-responses to be hampered by the completely illegitimate power of habit. We must combat it expressly by calling to mind on all occasions how great the gift is that we enjoy; also, what our situation was before we had received it and what our situation would again be if it were withdrawn from us.

Habit can dull our sense of the horror of particular sins

Neither should we simply get accustomed to the hard trials imposed on us by God — such as the loss of a beloved person, or again, the state of spiritual dryness. We should certainly bear them in patience, but at the same time clearly perceive their character as a cross, and endeavor to discern the meaning God intends them to convey to us.

Least of all should we suffer habit to make us obtuse in regard to sin. Repeated lapses into the same kind of sin may easily dishabituate us from a keen perception of the antithesis to value it embodies: we tend to consider the offense in question no longer as "so very bad," and allow certain channels to form in our mental world through which we may all the more glibly slip into that sin.

We must fight this tendency with the utmost determination, particularly in the following way. We should never repress (that is, dismiss or crowd out from our memory) any wrong we have done, nor content ourselves with a mere passive guilty conscience, but work out an explicit and active repentance of any transgression we may have committed, disavowing our wrong expressly before God, and accusing ourselves in Confession; whereby the barrier that separates us from sin is restored, the trench we filled up when committing the first sin is dug out again, and the *grooves of sin* are prevented from forming.

Habit may lead us to consider blessings as if they were due to us

Finally, habit has also the bad effect of tempting us to regard the blessings of God as something self-evidently due to us, something to which we are strictly entitled as it were. Habit is apt to make us not only ungrateful but arrogant. The unmerited gifts that the "Father of all lights" bestows upon us we easily come to claim as our legitimate property so that, should any new benefits we covet be denied us, we shall be inclined to believe ourselves wronged. We shall deem our temporary separation from a beloved person, for instance, an intolerable hardship instead of considering what an immense gift the union of loving hearts represents in itself.

He who is truly free knows — with a living knowledge — that everything is an unmerited gift of the merciful goodness of God; that before him we are beggars devoid of any claim whatsoever.

From our very existence, our vocation, and our redemption, to every ray of the sun that enlivens us with its warmth and its luster, and to every drop of water that quenches our thirst — everything is a gratuitous gift of His inexhaustible goodness. All the truths we are blessed in knowing, all beauty we are allowed to enjoy; every moment of good health and every bit of nourishment we take —

all these are undeserved benefits in no wise due to us. How often do we misuse the gifts of God; with how much ingratitude and indifference do we requite His blessings!

Yet, as soon as habit deludes us into misjudging our metaphysical situation, as soon as (under the influence of habit) our nature represents to us any possessions or privileges we enjoy as self-evident rights, we have *eo ipso* renounced true freedom. For all subjection to illusions, and in particular, all misconceptions of our situation relative to God, necessarily imply a privation of freedom.

Inordinate shyness restricts freedom

Finally, we may set aside one more form of unfreedom: that which has its psychological source in *shyness*. This should not be confused with that virginal bashfulness which causes a person to recoil from any too spontaneous manifestation of his interior life, and frequently to blush whenever the attention of others is focused upon him. The desire to hide, in the sense of shunning publicity, is in itself a fine and praiseworthy trait. But this desire of remaining unnoticed may reach a point where it becomes an obstacle to freedom, inasmuch as it constrains us to remain in our retirement even in situations that require us to intervene openly and to profess publicly our conviction.

He who is truly free will be happy if he can escape notoriety, but will also be ready to face the light of publicity whether restricted or wide, by expressing his opinion and making valid his standpoint in words or deeds as soon as the call of God demands it.

A certain type of person, however, is forcibly hindered from doing so by his inveterate shyness. People of this kind cannot manage to contradict an assertion, though in the circumstances it is objectively necessary. They are barely able to mumble a word when asked a question; they keep an obstinate silence in company, thus laying themselves open to accusations of pride. From mere shyness they sometimes display a definitely unkind behavior. The fear of being observed makes them feel insecure to the point of a veritable paralysis of will, which in circumstances may prevent them from performing imperative duties. Confession, too, is apt to be exceedingly difficult for them owing to their inhibitions.

To be sure, shyness of this kind is a natural disposition for which the subject is not responsible; but whoever aspires to true freedom must take care not to abandon himself to it. For it hampers one at every movement as does a strait jacket, and introduces into all situations an element of superfluous complication.

A person subject to this weakness should systematically seek to overcome it by ascetical practices adapted to the purpose. He must learn to fling himself entirely into the arms of God, in an attitude of holy unconcern. Just as a man's aversion to water is best cured by his jumping into it boldly and with closed eyes, a sufferer from shyness should — in the spirit of holy obedience to spiritual counsel, preferably — force himself to jump into the thick of certain embarrassing situations. Having again and again pierced the charmed circle, he will gradually get rid of his disability and become fit to follow the call of God unhampered.

Secretiveness may diminish freedom

The fear of disclosing certain secrets of one's life may similarly depress one's freedom. True, we are wholly justified in spreading a veil over our deep inward experiences, religious or personal, and in protecting them as far as possible from profanation by an incompetent and unsympathetic public. One who is bent on divulging and publicizing everything cannot but be a superficial person devoid of the virtue of discretion.

To this, however, should be added a twofold consideration. First, we must derive no pleasure from secrecy as such, and guard against wantonly inserting in our lives a great number of secrets. Secondly, we must not lapse into the habit of entering every situation *a priori* with a fear lest something we intend to keep secret should be revealed — a warped attitude of self-consciousness that is sure to prevent us from paying adequate attention to the theme of the given situation. For instance, somebody tells us about a grave inner crisis through which he is passing and seeks our help; yet, we listen to him only distractedly, being preoccupied by the possibility that in the course of the conversation something might come to the surface that had better remain hidden.

This concern about the safety of our secrets must never become the primary category under which we consider the various situations that make up our life; for this, again, might easily develop into a cramp of egocentrism numbing our response to the call of God.

It need not be emphasized that what has been said here does not in any way apply to others' secrets, which we are in duty bound to preserve.

Only true freedom enables us to respond properly to all legitimate goods

To sum up — true inner freedom means that we have relinquished our natural standpoint and live *through Him, with Him, and in Him*. This implies an unequivocal renunciation of the basis that had formerly provided us with a sense of natural security. Egocentric biases, complexes of fear, psychic cramp as well as laxity and self-indulgence of every kind — in a word, all illegitimate preoccupations, all that is not rooted in the call of God or in the appeal of true values — must be dislodged and stripped of their empire over us.

To all legitimate interests and obligations, on the other hand, we must remain and become fully alive. Hence, true freedom is not the equivalent but the *opposite* of those stoic ideals of apathy and ataraxy which require us to become insensitive to all goods, so that we derive a sense of mastery from being subject to no obligations. True freedom does not make us insensitive to either the sufferings imposed on us or the blessings lavished upon us by God; on the contrary, because we are free from all irrelevant and illegitimate ties, everything that bears on true values has a far deeper and stronger impact on our hearts.

And, because (under the law of true freedom) we seek before all else "the kingdom of God and His justice," all natural values present themselves to our eyes against the background of the supernatural; therefore, no natural good as such can attract or bewitch us to the point of enslaving us. Its power over us does not extend beyond the limit of its relevancy as viewed in the light of the supernatural. The comparative reserve we impose on ourselves in regard to all genuine goods of the natural order has no meaning but to make us completely free for integral allegiance to the highest good. Once more, the aim is not, as with the stoic, to get rid of all attachments, but to realize one's unconditional and unhampered attachment to God.

With our entire life informed by the consciousness of "the one thing necessary," all legitimate ties will assume their proper place as assigned to them by the will of God. True freedom means that, free from all illegitimate ties, we take account of the true hierarchy of values visualized in a supernatural light, and adjust all our attachments to it.

He who is truly free "abides in the truth." He lives his life in God, before God, and on a basis derived from God. He is no longer enchained to his nature, being able to say with St. Paul the Apostle, "And I live, now not I: but Christ liveth in me" (Gal. 2:20). The free, wide, universal air of the Liturgy breathes through his life.

Freedom means ultimate truth. He who has achieved true freedom is animated by that holy courage, steeped in humility, which says — "I can do all, in Him who is my strength." Nothing can confound him, for he knows the meaning of St. Paul's words: "If God be for us, who is against us? He that spared not even his own Son, but delivered him up for us all, how hath he not also, with him, given us all things?" (Rom. 8:31-32).

11

Blessed Are They Who
Hunger and Thirst After Justice

THE Sermon on the Mount praises those who "hunger and thirst after justice," and promises them that "they shall have their fill" (Matt. 5:6). With regard to the state of mind thus glorified, we may distinguish two main types of defective attitudes.

Indifference

First, there is the attitude of general indifference: the unimpassioned dumbness of the kind of man who lacks intensity in all things. This description applies to a great number of psychological varieties. Consider the type of person who is sunk in a sort of placid inertia or the superficial mind flitting from one object to another with no genuine interest in any one of them; the seeker for shallow pleasures or the philistine established in his smug mediocrity, who shuns all greatness, all heroism, all fervor, and contemplates the world through minimizing glasses, as it were; or again, the anxious man who dreads being *seized* by any object or inflamed by any overwhelming experience — all these have one trait in common: all spiritual hunger and thirst is alien to them.

They do not really hunger, they do not strongly yearn, either for a true value or even for a subjective pleasure; they evince only a languid and conditional interest in anything. It is to such souls that the Apocalypse of St. John refers in these words: "I know thy works, that thou art neither cold nor hot. I would thou wert cold, or hot. But because thou art lukewarm and neither cold, nor hot, I will begin to vomit thee out of my mouth" (Rev. 3:15-16).

Secondly, there are those who do hunger and thirst, not, however, after justice (that is to say, after something valuable in itself), but merely after things that in some way happen to appeal to them personally. Yet these, again, we must divide into two subclasses.

"Hunger" rooted in pride and concupiscence

The first group consists of those dominated by pride or concupiscence, the slaves of sensual desire, insatiably craving gratification; the avaricious; those engaged in a passionate pursuit of honors and prestige; those covetous of power. All these are not *filled*: they hunger and thirst for that only, however, which is of a nature to satisfy their pride or their concupiscence and yet fails to satisfy them when they possess it, but stirs up their thirst the more and makes them crave for further gains or lusts, so that their lives are comparable to an incessant hunt for gratification.

In certain cases belonging to this category, what the subject so passionately desires is not personal possession or pleasure in the primitive sense of the term but an *idol* — a fake ideal — for the sake of which he even makes sacrifices and endures privations of all kinds; in other words, he displays an apparently selfless service of "higher" aims.

Yet, the hunger and thirst many people evince for the victory of these idols is again only a product of their pride and concupiscence. This type of person is apparently enthused with selfless zeal for his idol; the idol may be an unrestrained urge-gratification, an idol of anarchy or of *master morality*, or of nationalism, or one of many others.

300

I say *apparently*, for actually his attitude, though formally it can be assimilated to a selfless zeal, yet, intrinsically and as far as its essential roots are concerned, is as much manifestation of pride and concupiscence as are the more unblushing forms of those vices. Nay, to kneel to an idol born of the spirit of pride may often imply a deeper gratification of pride than the one procured by proud pursuits of a crudely personal kind. The persons in this group, then, are not beneath hunger and thirst, but they do not hunger and thirst after the right thing; they are driven by *the zeal of bitterness*, the *zelus amaritudinis* "which separates from God and leads to hell" (Rule of St. Benedict, c. 72).

Egocentric hungering after one's own happiness

The second group under this division is made up of persons revealing a subtler kind of defect. These are filled with a thirst for genuine and noble gifts of fortune. They long for success in their work, for health and wealth, for freedom and the enjoyment of all beautiful things, for the bliss of loving and being loved, for conjugal happiness: in short, for whatever blessings life may offer. They are not dull and inert, not smug and sated; they know hunger and thirst; nor do they chase illegitimate joys or crave for specious goods.

Still, what they hunger and thirst for is not justice; what keeps them in tension is not value as such; not that aspect of creaturely goods by which they glorify God. Persons of this kind interpret happiness in terms of true and valid goods; yet in their exclusive longing for happiness — the mark of their basic egocentrism — they are ultimately incapable of fully understanding the high goods of life or, in turn, of bringing true happiness to others.

This is easiest to see with reference to the good constituted by a community of love. He alone who does not primarily seek for his happiness, as such, but forgets himself in his value-response to the beloved person — in other words, he alone who is able to give himself — can love in the full and genuine sense of that term. He alone, therefore, can experience the integral happiness of loving and of being loved — the unique mutual vision implied in a deep love-relationship. Yet, in fact the same thing is true, though less strikingly obvious, perhaps, of *all* high goods of life: our possession of truth, our penetration of the world of beauty (in nature and in art), and of the world of value in general.

He who is dominated by his thirst for happiness bars himself from access to true and deep happiness. In his possession and enjoyment of any good, he fails to reach the level of depth where that good reflects the light of God and reveals its ties with eternity. He always remains stuck on the plane of the perishable. The possession of no gift of fortune can ever bring him genuine satisfaction. It is as though every good he has secured spoke to him in the end only words of disappointment: "I am not what thou seekest"; and his hunger and thirst drives him, as it did Faust, further and further across the limitless plains of breadth rather than down the deep paths that converge in the Center, where alone peace and consummate happiness can be found.

Respect for justice without hunger for it

To these two classes of men — the souls that hunger and thirst either not at all, or not after justice — the standard antithesis, intelligible even on a purely natural level, is embodied by the type of man filled with hunger and thirst for that which is important in itself, objectively valuable, and pleasing to God.

They are not very frequently to be met with — the persons belonging to this category, who in the context of every situation attend above all to the question of what is objectively valuable and what is not; who consider everything *sub specie* of this question, instead of concentrating on the gratification of their subjective needs. Now here, again, we shall have to distinguish various grades of perfection. The lowest degree of this high-minded minority of mankind is found in that class of persons, still comparatively numerous, who do take account of the demands implied in objective value and of the commandments of God inasmuch as they are anxious to avoid any conflict with His will — so far as their own conduct is concerned.

Strictly speaking, it is still the goods of this earth that constitute the object of their longing and striving; they are guided by the purpose of achieving a fine career, of increasing their possessions, of acquiring honors and consideration; they envisage marriage or friendship in the light of the happiness it may provide for them.

But their pursuit of such aims stops short wherever it might involve a transgression of the commandments of God. They display a real interest in justice, accepting it as a corrective, that is, a check placed upon their primary and proper interests. As a loyal citizen respects the laws of the State and seeks to realize his wishes strictly within the limits of legality, so these men are ready to respect the commandments of God and to confine their pursuit of happiness to the limits prescribed by them. They respect justice, but they do *not* hunger and thirst *after* justice.

Furthermore, justice merely plays the part of a corrective for *one's own* conduct. Whether *others*, too, love justice is not a question that would deeply stir such minds; they are firmly intent on safeguarding only their own peace of conscience. Certainly they accord ultimate sovereignty to the commandments of God; but they are hardly devoured with zeal for the triumph of justice as justice. To a person of this kind we may not apply the Psalmist's words: "His will is in the law of the Lord: and on his law he shall meditate day and night" (Ps. 1:2).

In his respect for the commandments of God and for the obligations ensuing from values, an element of egoism is still perceptible; it is, after all, for the sake of his own peace that he endeavors to preserve his conscience intact and to remain in accord with God. We miss in him an eagerness for value as such, an enthusiasm for the beautiful and the good in themselves, the ardent desire to glorify God solely for His own sake. He does not deeply love God, for he does not regard Him as an incarnation of all value but merely as an omnipotent Master, whose will it would be foolish to defy.

Admittedly, such a person considers the moral order of the universe as an evident and unchallengeable rule. But it interests him predominantly with reference to the question, "What is forbidden; where are the limits of my good pleasure?"; not with reference to the question, "What can I do in order to glorify God; what is in conformity with the will of God; what is implied in my vocation; given a choice between two things, which is the objectively better one and related to a higher value?"

Hunger for justice (among other ends)

Accordingly, an entirely new level is attained whenever one's interest is engaged by the valuable and the significant as such: whenever, that is, justice no longer holds the place of a mere secondary corrective but attracts man in a primary and thematic capacity and is sought for its own sake.

This is the case with persons who are deeply moved and influenced by the fact alone that something good or beautiful in itself exists; who are not concerned solely with their own profit or happiness but evince a passionate interest in things that have no reference whatsoever to their personal prosperity; who can be *inflamed* with the desire of preventing an injustice or ensuring the victory of the good.

They look upon the moral order of the universe not merely as an insurmountable legal barrier to some of their personal cupidities, but as a positive higher good, which they not only respect but cherish. An act of generous forgiveness, a manifestation of indestructible fidelity or selfless love can evoke their enthusiasm.

The criterion of objective value holds their attention, therefore, not only in ruling their own behavior but in considering that of others, too. Any wrong done by others pains them, no matter whether or not it involves any personal disadvantage for them. Any injustice, impurity, unfaithfulness or falseness they experience as an evil, whether they notice it in themselves or in strangers.

Persons of this kind we may rightly credit with a basic, if imperfect, hunger and thirst after justice. For they know the happiness derived from the victory of the good as such — happiness of a quality that no advantage, no success, no accumulation of gifts of fortune can ever procure or equal. Still, their interest in justice is only one among others; in spite of its essential primacy, it has not yet blossomed out into a devouring passion of the soul that would obscure all other desires or concerns.

Passionate, unconditional supernatural zeal for the kingdom of God and His justice

From these, again, we must distinguish those rare personalities which, like Socrates, are wholly possessed by their preoccupation with value — who consider everything primarily from this point of view and let all other points of view fade into insignificance. Here we have a true and perfect hunger and thirst after justice on the natural plane.

With persons of this category, the passion for the victory of the good has acquired an unconditional and actual primacy over all other concerns; it has become, as it were, the form of their lives. What is the objectively right, the morally good, the valuable thing? — this query controls their orientation in all situations, relegating all desire for earthly goods and advantages into the background. It constitutes the self-evident rule of their attitude in regard to all objects; and it alone can evoke a passionate interest on their part. In a more permanent and universal sense, they suffer from the ocean of injustices and wrongs that fill the world. No personal success or happiness can dull the edge of their interest in the victory of justice or soften their pain at the triumph of evil.

Men and women of this kind are in constant danger of being misjudged; they are apt to scandalize many of their fellow beings. The reason is that their emphasis on the primacy of value tends to interfere with the quest of happiness that is natural to others. Their passion for the victory of the good constitutes a virtual menace to the framework of ordinary people's lives. Their ardent pursuit of justice cannot but be misinterpreted by those enfolded in the tissue of their ego-interests.

Ordinary men will mostly try to construe the behavior of such persons of exceptional nobility in terms of some hidden *ressentiments* or other motives of disguised self-seeking — there being no other explanation for such a passionate "taking sides" that they can conceive of.

Yet, those whom the Lord in the Sermon on the Mount calls blessed are not such as hunger and thirst after justice in the sense of natural morality only, but such as hunger and thirst after the *kingdom of God*; such as "seek first the kingdom of God and His justice." What *they* seek is not merely whatever is naturally valuable and *as such* glorifies God: it is (beyond that) the supernatural life, the victory of the God-Man Christ, the salvation of souls, the growth of the Mystical Body of Christ, and man's transformation in Christ. Socrates, so nobly obsessed by his eternal quest for the naturally good, is still a far cry from St. Francis of Assisi with his insatiable hunger and thirst for the kingdom of God.

It is not enough for us to seek *also* for the kingdom of God, to labor *among other things* for the consummation of that kingdom, or to take interest in the problem of the kingdom of God occasionally only, that is, whenever it happens to carry with it a close reference to problems of our personal life. We must seek *first* the kingdom of God. Our search for the kingdom of God and His justice must be the consuming passion of our souls. The empire of Christ over our souls, as well as in all other souls, must become the paramount theme of our lives. Day and night we must be swayed by the burning desire *that God be glorified in all things*.

For such has been the way of life of the saints. They, indeed, hunger and thirst after the kingdom of God, postponing all other concerns to the *one thing necessary*. Theirs is not a limited and conditional interest in the kingdom of God, like that of the rich young man of the Gospel, who would not decide to follow Christ; they are consumed with an unlimited and unreserved longing for Him. They live up to the rule of St. Benedict, "To prefer nothing whatsoever to Christ"; they are *undivided* in the sense of St. Paul (1 Cor. 7:33).

An ardor for the cause of God that knows no defeat is what meets our eyes again and again in the lives of the saints. Take, for example, an episode in the life of St. John of God. Seeing a young man engaged in conversation with a harlot, presumably with a sinful intention in mind, the saint knelt down before him and besought him in Jesus' name to abstain from the sin he was contemplating. Indignant at such an interference with his private affairs, the lad struck him in the face, exclaiming: "Mind your own affairs!" Imperturbably, the saint tendered him his other cheek and said: "Strike me as often as you like, only do not offend God." Such was the force emanating from this serene contempt of self, this unflinching love for God and an erring fellow creature, that the young man not only abandoned his sinful project but was converted and became a disciple of the saint.

Or again, think of this scene from the life of another saint, Don Bosco. On his journey through a forest he was attacked by a robber shouting, "Your purse or your life!" He recognized the bandit's voice as that of a former pupil of his, and spoke to him, deeply pained:

"Tonio, what a dangerous path you have chosen! You must change your life; you must confess your sins." No fear for his life, no thought of himself is present in the saint's mind; he is possessed by his zeal for the salvation of his fellow man's soul and for the kingdom of God. In this case, too, the force of a holy hunger and thirst for the kingdom of God prevailed upon the sinner. A few seconds later he was kneeling at the feet of the saint, and making his confession.

Hunger and thirst for the kingdom of God is the very stigma of the saints. They all are devoured with zeal for the honor of God and filled with an unquenchable thirst to win men's souls for God. But this, let it be clearly understood, is a *supernatural* zeal, not the enthusiasm and buoyancy of natural man — a zeal that is not merely directed towards God but grounded and anchored in Him, and informed by His Spirit.

Natural enthusiasm for the kingdom of God

For there is also such a thing as a natural zeal for the kingdom of God. The fact that our *aim* is supernatural does not by itself imply that our *attitude* is supernatural, too. For one thing, a kind of natural enthusiasm about the kingdom of God is sometimes to be met with, which is likely to flare up impetuously in certain moments but will not stand any hard test. It is deficient in constancy; whenever it encounters defeat or entails the necessity of a heavy personal sacrifice, it is apt to dwindle away. It lacks both ultimate earnestness and sterling solidity.

This kind of zeal is not rare in converts, some of whom have no sooner embraced the Faith than they are busy forming grand projects about extending the kingdom of God. Such short-lived fits of pious zeal, as contrasted with that *fire* which Our Lord came down to kindle on earth, are also recognizable by the fact that they are devoid of the virtue of discretion. These enthusiasts forget that no one is qualified to labor fruitfully in the vineyard of the Lord who is not also ready to drink the chalice; they have not pondered the parable of the man who wanted to build a tower.

Aggressive, destructive natural zeal for God

Apart from that, however, we know examples of a deep and persevering zeal for the kingdom of God which is still essentially on the natural level. There have been ardent fighters for the cause of God, enduring heavy sacrifices for the kingdom of God and continuing the struggle in the midst of all adversities, yet doing so in a mood of natural pugnacity, in a hard and rigid attitude — men who have failed to grasp the parable of the wheat and the chaff.

Think, for example, of the tragic figure of Pope Paul IV (Caraffa), who was burning with zeal for the house of God, who led a life of austere poverty amidst an environment reeking with worldliness, who would not have hesitated a moment to give his life for the reform of the Church, and yet, whose pontificate was to be so unsuccessful owing to his fanaticism, his asperity, and his lack of trust, that on his death bed he declared it to have been the most unfortunate since St. Peter's. A world's distance separates his *ethos* from that of his gentle, patient fellow friar, St. Cajetan.

Paul IV's zeal was of the kind that is not anointed with the holy oil of patience; that is not transfigured by *discretio*; that is apt to degenerate into an angry zealotry devoid of all kindness and trustfulness, and to dash forward with an impetuous fury stemming entirely from the natural man.

A person inspired by this kind of zeal, though his fervor is not deprived of charity towards God and his fellow men, will hardly escape the danger of becoming a fanatic and sinning against charity. For it is rather his great passionate nature as such than a full and unreserved surrender to God that feeds the flame of his struggle for the kingdom of God. True, his entire robust power is put into the service of God; but the aspect of dying unto one's self is absent. A life thus devoted to God falls short of being a life really and truly *based* on God.

Very different in character is the gentle, radiant, peaceful flame, the wholly spiritualized ardor that burns in him rich in patience and loving kindness, who may say of himself, "I live, now not I: but Christ liveth in me." Of such men alone can we predicate, in the fully adequate sense of those words, that "they hunger and thirst after justice," and "seek first the kingdom of God."

As regards the above-described cruder type of ardent souls, they too are in a certain sense *warriors of God*; but they are bent on changing the face of the earth *by violence*, on *forcing* the victory of the cause of God, on determining "the day and the hour" according to their own counsel; hence, the havoc they work often outweighs their constructive achievements. In a sense, they undoubtedly hunger and thirst for the kingdom of God; but that hunger and thirst is warped, to a greater or lesser degree, by its all too natural motivation and style.

Humble, supernatural ardor for the kingdom of God

Contrast therewith the zeal of a St. Dominic as, on one occasion, he meets an Albigensian innkeeper who is swearing and blaspheming; instead of expostulating with the unhappy fellow, the saint kneels down beside him and starts praying, and keeps on praying throughout the night, until at dawn he finds the heretic on his knees and sunk in prayer, too. What strikes us here is the wonderful way in which patience and a tireless zeal for God and the fellow man's soul interpenetrate each other. We see a blend of discretion and ardor, calm meekness doubled with implacable strength — in a word, that *coincidentia oppositorum* which is the mark of supernatural life.

The saint is so *dead unto himself* that his solicitude is altogether borne and guided by God, who "maketh his sun to rise upon the good and bad" (Matt. 5:45), and woos our souls with inconceivable forbearance.

The fervor of the saint reveals a rhythm that can no longer be measured by natural standards. He borrows, so to speak, the rule of his being from God; and may speak with St. Paul: "Gladly therefore will I glory in my infirmities, that the power of Christ may dwell in me" (2 Cor. 12:9).

No longer do we face here the massive impetus of a powerful nature — its place is taken by a soaring tranquillity; we discern an attitude completely embedded in the peace of God; an awareness (uniting the utmost devotion to detached serenity) of being nothing but an *instrument* of God, who also disposes of ways *other* than those which this particular servant of His has devised or is pursuing, nay, who "is able of these stones to raise up children to Abraham" (Matt. 3:9), and who therefore never depends necessarily on himself. Such a man is as though he had cast all earthly weight from him. He irradiates a mild and yet resistless energy which makes all natural impetus appear as impotent weakness.

In all our search and struggle for the kingdom of God, we must again and again examine ourselves as to whether we have reached the stage of such a *supernatural* hunger and thirst. It is not enough that we should *burn*: it must be the light, serene flame rising from a heart penetrated and lit up by the love of Christ. We must examine whether our zeal is tempered with holy patience; whether we are inspired by that tender, sensitive, attentive charity which is molded by the longanimity of God.

We must question if we are proof against the temptation of endeavoring to establish the kingdom of God by assault, by trampling on our fellow men. We must keep on our guard against the delusion that the paths we have chosen shall infallibly lead us to our goal. We must bear in mind the advice St. Ambrose gave to St. Monica, at a time when her son Augustine was still unconverted, that she should speak more with God about her son than with her

311

son about God. To that advice she conformed; and we know what was to be the reward of her holy patience.

Our hunger and thirst for justice and the kingdom of God is a necessary condition of our transformation in Christ. The glow that pervades it, however, must have its source not in our nature but in Christ. "For the charity of Christ presseth us," says St. Paul (2 Cor. 5:14): meaning that it is not merely his love *for* Christ but Christ active *in* his love that fills him and urges him on — not a natural love but one that issues from his participation in Christ, and that bears a quality entirely new and *sui generis*.

We must hunger and thirst for Christ Himself

But the justice referred to in the Sermon on the Mount does not mean the kingdom of God only; in the deepest sense, it means Christ Himself. After Him, whom the Church (Litany of the Most Holy Name of Jesus) names *Sol Justitiae* (the Sun of justice), must we hunger and thirst. When our heart says with St. Thomas Aquinas, "No other reward do we desire, O Lord, than Thee Thyself," and with St. Bonaventure, "May my heart ever hunger for Thee and be nourished by Thee, whose sight the angels desire; may my innermost soul be filled by the sweetness of Thy savor and ever thirst for Thee, the fount of life, the fount of wisdom and science, the fount of eternal life, the torrent of joy, the plenitude of the house of God" — then only do we hunger and thirst for true justice.

It is, then, Christ after whom we must hunger and thirst above all, yearning for the vision of His face and saying with the Psalmist, "Thy face have I sought, O Lord, Thy face will I seek" (Introit of Sunday within the Octave of the Ascension). A thirst no earthly good may quench should burn within us for the "water, springing up into life everlasting" (John 4:14); an insatiable hunger should be alive within us for "the Bread of Life."

To all created things we must address the question of the Bride of the Canticle of Canticles: "Have you seen him whom my soul loveth?" "Our loins girt and lamps burning in our hands" (Luke 12:35), we must await the Lord. May our whole life be impregnated and ordered by the holy desire that glows in St. Thomas Aquinas' words:

> *Jesus! whom for the present veiled I see*
> *What I so thirst for, oh vouchsafe to me:*
> *That I may see Thy countenance unfolding,*
> *And may be blest Thy glory in beholding.*

12

Holy Patience

FEW virtues bear such unequivocal witness to the fact that one's life is based no longer on one's own nature but on Christ, who imparts to us His divine life in holy Baptism, as does true patience. From the mysterious words of Our Lord, "In your patience you shall possess your souls" (Luke 21:19), we may glean an initial knowledge of the greatness and significance of this virtue.

Indolence is not the same as Christian patience

Here, again, let us do away at once with a possible misconception. Christian patience has nothing in common with a phlegmatic temperament and the sluggish rhythm of life such a temperament produces. There exists a kind of people who never grow impatient and are always willing to wait — either because they need much time for everything themselves and reveal a slow pace in all their vital manifestations, or else because nothing can rouse them from their indolence nor evoke on their part any but dull and spiritless reactions.

This natural disposition is not, as such, of any moral, let alone supernatural value; rather, specifically speaking, it must be considered a deficiency. In certain situations, it may of course prove to be comfortable and helpful; but frequently it will act as a heavy impediment inasmuch as it renders all wakefulness, ardent zeal or bold determination difficult of attainment.

Such a disposition of pseudo-patience may be a symptom of deficient vitality; or again, it may flow from a certain form of self-contained animal vitality unresponsive to all stimuli of a higher order. We are thinking of that signally healthy type of persons who, owing to a dull, bovine, but all the more solid vitality, are unlikely ever to lose their temper, and in their almost vegetative calmness face the impact of all things with brazen equanimity. By virtue of their robust nerves and a false sense of security, they preserve the consciousness of having the situation well in hand even though the results they have been aiming at take long to appear; hence, they are able to wait without lapsing into impatience.

Stoic indifference is not the same as Christian patience

Nor should Christian patience be confused, either, with that equipoise based on intellectual discipline and a kind of natural asceticism which we know to be a specific ideal of Stoic philosophy. The Stoic endeavors to acquire an artificial disinterestedness in regard to all things, thanks to which nothing can any longer perturb his composure. His aim in so doing is to safeguard his sovereignty amidst all situations; for he deems it inconsistent with his dignity to be agitated and buffeted about by the blows of fate. It is, we may well say, repugnant to his pride that he should admit his infirmity and his creaturely dependence on a higher power.

The reason why he exhibits no sign of impatience is that there is no longer anything that can move him deeply or touch him to the quick, no object to which he would abandon himself with his inmost being. His patience, then, is merely a manifestation of his indifference to all things except his own imperturbability — of his *apathy* and *ataraxy*, as the Greek names go — which of necessity also implies a loss of the response to values.

It is a purely negative accomplishment bought at the cost of his renunciation of a most necessary virtue: to wit, an ardent zeal for the victory of the good. On no such foundations can we base our obedience to the call implicit in the words: "Blessed are they that hunger and thirst after justice: for they shall have their fill." Of course, he who has no vital interest in anything can well afford to wait placidly; he is unlikely ever to lose his temper, ever to press onward tumultuously, ever to grow impatient.

Buddhist placidity is not the same as Christian patience

Another attitude that bears an outward resemblance to true patience but is essentially distinct from it is typified by the Buddhist mood of an even-tempered endurance in regard to all that comes to pass. This, too, implies a capacity for waiting indefinitely without falling into impatience.

What we are faced with here is not the psychological device for ego protection that the Stoa commends under the label of *ataraxy*: it is a fundamentally different attitude to the world of real things, and hence to that eminent and constitutive aspect of natural reality, the reality of time as such. To the Buddhist, all real being is mere appearance, devoid of true substantiality. His attitude, therefore, is that of detached contemplation of reality, dispensed from all obligations of action and accomplishment.

This position of a pure spectator, unfavorable to all activity and tension — in fact involving an aversion to all endeavors at realizing a purpose — precludes the very basis on which the virtue of true patience might unfold. Certainly it also keeps out impatience in the sense, that is, of uprooting the common presupposition (the importance of reality and of tasks ordained to its shaping) for the actualization of both impatience and patience, just as a lunatic can no longer commit any sin but can no longer display any virtue either.

In other words, the Buddhist doctrine eliminates the *problem* of patience and impatience, and that in a much more formal sense even than does Stoicism. For, whereas the Stoic philosophy bears upon our attitude towards things merely insofar as they affect our state of mind, the Buddhist modifies our basic relation to the world of reality and calls in question our general obligation to do our part within its framework.

Patience is opposed to petulance and to inconstancy

Passing, now, to the description of true Christian patience, we must at once signalize two distinct dimensions in which it unfolds. We mean that patience is opposed to two moral defects: first, to impatience in the sense of petulancy or a quarrelsome and violent behavior; secondly, to fickleness and inconstancy: the tendency soon to desist from a purpose if its realization seems to require a long period of time.

Patience in the sense of an antithesis to this last-named defect is closely related to constancy; yet, it should be noted that constancy comprises other elements besides patience. Lack of constancy may be conditioned by the lack of patience; but it may also come from superficiality, spiritual discontinuity, mere suggestibility or lack of selflessness (such as is found in insufficient love and zeal). He who is wanting in constancy does not necessarily lack patience; but whoever possesses constancy also possesses patience in the latter sense.

Furthermore, patience may reveal varying shades according to the different classes of good to whose pursuit it refers. We must use different criteria in discussing patience according as the good we are desirous of (without being able to obtain it immediately) attracts us as something that just happens to be agreeable to us in some respect, or as something that constitutes an objective good for us, or as something valuable in itself, or again, finally, as something that actually bears upon the realization of the kingdom of God.

Impatience is a form of self-indulgence

Insofar as the good we are pursuing belongs to the category of *what is agreeable or objectively beneficial to us*, it will be a question of that kind of patience in which the element of constancy is less stressed. Suppose we are longing for some legitimate good for ourselves: if its acquisition is rendered difficult by certain obstacles (unforeseen ones, in particular) or is delayed too long, we are apt to become impatient. For example, if we are hungry and have to wait for our meal, or again, if we have pains and the soothing drug is not directly at hand; similarly, if we fail to receive a letter at the time we have expected it, or if somebody we are to meet takes long to appear.

Here what our impatience refers to is always the element of time. It may be the period of time that must lapse before our strongly desired good can be obtained; it may be the oppressive emptiness of a spell of waiting as such; it may be, again, the long duration of some evil, however slight.

Thus, we are likely to develop impatience if we have to endure lasting pains, a tedious conversation that tends to prolong itself, or the importunate advances of bothersome persons. In short, three varieties of evils related to time may account for this kind of impatience: delay in the securing of a coveted good; any kind of lasting unpleasantness; and the boredom inherent in pure waiting as such, especially when the thing we have to wait for may not imply a great pleasure or be highly enjoyable.

Our impatience will mostly take the form of ill humor and anger directed against somebody who is really guilty of the delay that irks us, or possibly only a scapegoat whom we arbitrarily make responsible for our vexation. But the anger of impatience need not always tempt us into reproaching or grumbling at a person; it may find some other outlet. Thus, even in this case (though the theme of constancy as against fickleness does not rank paramount here), impatience often prompts us to renounce an aim because we cannot secure it expeditiously.

This form of impatience can be subsumed under the head of letting ourselves go. In investigating the deeper roots of this inward disharmony and rebellion, we shall have to distinguish a threefold motivation which underlies it.

Impatience springing from overestimation of goods or evils

First — the interest we take in the given aim we are pursuing is apt to be an inordinate one. It dominates us too strongly and too exclusively, so much so that it may push aside our interest in what legitimately demands our primary and invariable attention. The impetuous dynamism of certain trivial and transitory or intermittent interests overlies in an inordinate fashion our awareness of God, of our fellow man, or of other high values.

Our impatience, then, is a sign that we are still too much absorbed in outward concerns and momentary aims; that they are too important to us and at a given period occupy our field of attention too extensively. It is a sign that we have not yet arrived at the right gradation of our interests, which should take into account the objective hierarchy of values. Such is the case, particularly, insofar as our impatience corresponds to our endeavor to secure something agreeable or a practical necessity of the moment.

If, on the other hand, it is a question of enduring some outward evil (be it bodily pain, illness, annoyance or just boredom), our impatience betrays on our part too strong a reference to what gratifies and what is contrary to our inclinations, a certain softness and lack of distance in regard to our body or to the impact of disagreeable sensations as such. A kind of inner servitude, too, is implicit therein; a false reliance upon an imaginary *normal* situation exempt from evils, which we take to be self-evidently due to us to the point of making ourselves dependent upon it. Hence, whenever an evil, as is inevitable, befalls us, it cannot but arrest our attention wholly and turn it away from the higher values that approach and address us — from the love, for example, which other persons manifest for us, or above all, from God, who, we know, means to tell us something even by the evils which He permits to visit us.

In sum, the impatience we have in mind here expresses an automatism of self-indulgence, an attitude of uncontrolled allegiance to one's own nature. It signifies that one has not yet succeeded in establishing that distance between one's responsible self and one's unredeemed nature with the desires and impulses it harbors, which is a basic aim of all ascetical practice.

The Christian, however, must never abandon himself to the autonomous pull of his nature. Though he may pursue all kinds of licit objects with intensity, he must never install such a pursuit, as it were, in sovereign omnipotence. He must keep it always dependent on the sanction of his central personality and confront it with the rest of his valid interests — particularly, his tasks and duties. Yet, most people are prone to obey the impulse of their nature without submitting it to any control, on certain points at least: whenever, notably, the object pursued is not by itself illicit or fraught with sinful implications.

Impatience rooted in an illegitimate sovereignty of self

But there is a second root of the impatience we are now dealing with. A certain type of persons — who may be described as impatient *par excellence* — are apt to lose their temper not merely when obliged to wait for the realization of an object they passionately desire, but whenever they face a delay in the attainment of an aim they have once set up, even if that aim is a neutral or unimportant one as far as its actual content goes. They allow themselves unreservedly to be swayed by the weight which the thing they have proposed as an aim acquires simply on the strength of having been so proposed. The very failure of this chosen aim to find immediate accomplishment strikes them, in their obstinacy and arrogance, as an insupportable affront.

This unlimited subserviency to their own nature also creates in them an egocentric attitude, for they ascribe to any pursuit they are engaged in an importance over and above everything else. They recklessly disregard other people's needs.

This second source of impatience, then, lies in one's attribution of an unrestrained *formal sovereignty* to one's nature. That is why typically impatient persons are likely to manifest such a self-indulgence and lack of discipline not merely when they have to endure a strong pain or the frustration of a violent desire, but whenever *any* purpose of theirs suffers a delay in its realization.

Our impatience is a mark that we have quit the status of *habitare secum*, and are swimming with the current of a predominant impulse or the formal automatism of our nature. There is an analogy with a fit of anger in this type of self-importance, or even more closely, with an act of frivolous swearing and cursing. We then, giving free rein to impatience, stake, as it were, everything on one card and give away our whole person without the sanction of our central and responsible self.

In other words, and viewed from a different aspect, we sever the fundamental link with God that defines the constitution of our life as a creature. This second factor — the tendency to erect any purpose, once it has been set up, into a formal absolute — is more characteristic of impatience than is the first-named one, the inordinate stress attached to certain of our pursuits, for it bears a direct relation to our scorn for *time* as a dimension of objective reality independent of our will.

Impatience rooted in a prideful denial of our creatureliness

Hence, we may proceed immediately to the third and most basic factor of impatience: the assumption of a false position of *supremacy* above the universe, the non-recognition of one's own creatureliness, limitation, and finiteness. Thus illegitimately arrogating to himself a status of sovereignty, the subject clings to the illusion of being a lord over time. He would extricate himself from all dependence on the *causae secundae*, on the order and interaction of created causes. The impatient man experiences any obstacle to the progress of his pursuits as an injurious interference. He revolts at the check placed on human volition by the interval of time that must lapse between conceiving and attaining a purpose, and would conjure up the intended effect by a mere *fiat* — the likeness of a divine command.

Herein lies the primary and deepest sinfulness of impatience. It contains an act of *hybris*: an illusory negation of our human situation and the substitution of a supra-human position of mastery. For the givenness of time, with the ineluctability of waiting it involves, represents a specific limitation of our creaturely existence on earth. We are faced with a course of happening, a sequence of events in time, which is not of our making and which we cannot alter except within certain rather closely set bounds. We may not subvert its essential structure.

We have to reckon with a space of time interpolating itself between our volitive decision and the fulfillment of our purpose, and accept it as a reality imposed by God.

The impatient man insists on ignoring this reality; he behaves as though it were in his power to make the trees grow more quickly and the earth revolve more quickly around the sun. Impatience renders us hard, unkind, masterful, and in some circumstances, violent. It always implies a loss of depth.

Impatience differs from our legitimate deep yearning for the realization of a noble good

It should on no account be confused, therefore, with a consuming desire or a feverish yearning as such; with the deep tension of the soul towards a noble good, which may cause us to live through the minutes of waiting as though they were hours. Our fiery inward motion towards a high aim ardently longed for — such as seeing again a dearly beloved person after a long separation, embarking on a beautiful journey which fills us with magic anticipations, or the inception of a gratifying work which our mind has been passionately engaged in planning — should be well distinguished from impatience proper.

To be sure, even such a fine aspiration must never dominate us to the degree of a complete possession. We must always place everything in the hands of God — "Not as I will but as Thou wilt." But this inward tension towards a high good is something valuable by itself; it lacks the distinctive marks of impatience proper — it does not generate anger, scowling indignation, masterful rebelliousness. It should — it can — be informed and transfigured by an attitude of serene humility which keeps us constantly aware of the truth that the fulfillment of any aim of man is a gift of God.

This kind of tension differs from impatience proper by the fact, also, that it presupposes a high good as its object, whereas the impatience we have in mind mostly refers to trivial goods. Moreover, the former's sphere of objects includes goods whose realization is entirely independent of ourselves, whereas the latter bears more generally on such goods as we can at least help to bring about.

What irritates an impatient person is, above all, the too sluggish effect of his orders, his actions, his attempts to influence men's behavior or the development of a situation. His ill temper expresses a revolt against the relative and limited character of his effectiveness.

The foregoing analysis of impatience may help us now to describe the virtue of Christian patience, insofar as it refers to the securing of pleasurable goods or ego gratifications as such, to the endurance of pains or boredom, or again, to the attainment of legitimate natural goods of the higher kind.

Patience respects the hierarchy of goods

The patient man, in the first place, preserves the right order in the scale of his interests. The requirements of the moment, no matter how imperious, can never displace or overshadow his attention to higher values. The intensity of his attention to a thing will not be determined by its dynamic appeal, its aggressive presence at a given moment or the noise with which it is advertised, but by the objective weight of its content. His emotional accents are ordered in a fashion proportionate to the objective order of values. He possesses a prompt readiness to bear any cross that he cannot avert from himself without injury to charity or infringement of some duty.

He has the art of waiting, and he knows that, though he might justly reproach somebody with having caused him a needless loss of time, a loveless rebuke sometimes amounts to a greater evil before God than a measure of lost time. Our neighbor's sluggishness, too, as his other awkward and annoying traits, belongs to the things we must bear in charity.

It is because he generally refrains from letting himself go that the patient man achieves this order. He maintains himself at a certain distance from his nature and its stirrings. Even when intensely set upon attaining a purpose, he does not lapse from the status of *habitare secum*. He watches lest he overestimate a thing merely because he is striving after it at the moment. He is on guard against delivering himself over to the autonomous logic of that striving which tends to impart an undue weight to any chosen aim merely on the strength of its being chosen.

Patience never pursues limited aims inordinately

In the second place, he never engages himself totally for a partial aim — which means that he never becomes blind to the consideration he owes to others, restricting his vision to himself and his own affairs as an exclusive whole. He knows that such a total engagement is illicit; that God demands of us a confrontation of all things with Him and with one another. Still less would he push such a total engagement to its extreme limit, at the cost of sacrificing even his own important concerns of another order. He would not stake everything on a card, to the point of dissolving his fundamental nexus with God — as the Flying Dutchman who, impatient to round a cape more rapidly, wagers his soul thereon; or as Esau who sells his birthright for a mess of pottage.

Though we are at liberty, and in certain cases, in duty bound to do everything in our power to attain a legitimate purpose, no obstacle and no ill-success must ever be allowed to throw us off our balance. The true Christian is determined to preserve in all circumstances his open and devoted attitude to God: that basic constitution of his soul which guards him against ever losing hold of the *habitare secum*; for he is well aware that he cannot remain in communion with God except in such a state of composure and self-possession.

Patience recognizes the sovereignty of God over time

Above all, the true Christian never pretends to a false position of supremacy over the universe. Indeed, Christian patience issues from *religio*: the consciousness of being a creature of God, whose property we are, without whom we can achieve nothing, and in whose hands all our endeavors, actions, and accomplishments are placed. The true Christian assents to his creaturely dependence on God, and consciously derives from it the informing principle of his life. "My days are in Thy hands" (Ps. 30:16).

He knows that God is also the Lord over Time; that He has assigned to the course of events its temporal extension; that we must recognize the interval of time that separates the taking of a decision from the reaching of the intended aim as a reality willed by God: "All things have their season: and in their times all things pass under heaven" (Eccles. 3:1).

He loathes the *hybris* which lies in the pretension to override the autonomous operation of the *causae secundae* and to secure effects by a mere *fiat*. That is why patience in this first and inferior sense, too, is an integral component of a life centered in Christ. It contains a specific response to the omnipotence of God and to our absolute dependence on Him, as well as an acceptance of our creaturely finiteness. He who has patience abides by the Truth; the impatient man, posing at least in a partial sense as though he were God, submits to the bondage of the illusions of pride.

Patience is appropriate even when pursuing high goods

The second form of patience belongs to a much higher level. It refers to the realization of things valuable in themselves, and in particular, the spreading of the kingdom of God. It is in this context, again, that the second dimension of patience — that which makes it akin to constancy and perseverance — assumes its full significance. Here it is a question of intrinsically noble and all-important aims, whose furtherance we *ought* to seek with impetuous zeal. The moral advancement of ourselves and of others, the triumph of justice, the dissemination of the true Faith, the conversion and the progress of a soul specially entrusted to our care — these, to be sure, are things for which we must yearn in our every fiber and strive after with our whole being; our concern for these can never be too intense.

Woe to those who can take but a moderate and conditional interest in these aims. With a burning eagerness should we engage in their service; for "the kingdom of God suffers violence." So far as these things are concerned, it would be wrong of us to take our time. Rather we should emulate the response of St. Matthew the Apostle to the inexorable call, *Sequere me*: "Jesus... saw a man sitting in the customhouse, named Matthew; and he saith to him: Follow me. And he arose up and followed him" (Matt. 9:9).

Thus, too, did St. Peter and St. Andrew leave their fishing nets and all their work and, without glancing back, follow Christ. No less immediate and wholehearted was the response of St. Anthony, who, upon hearing the words of the Gospel, at once went to live as a hermit in the desert. No less eager and integral, many centuries later, was the response of St. Francis of Assisi.

And yet, even in this zeal, holy patience is absolutely necessary, and an essential part of holiness. For holy patience means our response to the truth that it is *not we* but God alone who determines the proper day and hour for the fruitful performance of certain actions and even more exclusively, the ripening of our seed and the harvest of our labors.

The rapidity of our immediate response may sometimes differ in our inward dedication and our outward actions

A keen distinction must be made between our *inward dedication* to God and to His kingdom in ourselves and in others, and our *action proper* (on ourselves and on others). The call of God once perceived, our response cannot follow quickly enough. We should immediately and unconditionally respond to the *sequere me*, giving ourselves to God without demur or reserve as did Mary: "Behold the handmaid of the Lord: be it done to me according to thy word." All hesitation here would be a perilous error.

But this unhampered inward dedication to God does not by itself involve the performance of all single acts which it entails in a general and essential sense. Particularly does this caution apply to extrinsic and public action, that is, the works of the apostolate.

Certain saints — among them, as we have seen, St. Francis and St. Anthony the hermit — immediately drew the full consequences from their conversion. But this is a great privilege of grace. Our sense of discretion must enlighten us about whether we may take the decisive step with its full implications at once, or had better remain for a period in inward maturing. There exists a danger of skipping over necessary stages.

Sometimes it also happens that a sincere but not so highly privileged Christian, instead of awaiting a more unmistakable and concrete call of God, overreaches himself in a kind of natural enthusiasm and anticipates certain acts fraught with grave obligations, without being able to posit them with a true inward decisiveness. Many converts immediately want to enter a religious Order, though they lack actual vocation and have not measured the whole significance of such an enhanced dedication to God.

The Church knows this danger; that is why she requires an adequate interval of inner maturing for all great steps in religious life. Unless a particular and a rare grace makes up for it, man needs an appropriate space of time for all deep and great things.

The attitudes deep things require cannot, in general, attain their complete validity and reality except after a period of organic development, whose length varies greatly according to each case. For every deep, fateful *word* there is a *fullness of time* in which alone it can be legitimately and fruitfully spoken. Anticipate it hastily by acting without discretion, and your utterance of it will be shadowy, devoid of maturity, and invalid. Again, let the "destined hour" pass unused, and you will no longer be able to speak that *word* except in an empty and purely formal fashion.

It is touching to read how the chamberlain in the Acts of the Apostles hastens to be baptized by the deacon Philip; for him, thanks to a special grace of God, the destined hour — the *fullness of time* — was at hand there and then. But the Church by no means modelled her general practice in admitting converts upon these cases, recorded in apostolic times, of an instantaneous and definitive conversion.

On the contrary, in the first centuries she imposed on the catechumens a long course of preparation through the successive stages of which they had to pass before being admitted to Baptism. Even today, every adult baptism must be preceded by a certain period of instruction and maturing. As regards the preparation for monastic life, the Church only allows the taking of temporary vows at first; final vows require a preparatory stage. Nor does she admit a definitive private vow of virginity without an antecedent temporary one. Thus, in forming these decisive resolutions concerning our inner and personal life, too, we must exercise holy patience, and accord time the significance in human affairs with which God has invested it.

Evangelization also calls for patience

Even more does the same caution apply to the apostolate or our activity devoted to the winning of other people's souls. Anxious as we may be at once to communicate the Truth we have unmeritedly received and to light up other souls with the fire Christ has kindled in ours, we must always bear in mind that we ourselves cannot fruitfully sow before the divine seed has unfolded to a certain degree in our own souls — which, again, means a period of maturing.

Undoubtedly a special grace of God may overrule this, too; but generally speaking, a time of silence must precede the time to speak. St. Paul, after his conversion, lived in silence for several years before he started his work. Nay, the Savior Himself only began His public activity after thirty years of complete privacy; not that He, in whom the fullness of Divinity resides, needed a process of maturing: but He chose to give us an example of the rhythm which God has imposed on human life.

Notwithstanding all our zeal, then, we must observe the obligation of patience even as workers in the vineyard of the Lord. With careful discretion we must try to perceive the striking of God's own hour for our work to start in His vineyard rather than insist, in a spirit of natural enthusiasm and impatience, on determining it by ourselves. Suppose we are animated by a glowing zeal: if, at the same time, we have patience, we may be infallibly sure that we no longer live by our nature but by a supernatural principle of life.

To be sure, we are not in all circumstances obliged to make the time of our action dependent on the degree of receptivity we may suppose to exist in the souls we deal with. There are cases when, with St. Paul, we must set forth the truth *opportune, importune* ("in season, out of season"). Yet, even then, we are not relieved of the duty of patience; for St. Paul says further: "Reprove, entreat, rebuke in all patience and doctrine" (2 Tim. 4:2).

Still more is patience our duty in regard to the blossoming of the seed which we are allowed to sow in the Lord's vineyard. As Pascal wrote, "Christ wills us to fight with Him, not to conquer with Him." We must be humble enough to renounce any pretension to determine ourselves the time of the harvest. While doing everything in our power to hasten the extension of the kingdom of God for which we are working, we must let God alone decide when He shall grant it.

Even in cases when our business concerns some object eminently pleasing to God, which indeed we ought to pursue with consuming zeal, we must not cease saying, "Not as I will but as Thou wilt." At the start of his activity, St. Dominic lived for four years among the Albigensian heretics without converting a single one of them. Yet, he became neither impatient nor discouraged; he did not give up his effort. By the end of his life, he and his sons had converted sixty thousand people. It is in this higher sphere that the second dimension of patience — the aspect of perseverance and indefatigable zeal — reveals its full importance.

Holy patience frees zeal from impatience

Once more, we encounter here the fact, repeatedly stressed in the foregoing pages, of an organic mutual union on the supernatural plane between aspects apparently antithetic. The nearer we draw to God, the more we see develop in ourselves a *coincidentia oppositorum* — a reconciliation between two equally valid demands which seem to imply an opposition or at least a tension.

It is only on a basis derived from Christ that we can achieve an accord between these two attitudes: hunger and thirst after justice and holy patience. In the natural framework, zeal appears inseparable from impatience.

But the saints accomplish the miracle: on the one hand, they say with the Apostle of the Gentiles, "The love of Christ presseth us," and live up to the message of Christ, "I am come to cast fire on the earth. And what will I, but that it be kindled?" (Luke 12:49); on the other hand, they await in holy patience and inward peace the time when God shall choose to manifest the fruits of their labors.

What holy patience expresses is a living recognition of the truth that the Lord God alone can bring forth the fruit; that, even in this highest sphere, man — with whatever blessings of grace — can do no more than disseminate the seed he has received from God, thus establishing the conditions for the operation of grace in his fellow man's soul. As St. Paul puts it: "I have planted, Apollo watered: but God gave the increase" (1 Cor. 3:6).

Holy patience is an ultimate act of surrender to God

Holy patience, seen from another angle, embodies an ultimate act of our surrender to God, and *therefore* a status of consummate self-possession. For only in the measure that we have surrendered our inmost being to God do we possess ourselves. He who has holy patience has accomplished the process of dying unto himself, and entered the peace of Christ which "surpasseth all understanding." "In your patience you shall possess your souls" (Luke 21:19).

In holy patience, we become children of Him who with inconceivable longanimity "maketh his sun to rise upon the good and bad and raineth upon the just and the unjust" (Matt. 5:45) and who does not weed out the cockle but sorts the chaff from the wheat at the harvest only.

In this sense, holy patience may be described as a sister of wisdom and of contemplation. As these virtues cause us to consider and appreciate everything in a perspective centered on God, thus evoking to the full the beauty and depth of all things, so also in the attitude of patience we emphatically *let God act*, thus allowing all things to unfold from above — as proceeding from their Origin — and by so experiencing their operation again render to God what is God's.

Holy patience is the fruit of faith, hope, and charity

Holy patience is a fruit of faith, hope and charity. Faith teaches us that God the universal Lord is also the Lord of Time; that He alone appoints the proper hour to everything; that we must place the success of all endeavors, including such as are eminently pleasing to Him, in His hands; that we must believe in the possibility of success though no pledge of it be visible to the human eye; and that consequently we must labor for the kingdom of God whatever the odds seem to be.

Hope keeps us from getting discouraged in spite of all failures and all delays in achieving success and expects "against hope" everything from the goodness of Him "with whom nothing is impossible." Charity impels us to love God and His holy will above everything, and prevents us from expostulating with Him or renouncing our work in His vineyard on account of any defeat sustained. Particularly is patience an offspring of charity insofar as it is assimilable to constancy and perseverance – an offspring of the charity, that is, which in St. Paul's words "beareth all things, believeth all things, hopeth all things, endureth all things" (1 Cor. 13:7).

The fruits of holy patience, finally, are meekness and that inner peace of Christ "which the world cannot give." Patience, then, is closely related to the very flower and perfume of Christian life.

Holy patience acknowledges man's creaturely status

It constitutes one of the basic traits that distinguish a true Christian *in statu viae*, in the sense even that it connotes in a twofold fashion a specific reference to the character of earthly existence as a *status viae* — a journey destined to lead us to our ultimate goal. First, it expresses our assent to our creaturely and finite condition, and more particularly, our response to the significance of time as an aspect of the divine plan of creation, as an essential constituent of the *status viae*, the world of "that which passes" in contradistinction to eternity. Second, patience represents a basic condition for winning through to our eternal salvation, since it implies a capacity for waiting without despairing of our effort for the kingdom of God, an attitude of perseverance in the midst of all obstacles and all sufferings, an intrepid hope for victory, and a humble but sustained preparation for eternity.

Not only is patience an indispensable virtue; beyond that, it discloses a formal apprehension of the basic condition of *status viae* and of the relation between terrestrial life and eternal life. Thus are the mysterious words of Our Lord on patience related to these others: "He that shall persevere to the end, he shall be saved" (Matt. 24:13).

He alone who possesses patience — encompassed by disappointments, worn down by defeats, painfully aware of the narrowness of the road to salvation — can yet give proof of the constancy demanded by God, and hold on to the *one thing necessary* with a devotion not only unflagging but ever increasing. In him alone can the hunger and thirst after justice unquenchable on earth — which is Christ Himself — and the undying fire that the Lord came down to kindle, burn throughout his entire life. Only the patient man, who lives by Christ, can persevere unto the end: "In your patience you shall possess your souls" (Luke 21:19).

13

Blessed Are The Peacemakers

PEACE is a basic word of the Gospel; it occupies a central place in Christian revelation. Indeed, it is the primal word addressed to mankind by the message of the New Covenant: "Glory to God in the highest: and on earth peace to men of good will" (Luke 2:14). Again, in His parting speech to the disciples, Our Lord says: "Peace I leave with you: my peace I give unto you" (John 14:27).

The object of the Christians' Advent longing was, above all, the Messiah, the bringer of peace, who would heal the strife of the world; the strife that, more tangibly than anything else, expresses the disharmony of a fallen creation. A touching desire and hope for peace cries out in the vision of Isaiah the prophet: "The wolf shall dwell with the lamb: and the leopard shall lie down with the kid. The calf and the lion and the sheep shall abide together: and a little child shall lead them" (Isa. 11:6). And the Psalmist sings: "Justice and peace have kissed" (Ps. 84:11).

At Christmas, the Church hails the Savior as *princeps pacis*, Prince of Peace. In the High Mass of earlier times, the faithful before receiving Holy Communion exchanged the *osculum pacis* — kiss of peace — as a sign that all discord among them had been obliterated. On Holy Thursday, in the Liturgy of the Washing of the Feet, the Church sings: "Let malicious upbraidings cease; let

wranglings cease. And may Christ, our God, be in the midst of us."
Pax is the motto of the Benedictines; *Pax et bonum*, that of the
Franciscans.

Peace is a central theme of Christian revelation

No one who does not love peace as a high good, and whose
heart is not scorched with pain at the sight of strife or by the
thought of disharmony, has ever really understood the Gospels or
can ever truly love Christ. Our imitation of Christ — and the more
so, our transformation in Christ — necessarily involves a love for
peace, a concord of hearts, a horror of all forms of discord, disunion,
and dissension.

Nothing evokes more constant blame from St. Paul in his
epistles than the *dissensiones et contentiones* arising in the Christian
communities. Again and again he urgently admonishes the faithful
to keep peace among one another: "I beg of Evodia and I beseech
Syntyche to be of one mind in the Lord" (Phil. 4:2). It is a specific
stigma of abysmal separation from God to maintain a quarrelsome
and cantankerous attitude, a morbid delight in conflicts and bick-
erings, a perverse pleasure derived from disharmony.

However, an essential love for peace and aversion to strife is not
enough. It does not by itself vouch for our being actually able to
behave as peacemakers and to overcome the temptations of enmity
in the evolving situations of life. The immanent logic of various
events and relationships, with their autonomous demands and the
interests implied in them, are only too apt to entangle in discords
and conflicts even such men as essentially love and seek peace.

To begin with, we must make a fundamental distinction. The
dangers to peace arising from a multiplicity of social contacts and
oppositions require a different treatment, according as they originate in a situation whose theme is supplied by our interests as such
(even though taken in a wide sense) or in a situation in which we

are striving for some high objective value — in the extreme case, the kingdom of God itself. Let us next consider the first type of situation.

Dangers lie in a peace rooted in our own interests

There is a kind of people who, though by nature peaceloving and far from quarrelsome, are so touchy as to feel insulted and wronged on the slightest provocation. The sense of being injured will incite them to acute outbreaks of anger or to more latent reactions of ill temper and sulking, and thus involve them in clashes and disagreements.

Against this susceptibility, which is wholly incompatible with a life conceived in the spirit of Christ, we must wage a relentless fight. Whenever we feel offended, we should at once examine before God whether we are not really only indulging our susceptibility, without having suffered any objective wrong at all.

Perhaps the "offender" has done no worse than tell a truth which irritates us because it is unpalatable to our pride. Or again, it may be our jealousy that makes us fretful. Our egocentric squeamishness, too, may often present other people's actions or utterances in a false and distorting light. Sometimes, again, it is our distrusting disposition that incites us to look for a sting of insult or an edge of malevolence in whatever people say. It may also happen that a stranger's words unintentionally strike upon a sore spot in our emotional system, an inferiority complex for instance. We then feel offended and unjustly put him down as tactless.

In view of these numerous possibilities of error, it is a Christian's duty always to examine, with a wholesome mistrust of himself, the objective side of the question when he feels wronged or insulted. Confronting his feelings and their occasion with God, he must attain to a freedom of mind enabling him to ascertain, with his vision unblurred by any subjective biases, whether he has suffered any wrong in the objective sense of the term. If this proves not to be the case, he must wholly and thoroughly dissolve his rancor — have it "shattered upon Christ," as the Rule of St. Benedict puts it — and approach the misjudged "offender" with particular friendliness.

A great many people shirk this duty because, in their general reliance upon their nature, they implicitly trust its reactions and unquestioningly interpret their moods as the index of an objective fact. They deem their subjective state of mind the more sensitive instrument, whose findings cannot be tested and corrected by the clumsier methods of intellectual analysis. This overvaluation of one's subjective impressions is a tremendous mistake; for in truth, their legitimate role is not to outrun or supersede objective thinking but merely to provide it with initial stimuli and with part of its materials.

We must forgive all objective wrongs we suffer

If, on the other hand, an objective wrong has been inflicted upon us, we must endeavor truly to forgive it. To be sure, the experiences we have had with a person (inasmuch as they disclose to us the general defects of his character, apart from our personal interests on which they have happened to impinge) may warrant on our part the drawing of certain consequences.

We may decide no longer to trust him. But we must not let a state of conflict establish itself. In confrontation with Christ and remembering His words, "Love your enemies: do good to them that hate you: and pray for them that persecute and calumniate you" (Matt. 5:44), as well as the many wrongs we have ourselves perpetrated upon others, we must truly and honestly dissolve all rancor, all embitterment, all enmity.

We must definitively expunge the debt our offender has contracted towards us. We should face him in serene charity, without any sullenness or cramped self-consciousness. The negative consequences we cannot help drawing in his regard must, without any trace of irritation and asperity, exclusively imply a noble and serene sorrow.

Ignoring objective evils does not establish true peace

Moreover, the attitude of rancorous enmity is not the only antithesis to the Christian spirit of forgiveness. Another attitude opposed to it is that of simply ignoring the wrong inflicted upon us, as though nothing had happened. This aberration may result from laziness, from faintness of heart, or from a sickly, mawkish clinging to outward peace. We hold our comfort too dear to fight it out with our aggressor; or again, we feel terrified at the thought of any tension or hostility, and fear lest a sharp reaction on our part should exasperate the adversary; or perhaps we yield just out of respect for the abstract idol of peace.

This is a kind of behavior far remote from the genuine love of peace or from a genuine spirit of forgiveness. It can never achieve the true harmony of peace, but at best a superficial cloaking of enmity, a mood of false joviality which drags our souls towards the peripheral.

Also, people who behave thus fail to consider the moral damage that their supineness is likely to inflict on others. It is very often necessary to draw a person's attention to the wrong he has done us — in fact, necessary for his own good. To pass over it in silence may easily encourage him in his bad dispositions.

But we cannot reproach him to good purpose — that is, without provoking strife, unless we have ourselves attained to that serene attitude cleansed of all impulsive resentment; in other words, unless we have truly forgiven him. When we have risen above the narrow logic of the situation and ceased to face our fellow man as an antagonist with whom we are locked in strife on a battleground;

when we have acquired in Christ that holy freedom, that humility before God and the human soul — His image — which confers upon us a sovereign detachment from the immanency of the situation, then only shall we be able to correct our offender in a manner really conducive to his good. Again, when we have risen above the mood of regarding his awareness or admission of his wrong as a satisfaction to ourselves, then only shall we be able to ponder judiciously and to decide pertinently whether or not it is necessary for us to remonstrate with him for his good.

Peace between friends requires that all wrongs be confronted and forgiven

All this refers to our disagreements with comparative strangers, persons with whom we are not linked by close bonds of friendship or love. Where such bonds do exist, the case is essentially different. Here it is strictly required by the *logos* of the relationship that our partner shall recognize and regret the wrong he has done to us. Here we must not quit the common level on which we are joined with him, for by so doing we should act against the spirit of the relation that unites us, and indeed, implicitly disavow our friendship. In this case, the other person has a legitimate claim to the continuance of our being partners.

Most certainly we must forgive him, too; but here we must desire that he recognize and repent of his wrong, not merely for his own good but for the sake of our relationship itself — of the restoration of that intimate union of hearts which essentially demands the clearing up of all misunderstandings and the healing of all disharmonies. For that union of hearts is an objective good which we must guard and cultivate, and which imposes certain obligations on us.

True, here as in other cases we must not let the autonomous mechanism of the situation run away with us and must carefully refrain from repaying an injury in kind. As victims of an aggression *hic et nunc*, we must — under these specific conditions, too — detach ourselves from the situation of the moment and answer all gestures of irritation, all moral blows, with kindness and charity only.

Yet, here we can on no account content ourselves with an act of inward forgiveness: at the proper moment, we must in love draw our friend's attention to his wrong and maintain our desire for his redressing it. However, we cannot do this in the right way before we have truly forgiven him, before all bitterness and irritation on our part have yielded to a purified, unselfish pain.

Our admonition should not bear, properly speaking, the note of a reproach. It should rather be in the character of a humble and amicable exposition of our grief, a gentle invitation to our friend to consider the matter in a valid perspective and to collect himself anew, taking his start from that incident on a plane of spiritual earnestness and love. Nevertheless, it remains true that the full harmony implied by the objective *logos* of the relationship is not reestablished before our friend has understood and admitted his wrong, until he has asked our pardon for it.

To insist on this condition is not to postpone but to uphold the value of peace. By so acting, we still keep aloof from strife. Our demand that our friend revise his conduct springs from our longing for an unsullied harmony and an enduring intimacy in our relationship with him; that is to say, for peace — perfect and undisturbed.

Ways of dealing with violations of our rights

The safeguarding of peace presents an even more difficult problem when the offense in question is not merely one against charity — an act of unkindness or discourtesy, say — but an infringement of our rights, which we cannot refrain from defending. To take a few typical cases — somebody assumes a patronizing attitude towards us and would illegitimately restrain our freedom of decision or is about to appropriate something that by rights belongs to us, or again, arrogates to himself certain claims on third parties who are really under our supervision: gives orders, for instance, which it is our exclusive right to issue, and the like. We cannot brook such things in all circumstances, let alone permanently; yet on the other hand, our insistence on our rights obviously entails the danger of dissension and conflict.

In such cases, we must begin by forming an unbiased view of the matter, so as to ascertain whether, objectively speaking, it is really we and not the supposed offender who is in the right, or whether the problem is not a complex one, with rights and wrongs in some way divided. On no account must we simply abandon ourselves to the natural automatism of our defensive reactions. Before deciding on our course, we must arrive at a detached judgment, which we should maintain as though it were not ourselves but a third party whose rights were encroached upon.

When, in confrontation with Christ, we have acquired an inward readiness to renounce the right thus challenged, should that be God's will, when we have performed the mental act of putting ourselves in our antagonist's place and envisaging the matter with roles reversed, as it were, and so gained the conviction that the right we attribute to ourselves is indubitably valid and not merely a putative one — then only have we created the necessary condition for taking action in defense of our claim, should further considerations decide us to do so.

Sometimes, the situation being unequivocal, it is very easy to arrive at such an impartial and sober judgment; in other cases it is apt to be more difficult. Having made sure, then, that our rights have in fact been interfered with, we must further examine before God whether the right in question is of such objective value as to justify us in risking peace in order to vindicate it. To a Christian, the mere fact that some right of his has actually been tampered with does not by itself constitute a ground for conjuring up the danger of strife. In many cases, it may be more pleasing to God that we renounce our legitimate claim; particularly, sometimes, in controversies concerning our material possessions.

On other occasions, however, it may be our duty to take up the challenge: thus, for instance, when somebody is bent on curtailing our legitimate freedom of decision. In such cases we must oppose the encroachment, and therefore cannot shape our conduct with a view to avoiding a conflict at any cost. For our freedom is not ours to give away; it has been entrusted to us by God as an essential instrument for us to do His will.

Even in the midst of conflict, we must remain eager for peace

Still, whenever we have to defend our rights, we must do so in such a fashion that we avoid getting caught in the self-enclosed automatism of conflict. Steering clear of all irritation and malice, we must always preserve that inner freedom — that spirit of detachment — which looks upon everything in the perspective of God's will and of objective right, as though the rightful claims of an unidentified third party, and not one's own, were concerned.

As a first step, we should try amicably to persuade the offender to desist from his course; if this attempt fails, we should ask a third party to arbitrate the conflict. Again and again we should endeavor before God to evoke in ourselves that charitable attitude, free from all admixture of personal enmity, which makes us experience discord as a grievous thing.

We ought never to think ourselves dispensed from the essential pursuit of peace — justified, that is to say, because of the unreasonableness of our adversary, in giving free rein to the autonomous dynamism of conflict and tolerating in ourselves an essentially inimical attitude toward him.

Every further step imposed on us by the aim of protecting our right should impress us with pain. We must never lose our awareness of a fundamental duty of charity in regard to the person in question.

Never, in particular, must the immanent evolution of the conflict (which, once set in motion, cannot be stifled so far as the objective order of events is concerned) come to determine our moral orientation. We must not be seduced into enjoying the wrangle or the blows we may manage to inflict on our antagonist. In other words, it is not enough that we ponder the matter before God at the beginning of the struggle, so as to decide whether we should embark upon it at all. During its entire course we must continue confronting ourselves with God again and again, lest its autonomous dialectic should become the law of our inward attitude.

Even though engaged in a conflict we could not possibly avoid, we must remain *lovers of peace*, who would at any time prefer a peaceful solution to a victory over the adversary obtained by means howsoever licit.

Oversensitivity to one's rights can be a vice

Notwithstanding the fact that in certain cases we are bound to defend our rights, we must never allow our mere displeasure at being threatened in some right of ours to become a motive of our conduct. There are people who feel upset by the fact alone that their sphere of rights is trespassed upon, though the offense referred to some good about which they care but little. Such a person will, for instance, if living in a tenement house, resent his neighbor's indulging in some noisy occupation (beating carpets, say) outside the hours legally reserved for such work, not because he is sensitive to noise but in view of the disrespect for his rights involved in the thoughtless neighbor's behavior. Or again, it arouses his anger when a stranger takes his seat in a railway carriage, though there be other empty seats nearby just as convenient.

Such people, then, jealously watch over the respect shown to their rights as such, independently of the interest they actually take in the good that their right happens to cover in the given case. The fact is that they attach an immense weight to the question of whether their person is treated with due esteem, which implies a scrupulous respect for their rights. Thus, if some property of theirs is stolen, they are much less grieved by the loss of that good than shocked by the sacrilegious interference with their range of rights. Hence, it does not lessen their fury if, owing to insurance, they suffer no material damage through the theft.

Something of this abstract sensitiveness about one's rights is present in practically all of us. The saints alone are entirely free of it. However, it is inconsistent with the *ethos* of the true Christian and should be diligently repressed. For, apart from its constituting a specific source of discord, it obviously harbors a residuum of proud self-assertion and of petty self-importance.

This attitude, again, must be precluded from contributing to the motivation of our conduct and tinging our state of mind in cases when we are compelled to resist an aggression. Even should we deem it necessary to uphold some right of ours merely in order to curb the insolence of a reckless aggressor and prevent the establishment of a precedent that would place us in a false situation relative to him, we must remain inwardly free of that sensitiveness concerning our rights, and make our claim valid in a manner as though it were somebody else's.

Cowardly acquiescence is not the love of peace

Of course, as has been pointed out above, a spineless disposition to abandon one's rights is no more in keeping with the true love of peace than is the obsession with one's rights as warned against here.

Not to defend one's rights, out of sheer cowardice or love of comfort, has nothing to do with the true spirit of peace. For these chickenhearted characters who would swallow any insult do not derive the principle of their conduct from a response to value; it is not the true value of peace that attracts them. They automatically obey the inclination of their nature, to which it comes easier to yield a right or to lose a possession than to sustain any conflict.

Not unlike a suggestible person who without critical reflection adopts alien opinions and outlooks just because he is exposed to their contact, these weaklings surrender anything for the asking, not on the ground of any conscious deliberation or of any reasoned conviction that would make them prefer surrender to strife as the lesser evil, but because they succumb to the dynamic superiority of others before they could even make an express decision. Such are the helpless "softies," pushed aside or exploited by anybody coming their way, incapable of opposing any resistance (independently of any question of value, nay, even of the question as to pleasantness and unpleasantness), a defenseless prey to any attack.

The kind of peaceable souls we have just been describing lack that basic response to value which is a prime condition for all true love of peace. They are unable, therefore, to ponder the essential problem as to whether their yielding does moral damage to the aggressor or not. For this, too, we must examine before God — in addition to the question as to the value of the threatened good — before we decide between offering resistance or abstaining from it for the sake of peace. Our renunciation may encourage the offender in his unrighteous course, and habituate him to disregard the rights of others to the detriment of many, and above all, of his own soul.

Even in conflict we must maintain inward peace

It is clear, then, that true love of peace cannot dispense us from fighting for our own rights. There is no commandment enjoining man to behave peacefully in all circumstances and to abstain invariably from struggle and strife. It can be our duty to defend some right of ours.

Yet, "blessed are the peacemakers" implies two demands upon us: first, that we shall not decide to engage in a struggle unless, having examined the case *in conspectu Dei* and in a state of full inward peace, we are convinced that it is our duty to uphold our right.

Secondly, that even in the course of a conflict which we had to take upon ourselves, we shall abide in a state of inward peace; that our attitude shall always remain a detached one, undefiled by bitterness and rancor, connoting no enmity but, on the contrary, charitable kindness towards our adversary; that we shall experience the conflict as a great evil, as a heavy cross we have to bear in pain.

In other words, so far as our state of mind is concerned, we must wage the conflict as though we waged it not. During all its phases, without ever allowing ourselves to be submerged by the blind automatism of strife, we must keep alive in us the longing for peace and, as far as our duty to right permits it, the immediate readiness for peace.

The spirit of peace may sometimes call us to fight for the kingdom of God

So much for the case where we must protect our rights against an aggressor. Let us turn now to the other type of situation: when we have to take our stand in defense of an objective value as such — in the supreme case, the kingdom of God itself. Here, evidently, to evade the struggle is much more difficult. For, mindful of the words of Our Lord, "I came not to send peace, but the sword" (Matt. 10:34), we should be warriors of Christ. The holy Church on earth is called *ecclesia militaris* ("the Church militant"). We cannot at the same time hunger and thirst after justice — an inherent basic attitude of the true Christian — and be at universal peace with the doers of evil and the unjust. The meek St. John the Evangelist goes so far as to advise the faithful against greeting heretics (2 John 10-11).

How are we to reconcile our character as a *miles Christi* (a "warrior of Christ"), who in St. Paul's words shall proclaim the divine truth *opportune, importune,* and intrepidly oppose or even combat evil, with our love for peace and our eagerness to avoid all strife?

In order to solve this difficulty, we must first of all understand that an outward truce with evil — that is to say, a passive toleration of all objective wrongs, an attitude of silence and of letting things pass which in some circumstances has the appearance of consent and sometimes actually results in consent — can never derive from a love for true peace. For the real value of peace resides in its being an outgrowth of love and an expression of genuine harmony.

The unison we pretend to establish with evil — the attitude of coolly allowing a power of wrong to unfold — neither rests on actual love nor reflects true harmony. Rather it is a product of weakness and involves a defilement with evil, a participation in the wrongdoer's guilt. Through our feeble submission to evil we merely increase the disharmony that lies in evil as such and aggravate the discord that is implied in all evil, in all wrong that offends God: a discord deeper than the one implied in the sheer fact of conflict, however fierce.

It is, on the contrary, our struggle against evil that must be recognized as a necessary consequence of a true love of peace, inasmuch as it also means a struggle against discord and an endeavor to limit its empire.

It is not in our power to prevent evil from raising its head at this or that point, but we must strive to restrict its reign within the narrowest limits possible or else we connive at its expansion and thus actually contribute to the evil of discord. God alone, not a peaceable behavior as such, is the absolute good. Our fight for the cause of God is necessarily also a fight for true peace, seeing that the latter coincides with the victory of the kingdom of God. Therefore, the spirit of peace which must animate a true Christian will never restrain us from fighting for the kingdom of God. It will determine a basic difference in quality between that fight and any merely natural conflict.

Our struggle for the kingdom of God must not be mixed with self-interest

In this context, again, a true Christian should first examine whether his zeal for the kingdom of God is not alloyed with some sort of personal interests, for that might easily be the case. Only too often, the fact that something objectively valuable is at stake provides us with a pretext for ruthlessly safeguarding our own interests on the strength of their incidental nexus with that higher cause. That is why it is necessary, before taking action, to consider the elements of the situation carefully before God — mistrusting our nature and the possible subconscious currents in our mind — and to probe our motives until we have gained a full certitude with regard to their character.

Be it understood: the fact that, in a given case, our struggle for the kingdom of God happens to converge with the line of our personal interests need not — nay, in certain circumstances, must not — prevent us from conducting that struggle to the limit of our forces. But neither must that fact be allowed to tinge in any way, to modify the quality of our combative attitude. We must carefully keep one thing apart from the other, and never for a moment stick the pretentious label of a *fight for the kingdom of God* on what is really an action meant to subserve our own welfare. In no wise must our pure, selfless, serene zeal for the kingdom of God be contaminated with the base coin of self-assertion.

We must not even struggle as if it were our own cause

Nor is that all. Even though we are standing for the kingdom of God, with no trace of personal preoccupations tarnishing our zeal — though we were acting perhaps, in effect, against our personal interests — the *ethos* of our struggle might still be overlain with aspects that render it closely akin to a conflict waged on behalf of one's own interests but under high sounding watchwords.

Thus, this is the case if we wage the fight for the kingdom of God after the fashion of a fight on our own behalf, making it *our cause* in a qualitative sense, conducting it, as it were, with the massive reaction of our nature. Many men, even good men, pursue an aim conceived purely in terms of objective value, simply because *they* have set it up as an aim and devoted themselves to it exactly as though some private and passionately desired aim were at stake. Entirely subject to the sovereign automatism of their formal purpose, they conduct the struggle with all their natural register of moods; with all the harshness, bitterness, irritation, and petulance of one who is bent on asserting himself.

To fight in this way is incompatible with a true love of peace. Our fight for the kingdom of God must be not only motivated but informed by our response to value lifted to a supernatural plane. Its spirit must be derived not from our own nature but from God. This will find its main expression in our constant endeavor to fulfill St. Augustine's demand: "Kill the error; love him who errs."

While passionately combatting an injustice, attacking a false doctrine, struggling to save a fellow soul, or pitting our forces against an expanding evil, we must never lose our living charity for the sinners and the misguided, but always remain solicitous about *their* good, too. Our very indignation, our tireless resistance, our stubborn advocacy of the good, our inexorable opposition to evil — these must, in all their phases, be permeated by the light of love and thus cleansed from all acrimony and fanaticism.

We must remain continually aware of the dangers inherent in struggle as such

The danger to be feared is that we might possibly assume such a truly Christian attitude when engaging in the struggle but desert it later, succumbing to the autonomous dynamism of hostility. That is why it is so important for the *warrior of Christ* again and again to actualize before God the meaning of his fight and to soften his heart in a supreme love for God, beholding his antagonists as brethren gone astray. He must always remain aware of the danger inherent to all fighting and never regard combative action as a neutral instrument which one may use freely if only it is ordained to an aim pleasing to God.

On the contrary, our activity with all its details must be altogether directed and colored by an ethical conception informed, in its turn, by our aim: the glory of God and the eternal welfare of our fellow men. This kind of fight must be widely different, not merely as regards its object but also as regards its formal character, from a fight waged in a natural spirit and destined to protect our interests.

In particular, we must guard against placing ourselves on a level with the adversary and from being infected with his spirit and morality. It must be an unequal fight — with a sharp contrast between his and our motives, principles, and methods. For our fight for the kingdom of God is by the same token a fight for true peace, whereas the fight of the children of the world is a fight for something that essentially implies strife and disharmony.

The "peace of Christ" is inner peace

Two further supports must be mentioned on which to found the right attitude of a lover of peace engaged in fighting. One is patience, of which we have treated in the preceding chapter, the other is inward peace. The lover of peace preserves his patience while waging a struggle. He *lets God decide* about whether he shall himself live to see that struggle crowned by victory; he conducts it without that violence which is the infallible mark of impatience. For he only fights in order to serve God and therefore with a complete detachment from self.

In accordance therewith, inward peace is the central condition for abiding by the spirit of peace in the midst of an indispensable struggle for the kingdom of God. Of this second dimension of peace we shall have to speak now: the peace whose possession is most necessary for the true Christian and to which Christ was eminently referring when He said: "Peace I leave with you: my peace I give unto you: not as the world giveth, do I give unto you" (John 14:27).

Lack of inner unrest is not necessarily the peace of Christ

We shall only do justice to the full importance and value of peace if we realize that the peace Christ came to bring was, above all, inward peace. Let us state at once that here, too, apply both antitheses: that antithesis between peace and discord, and between true peace and false peace. The absence of all inward unrest is by no means invariably a good. It is a good on the condition only that it comes from a harmony with objective good and expresses a response to Truth. Sated contentment or a peace of mind due to thoughtlessness or illusion, is not a good but an evil — no matter how pleasant it may subjectively feel.

It must be emphasized, however, that this false peace differs radically from true inward peace objectively grounded, not only in view of its ultimate worthlessness but also as regards its experienced quality. The relevant question, then, is not "How can we avoid all inward unrest?": it is, "How can we find true inward peace?"

What we have said in reference to outward peace also holds true in the present context: not peace as such, but God, is the absolute good. The only decisive question always remains this — "When are we united to God; when do we behave in a fashion pleasing to God?" And the distinctive high value of true peace lies primarily in the fact of its being the fruit of a true union with God and an expression of the right response to God.

The value of an attitude depends on its adequacy as a response to a good

The value of an attitude depends on whether it embodies an adequate response to a genuine objective good — to what is truly valuable in itself. Hence, it has to be judged by the two following criteria. The important thing is, first, whether in a given case our will, our joy, our enthusiasm, our longing, our love (or our sorrow, our indignation, our fear, our repulsion) is each directed to an object to which such a response is proper and due. Malicious joy, delight taken in another's misfortune is bad; delight experienced at the moral progress of a fellow being is good. Enthusiasm evoked by an idol constitutes a negative value; as a response to a true good, it itself is a valuable thing.

Moreover, it is from the object that the attitude derives not only its moral *sign* but its distinctive note and quality. We know nothing definite about the specific quality of an act of love or of fear, of a mood of joy or enthusiasm, until we know the object to which it is directed.

Its value lies secondly in its consonancy with the hierarchy of values

The value-test of an attitude lies, *secondly*, in whether the intensity of our response, the role which an object plays in our soul's life, is consonant with the objective order of values. Thus, our joy about someone's conversion should be greater than our delight in a brilliant intellectual achievement.

Above all, what is intrinsically important or noble should delight us more than what is merely agreeable to us: for example, we should rejoice at having found God more than at having gained some earthly treasure.

Hence, it follows that so long as we have not found God it is good for our spirit to be restless. Suppose the mere possession of earthly goods could satisfy us to the point of undisturbed happiness: this would mean a counterfeit happiness, a false harmony, and therefore a negative value. To be sure, we have seen (in Chapter 11) that earthly goods never can really gratify our longing; but the illusion that they can do so is obviously worse than valueless.

Inner peace is possible only in God

So long, then, as we are separated from God, as we have not found Him and are not reconciled with Him, we *should* have no peace. Blessed are the Advent souls, unsatisfied in the world, awakened to the truth that God alone can give us true peace, witnesses to St. Augustine's, "Restless is our heart until it reposes in Thee." Unhappy, however, are the restless who find not God, though He has spoken to us; who flee communion with God; who refuse due response to the fact of our redemption by Christ.

Those who are content in this world are farthest from God

We must not seek peace for its own sake, and on no account must we seek any and every kind of peace, but seek God and content ourselves with that peace which He alone can give our soul. Those restless in the world are nearer to God than those satisfied in the world. For the former at least take account of Truth insofar as they (in this fundamental sense) give the world the response due to it, and experience the objective evil of separation from God subjectively, too, as the evil it is. But they are unblest insofar as they do not recognize the *whole* Truth but pass by the true metaphysical situation of man — and, in particular, the radical change it has undergone owing to the Redemption — without yielding to it the right response.

Our transformation in Christ necessarily implies true inward peace. Yet, those are most remote from God who possess a false peace; those who, absorbed by purely terrestrial goods, are sated and content without God; those who smugly reject the knowledge that no creaturely thing can ultimately quench our thirst; those who escape being disquieted by the incertitude of the future and the impermanency of all earthly things, because they are too busy with the concerns of the moment ever to collect themselves at all. They live thoughtlessly as though this life were never to end; as though the warning which the holy Church addresses to us on Ash Wednesday, "Remember, man, that thou art dust and unto dust thou shalt return," had no validity for them.

Some of them squander away their lives in shallow pleasures; others, again, are so engrossed in their daily concerns that, though not leading an agreeable life at all, they simply find no time to stop and think. The complete enslavement of their attention to the practical task immediately ahead deprives them of any leisure for feeling their want of peace. Like beasts of burden, they tread along their path in dull monotony, without ever becoming sufficiently awake to feel distressed by the meaninglessness of their lives.

Those who sense the disharmony of the world are closer to God

By comparison with them who have peace in this sense, those who sense — and suffer from — the disharmony inherent in a world severed from God are by one degree nearer to the truth and thus to God Himself. Those who are searching restlessly and ceaselessly for true happiness; who are disappointed by every earthly pleasure or possession which would masquerade as an absolute; who are disturbed by the idea of death; who feel secure neither in themselves nor in the world; who face the future with anxiety, and are deprived of peace by their worry about whatever they love — they at least experience the insufficiency of a world grounded upon itself alone.

Just because they vaguely feel, without correctly interpreting it, the disharmony implied in their separation from God, they are no longer so widely separated from God as are those entrenched in a false peace.

Those who consciously suffer from estrangement from God are closer yet to Him

Even closer to Truth are such as, while equally lacking peace, consciously and explicitly *trace* their want of peace to their disunity with God. Such are those who are not without belief in God, yet keep on doubting; who hear the call of God but are reluctant to part with illicit joys; who are dragged to and fro between God and the world; who, held by the spells of sin, would yet wriggle themselves free; who, were it but possible, would fain serve two masters.

These are the souls that most deeply *experience* disharmony, are most restless, and are most tormented by their knowing no inward peace.

The objective fact of their disunity with God is unquestionably a terrible evil, but the fact that it impinges upon their minds in the form of distress and anguish — robbing them of peace — is highly valuable, for it forces them into an awareness of Truth by one degree less indirect than is present in those who merely suffer from the immanent disharmony of the world without viewing it explicitly in terms of a disjunction from God.

They at any rate surmise the bliss that lies in a union with God; they recognize the seat of true peace and the central cause of their want of peace. They have taken profit from their trouble to the point of laying bare its real root. They have advanced as far as to evince an express yearning for God, though they still feebly evade a clear and unequivocal decision for God. Of such a kind was the tribulation St. Augustine suffered before his conversion, the unrest of which he was to give so moving and magnificent an account in his *Confessions*.

Inner peace comes only to him who attains full reconciliation with God

Inward discord, as we now see, is not an absolute evil but an adequate response to the world taken in separation from God; it cannot and must not be overcome except by man's awakening to the Truth and his adequate response to the fact that beyond and above all the disharmony of the world, God the infinitely Glorious and Blissful One, who is Love, is enthroned. It will disappear when man becomes aware of his metaphysical situation, particularly as modified by Christ's redemption of the world.

The nagging unrest of him who doubts and of him who writhes in the fetters of sin, the most deeply painful experience of unrest will dissolve as soon as he achieves an unequivocal surrender to God: peace will come to man when he lets himself fall into the arms of God and — submitting to the grace that makes him into a member of the Mystical Body of Christ, whose sins are washed away by the Blood of the Lamb — attains to a reconciliation with God.

Every one of us feels something of this same unrest, whenever he is aware of deviating from the paths which God has proposed to us; whenever his conscience warns him of a separation from God. No sooner do we turn back and renounce what has been separating us from God than our unrest commences to dissolve; but until we have repented of our wrong and been forgiven by God, our peace will not be completely restored.

Inner peace requires a unified life ordered to goodness

The first and most obvious mark of inward peace, then, is a formal unity of our essential direction of life; an absence of different basic directions at loggerheads with one another; a liberation from unrest and incessant searching; the integral ordination of our interests and pursuits to an ultimate life-purpose.

But this formal unity — this inner coordination and convergency — is not all that inward peace implies. It also implies a unity with *the good*; a participation in the harmony implicit in the good as such. No matter how integrally (in a purely formal sense) we give our attention to what gratifies our pride and our concupiscence — without ever flinching from this our course; without being haunted by any pangs of conscience — we still live in a state of disharmony and can never taste true peace, which emanates from the intimate beauty of values.

All attitudes opposed to value carry in them a germ of discord, a principle destructive of community. In values alone dwells a *virtus unitiva*. They alone, therefore, can fill us with true concord and harmony, which is a positive state of the soul, implying far more than a mere absence of instability or inward division.

Clearly, nothing could be more unlike true peace in its quality than the state of mind characteristic of high pride. The proud man, self-contained and seemingly free from all inner contradiction as he may be, through his fierce contempt for objective values inevitably becomes tainted with the disharmony attached to all negation of the good.

Inner peace also requires a personal relation with God

Yet, even our participation in the good does not by itself give us what may *most properly* be called inward peace; for the latter requires our incorporation, not only in the realm of values and their harmony, but in *the living God*, in the holiness of the Almighty Lord, who is the Good *per se* and who reveals Himself in Christ.

Inward peace, at its highest, means even more than our participation in the light of values, our reception of the tranquillity and simplicity conveyed by their power, our being integrally permeated with the tone of their accord and harmony. It means, beyond that, that clarity and limpidity of the soul which nothing except a real link, a personal communion, with the thrice Holy One can accomplish in the soul; that enlightening of which the Prophet Isaiah says: "Arise, be enlightened, O Jerusalem: for thy light is come, and the glory of the Lord is risen upon thee" (Isa. 60:1).

To sum up — true peace, the peace Christ means when He says, "My peace I give unto you," includes three main aspects.

First, a more formal one: a state of inner concord and unity takes the place of strife and division among conflicting orientations, of indecision concerning the ultimate directions of life. By contrast to an unappeasable disquietude — a fidgety groping for what might prove to be *the real thing* and the secret of true happiness — there is the valid recognition and enduring possession of the aim that makes life worth living; the state of resting in an ultimate which gives to everything else its meaning and renders all further search unnecessary. It is the attitude which fills the soul of Simeon when he exclaims: "Now Thou dost dismiss Thy servant, O Lord, according to Thy word in peace: because my eyes have seen Thy salvation" (Luke 2:29-30).

True peace may only be established on the highest good

The second main aspect of true peace refers to its *objective foundation*. The good in which we repose must be of a nature to justify this attitude of ours. It must in truth be the highest good: a good that, once found, really does render all further quest superfluous and inappropriate. This principle of objectivity — a general presupposition, strictly speaking, of all valuable attitudes in man — is what prints upon true peace the seal of validity and sets it apart from all kinds of illusory peace based on this or that deception. And the highest good, which alone can validate our peace, is also the only one that can *satisfy us completely.*

True peace involves our participation in the harmony of values

Finally, true peace implies a *participation* in the *immanent harmony of values.* When truly at peace, we are illuminated by the light irradiating from values; whereas our surrender to what panders to our pride and our concupiscence is bound to darken us inwardly. It is here that we touch the nerve of positive peace and gain sight of its proper quality.

By its incorporation and its habitation in the realm of values, the soul becomes, as it were, wide and luminous, soaring and lithe as these values. Its participation in the good opens it up to the *virtus unitiva* of values, and thus infuses into it a new principle of unity and harmony.

The spiritually unprivileged — whether depraved or merely primitive or obtuse — and those entirely concentrated on what is gratifying to their desires, do not know this peace. They allow themselves to be filled by something that, notwithstanding the moments of pleasure it procures, is utterly devoid of this principle of intrinsic harmony, which liberates and at the same time collects the soul, takes all harshness and cloddishness from it, and adorns it with a luster of supple serenity.

For what subserves the mere aim of gratification cannot give more than a dull pleasure, behind which lurks a sense of surfeit and inanity, and which renders us egocentric and heavy. The pursuit of mere subjective gratification condemns man to ever increasing emptiness and bluntness.

Wickedness is the antithesis of true peace

Even more glaring is the contrast between the last-described aspect of true peace and the inward complexion of the wicked who, in their spasm of pride, do not merely ignore the world of values in the sense of a blind indifference but scorn objective value and defy God in an attitude of hatred and resentment. These unfortunates are ridden by what might be termed the counter-principle to peace; they carry in their souls a poison which represents a radical antithesis to the immanent harmony of values. They incarnate the spirit of discord and actually hate true peace: it might be said that they live *at war with true peace*.

Whereas the slaves to dull concupiscence may typify the state of a false peace, characterized by the absence of true *concordia* — of the luminous harmony inherent in true peace — the mental complexion of the proud haters of objective value (the state of mind epitomized, at its highest, by Satanism) embodies the qualitative opposite of true peace. Men of this kind absorb and assimilate as it were, the immanent disharmony of all typical negations of value, and appear incessantly to work at the decomposition of their own souls.

True peace comes from intimate communion with God

Yet, true peace, the peace of Christ, contains more than the harmony we owe to our participation in the realm of values: it connotes, as its consummation, that entirely distinct supernatural quality which arises from our *communion with God* alone, "through Him, with Him and in Him."

Just as the world of the supernatural beauty of holiness towers high above all natural values — as a thing of unimagined novelty and greatness by contrast to even the highest natural beauty — so an unmeasurable gulf yawns between the immanent harmony of all values and the infinite harmony of Christ the God-Man. Only think of the peace displayed by a lofty figure of antiquity like Socrates! Plato's wonderful dialogue (the *Phædo*) portrays him, two hours before his death, peacefully meditating on the immortality of the soul, awaiting death in placid composure as the most important moment of life, serenely aware of the metaphysical situation of man (as far as it is knowable to our natural faculties), rejecting all suggestion of flight as injurious to the State.

And compare with *that* noble sight the peace of the Christian saints! Francis of Assisi, say, who, almost blind and his body on the verge of collapse, composed his jubilant *Canticle to the Sun*; or again, the behavior of the martyrs, facing a horrible death by torture, in holy peace and filled with celestial joy. Witness the epistles of the apostolic Father of the Church, Ignatius, or the record of St. Agnes' words.

Different from all merely natural peace, however perfect, is the peace emanating from the saints: this blessed harmony entirely *sui generis*, this flowering of the supernatural life implanted in them by Baptism; this soaring peace resplendent with Redemption and ringing with the note of victory over the world, which could never arise from their mere participation in the intrinsic harmony of values but alone from their harmony with God the thrice Blessed.

Peace through our being "sheltered" in the living God

In close connection with the peace of such communion with God, we perceive one more mark of true peace, which is a state of "being sheltered" proper to the soul that rests in the living God. In contradistinction to the metaphysical precariousness of the state of man left to himself, to the anxiety that must fill everyone who draws the full consequences from the concept of a world without God, to the fearful unrest oppressing one who has awakened to the metaphysical situation of man unreconciled with His Creator —

and knows "how terrible it is to fall into the hands of the living God" — he who is redeemed by Christ experiences that he is sheltered in God.

The world of values, the realm of impersonal ideas, cannot relieve us of the unrest that arises from our anxiety in facing the dark gate of death, from our concern about everything we love, from the irremediable insecurity of our fate. But he who takes shelter in the infinite love of a personal and almighty God may say with the Psalmist: "But I have put my trust in Thee, O Lord. I said: Thou art my God; my days are in Thy hands" (Ps. 30:15-16). He knows that God loves all those who are particularly dear to him infinitely more than he could love them himself; that "the very hairs of their heads are all numbered." He has received from Our Lord's mouth the words: "Fear not, little flock, for it hath pleased your Father to give you a kingdom" (Luke 12:32).

Indeed, let us imagine even a condition in which no evil would threaten us any longer and in which we might eternally contemplate impersonal values; a condition like dwelling in the *heaven of Ideas* which Plato puts before our eyes. Such a mode of being would still carry with it an ultimate note of forlornness and anxiety. In this apersonal world, we should still be abandoned to ourselves and closed up in our finiteness. We cannot be sheltered as finite persons, except in an infinite *Person*, who alone can fully comprehend us and lift us from the state of dereliction that is inherent in our finiteness. Only a personal face-to-face relationship with the infinite person of God can make us participate in infinite being. The almighty God alone can thus hold and sustain us so that we may say to Him: "Into Thy hands, O Lord, I commend my spirit."

Deep peace may yet be disturbed by lesser disharmonies

So much, then, for the essence and the aspects of true inward peace. Every living member of the Mystical Body of Christ, aware of Redemption and in the state of grace, possesses this true peace. Yet, although to the redeemed is given peace in the basic metaphysical sense, on the plane of their human existence they still may be inwardly torn and experience disharmonies.

Only a false response to our metaphysical situation can deprive us of peace essentially; but various false attitudes to purely creaturely things may still disturb the harmony and damage the peace of our souls. Even though the adequate basic response is firmly established in the concept and the conduct of our life, its victorious extension to all single departments thereof and the concrete realization of everything it implies will still mean a further ascent to higher religious levels. This is precisely the course we must follow in the process of our transformation in Christ; a course which also implies a strengthening and a qualitative enhancement of the basic response itself.

So long as we do not live integrally by Christ and in Christ, we may possess metaphysical peace to a certain degree and yet, on the plane of human relationships, suffer many disturbances of our concrete psychic peace, which may even adversely react upon the permanent state of our soul and diminish its harmony and integrity. Thus, it may happen to us to be torn between two great affections which, though neither of them is bad in itself, are yet incompatible with each other. Many a one, again, falls a prey to disharmony because he has chosen a career which is either altogether unsuitable for him or in which he does not feel in his right place.

There are, further, those who lapse into a state of inner discord as a consequence of having repressed a number of deeply stirring experiences instead of dealing with them in the clear light of consciousness and thus disposing of them as a source of trouble. Such persons often suffer from inferiority complexes or psychic spasms of various kinds. Their souls are caught in a state of disorder; they are full of inner contradictions. Their interior is darkened with unfreedom, lack of peace, and painful tensions. They torment themselves with unnecessary problems or fears. They feel, as it were, ill at ease with themselves; they are at odds with themselves.

As a specific factor of disharmony we may recall here that excessive self-observation — which has been treated in Chapter 4 — a reflective over-concentration on one's self, which prevents all true contact with the object and destroy the power of experience. Persons of this type can never stop looking at themselves; they always contemplate themselves from the outside, as the central object in their field of vision, which they restlessly scrutinize now from one angle, now from another. Sufferers from hysteria furnish the most characteristic cases of this kind of disorder.

Only surrender to God can heal lesser discords

This psychic lack of peace, too, can only be healed by forces derived from our surrender to God. To be sure, one can be originally free from the illness described above without being religious. There exists an unreflective, uncomplicated, "natural" kind of man, who, blessed with a happy disposition and fortunate conditions of life, goes his way unhesitatingly without ever becoming a prey to that habitual psychic disintegration — although, adhering to a purely human plane he cannot (as we have seen) possess metaphysical peace.

But his is a harmony of a merely accidental kind, apt to collapse in the face of any serious test; nor can it, in a qualitative sense, be called true harmony at all, for the latter implies more than a mere absence of psychic disorder. This relaxed, healthy flux of life reveals at best the breadth, not the depth of true harmony. Such persons are mostly childlike, deficient in consciousness; they are far from knowing the positive peace of an inward order and true simplicity.

Above all, there is no possibility for them to overcome inner discord, once it has arisen on a mere natural plane. There is no way back to a lost ingenuousness, childlikeness or naturalness.

The disturbance evoked by conflicting experiences cannot be overcome except by their confrontation with God (from which, as we know, results their effective confrontation with one another, too); by an attainment of full consciousness before the face of God, which renders even the most hidden chambers of our heart penetrable to the light of Christ — the serene light that clarifies and brightens up all things.

Whatever is cramped, repressed, entangled, unsettled in us must be spread out before Christ and put up to His judgment, and hence receive its valid solution from *His* spirit. Our failure to examine and set right these things must be made good; whatever works mischief in the obscure corners of our soul must be brought to light and, as it were, be "shattered against Christ."

In the humble attitude of a surrender to God animated by supernatural love, all inner discord finds its solution. Then will not only all disharmony vanish but true positive peace become free to take up its home in the soul. It is the supernatural peace which flows from our "sharing in Christ," and which the Church in the Litany of the Sacred Heart calls *pax et reconciliatio nostra* ("our peace and reconciliation"); the indestructible harmony derived from our resting in the victorious power and the all-pervasive light of Him by whose grace "Night shall be light as the day" (Ps. 138:12). Peace will then fill our soul without barrier or obstacle, lending it that serenity which is an unmistakable mark of the saints.

In addition to the above-discussed *habitual* forms of our lack of peace, we must note certain more *transitory* forms. In these derangements we have to distinguish different elements.

All heinous attitudes destroy peace of soul

We begin with the gravest one — that which constitutes a material, intrinsic antithesis to peace as actually experienced. What is meant here is a specific type of disharmony, distinct from the general aspect of disharmony which is inherent in all sorrow, pain, and displeasure, and which may engender lack of peace but does not involve it of intrinsic necessity. (For one may feel a deep sorrow while being entirely at peace.) The disharmony we have in mind here bears a characteristically unhealthy note suggestive of inner strife and decomposition.

Once more, a distinction imposes itself: that note of decomposition may reveal a specifically *poisonous* or a specifically *oppressive* tinge. The former belongs to morally reprehensible attitudes only, but not to all of them. It should not be confused, again, with the general aspect of disharmony attendant on all sin as such, which is a consequence of our separation from God and finds its expression in our guilty conscience.

The specifically "poisonous" experience of disharmony which concerns us here is always present in a certain class of attitude, even though the subject may not evince a guilty conscience at all. It is a never-absent concomitant of hatred proper. All heinous attitudes exude, as it were, a venom which is responsible for this corrosive experience of disharmony. To be sure, the hater would apply that venom not to himself but to the thing he hates; yet, whatever satisfaction he may derive from thus mentally injuring and corroding the object of his hatred, that venom inevitably affects — eats, as it were — his own soul. The state of mind into which we are driven by hatred, vindictiveness, envy, jealousy or malicious pleasure necessarily embodies a radical antithesis to true peace — and that in a sense more specific than the one implied by sin and our separation from God as such. So long as we harbor this venom in us we can certainly never attain true peace.

Depression engenders disharmony in our soul

The second variety of such an intrinsic disharmony, with its specifically dark or dismal tinge (as distinct from the tinge of *poisonous virulence*) accompanies all forms of the *depressive* states of mind. It need not originate in any morally reprehensible behavior or intention. With its leaden atmosphere of gloom, it exercises a suffocating rather than a corrosive effect on our soul and our interior life. It might be compared to a kind of mildew blighting our entire mode of experience. Its action is, if not a poisoning, a palsying one — with the subject playing a much more passive part than in the case of disharmony issuing from hatred.

Whereas, in our heinous attitudes, we in a sense produce ourselves the venom whose toxic effects we cannot escape, the darkness of such depressive states of mind we suffer as an affliction imposed on us entirely from without.

Excitement and agitation disrupt our peace of soul

The second, more superficial, antithesis to inward peace consists in a formal — rather than intrinsic — derangement of our psychic order. It attaches to the various types of excitement or agitation.

By this we do not mean, of course, that inward tension which is inherent in every ordination to a future aim: that is, in every volition, in every anticipation of a joyous event, in all expectation and hope, in all longing and desiring. Tension in this sense, though it undoubtedly contains in contradistinction to the purely contemplative states of mind (such as the meditation of a truth, the delight taken in present beauty, the experience of loving attention to a person) an element of unfulfillment, is not necessarily opposed to inward peace.

Even less do we mean by *agitation*, that inward tension and intensity which goes with every keen, alert or important experience, whether contemplative or active — as distinguished from relaxed states of mind, devoid of all stress of activity, whether purely immanent or transient, and best typified by recreation. The spiritual tension involved by all experiences in which high values move us or in which we respond to them — a tension that, far from disappearing, shall reach its apex in eternal beatitude — obviously implies no opposition whatsoever to inward peace. Rather, it belongs to the very consummation of that peace.

What we are speaking of, then, is agitation in the narrower and more trivial sense of the word, indicating a derangement of the psychic equilibrium and an interruption of the normal course of psychic life.

Insofar as agitation, in this sense, prevents us from a downward concentration, diverts us from contemplative attention, and hampers our pursuit of definite and permanent aims, it evidently interferes with our inward peace. It constitutes, not a material, qualitative or intrinsic antithesis to peace as does disharmony proper, but at any rate a formal or structural one.

There are manifold varieties of agitation, too. It interferes with peace most manifestly when it takes the form of what we sometimes call *psychic alteration*: the specifically upset state of mind.

The quality of psychic agitation is an ultimate datum which we cannot reduce to anything else. It can only be grasped in an immediate experience. Its presence taints our whole vital rhythm with disorder. It is characterized by a thoroughgoing confusion, a sort of topsy-turvydom in the succession of our affective states. In the place of their normal nexus and progress, there prevails a tendency in the mind to swing to and fro without an aim: to flit impotently round one point, without arriving at a conclusion or achieving any result; to stick endlessly to one topic, or again, to buzz forth to a new one every moment.

We try spasmodically to flee from what is the cause of our agitation, only to return to it again and again from the most varying directions. Without mustering up sufficient strength or courage to deal with it thoroughly and sensibly, we yet constantly remain under its spell.

Moreover, the sufferer from this condition loses touch with the outside world, with the objects and persons that surround him. Not being able to shake off the spell of the thing that excites him he becomes incapable of responding to the *logos* of a new task or situation. He grows egocentric and apathetic. Imprisoned in a strait jacket, as it were, he can neither relinquish nor really find his own self. In a word, he loses the capacity for composure or recollectedness, for the *habitare secum*; and in such a dishevelled state of mind, when he has lost his head — he is liable to display unpredictable, irrational reactions.

Sometimes we say of such a person that he is "beside himself"; yet, we might not unreasonably call him locked up within himself, for he certainly is the slave of a subjective concern. Anyhow, he is devoid of any adequate perspective for the world of objects. In this state of alteration we are faced with a specific form of depersonalizing obsession and inner enchainment.

In addition to it, there are other, more superficial, forms of agitation, which are also opposed to inward peace, but whose upsetting action is a more limited one. For example, the agitation that grips one who is subject to what is called a *paralyzing fear* — hypnotized, as it were, by the approach of the dreaded evil — or again, the kind of excitement, much more peripheral for all its explosiveness, which accompanies anger and impatience.

Depression can paralyze the soul

Depression, further, which we have treated above as a source of intrinsic disharmony, also reveals an aspect of formal opposition to peace. Whether evoked by care and anxiety, by a humiliation, or by any situation apt to elicit a feeling of inferiority, depression not only impedes the qualitative experience of peace as such but also entails a formal disorder in psychic life, not identical with, but in some ways similar to the one due to agitation.

He who labors under a severe depression will exhibit, not the specific fitfulness and unrest of agitation, but a similar tendency to evade dealing with the cause of his trouble in conscious clarity, and to let himself be possessed by it in an illegitimate fashion.

He, too, is stuck to something — not in the sense of circling around it restlessly, but in the mode of torpor and stagnation. He, no less than the excited type, loses touch with things and persons, and becomes egocentric, without, again, finding himself or preserving an adequate view of his experiences and aims. To him, too, we might apply the simile of the strait jacket. Or, since in him the place of a senseless and spasmodic activity is taken by a morbid passiveness, we might vary the metaphor and describe him as a person living under a glass cover. An experience — a blow, an impression, a situation — which he has not been able to digest sticks, as it were, in his throat. In his paralyzed state, he cannot get over it, nor advance further. Resilience, hope, and confidence are stifled in him.

Material and formal elements of disharmony sometimes combine in us

Both types of *actual* or *psychic* lack of peace — the *intrinsic* and the merely *formal* one — imply that some aspect of an experience or an event acquires a subjective emphasis out of proportion with its true significance. The subject accords to it a place in his life which is in no way justified by its objective content.

As we have noted in the context of depression, the derangement of our inward peace may combine, in the concrete case, the material aspect of qualitative disharmony with the formal one of an immanent disorder among the subject's mental concerns. In fact, this is what happens most frequently. But that is no reason for abandoning the clear distinction between the two types of psychic factors militating against inward peace.

With regard to this double aspect, *psychic* or *actual* peace presents a clear analogy with the *habitual* or *superactual* one. Just as habitual peace is characterized by a formal and a material element — simplicity and unity on the one hand, the soul's participation in the qualitative harmony of the Good on the other — actual peace, in its turn, admits of a distinction between its formal and its material sides: the state of *habitare secum*, of an immanent psychic order, as opposed to the disorder of agitation; and again, the quality of intrinsic harmony as opposed to the note of disharmony, be it of a virulent and poisonous or of a leaden, dismal tinge.

Outward factors may also disturb our inner peace

Now as to the various outward factors that may, even though we be habitually at peace, disturb our peace on the plane of *actual* psychic life, these are, generally speaking, evils which have befallen us or which threaten us: more particularly, cares or preoccupations of all kinds. The proper root of the disturbance, however, always lies in a false mental attitude within ourselves which allows these outward factors to act upon us disproportionately or lures us into opposing them with exaggerated or irrational reactions.

A threefold division commends itself here. Our inward peace may be marred, first, by an attitude which in itself is morally reprehensible, such as envy, hatred, jealousy, or, at a different level of relationships, impatience.

It may be interfered with, secondly, by responses which are not in themselves condemnable, nay, which in the context of a purely natural outlook appear rational and justified; which, however, in view of an interpretation of the universe as derived from Revelation, and particularly of the consequences of the Redemption, imply, on man's part, an inadequate response to his essential situation. Especially, the manifold varieties of fear and dread fall into this class.

A disturbing effect may also issue, thirdly, from responses which in themselves are not only justifiable but even necessary, and also retain their legitimacy if confronted with Revelation and Redemption, but which need correction or modification, for they contain a kind of sting and are, until that sting be removed, apt to upset our inward peace. Distrust, indignation, and sorrow, as well as the consideration of fighting for a good cause, enter into this category.

Inner peace may be overthrown by reprehensible attitudes such as jealousy

Let us take these three groups of peace-destroying factors in turn.

First, those emotional reactions which are open to moral criticism. The most important case, here, is that of jealousy. We do not mean jealousy in that broader sense of the term in which it is not deserving of reproach at all — the pain one necessarily feels when a beloved person ceases to reciprocate one's love; a pain that is likely to be increased by the fact of that person's transferring his or her affection to another — but jealousy in the stricter sense.

What we mean is a bitter, irritated, malignant attitude linked to the situation of personal rivalry. In all its manifold forms — whether it refers to a rival's success or fame, the preference accorded him by a third party, or the fact that a person whose love we covet leans towards him instead of responding to us — jealousy constitutes an egocentric attitude.

The jealous man measures himself with another, begrudging his rival — in rebellion against the dispensation of God — what he would fain have himself. Rivalry as such is what specifies jealousy — the fact that, apart from being displeased with our lack of a certain good, we feel irritated by another's possessing it.

Jealousy includes, then, both the simple distress over being deprived of the good one desires — or, more exactly, a peevish and sullen kind of reaction to this evil — and a specific interest in having no one else possess that good either: the aspect of competition and rivalry. Thus, in the case of infidelity on the part of a beloved person, our jealousy never fastens upon the unfaithful person alone; it also attacks the successful rival. We seek to humiliate, to depreciate, to confound our rival in some fashion. We view him with unfriendly eyes and delight in any self-exposure into which he may blunder.

Now jealousy, whether groundless or "justified," always connotes a specific unrest. Aimlessly and endlessly, the jealous one revolves round one theme. He keeps a constant watch over the behavior of the object of his jealousy, prying into his movements with insatiable curiosity; he is astir with irritation, and his life is poisoned by a distinct kind of unrest.

To sum up, jealousy is opposed to peace in a twofold sense. On the one hand, it reveals a poisonous tinge of disharmony, qualitatively inconsistent with peace. On the other, it reveals the typical alteration which we have called a *formal* opposition to peace: the state of swinging to and fro and of circling round one point, the loss of contact with the universe of objects, and so forth.

Envy differs from jealousy in that it is opposed to peace because of its aspect of poisonous disharmony only; it does not imply the specific marks of a structural disintegration of psychic life. It is the same with hatred, *schadenfreude* ("malicious joy"), and similar attitudes. Against this must be said, however, that hatred, envy, and malicious pleasure display the note of poisonous disharmony to a much higher degree than does jealousy, as they involve a greater moral fault than jealousy does, and separate us more sharply from God. Only from the specific point of view of actual or psychic derangement of peace does jealousy present a particularly typical case.

Now, jealousy is one of the things that cannot subsist before the face of Jesus. Whenever it raises its head within us, we must take care immediately to disavow and to uproot it. It must be "shattered against Christ," as it were, dissolved by the glance of His love. Thus will the peace, too, which it has driven away, return to our mind.

The case of jealousy presents some analogy with that of impatience, although the latter interferes with peace in a more purely formal and far more superficial way. Impatience as such entirely lacks the aspect of virulent disharmony. The unrest it evokes, though apt to be very drastic in a sense (no other emotion, except anger, makes one so quickly lose one's self-control), does not exhibit the specific marks of what we described above as psychic alteration. It has much less tendency to work a destructive effect in the depths. Its very explosiveness is linked to its transient character. Withal, impatience constitutes a typical and irksome danger to outward peace. (Ch. 12 considered ways to uproot it.)

Inner peace may be upset by non-reprehensible attitudes such as fear or anxiety

Among the second class of factors that may upset our peace of mind, fear — or, more precisely perhaps, anxiety — ranks foremost. Anxiety is not, by itself, a false and immoral response. There are things we justifiedly fear or dread; nor is there anything intrinsically evil about anxiety. It does not, therefore, carry within it what we have attempted to characterize as poisonous disharmony; yet it is associated with that leaden tinge of disharmony which we have seen to belong to the graver states of depression.

Above all, anxiety impinges on our peace in the sense of its formal or structural derangement. There are kinds of anxiety which plunge us into a state of alteration: what may, in particular, exercise such an effect is the torturing vague fear of some uncertain or indeterminate but grave evil: take, for example, our concern about a beloved person of whom, without being able to account for the delay, we have had no news; or again, our fear lest we should lose the affection of a beloved friend. Such anxieties may bring in their trail all the disturbances characteristic of psychical alteration. Furthermore, there is a specific variety of paralyzing fear. When seized by this, we stare at the approaching danger in a helpless state of numbness, like a bird hypnotized by the cat poised to jump.

Now, as has been hinted before, anxiety, justified as it may be in the world, became a false response after the Redemption of the world by Christ. "In the world you are afraid: but be of good cheer, I have overcome the world." A true Christian must no longer abandon himself to oppressive or benumbing anxiety. He must conquer it with the weapon of his confidence in God; his consciousness that nothing can separate him from the love of Christ — in the spirit of the Psalmist, saying: "For in Thee, O Lord, have I hoped: Thou wilt hear me, O Lord my God" (Ps. 37:16). He must endeavor to rise above his anxiety with the strength derived from his resignation to the will of God, from the virtue of hope, from his awareness of being sheltered in the Divine Love. Thus, will he regain the peace he has lost through anxiety.

Inner peace may be disturbed by legitimate responses

In regard to the third type of peace-disturbing factors, the situation is vastly different. Mistrust; indignation; the struggles we inevitably have to face on earth; the manifold forms of sorrow and pain that beset us in this valley of tears — here are attitudes and states of mind which have not been rendered invalid even by the Redemption. And yet they, too, may — if we abandon ourselves to their autonomous strain — dislodge our inward peace.

Necessary mistrust may threaten our peace

In particular does this apply to mistrust. Whenever we grow to mistrust a person and start to look behind all his actions and utterances for something different from what they pretend to mean, a specific form of peacelessness is likely to arise in us. We are searching restlessly for something hidden. We tentatively interpret that person's behavior along varying and contradictory lines. We fall a prey to constant doubt, which cannot but make us prejudiced and diminish our freedom. Our primary, basic contact with the person in question becomes envenomed and atrophied.

This may easily impair our attitude of openness to our fellow beings in general, and, as it were, throw us back on ourselves. We may thus become wrapped up in ourselves and develop traits of egocentrism. The habit of observing the person we mistrust from the outside, from a remote point of vantage, with the resulting compulsion to decipher his every gesture and expression, impregnates our mind with a sense of insecurity most adverse to peace, and interferes with the healthy rhythm of our psychical life.

Yet, in various situations we have to be mistrustful, lest we should be deceived and our confidence abused. Within the framework of terrestrial life, it is not permissible for us to indulge a debonair confidence in everybody and everything, glibly putting aside all mistrust, merely in order to avoid the oppressive experience of not being able to *expand* freely, unchecked and unreserved.

For man to insist upon this is definitely illegitimate; in fact, it amounts to a form of easy-going indolence and self-indulgence. The truth is that again and again life places us in situations in which we can hardly afford not to mistrust people. However, we must learn how to do so in a fashion not impairing our inward peace.

To begin with, we must in general train ourselves not to have our equilibrium upset by every outward disharmony. We should firmly avoid depending on a naturally harmonious situation and presupposing it as a matter to be taken for granted. God and His Kingdom, the eternal happiness that is our goal — these are to constitute the pivot of our life and the indestructible source of our inner harmony.

As for this "valley of tears," we must in our general outlook reckon with its inherent disharmoniousness. The basic answer thereto is contained in the Psalmist's words: "My heart is ready, O God" (Ps. 107:2). So long as our center of gravity lies in God, no outward disharmony — though we may not escape suffering from its effect — will be able to unsettle our balance.

If, whenever we perceive in us the germs of mistrust, we at once proceed to collect ourselves in God and to spread out the whole situation in His light; if we thus wake into awareness of reality in the proper and eminent sense (supernatural reality) and revive our affiliation to that reality — then the object that has aroused our mistrust will, on the one hand, lose its power to trouble our equilibrium, and on the other, reveal to our eyes its comparative insignificance in the scale of universal being.

We must then carefully examine in the sight of God whether our mistrust is in fact objectively grounded and not perhaps a mere outgrowth of a mistrustful disposition on our part. If, in the light of such an examination, it proves to be warranted, our task will next be to keep it within the limits of its objective justification. We must not start doubting everything, but on the contrary, must stand firm against the lure of glib generalization. In brief, we must resist being carried away by the automatism of mistrust. We must endure the suffering that results from our being thus disappointed in someone, rather than seek to ease it by simply withdrawing our love and separating ourselves from that person.

Our endeavor should be to rise above the situation, and, instead of having our attitude imposed by the behavior of our partner, consider him in a spirit of merciful love, observing at the same time the necessary caution. We must not allow ourselves to be thrown back upon ourselves, nor get immured in ourselves.

Most of all should we guard against the extension of such a state of mind to our general attitude, beyond the limits of our relations with the offender himself. In other words, what we ought to do is to confine our mistrust within the limits of its objective validity, thus subordinating it to the teleology of our life rather than permitting it to control the latter. We should also strive to incorporate that objectively necessary mistrust in a comprehensive attitude of charity, and so have it shaped by the supremacy of love rather than have our mental complexion defiled with a heinous tinge.

If we have thus circumscribed and tamed our distrust — without, until the grounds for it disappear, suppressing it — the destruction of our inner peace will be prevented or repaired, though we shall still be afflicted with the residuum of pure and venomless chagrin.

Sorrow may darken our inner peace

However, a deep sorrow itself, while it never bears that specific note of peacelessness which marks the unchecked raving of mistrust, may darken our inner peace. Sometimes a person stricken with real grief will revolt against his misfortune. Unable to digest it and to pass on, he will cleave to his grief and owing to his oppression by it become paralyzed in all his vital functions. When the sorrow leads to despair or to expostulation with God, a climax of inner peacelessness is attained.

It is utterly false to hold that we ought *not* to sorrow over a real misfortune. (For more about this subject, see Chapter 16.) Any attempt to evade the cross, be it by a mental technique of dulling ourselves to pain or by fostering in ourselves the illusion that we are, essentially, no longer in the valley of tears but in the realm of eternal happiness, is hopelessly mistaken. We should not try to overleap suffering.

True, Jesus by His crucifixion has redeemed the world and cleansed all suffering from its poisonous sting. Yet, Jesus also spoke the words, "If any man will come after me, let him deny himself and take up his cross" (Matt. 16:24). The cross awaits us inescapably on our life-path; and we have to accept it. We should, however, take it in imitation of Christ, and endure all suffering in the spirit of Christ, in Christ, and with Christ. If governed and shaped by those two eminently Christian attitudes of mind — resignation to God's will and patience — all suffering will become transfigured and pleasing to God.

Sorrow and suffering can be transfigured by patience and resignation to God's will

Patience in general, of which we have treated earlier, is, of course, implied in the virtue of acquiescence to God's will. Full subordination and surrender to God's absolute kingship contains an inward assent to everything that faces us inevitably and is thus the result of a decree or at least a permission of God. "My Father, if it be possible, let this chalice pass from me. Nevertheless, not as I will, but as Thou wilt" (Matt. 26:39).

In these words of Jesus, all aspects of our right attitude to pain are condensed: the subordination of all our desiring and longing to the will of God; our recognition of His absolute mastery, which bids us say at every joyful or sorrowful event, "Behold the handmaid of the Lord: be it done to me according to thy word"; our response to the infinite wisdom of God, who says to us, "My ways are not thy ways"; our awareness of the infinite glory of God and of the sublime fact that whatever has been accomplished expresses a decree or at least a permission of the holy will of God; and finally, our knowledge that "all turns to bliss for those who love God."

Here is, in a word, resignation to God's will — a thing impossible except as a response to the concept of the universe that is conveyed to us by Christian Revelation. It does not dissolve suffering, but it transfigures suffering and removes from it that sting which threatens to destroy our inward peace. It prevents us from remonstrating with Providence. Resignation to the will of God — our total surrender of self to God and His infinite love; our knowledge of being sheltered in Him, *per ipsum, cum ipso, et in ipso* ("through Him, with Him and in Him") — this, above everything else, is what strips all worries and evils of their power to disturb our peace.

Depression can be diminished by patience and resignation to God's will

It also plays a decisive part in our mastering of depression and the specific lack of peace it entails. Whenever something that is not a true evil but merely appears as such to our pride or our inordinate covetousness preys on our mind, we must attempt before Christ to uproot from our soul this unfounded sensitivity. The depression and its peace-disturbing effect will disappear when we succeed in dissolving before the face of Christ this illegitimate field of susceptibility. No doubt, this may often prove a laborious task, and require a long ascetical training. Yet, it is the more necessary because in this case — just as with jealousy, and particularly with hatred — the attainment of inner peace is closely linked to the victory over an actual moral defect in us.

If, on the other hand, the cause of our depression *is* a true evil, what we should do is not to try and banish it from our conscious-ness, conceal it from ourselves, or explain it away — and so provide it with a harmful subconscious hold on our mental life — but to set it clearly and consciously, confronting it with Christ, in the place that is objectively due to it within the universal framework of reality. We must then try to accept it consciously and expressly in an act of resignation to the will of God.

If we thus receive that evil as a cross from the hands of Christ, submitting to it expressly — taking it upon us actively, as it were, rather than merely enduring it in passive helplessness — it may still hurt no less, but it will no longer weigh us down, no longer affect us as a paralyzing poison, no longer warp our peace of mind. Finally, as regards future evils whose incidence is still uncertain, we must lay them in the hands of God, and from Christian resignation and confidence in God derive, in reference to those specified menaces, too, the attitude thus expressed in St. Paul's words: "Be nothing solicitous" (Phil. 4:6), or in the Psalmist's: "Cast thy care upon the Lord" (Ps. 54:23).

We must truly bear the burden of care, but strive to retain our inmost peace while doing so

This is not to say that we do not have to bear the burden of concerns about future evils. Some people are inclined to shut out and pass over such concerns in a false way. They ease their consciences with the happy formula of "confidence in God," whereas in fact they are just easy-going, and intent on avoiding unpleasant matters as long as they can possibly manage it.

We should, in truth, accept all burdens that God imposes on us, including the burden of care. We should, accordingly, prepare for all trials we see coming, and, so far as it is within our power, try to avert an evil not yet accomplished. However, the acceptance of this burden must not take away our peace. If in a general sense we acquiesce in bearing our cross; if we succeed in getting rid of the tenacious, secret resistance of the *old man* in us against everything that hurts our nature; if we are ready to receive everything God has meted out to us as a gift of His love and a means of our sanctification; if we surrender all *self-evident* claims to happiness and shake off the illusion that even on earth a state of undisturbed bliss might, after all, be attained — then we shall be able to face the threat of approaching evils, too, without losing our inward peace.

No sane man will deny it to be implicit in our terrestrial situation that the threat of great evils which close in upon us —

when we have reasons to apprehend, say, the loss of a beloved person — should afflict us with anguish and care; nor are these compatible with a state of unruffled calm and unimpaired peace. Yet, in the midst of all the inevitable alarm, in our deepmost soul we can and must preserve that serene peace which flows from our surrender to God's will and our firm belief that "God is love."

We must remain recollected in the midst of cares

Another condition, too, has to be fulfilled so that amidst all tribulations of life we may safeguard our inward peace. We must maintain a *recollected* mode of life. We have seen earlier the necessity of recollection and composure as a precondition to our transformation in Christ. That motif is bound to reemerge in the present context. If, indeed, we conduct a bustling and fitful sort of life with one aim chasing the other, involving a breathless succession of disparate tensions — a sort of life which never gives us time to pause and to meditate, nor allows any possibility of a contemplative attention to God — we shall be exposed to incessant derangements of our peace.

How could we, amidst the turmoil of such a life, develop the habit of confronting everything with God and of thus subjecting all our single preoccupations to an intrinsic order? How could we dwell in the depths of reality and the realm of eternal values; how find ourselves?

On the contrary, pushed about and unduly possessed by our rapidly alternating tasks (all of which carry in them the impetus of urgency), we are at the mercy of the autonomous mechanism of each in turn. In our constant attention to present and fugitive actuality, even should the matter in hand be ever so profound and important in itself, we are hopelessly incapable of setting ourselves, *in conspectu Dei*, at a distance from all things, including our own ego.

Yet, this distance, as has been shown, forms an indispensable prerequisite for the neutralization of any kind of depression and excitement.

Even aside from this, a hyperactive and one-sidedly pragmatic rhythm of life — in which contemplation is doomed to wither — involves as such, in a general sense, a certain formal lack of peace. The restlessness, the speed, the nervous fatigue inherent in such a mode of life, the feverish rhythm of work and the bondage to the imperative of doing that are inseparable from it, inevitably plunge man into a state of peacelessness.

This is not the peacelessness of disharmony or of a subverted equilibrium (which is the note, for instance, of jealousy), but at any rate the peacelessness of a peripheral, centrifugal mode of being, of an endless rushing and routing. It, too, forms an antithesis to positive peace. Such bundles of energy, bursting with dynamism and delivered up entirely to the concern of the moment, who can never allow themselves a spell of emerging from the immanent logic of their activities, essentially carry with them a suggestion of peacelessness. Not for them is the state of *habitare secum*. True peace, then, is inseparable from recollection.

Composure is not the same as recollection

Composure of mind, of course, seems to be possible without true peace. There are people who manage their affairs slowly and comfortably, without any hustle and bustle at all, and who nevertheless cannot be described as being truly and inwardly at peace. But such people, though the slow cadence of their vital manifestation creates an impression of calmness and composure, are too indifferent, empty, or irrelevant to be really recollected.

What matters in this regard is not the quick or slow cadence of one's reactions, nor the tense or relaxed quality of one's vital rhythm. It is, rather, the presence or absence of concentration and contemplation; one's tendency towards the *depths* or the *periphery*; whether one's attitude of mind tends to be reflective or dissipated; whether one lives in a mode of unity and continuity, or as a puppet actuated, from moment to moment, by the heterogeneous flux of events, impressions, and aims — a slave of imperious automatism. Such automatism may be seen, too, when we engage too readily in a great variety of work, though all the activities we embark upon be in themselves legitimate.

Inner peace calls us to have our spiritual roots in God

The true *actual* peace of the soul depends, finally, on that *superactual*, habitual, constant attention to God, that sustained consciousness of having our roots in God, which allows our interior world to be penetrated by a ray of His infinite peace. This conveys to us a foretaste of ultimate harmony and protects us against inward disunity and unrest.

It is implied in this true peace that we shall never be wholly submerged by the vortex of successive tensions which we have to endure. We shall never so forget the true and perennial order of things as to overestimate the task of the moment merely because we are caught in the tension of our effort to realize it.

Lack of inner peace renders happiness impossible

Lack of peace constitutes a threefold evil. First, if experienced as such, it is essentially inconsistent with true happiness — most of all, the lack of peace associated with alteration and with depression. It is not, of course, in our power to eschew all unhappiness. On earth, no human being can escape the cross. And particularly, no Christian: even should he be spared all trials in his personal life, he would still suffer from the multiform manifestations of that basic disharmony which is a consequence of original sin. But, provided that we give God the right answer, it is in our power to avoid peacelessness.

Moreover, man's longing for true happiness — nay, for a blissful life — is something that God has implanted in the heart of every one, and so we are justified in looking upon any unhappiness which we have ourselves guiltily caused as a veritable evil, a thing that ought not to be. Apart from other reasons, then, we should shun whatever is opposed to peace inasmuch, also, as it constitutes a poison for our happiness, a subjective evil of which we are legitimately anxious to rid ourselves.

Lack of inner peace springs from a disorder which constitutes an insult to God

The second and more important reason why lack of peace means a real evil consists in the insult to God which lies at its root. This is most patently true in regard to the type of peacelessness that springs from attitudes immoral in themselves — such as hatred, envy, or jealousy — which fill us with the poisonous disharmony proper to them.

Here our lack of peace is plainly caused by an attitude that insults God and separates us from Him. Our peacelessness represents a symptom of the disease which has befallen our soul. It is a product of the sinful attitude which in objective reality separates us from God and which therefore cuts us off from the source of all peace.

In its other forms, too, our loss of inward peace always presupposes some devious attitude on our part. It always indicates a state of mind in which we fail to give the proper and adequate response to the situations and events we are faced with, and in particular, a failure to respond to everything according to what it is and means *in conspectu Dei*. Such is, as has been shown, the central defect that underlies all disorders of our inward peace.

Lack of inner peace separates us from God

And finally, not only does our lack of peace originate in some cause that isolates us from God; in its turn, it reaffirms and increases our separation from God. It constitutes a formal obstacle to our full awareness and loving contemplation of God, to our delight in His infinite beauty.

By contrast to the above discussed second aspect of peacelessness, this third one is most clearly visible in cases where the root of our lack of peace is not an expressly evil attitude — not one that would by itself banish us far from the face of God. Whenever, for instance, we fall a prey to anxiety degenerating into a state of depression or alteration, this condition will in a purely formal sense prevent us from reposing in God, and make us incapable of mental prayer as well as of every genuine act of contemplation.

For one thing, we are too much possessed by what depresses or agitates us to be capable of an adequate attention to God. In general, as has been pointed out, we are then cut off from all contact with the universe of objects. Furthermore, the unhealthy condition of our vital rhythm prevents us from recollecting ourselves and from all concentration towards the depth of our being. Lack of peace, then, is a disease of the soul which shuts us off from what is outside the ego and thus in a purely formal sense separates us from God.

Lack of inner peace separates us from other persons

Nor does it separate us from God only. It also makes us unable to attend to other persons according to the will of God. And so, inasmuch as it renders us egocentric, our lack of peace also causes us to offend against charity.

Under its action, we become indifferent and lose the capacity of adequately dealing with the multifarious tasks which life imposes on us. It saps our working-power and undermines our faculty of coordination. It makes us scatterbrained and is thus responsible not only for many omissions but for many mistakes on our part.

Lastly, it also diminishes our readiness to keep peace with others. Our inner state itself being peaceless, any attack or insult on the part of others — be it even a merely putative one — will easily provoke us to a heated reaction and thus lure us into discord and conflict.

Nor can we, in such a condition, conduct a struggle for the kingdom of God except in a mode of rancorous irritability unworthy of the cause. For this great task in particular, so difficult to pursue without increasing the amount of strife in the world, inward peace constitutes a strict formal condition.

Therewith we return to our starting point. For our ability to preserve the spirit of peace and our love for peace in the midst of that struggle for the kingdom of God which *in statu viae* we have to wage as a warrior of Christ, there is (apart from the virtue of patience) no precondition equal in importance to this one: that we ourselves possess true inward peace and keep it intact throughout the struggle.

Inner peace is possible only for those who have given themselves unconditionally to Christ

To be sure, the significance of true inward peace is not limited to its being a condition for outward peace. It constitutes a high good in itself. Indeed, it is so intimately linked to our transformation in Christ that it cannot, in the midst of all the threats to it, fully and sustainedly unfold except in such as have given over their souls to Christ.

This can be affirmed in reference to each single aspect of inward peace as analyzed in the foregoing pages. In him alone who really and truly prefers nothing to Christ; whose life is shaped and remodelled by a total surrender to Christ; who follows Christ *relictis omnibus* ("leaving everything behind"); who is undivided and unhampered by any inward resistance in belonging with all his soul and will to God (whose property, to be sure, we all are in metaphysical fact) — in him alone who is thus turned towards God and incorporated in Christ may the inexpressible sweetness of the peace of Christ, which in St. Paul's words "surpasseth all understanding" (Phil. 4:7) spread out in all its wealth, undisturbed by any accidental agents of disorder.

He alone who has established in his heart the words of the Lord, "Seek first the kingdom of God" and who no longer hungers and thirsts for anything but justice (that is, ultimately, Christ), possesses that supreme freedom which permeates his soul with true inward peace.

True peace only blossoms out of a life entirely rooted in Christ and illumined by the *lumen Christi*; of the experience of having tasted the untellable sweetness of Him whom the holy Church thus glorifies in her chant —

> *Jesus dulcis memoria*
> *dans vera cordis gaudia,*
> *sed super mel et omnia,*
> *ejus dulcis præsentia.*

> Jesus, the very thought of Thee
> With sweetness fills the breast;
> But sweeter far Thy face to see,
> And in Thy presence rest.

Of that supernatural inward harmony, which nothing can destroy any more, he alone partakes whose heart has been wounded by Jesus and molten in His love; who is drunk with the sweetness of His love, and able to sing with the Church —

> *Nil canitur suavius,*
>   *nil auditur jucundius,*
>   *nil cogitatur dulcius*
>   *quam Jesus, Dei filius.*

> No voice can sing, no heart can frame,
>   Nor can the memory find,
> A sweeter sound than Jesus' Name,
>   The Savior of mankind.

It is the Holy Spirit — "rest for the weary, refreshment for the pining, solace in the midst of woe" (Pentecost Sequence) — who imparts to the soul an imperturbable poise and a serene calm, the character of *habitare secum*, the soaring lightness of a full inner freedom.

He, whom the Church calls "light of the heart, sweet guest of the soul," fills us with that supernatural light which takes away the poison of enmity, dispels the gloom of depression, and dissolves the spasm of agitation. The consummate peace of the "redeemed," the peace of those whom the blood of the Lamb has reconciled to God, is borne up by the consciousness that He "in whom we live and move and are" (Acts 17:28) is eternal Love; that "He hath first loved us" (1 John 4:10). That peace is the fruit of a supernatural love for God.

For no earthly power can shatter his peace who, like the merchant in the Gospel who gave away everything he had for one costly pearl, no longer seeks anything but Christ. He knows "that neither death, nor life, nor angels, nor principalities, nor powers, nor things present, nor things to come, nor might, nor height, nor depth, nor any other creature, shall be able to separate us from the love of God which is in Christ Jesus our Lord" (Rom. 8:38-39).

This peace is a thing immeasurably precious in itself, and most pleasing to the eyes of God; it is the special gift of the Paraclete whom Christ has promised us before His leavetaking: "My peace I give unto you" (John 14:27).

Inner peace engenders outward concord

This inward peace, then, is infinitely more important even than all outward concord; however, it is not separable from the latter, but engenders it of necessity. If inward peace reigns in a man's soul — as it does in the saints' — it removes from any struggle he may have to wage the venoms of asperity and irritation, of harshness and malicious enmity. With him, the struggle for the kingdom of God becomes visibly and tangibly a struggle of Peace against Peacelessness.

Such a fight is always waged in the ultimate interest of the opponent, too — according to the words of St. Augustine: "To kill the error, to love the erring one."

It is a fight waged with weapons entirely different from those wielded by the adversary — with the weapons of Light. Such a struggle is inscribed with the words of the Lord: "Father, forgive them, for they know not what they do" (Luke 23:34). For they who possess true inward peace irradiate peace even when fighting for the kingdom of God. From their being emanates an intrinsic harmony, the reflection of the infinite harmony of God; from their whole bearing and doing issues a mild and soothing light, which melts away all grimness and embitterment.

A true *warrior of Christ* is firmly entrenched in the Absolute. He conducts his actions sovereignly from an irremovable point of vantage, against which all the poisoned arrows sent by his adversaries prove powerless.

Such a style of warfare tends to disarm the antagonist and to communicate to him something of the serene calm that tints it; even to draw him irresistibly into the orbit of that victorious yet mild and redeeming light.

We must also be peacemakers

But there is one more thing we must remember. The Lord says, not merely, "Blessed are they who are at peace," but, "Blessed are the *peacemakers*." It does not suffice to love peace and to preserve it amidst inevitable conflicts; beyond that, a true Christian must also and everywhere act as a peacemaker. Wherever we witness a struggle over earthly goods or a struggle for the kingdom of God that takes the form of a mundane strife, we should be pained and grieved at the sight.

We should diligently try, in the first case, to mediate peace, and in the second, to inject the spirit of peace into the inevitable struggle for the kingdom of God and to restore that struggle to its true character. In this function of peacemakers, too, it will be most needful for us to possess true inward peace in ourselves, and that in a measure which renders it effective even by mere spontaneous *irradiation*.

All saints were peacemakers and brought peace wherever they went. A scene from St. Francis' life may provide the most touching illustration for this. Shortly before his death the saint was lying, gravely ill, in the episcopal palace at Assisi.

"The first thing Francis learned there, after his arrival, about the affairs of his native town" (we quote from Jörgensen's *St. Francis of Assisi*) "was that an open feud had broken out between the Podestà and the Bishop. The Bishop had pronounced an interdict against the Podestà; the latter, in his turn, had forbidden the burghers all traffic with their spiritual head. 'It should greatly shame us,' said Francis to his brethren, 'that none of us is working for peace here!' And, eager to do what was in his power, he wrote two new strophes of his *Canticle of the Sun*, and thereupon invited the Podestà to the episcopal palace where he lay bedridden, asking at the same time the Bishop to lend his presence. When the two enemies, and all others Francis had wanted to be present, were gathered in the Piazza del Vescovado (the same place where, nineteen years before, Francis had given his sumptuous robes back to his father), two friars of his brotherhood came forward and sang the *Canticle of the Sun*: first its original text, then the addition newly written by Francis —

> *Laudato si, Misignore, per quelli ke perdonano*
> *per lo tuo amore*
> *et sostengo infirmitate et tribulatione,*
> *beati quelli ke sosterrano, in pace,*
> *ka da te, Altissimo, sirano incoronati.*

> *Praised be Thou, O Lord, for those who give*
> *pardon for Thy love*
> *and endure infirmity and tribulation;*
> *blessed those, who endure in peace,*
> *who will be, Most High, crowned by Thee!*

"While the two friars sang, all stood there with folded hands as when the Gospel is read in church. But when the chant was ended, with the last *Laudato si, Misignore* still in everybody's ears, the Podestà made a step forward, knelt down to Bishop Guido, and spoke: 'For love of our Lord Jesus Christ and His servant Francis I forgive you from my heart and am ready to do your will, as it pleases you to bid me!' The Bishop then bent down, and drawing his former enemy to him, embraced and kissed him, and said: 'According to my office, it would befit me to be humble and peaceable. But of my nature I am inclined to anger; therefore thou must bear with me.' And the brethren went in and told Francis of the victory he had achieved with his song over the evil spirits of strife." "Blessed are the peacemakers, for they shall be called the sons of God."

In every one of us the desire must be alive to attain inward peace, to keep peace, and to serve the peace of others. As the disciples of Him about whom St. Paul says, "Christ is your peace" and whom the Church at Christmas calls *Princeps pacis* ("Prince of peace"), we must possess, irradiate, and spread peace. We must always stand witness to this primary word of the Gospels, thus giving proof that we are true disciples of Christ: "Taste and see that the Lord is sweet."

In truth, he alone who has *tasted the sweetness* of the Lord can imagine what true peace is, and burn with desire for that peace. They alone can be truly transformed in Christ who say with St. Augustine (*Confessions* 10.27): "Thou hast called me aloud, and pierced my deafness; Thou hast shone and sparkled, and chased away my blindness; Thou hast spread a sweet perfume; I have breathed it in and am longing for Thee; I have tasted, and now I hunger and thirst; Thou hast touched me, and lo! I burn with desire for Thy peace."

14

Holy Meekness

ST. PAUL refers to meekness as one of the fruits of the Holy Spirit. It derives, indeed, from supernatural love; in particular, it presupposes patience and inward peace.

Meekness is comprehensible only in the light of Revelation

Mansuetude, or true *meekness* in the Christian sense of the word, belongs to the virtues that can only arise in us on the basis of Revelation. It is not accessible nor even understandable to us until we become aware not merely of the metaphysical situation of man but of the entirely new world of the supernatural, implying a collapse of all purely natural measures.

It requires an awareness of the new light that issues from the words of the Sermon on the Mount — the words which revolutionize all canons and rules of the natural world to a status of merely relative validity. Meekness can have no meaning for us unless we know that God, the Lord Almighty, Creator of heaven and earth, is *Love.*

It is Christian Revelation which promises ultimate victory, not to natural strength nor to superior power but to those "who are meek and humble of heart." "He hath put down the mighty from their seat and hath exalted the humble" (Luke 1:52).

God has redeemed mankind, not by force but by the God-Man's death on the cross. And, what Christ has bidden us to do is not to spread His truth by sword and fire but to proclaim it as prisoners of His love. The *ethos* by which we are to overcome the world is that of a humble and gentle charity. "Blessed are the meek: for they shall possess the land" (Matt. 5:4).

True meekness, then, cannot blossom except in those who have seen the light of Christ — *lumen Christi* — and grasped the wholly new order of the supernatural. It is a privilege of those who have read the secret of true strength: the strength that is pleasing to God. Accordingly, holy meekness is not only a lovely flower of the Christian *ethos* but a central virtue of the true Christian, who reflects the primary law of the supernatural order. It contains the key to the supernatural power of Him who spoke the words: "Learn of me, because I am meek and humble of heart" (Matt. 11:29).

A phlegmatic person is not thereby meek

At first sight meekness would seem to be, chiefly, the opposite of what is called a violent temper. By contrast to the petulant, irascible or irritable character, the meek or gentle person is one who patiently bears opposition or even insults, and always preserves a calm, kind, and amicable attitude. Even if he feels compelled to blame someone, he will do so in a kind and suave manner without any harshness, acerbity or anger; without using any offensive language. What else could meekness be?

However, this view is inadequate.

Meekness is by no means unequivocally determined by its being antithetic to anger and violence. The fact that a person quietly swallows any insult is not necessarily a sign of true meekness in him. It may also be due to a cool and sluggish — as it is sometimes called, *phlegmatic* — temperament. Such a person keeps his temper because, with his thick skin, he does not feel hit by an insult; his love of comfort does not allow him to display any explosive reactions.

Now the phlegmatic temperament differs from the virtue of meekness, first, by being a mere natural disposition, whereas meekness is a virtue born of a free spiritual attitude. Secondly, the phlegmatic behavior has something heavy, listless, lusterless about it, whereas there is proper to meekness a note of soaring and luminous suppleness.

Good-natured joviality is not meekness

However, not only a dull and indifferent temperament but also the good-natured joviality of the typically sociable kind of person, the good mixer, is a thing utterly different from meekness. True, joviality is not only a mere disposition but expresses a personal attitude proper; but its *quality* is widely different from meekness. It does not convey the sustaining warmth of love; it springs from a need for surface harmony. The *good fellow* takes everything in a friendly spirit — for the sake of his own comfort rather than out of his consideration for others.

This jolly attitude has something unimportant, superficial about it; you will find it in such persons only as are incapable of a deep fervor and strong self-dedication. It is incompatible with a great and vigorous personality, with the hunger and thirst for justice; generally it is coupled with a certain laziness and shallowness.

It is usually a man of this type whom we are wont to call, with a kind of benign contempt, a mere cipher. Frequently, such people are of an inordinately yielding disposition, with their weakness easily exploited by the unscrupulous. Their freedom from anger and harshness is bought at the cost of grave deficiencies.

Meekness is not the cultivated indifference of the Stoic

Nor, again, should meekness be confused with the aloof composure or *ataraxy* of the stoic. The cool self-control of the latter, who refuses to be affected by an insult, is colored by indifference and neutrality: a mood far removed from the warm breath of charity exhaled by Christian meekness. What underlies the meekness of the stoic is not loving kindness nor a value-response in reference to a fellow person but a habit of apathy and self-discipline, acquired by sedulous training and cultivated as an end in itself.

Meekness is the manifestation of inward charity

True meekness is not a matter of outward demeanor only; it does not consist in the mere avoidance of angry outbreaks or other manifestations of an unbridled temper. Certainly it implies all that — but implies it *as* the manifestation of a charitable inward attitude. A man who is inwardly seething with anger and full of enmity towards his fellow but, controlling himself through will power, succeeds in keeping up an appearance of friendliness, is not therefore meek in the sense here reserved for the term. To disavow within ourselves any inchoate impulse of anger, to be intensely aware of its ugly disharmony, to have it shattered by the contact of Christ before the need could even arise to curb it — this is what constitutes true meekness.

Meekness is far more than self-control

Mere outward self-control, when our anger is checked in its manifestation while its venom subsists within us, falls entirely short of that virtue. Nay, even at the stage of formally disavowing our anger but remaining nevertheless inwardly excited, we can only be credited with the *pursuit*, not with the *possession* of meekness.

Accordingly, meekness is distinguishable from self-control even as regards its outward appearance. A somewhat discerning observer will easily distinguish one from the other. An act of iron self-discipline always impresses us with a sense of hardness, whereas an act of meekness irradiates the mellow brightness, the supple harmony of loving kindness. The former, besides its value in preventing a threatening clash, may force our respect; but it invariably lacks the irresistible disarming effect of true meekness.

Meekness bears mainly on our behavior towards our fellow men. It is specifically opposed to *two* sets of qualities: first, to everything brutal, uncouth, coarse-grained, and violent; secondly, to all modes of hostility, to the subtly or pointedly venomous as well as to the massive or rabid form of hostility. Let us next turn our attention to the first-named aspect.

Meekness rejects every brutal, forcible relation to others

He who possesses the virtue of meekness has grasped the essential evil that lies in all brutal force. He is aware of the sublime structure of the spiritual person; of the depth and the delicacy that characterize all valid acts in the realm of that spirituality; of the gulf that divides the laws of physical reality from those in the realm of personal life. He knows the difference between things *made* and things *created*: a difference whose archetype we find in that formula of the Creed, *genitum*, *non factum*, and whose many analogies pervade the created universe.

Hence, he would never attempt to enforce by mechanical and extrinsic means what is capable of realization only by way of an organic unfolding. He loathes treating personal realities after the pattern of techniques dealing with the world of mechanism. Utterly averse to the very idea of attaining an end by violence, he will also be disinclined to combat the evil in the world by mere mechanical methods.

He experiences intensely the incompatibility between every-thing brutal or forcible and the spirituality of the personal mode of existence. The preciousness and nobility inherent in the highest sphere of created being, that of the spiritual person, are always present to his eyes.

Meekness is a tender, explicitly spiritual attitude

Not only does meekness imply a specific awareness of this particular status of personal being; it is, itself, something definitely spiritual — the expression of a predominance of spirituality in man. The type of person in whom true meekness prevails must be distinguished, not merely from the obviously contrasting type — the *material* type, stamped as it were with the unlit dullness and mechanical clumsiness of matter; he must also be clearly distin-guished from another type of character with whom he is more easily confused, namely the man endowed with a certain soft and tender kind of vitality, not conditioned by any vigorous instincts, and displaying the flow of life in the form of a soft, flexible, eminently *organic* rhythm rather than of explosive urges and robust pulsations.

In the meek person, there shines the tenderness which is specifically proper to the spiritual. His being breathes the victory of the spiritual sphere over the material and vital. In the meek man a spiritual principle has stamped the whole man with its imprint and conferred its radiant bloom upon him.

Meekness does not try to dominate as do the spiritually "hard"

At this stage, however, one more distinction becomes neces-sary. There exists, too, a spiritual type of man who also lacks meekness. Persons of this type are not brutal nor mechanical in attitude — which would contradict their being spiritual — yet they reveal what might be called a *cramped* character. In such persons, everything is controlled by the mind. They are in no way swayed by unconscious vitality. Their conduct is governed entirely by the free center of their conscious personality. In them, the attitude of intentional meaningful response to being has attained to full maturity, but nevertheless, there is something highly strung, something hard and cramped about them.

In their stern idealism, they are set on enforcing, in their own lives at least, what they know to be right and desirable. They overestimate man's range of power and place a one-sided trust in the efficacy of his will. They are deficient in inward suppleness; they know no melting or serenity.

On the contrary, he who is graced with meekness is eminently supple and serene — tender, relenting, in a sense relaxed, as though soaring in a luminous medium of freedom and peace. He would enforce nothing; he accords everything the time required by its inward law of unfolding. Despite all its fervor and intensity, his effort retains a quality of gracious, unhardened mellowness.

For all its supra-vital rationality and morality, the cramped character we have described above still implies an infringement, however subtle and hidden, of the inward law of spiritual and personal reality. A person of this type transfers, in some way, methods of the infra-spiritual world to the sphere of the spiritual person. He applies purely spiritual forces — his conscious will, in particular — according to the pattern in which our spirit can operate upon material things. Thus, in a sense, his aggressive spirituality, genuine though it is, means a treatment of things spiritual as though they were material.

Meekness respects the spiritual sphere and its laws

But meekness, as we have seen, implies not only the *supremacy* in man of the spiritual element, but also his *respect* of the spiritual sphere and its particular laws. He who has true meekness treats spiritual reality according to its proper nature. In dealing with what is spiritual and personal, he adapts his methods to the fact of its fundamental difference from all other realms of being. This is precisely the virtue in which the cramped and violent man is found wanting, be he ever so much actuated by spiritual motives and ever so rational in the choice of his attitudes.

Meekness acknowledges the impotence of force in the spiritual realm

Moreover, true meekness implies the knowledge that in relation to the spiritual sphere — that is, the plane of reality for which meaning is constitutive — violence is not merely inadequate but also inefficacious. The truly meek man is aware that on this plane, forcefulness is far from being the really victorious force; that real spiritual power is of an entirely different and more sublime nature — a power which essentially operates through the medium of the intelligible.

Above all, the fact of Christ is sealed upon his soul, the redeeming merciful love of God, of which Paul the Apostle says: "The goodness and kindness of God our Savior appeared" (Titus 3:4). Brutal or mechanical force is still incomparably more inadequate to and incompatible with the supernatural than it is with the natural sphere. The hidden operation of grace is incomparably more *organic* than even the most sublime spirituality within the confines of natural being. Every attempt to force a conversion or to secure the unfolding of grace by mechanical outward means, is even far more preposterous than are all forcible methods applied to the mental world.

The concept of force of violence is not, of course, limited here to attitudes into which an inimical intent enters. It is applicable wherever men, fatally mistaken in their views of spiritual (let alone, supernatural) ends, plan to impose the Good on others by force, or at any rate trust the efficacy of mechanical means in securing its acceptance. Such men, even in proposing to help their neighbors and to heap benefits upon them, are essentially guilty of using violence. They adhere to the principle of violence.

Not so, the person imbued with true meekness. Even when fighting an evil power, he never lapses into violence. Even in such a situation his whole behavior, inward and outward, is based upon his recognition of the particular character of spiritual — and even more so of supernatural — reality. He is reverently aware of the structure of spiritual reality, translucent with meaning. He is filled with awe before the mystery of the operations of grace; he has understood the parable of the wheat and the chaff.

Notwithstanding his adamant insistence on the truth, according to St. Paul's words: "Preach the word: be instant in season, out of season: reprove, entreat, rebuke" (2 Tim. 4:2); notwithstanding his intransigence and heroic strength of soul — he preserves that reverence for the structure of personal being and the more sublime mystery of grace, and so he invariably keeps aloof from violence and bitterness.

Nor does this apply to his outward conduct only, but to his innermost attitude as well.

Meekness is a manifestation of tender, holy love

Turning, now to the second main aspect of meekness — its antithetic relation to violence as an expression of enmity — we shall be able to gain an even clearer view of its specific quality.

Meekness presupposes love; and with it an insight into the beauty of the human soul — the preciousness of the spiritual person as an image of God and a vessel of grace. It flows from our recognition of the beauty of love, goodness, and harmony, and of the hideousness of enmity, strife, and disharmony.

Still more, true meekness presupposes a mind conscious of the face of Christ, of His holy goodness and mildness. It presupposes a soul touched by His love, which softens all hardened fibers and dissolves all crampedness. It implies a taste of that peace whose concept we have tried to convey in the previous chapter.

Beyond the knowledge of these things, it requires a full response thereto. What constitutes the specific domain of meekness is the *manifestation of love*: the way in which love — the personified *intentio benevolentiae* as it were, condensing in it the whole personality of the subject — stretches out to reach the beloved person. In other words, meekness represents a certain consequence of benevolent, transfigured, holy love: that is, the way in which we spiritually embrace the beloved person.

The attitude of love implies, as we know, two basic elements: *the intention of union (intentio unionis)* and *the intention of well-wishing (intentio benevolentiae)*. In addition to these, there are many other elements to be found in love: the tone of inner suavity, the elements of fervor and audacity, and the act of a heroic self-abandonment.

The aspect of which meekness embodies a specific expression is that of a *serene mellowness* inherent in the perfect attitude of love: the softening quality of love by virtue of which it becomes, as it were, a tangible substance, which might be described as *fluid goodness*. Meekness is comparable to a seal which this element of love impresses on our whole essence, thus conferring a specific stamp upon all forms of our communication and intercourse with other persons.

Our inward attention to the fellow person (the way we think of him, judge him, appraise him inwardly), our tone of voice when speaking to him, our choice of words, our rhythm of speech — all this as well as all other details of our behavior towards him will, if we possess true meekness, be informed by that particular element of love.

Accordingly, all kinds of enmity, hatred and irritation — in view of the trait of venomousness peculiar to them — are evidently antithetic to meekness.

Coarseness, roughness, and violence are explicit antitheses of meekness

However, what constitutes a more *specific* antithesis to true meekness, its polar opposite as it were, are the qualities of roughness, coarseness, hardness, and violence. These are eminently opposed, not only to love as such, as are all modes of enmity, but to that particular quality of love in which meekness is rooted. The irascible, brutal, violent kind of person, bent on overriding another's will, on beating him into submission, is he who forms the really specific contrast to the man endowed with the virtue of meekness.

Meekness does not "harden," even when attacked

He who possesses this virtue will always, even though he be attacked or injured, preserve that radiance of loving kindness: that soft bloom of a sublime spirituality entirely ordained to the intention of charity. It is as though he never accepted a provocation. Even though faced with an enemy, he does not exchange the garment of love, the unarmed innocence of loving kindness, for a coat-of-mail which would harden him and protect him against the arrows of his assailant. Instead he tenders his vulnerable heart, unshielded, to the impact of those arrows, without steeling his heart against them. He endures the wounds inflicted upon him. No attack will impel him to abandon that specific openness of the soul which is a chief characteristic of love.

We all know the peculiar kind of hardening that takes place whenever we have to cope with an aggression. So long as we are treated with charity, we in our turn display a charitable openness of heart; as soon as we become the victims of an insult, we close ourselves; we stiffen and bristle. All our mellowness has disappeared; we oppose a hard coat-of-mail to the arrows of our adversary. To put it more explicitly, we either withdraw behind the walls of defensive seclusion or else turn upon our enemy in anger, returning blow for blow and meeting him in the destructive fury of enmity.

It might be said that fallen man bears in his soul a number of different fields of sensitivity, which receive and at which are aimed the different attitudes of others directed towards us. Insult, abuse, and mockery, notably, are aimed at a certain field in our soul which is keyed to the theme of honor. If that field of sensitivity is touched by the injurious word or gesture, the offender has realized his specific intention. This region of the soul is the habitat of harsh and irascible reactions *par excellence*. The sores which come about here give rise not to the straight pain of chagrin but to the venomous, bitter itch of irritation and resentment, which stirs us into a fighting position.

Sensitivity or susceptibility of this kind is founded in a certain deeply rooted attitude of self-assertion. In the saint, who has definitively risen above this attitude, the sensitivity that originates in it has been deprived of its base and meaning, and hence dies away. An insult no longer wounds him according to its specific intention but merely as an act of uncharitableness. It irritates him no longer, though it still distresses his heart.

The position of defending one's honor creates a shuttered attitude against one's fellow men. Persons strongly centered on that motif — those eminently fanatical about their "honor" — are therefore hard in their general attitude towards others. They are, so to speak, always on the *qui vive*, always on the lookout for insults to their dignity. In the ordinary sort of person who, though not a saint, is not thus abnormally anxious about his honor, the reaction of becoming hard and sealed up only appears after he has actually been defied or insulted.

The meek man, then, is distinguished by the fact that he does not know this gesture of hardening his soul but remains, even in the face of an enemy, in the position of that soft, unguarded openness which is love's mode of appearance. In his soul, the sensitive region of honor is blotted out. So also are other sensitive regions that foster some variety of the attitude of fierce resistance to an attacker: the region of specific sensitivity about one's rights, for instance.

Meekness does not close off the soul, as does sulking

There are also, however, attitudes in which we remain *soft* and which nevertheless are surpassed by the man endowed with true meekness. Certain people react to offenses or insults, to unjust or contemptuous treatment and so forth, by the attitude of passive ill temper described as sulking. As distinct from the combative rebound of irritation, sulking is not an irascible mood of the soul. The sulker does not stiffen into a fighting position; he lapses into a specific egocentric variety of softness. The overdelicate, squeamish sort of people seize every opportunity to feel hurt and to brood over the offense suffered.

What exactly is *sulking*? It is a peculiar way of withdrawing into ourselves, very frequently associated with tears of commiseration for our own unhappy self. With a lump in our throat, we take a sort of mournful delight in imagining how the person who has wronged us would feel at this moment if he heard that we had met with a disaster.

We are itching, not to avenge the insult we have suffered by retaliating in kind, but to punish its author by shaming him. We wish so to arrange and manifest the consequences of his conduct (perhaps by inveigling him into a new set of circumstances in some way analogous to the former situation), so that his guilt, or at any rate his selfishness, callousness or whatever fault we attribute to him, will appear in a glaring light. We derive an unhealthy joy from representing to ourselves the chagrin and contrition of the guilty one as he becomes aware of what he has forfeited by his act of inconsiderateness, or as he sees us in a condition that reveals the gravity of his offense.

Sulking, then, implies an act, not of hardening but of *closing to*. Whereas the truly meek one always remains open (even to an enemy), the sulker, even though remaining soft, lets the lids of his soul fall, as it were. He quits the kindly, serene attitude of love. Also, the resentment of sulking implies an inward crampedness in the place of freedom.

Moreover, softness in the sulker takes on a spineless quality incompatible with all strength of soul. Only an effeminate weakling can gain comfort and pleasure from wallowing in self-pity. Inseparable from sulking is an attitude of self-importance and self-centeredness. This, again, means a sharp contrast to meekness, for which a selfless attention to the fellow person — as expressed in the glance of love — is absolutely essential.

Whereas he who possesses meekness is ready to endure a wrong charitably, the sulker, though he too suffers it without retaliating, cannot be properly said to endure it. He only does so ostensibly: in reality, he forbears from hitting back precisely in order to make the offender's guilt more conspicuous and thus to hurt him.

The meek man forgives the wrong his adversary has committed. The sulker, far from forgiving it, definitely resents it and charges his enemy with it no less than does the irascible man. The meek person is wounded by an uncharitable act, but it is powerless to deflect him from charity; in the sulker, however, a sting is left behind: he continues cleaving inwardly to the wrong with which he perpetually reproaches the offender — perhaps, indeed, more so than does the man prone to explosive anger.

Sulking is motivated both by pride and concupiscence

The sensitive person, with a penchant for sulking, is hungry for love; not that he is himself rich in love and eager to see his love reciprocated, but he craves the soft comfort of being ensconced in a snug corner, the gratifying sensation of being petted, cajoled, and pampered. He is generally of a soft-fibered type. He is greatly attached to the amenities of life; he spoils himself and wants to be spoiled by others. He is indignant at being roughly handled, not because uncharitableness as such wounds him but because he is shocked by an experience opposed to that of caresses and blandishments — his chief source of pleasure.

Two motives, then, underlie the attitude of sulking. In the first place, pride: that is, an essential and seemingly self-evident claim to importance; a need felt for riding high on the consideration of others. Secondly, a certain type of concupiscence, which renders the subject particularly susceptible to the charms of velvety cushions, figuratively speaking; of being softly treated, and spoiled. Such a person is, first of all, soft towards himself. In a general sense, he lets himself go, allured by the mirage of a life in which there are no harsh winds at all but only softly whispering breezes. He is, in fact, much too egocentric to be capable of the true happiness of being loved.

True love would require on his part the capacity of loving others, which implies a readiness for heroic self-surrender. An uncharitable treatment does not wound him by reason of its intrinsic ugliness and the virulent malice it contains. It irks him because it inflicts upon him an unpleasant experience of roughness and harshness, and troubles the tepid atmosphere in which he feels comfortable. To sum up, his softness does not imply in him, as it would in a hard and irascible character, a great wealth of love, but merely a feebler and less spirited nature. Softness in this sense is anything but a value.

The softness in meekness is penetrated by active goodness

The softness inherent in meekness is of a vastly different type. An abyss yawns between both also with respect to their quality. Meekness is penetrated by a sublime flavor of active goodness. It is the transfigured softness proper to supernatural love, which, St. Paul the Apostle says, "Beareth all things, believeth all things, hopeth all things, endureth all things" (1 Cor. 13:7). It presupposes true freedom — freedom from all spasms of egocentrism.

In him who has attained to true meekness, there no longer remains any field of sensitivity to his treatment or appraisal by others except *one*: a heart warmed and made happy by the enlivening ray of pure love. Wounded by the dart of malice and hostility, blood flows from his wounded heart, yet at the same time he is neither embittered, irritated, nor sick with pettish resentment. Vituperations and insults, slights and injuries, acts of hatred or of contempt — they all no longer affect him with their specific venom, by tearing at his pride or grating on his sense of self-importance, but solely and exclusively in their quality as antitheses to love. The meek Christian is anything but insensible. He by no means views an offense inflicted upon him in a spirit of unimpassioned neutrality. By reason of the uncharitableness it represents, it will on the contrary bore into his heart — without, however, any poisoning or narrowing effect.

Meekness is compatible with ardent zeal and intrepid strength

Hence, the softness of meekness is consistent with ardent zeal and intrepid strength. St. Stephen, whom the Acts of the Apostles (6:8) call *plenus gratia et fortitudine* ("full of grace and fortitude"), is at the same time a shining example of true meekness. The brief account we read there of his conduct during his stoning reveals to us clearly his sublime meekness. No trace is seen here of a fighting hero's posture; none of the stubborn resistance of a purely natural virility; nothing of hardness or bitterness of any kind. In his victorious love of God, as also in his mild and forgiving love towards his murderers, he offers his heart, clad in the soft garments of charity, to their implacable hatred.

Jesus is the model of meekness

But it is in Jesus our Lord that we discern holy meekness at its purest. He lets Judas kiss Him; suffers Himself to be wounded by the touch of His treacherous apostle: "Friend, whereto art thou come?" (Matt. 26:50). The dolorous words, "You are clean, but not all" (John 13:10); His exposure of His most holy heart to the wrath of His pursuers; His attitude of sorrowful mildness and forgiveness, remaining fully open even in the face of His betrayer and of His slayers: "Father, forgive them, for they know not what they do" (Luke 23:34); that glance of a wounded yet generous and serene love, which lighted on Peter the Apostle after his denial of the Lord, kindling in him a fire of charity never to be extinguished again: here is holy meekness, a force issuing from inalterable and triumphant Love, a force infinitely more irresistible than any natural power on earth.

Here, indeed, is the new accent, the new idiom of the Gospel: the new gesture — mirrored in a thousand forms of expression — of redeeming Love, which the world does not understand but by which it is bound to be overcome. "Blessed are the meek: for they shall possess the land."

Holy meekness embodies transcendent power

It constitutes a specific test of our possession of a supernatural spirit if we comprehend the sublime beauty of holy meekness and recognize the transcendent power it embodies. Whoever still seeks for strength in some kind of natural heroism proves that, though he may have grasped certain truths of the Faith, he is as yet enslaved to a pagan idol of *virility*. The weaponless candor of holy meekness impresses him as something feminine; he deems it inconsistent with the spirit of virility.

Many a Christian is inclined to this error. In reaction against a well-known sickly, sweetish disfigurement of Our Lord's person in a certain insipid brand of devotional images, songs, and pious books, such Christians would read into the person of the God-Man a natural *ethos* of virile heroism. Combatting one mistake, they thus fall into the opposite one. Every attempt at thus dwarfing the stature of Him from whose "brightness a new light hath risen to shine on the eyes of our souls" (Preface of the Nativity) to the measure of purely natural categories — be it that of a placid kindliness or warlike courage — is in itself preposterous.

Holy mildness and meekness are as far remote from feminine fragility, let alone weak sentimentalism, as are the conquering solemnity and supernatural force of the *Kyrios* and *Victor Rex* from natural heroism, let alone a crabbed emphasis on virility. Nor do these two supernatural aspects merely stand side by side; they are indissolubly linked together. The holiness and supernatural sweetness of him "who is meek and humble of heart"; the heart that, unshielded, lies open to any attack: *fons totius consolationis* ("fount of all consolation": Litany of the Sacred Heart); the suffering, holy, redeeming Love — this is what brings us to our knees and reveals to us the divine power of Him of whom St. Paul says, "All things were created by Him and in Him; and He is before all: and by Him all things consist" (Col. 1:16-17).

The primal truth of Revelation — that "God is Love" — flashes up in the all-redeeming love of the Lamb "who taketh away the sins of the world." Of the Son of Man (whom the Church thus glorifies in the Sequence for Easter: "To a Father kind, rebellious men / sinless Son hath led again"), St. John says: "And we saw his glory, the glory as of the only begotten of the Father, full of grace and truth" (John 1:14).

Consider the image which the holy Liturgy presents to us of the Lord. According to the mystery proper to each feast, Christ appears to our eyes now in His infinite mildness and meekness (as in the Vesper of the Most Holy Name of Jesus), now in His victorious Divine power (as in the Sequence for Easter); now again, in both attitudes immediately united one to the other, as in the commemoration of the Passion on Good Friday: *Popule meus, quid feci tibi?...Agios o Theos; Agios ischyros; Agios athanatos.* ("O my people, what have I done unto thee?...O holy God; O holy, O mighty One; O holy, immortal One.")

For these attitudes are, in truth, not two opposites but two sides of one and the same Being, Divine and Human; their union denotes that specific mark of God, an apparent *coincidentia oppositorum*.

Those, then, who possess a supernatural spirit may be known by this — that they do not feel shocked or baffled at the meekness and the holy innocence, the love unarmed and disarming, of Jesus; that, instead, they sink to their knees before the Lamb who "taketh away the sins of the world," and who spoke the words, "I am meek and humble of heart"; that they say in adoration with St. Thomas the Apostle, "My Lord and my God."

We attain holy meekness by dwelling spiritually with Jesus

How can we attain to holy meekness?

In order to stay habitually in the soft, gentle, open attitude of loving kindness, we must, above all, constantly elevate our eyes to the face of the divine Savior. Whatever aggressions, insults, injuries, and humiliations we suffer, we must immediately bring them into the light that emanates from this most holy Face. In fact we should aim at dwelling in that light so permanently that our very first awareness of an injustice or slight inflicted upon us will be already impregnated with the spirit of meekness and free from any trace of the poison of resentment. "Learn of me, because I am meek and humble of heart" (Matt. 11:29). Such a sustained vision of Jesus and His Sacred Heart, "the propitiation for our sins" (1 John 2:2); a constant breathing of the air of His holy charity — can alone maintain us in that state of inward fluidity and suppleness.

True, the acts of meekness unfold in our attitude towards our fellow men; but meekness cannot thrive in us unless our eyes meet the glance of Jesus; unless we lay ourselves open to the sunlight of His love and in love surrender ourselves to Him. "My soul melted when he spoke" are the words of the spouse in the Canticle of Canticles (Song of Sol. 5:6). St. Gregory in his Homily on Luke 7:42 comments upon them: "For the soul of a man that seeks not his Creator is hard, because it remains cold in itself. But once it is seized with an ardent desire to follow the Beloved, it hastens to him, molten in the fire of love."

True meekness then cannot flourish in us unless our vital union with Jesus precludes the possibility of any attack from subjecting us to the control of its autonomous logic. It cannot exist in us unless our heart is pierced and conquered by the love of Him who said: "A new commandment I give unto you: That you love one another, as I have loved you" (John 13:34). This is the point of vantage from which we may conjure up, in its full and compelling reality, the vision of the sublimity of spiritual personality and of the incompatibility of all brute force with the laws of the spiritual sphere.

It is in the light of Jesus' face — of His transfigured nature as Man — that we shall catch a bright glimpse of the nobility of man *qua* spiritual person. It is here that we gain a corresponding insight into the preposterous inadequacy of all mechanical and massive methods in the face of the particular structure of spiritual personality. Only thus shall we fathom to the full the odiousness as well as the futility of all rough and violent modes of behavior. We must come to abhor their very principle in our innermost hearts; we must loathe it still more in its association with an intention of enmity — whether or not expressly manifested in the form of actual anger.

But, as suggested above, our sustained vision of Christ will not merely keep us alive to the value of meekness and aware of the inferiority and ugliness of its opposite. It will also help us to abide in the mild, detached, unshielded inward attitude without which we cannot behave with true meekness towards others. A particle of the mellow splendor of Christ will radiate into our own heart. It will soften and refine our inward life and dissolve all cramped ego-obsessions in us. It will even, at a higher stage of virtue, prevent them from arising at all.

Meekness presupposes the humility inherent in patience

Furthermore, meekness presupposes patience. As has been shown in Chapter 12, an eminently spastic and hardening effect issues from impatience; this cannot but sap the very foundations of meekness. But there is an even more specific consonance between these two virtues. Meekness, just as patience, implies one's abstinence from assuming a false position of sovereignty above the universe — from feeling as though it were one's due to be an absolute master. The humility inherent in patience is what underlies the softness — the absence of hardening — that is proper to meekness. In meekness lives the basic gesture of serving set forth in the words of Our Lord: "The Son of man is not come to be ministered unto, but to minister" (Matt. 20:28).

The natural illusion of a *position of sovereignty* is closely linked to the natural tendency to enforce whatever seems desirable. Once we feel it self-evident that we should be master over things we cannot help dealing with everything in a certain mode of hardness. Inversely, the basic gesture of service necessarily implies a tone of softness in our way of approaching the outside world. Thus, we see

417

it confirmed that meekness, even though actualized in our relations with created beings, is in its essence conditioned by our position towards God.

Meekness also manifests itself in kindness toward animals

More exactly, as we have seen earlier, meekness becomes actualized in our relations with our fellow men. To be sure, this field of relations constitutes its primary domain of unfolding; but a reflection thereof extends to our behavior towards *all* created things. In the first place, this applies to sentient beings inferior to man: that is to say, the dumb animals. He who has true meekness will never be cruel to animals. Whether he particularly sympathizes with an animal or not, he will never handle it roughly nor deny it a certain attention according to its specific character as a living being.

In an analogical (and by no means irrelevant) sense of the term, he will treat animals with charity, rather than unkindly pushing a brute aside as a mere troublesome *alien body*. Even though they happen to disturb him, he will maintain the kindly attitude of gentle softness. In particular, he will shun the false position of sovereignty in this relationship. Subject though animals are (in a sense) to the domination of man, he will utterly abstain from playing the despot. He will respect the character of a creature, the nobility and individual distinctness of life as such, the greater subtlety of the structure of organic life as contrasted to the mechanical forces of nature; he will, as it were, respect the right of these beings to an exercise of their dispositions within certain limits.

The all-pervading breath of loving kindness founded on humility will manifest itself, beyond an avoidance of all brutality, in a gesture of condescension and understanding, an attitude of friendly attention to the animal's distinctive nature. Furthermore, true meekness will leave its trace even on the manner in which a person approaches and treats lifeless objects. Even where inert nature is concerned, the fundamental antithesis between meekness and the false position of sovereignty — the illusion that man can be an absolute master of *anything* on earth — remains applicable and valid.

Meekness actualizes our inner peace in relation to others

The manner in which the meek man passes through the world breathes, in its every phase, that soft and serving attitude entirely detached from self-assertion. Whatever defects occur in his environment, he shows no eagerness to ferret them out nor to lay them bare, and much less, to fall upon them in a spirit of enmity. On the contrary, he would mildly cover them up and approach charitably those disfigured by them. The weapon with which he fights all disharmony is the radiance of his own indefectible harmony.

Inward peace is all the more an indispensable condition of meekness. He alone who preserves inward peace (removing from its path the obstacles we have listed in the preceding chapter) can possess that mellow harmony, free from all crampedness and all venom, from which meekness draws its nourishment.

Meekness *is* but the actualization of this inner harmony on the plane of our relationships with others: the shaping of all our reference to, and treatment of, our fellow men by the principle of a spontaneous, unhampered, overflowing charity. This dependence of meekness on patience and true peace makes it doubly evident that true meekness is unattainable for anyone who does not live through and in Christ.

Meekness alone achieves true victory in the world

"Blessed are the meek: for they shall possess the land." The meek, who in truth follow Christ and in all situations keep faithful to their primal response to the love of Christ — they shall obtain the promised land of eternal beatitude. Yet, already on earth they are irresistible: for them is also reserved true victory over the world. For it is they who challenge all evils in the world with the weapons of light; who resist all determination by the immanent automatisms of worldly concerns; and who confront all enmity with the superior power of an inalterable, soaring charity. True meekness is the token of our being thus anchored in the supernatural; the seal of the true and ultimate freedom that resides in suffering, serving, world-re-deeming love.

In meekness is revealed the operation of the fundamental law of victory over the world: the principle of not returning like for like — of opposing the spirit of the world by an integrally new and different one, as expressed in the words of the Lord: "Love your enemies; do good to them that hate you" (Matt. 5:44). Meekness is likewise incarnate in the words, "If one strike thee on thy right cheek, turn to him also the other" (Matt. 5:39).

It means no passive toleration of all wrongs, no dull acquiescence in the dominion of sin — rather, it means true warriorship in the cause of Christ. However relentless his fight against sin, however ardent his zeal for the victory of the kingdom of God, the true *warrior of Christ* remains meek: he is melted by the love of Christ once it has been evoked in him by his glance upon the Savior who suffered and died for love.

"For they shall possess the land." In his Homily on the words of Our Lord — "Behold I send you as sheep in the midst of wolves" (Matt. 10:16) — St. John Chrysostom with sublime mastery expounds this victory of the meek over the world. He paraphrases the words of the Lord: "When you start on your way, behave with the meekness of sheep, although you prepare to meet wolves, nay, to betake yourselves into their midst. For by this shall I reveal my power most visibly, that wolves shall be overcome by sheep, whereas the sheep, though exposed to the fangs of wolves and bleeding from innumerable wounds, shall not only *not* perish but

420

even change the wolves into their own nature. Surely it is greater and more wonderful to win the soul of the foe, to turn his mind into its opposite, than to kill him....So long as we are sheep, we conquer. Should a thousand wolves encompass us, we should win them over and emerge victorious. Yet if we become wolves, we shall be conquered. For then shall the Shepherd (who leads to pasture not wolves but sheep) withdraw his assistance from us. He shall turn from thee and abandon thee, seeing that thou makest it impossible for him to reveal his power. But if thou abidest meek, thy victory shall be his work." (St. John Chrysostom, *Homily 34*.)

In truth, the meek will emerge victors over the world, because, in their struggle for the kingdom of God, they know no weapons except that by which Christ has redeemed the world and vanquished our hearts; because they have cast all other — all natural — weapons from them, countering all enmity and unruly fierceness of evil with the offer of their unshielded heart, which is ready to bleed to death for the sinner's sake also.

If spoken by the meek, the word of truth which like a sword, severs soul and body, subtly insinuates itself like a breath of love into the innermost recesses of the soul. For the meek is reserved true victory over the world, because it is not they themselves who conquer, but Christ in them and through them.

15

Holy Mercy

MERCY is a specifically divine virtue. If humility is a virtue specifically befitting the creature, so that it can be attributed to God only insofar as He is the God-Man, and that in a merely analogical sense, mercy, inversely, is the divine virtue *par excellence*, which cannot be attributed to man except by analogy.

Mercy is the condescending, forgiving love of God for sinners

Mercy primarily means the condescending, forgiving love of the absolute Lord, the Epitome of all values, who bends down to us without our deserving it at all. Mercy becomes most manifest in reference to *sinful* man. None of the Gospel texts impresses mercy on our consciousness so clearly as does the parable of the Prodigal Son. It is love in its particular quality as mercifulness that strikes us in the conduct of the father as he goes to meet his returned son, receives the contrite one with love, and even kills a fatted calf for him.

But the Gospel as a whole breathes the spirit of mercy; for the mercy of God constitutes a central point in Christian Revelation. It upsets the ancient conception of the world, to which a God bending down in love to a creature would have meant an inherent contradiction. It is a stumbling block to the Pharisees, who expect everything from justice founded on the fulfillment of the law. The mercy of God, this primal word of the Gospel, speaks to us movingly from the parable of the Samaritan; it addresses us as a warning in the parable of the master who released his servant from his debt; it overwhelms us in Our Lord's death on the cross, who, dying, prays for his slayers.

The Gospel calls us to be merciful

Not only does the Gospel reveal to us the mercy of God: it also enjoins upon us to be merciful on our part. Our transformation in Christ requires us to share even this specifically divine virtue. "I will have mercy and not sacrifice," says Jesus in the house of the publican (Matt. 9:13). The merciful are above all pleasing to God; in fact, our mercifulness is the condition on which we in our turn may find mercy in the eyes of God.

Mercy presupposes misery in its object

Mercy obviously connotes love; it means, however, not love pure and simple, but one particular variety of love. We may best grasp the specific quality of merciful love by considering that mercy presupposes in its object some misery, some wretchedness. This is by no means generally true of love. The love uniting the Persons of the Holy Trinity does not possess the quality of mercy at all; nor does, except accidentally, conjugal love or the love of friendship.

Mercy, then, responds to misery in the one received or succored in love; moreover, it implies an attention to which its beneficiary has no *claim* proper — in other words, a gesture of condescension. It might be surmised, therefore, that mercy is the same thing as *compassion*; but that would be a grossly erroneous conclusion.

There is, in fact, a fivefold difference between compassion and mercy.

Mercy responds to our metaphysical situation; compassion responds to particular sufferings

First, compassion always refers to some concrete suffering in a definite person. We *pity*, in the sense of compassion, a person who is grievously ill or poor, or a prey to some other grave affliction. Mercy, to be sure, equally connotes an attitude of pity; but here our commiseration refers to the misery of the human creature as a whole, although represented or manifested by a given concrete case.

The true object of mercy is not this or that misfortune as such but the general helplessness and frailty of man under the sway of original sin. The particular suffering in question is not here relevant except as an expression of the universal misery inherent in the metaphysical situation of fallen man. The glance of the merciful penetrates into the abysses of man's situation in this "valley of tears"; against this background it also perceives in peculiar clearness the nobility of man *qua* a spiritual person created in the likeness of God.

With a vision much deeper than that of the compassionate, the merciful one always sees the creature in the light of its metaphysical situation and considers the special circumstances of its case, too, *in conspectu Dei*. Hence, there is a certain trait of spiritual gravity and heroism proper to mercy, but not to pity as such.

Compassion suffers with the sufferer; mercy does not

Secondly, genuine compassion implies a state of suffering in the subject himself; *con-passio*, indeed, means *suffering with* someone. He who evinces compassion is in some sense implicated in the situation of the one he pities. Mercy, on the other hand, is not itself associated with suffering, or else God — in His infinite beatitude, to which no shade of suffering attaches — could not be merciful. The subject of mercy in no way becomes a sharer in the situation of its object; he (in a very specific sense, to be sure) *controls* that situation from above.

Compassion is between equals; mercy is toward an inferior

By this we have already hinted at the third point of difference. Compassion presupposes a fundamental situation embracing its subject and object alike: it constitutes a relationship *inter pares* ("between equals").

Mercy, on the contrary, presupposes a superiority on the part of the merciful one. In the sense of *intentional* awareness, he certainly *assimilates* or *comprehends* the suffering of the creature he pities, but his own center of vision, his own spiritual locus as it were, is outside and above that suffering. Therefore, a gesture of condescension is inherent to all mercy: the merciful one *bends down in love* to the misery that has evoked his commiseration.

Compassion, on the contrary, not only does not require a gesture of condescension but is actually altered and spoiled by its presence. Once condescension enters, we have in the place of genuine compassion a proud attitude which is most likely to insult the person whom it is supposed to comfort. For compassion is eminently a corollary of an all-embracing solidarity of suffering mankind; it essentially demands, on the subject's part, an attitude of meeting the pitied one on a level of equality. Though it always refers to some concrete affliction of definite persons, it does so taking for granted the fundamental human situation, *common to all*, a constant background.

In contradistinction to this, mercy among men is but an analogue of the mercy of God: it is only possible as a participation in the latter, an imitation of the attitude of loving condescension whose primary subject is God and God alone. Therefore, mercy is an eminently supernatural virtue, requiring as its basis the Christian *ethos*. Every attempt to realize it on a purely natural plane is bound to fail — to result, that is, not in true mercy but in the irritating hybrid of a "superior" compassion.

Mercy is more spiritual than compassion

Fourthly, compassion — a specifically human motive of behavior — presupposes the vulnerable human heart as such. It implies a particular kind of sensitive understanding for the suffering creature, an organic sympathy, a certain feeling of sameness, as it were. Mercy constitutes a response very much more spiritual in character. In it, too, lies an ultimate understanding — a type of understanding, however, which is the privilege of one whose vision measures its object in a perspective of distance and height.

The merciful man thus approaches that object from above — from the altitude of his own response to the condescending love of God, not from a self-assumed position of superiority. He understands the pitiable object indeed, in a much deeper sense: somewhat as God, just because He is infinitely above us, is nearer to us than we are ourselves. This is what we meant by saying that the merciful one "controls" the situation which surrounds the wretched creature inasmuch as he views it in a light borrowed from God and comprehends it from above, conspiring as it were with the divine act of mercy.

Mercy presupposes that the merciful can give help; compassion does not

Finally, he who posits an act of mercy does so in reference to a kind of situation in which his intervention may effect some change.

This is obviously always the case with God; in regard to us men, however, the presupposition is fulfilled in a very limited measure only. Compassion, again, is not linked to this condition. Suppose a friend of mine is grievously afflicted by the death of one dear to him — I may vividly sympathize with him and share his sorrow fully, but the case presents no occasion for the exercise of mercy.

This point of difference is connected with the inherence in mercy of a certain aspect of superiority. One's pity cannot have the character of mercy without one's controlling the situation, in some way, from above. This, again, is impossible unless one is in some measure able to help: to mold the situation and not merely to deplore it.

Who *can* exercise mercy? A person in health who can assist the sick; a priest who, by virtue of his office, can cure the wounds of the soul; also, anyone who may remit a debt, renounce a right, or waive a claim for the benefit of another.

Mercy is an antithesis to justice

Having thus clearly established the distinction between mercy and compassion, let us now examine another fundamental aspect of mercy: its antithetic relation to strict justice. *Merciful* love — not, as is sometimes thought, love as such — embodies, indeed, an antithesis to justice. For it connotes an excess of loving kindness which is over and above the measure of merits. Well we know what our fate would be if God weighed us according to the measure of justice only: therefore do we pray, "If Thou, O Lord, wilt mark iniquities: Lord, who shall stand it?" (Ps. 129:3).

Yet, evidently, this *surpassing of justice* has nothing in common with injustice. Mercy is not an antithesis to justice in a sense implying a negation of the value of justice. It comprises the latter *per eminentiam* — by overflow, as it were. All that makes up the value of justice is contained to an even higher degree in mercy.

God does not cease to be supremely just by being supremely merciful. "King of majesty tremendous, who dost free salvation send us, Fount of pity then befriend us!" (*Dies Irae*)

Certainly this union of justice and mercy is possible in God the absolutely Simple One, who embraces the fullness of Being and in reference to whom we may speak of a *coincidentia oppositorum*. But how is *our* mercy related to justice? What kind of situations are there in which we may and ought to follow the promptings of mercy?

There are two main lines along which mercy unfolds. It may be exercised, first, towards persons against whom we have a legitimate claim: who, for example, owe us money or some kind of service; or again, who have done us some wrong. We may, secondly, behave with mercy towards persons afflicted with any sort of misery towards whom we have no special obligations, be it in the sense of duties inherent in our office (in the widest use of that term) or of obligations implied by a particular personal relationship. It is mercy of this kind that directs us to succor, say, a strange person who is wounded or one who is destitute; or again, one who is despised and ostracized by all.

Mercy can be exercised toward those against whom we have a claim

But let us first examine the type of mercy which involves the waiving of a claim. What is meant here is, of course, our renunciation of a valid right of our own. Mercy impels us to overstep the measure of justice in a case where justice would operate to our personal advantage.

When, on the other hand, we have to decide about the conflicting claims of others — acting, for instance, as an arbiter between two contestant parties — we are not at liberty to transgress the measure of justice. We have no right simply to cancel the debt which an indigent person owes to a prosperous one. By all means, we may — having regard to the particular circumstances — try to persuade the creditor to show mercy, but we are not in a position to substitute in our own right clemency for justice. Yet, we may well do so if the creditor is ourselves.

Even in this case, however, our surrender of the claim in question may not always be an act of true mercy, nor even always the right thing to do. If it is a debt we remit, it must, first of all, be owed us by a poor man — one who, not only as regards the given juridical case but in a more comprehensive sense also, is in a weaker position than we are. To remit a debt owed by a rich man has obviously nothing to do with mercy. The misery to which our mercy responds cannot consist in the weaker position alone in which every debtor as such has placed himself. It must attach to the situation of the debtor beyond this particular indebtedness, too.

It is further ill-advised on our part to renounce our right if by so doing we are likely to inflict upon our debtor a moral damage. Some people seek to capitalize on the magnanimity of others; to help them to success cannot but confirm them in their unrighteousness, whereas a stern treatment may provide them with a salutary lesson. In such cases, yielding one's right is not an act of true mercy but a mere indulgence of faintheartedness and guilty weakness. There are, as a matter of fact, several types of complaisant attitudes which, though they lack all intrinsic kinship with mercy, may easily be confused with it by a superficial observer.

Yielding to others out of fear of conflict is not mercy

Some people are simply too weak to defend their rights. They shun every dispute, abhor every act of resistance, and feel unable to sustain any conflict. With some of these the matter is chiefly faint-heartedness; with others, helplessness; with others again, sloth.

In any case their renunciation of rights is an outgrowth of weakness rather than of love. It is not pity for the other party that impels them to yield: rather it is their preoccupation to escape the discomfort inevitably involved in taking a stand. Such people would sooner abandon many things dear to them, and accept great sacrifices — both material and moral — than engage in any kind of struggle. Whenever they are faced with the necessity of claiming or insisting upon anything they immediately feel as though *they* were in the weaker position. Their dread of conflict, and not the state of right, is what in their minds supplies the determinant note of the situation. Their pusillanimity presents a glaring contrast to the active and heroic, the majestic attitude of mercy.

Pliability is not mercy

Another kind of weakness, nobler than that which is colored by cowardice or inertia, should still be carefully distinguished from genuine mercy. What we have in mind is the behavior of those softhearted people who will never refuse any request nor inflict any displeasure on others.

Unlike the truly merciful, they by no means view the situation from a higher plane. They do not take their departure from that ultimate love which considers the objective good of the fellow person over and above any immediate advantage or amenity. They are slaves to their instinct of compassion.

In other words, they fall short of an adequate response to the situation, in that they do not extend their compassion beyond the range of the present moment, nor care about their fellow's well-being in an integral and permanent sense of the term. Theirs is an inordinate compassion, which does not arise, as does mercy, from a confrontation of the problem on hand with God and His holy will. Such compassion delivers them over entirely to the dynamism of the momentary situation, which determines their conduct without any counterweight. Such is the compassion of an unconscientious nurse who secretly tenders the coveted syringe to a morphine addict writhing in the torments of a curative treatment.

Indiscriminate generosity is not mercy

Lastly, there are people who, owing to a certain generous disposition, are ashamed to make their rights valid even when this would be the objectively right course. They shy at the idea of taking any advantage of their stronger position as a hierarchic superior, a creditor, a victim of outrage. Thus, they fail in their duty to reproach a person, or to seize him with a peremptory demand, even though this were in conformity with his objective good. Such a type of behavior, again, is not inspired by mercy.

Mercy is rooted in concern for the good of another

For if I am truly merciful I shall derive the principle of my conduct towards others from that ultimate love which is above all concerned precisely with the good of the person in question — regardless of whether it is easy or hard for my own nature to insist upon my right. This — and not pliancy or tractability as such — is the essential mark of mercy, that, by virtue of my participation in the love of God, I relinquish my nature as a central frame of reference and shatter the narrow perspective in which I would see things and situations merely with my own eyes.

And this transformation implies that the instinctive tendencies of my nature, whether in themselves more possessive or more yielding, will no longer play any decisive part in the shaping of my conduct.

He who is guided by true mercy, then, will yield his right on the supposition only that he does not, by so doing, bring moral harm to his debtor. Consider the parable of the Prodigal Son more

closely, and you will immediately discover that the doctrine underlying it is by no means that of indiscriminate forgiveness. To be
sure, the father hastens to welcome his spendthrift son, but he does
so in response to the youngster's repentant homecoming. The
presupposition, in other words, is that the disaster his son has
brought upon himself has evoked in him a sense of his guilt and a
resolution to change his ways.

On the contrary, had he been supported by his father after he
had eaten up his fortune, he would — far from having remorse and
undergoing conversion — only have been consolidated in his sinful way of life. Unlike those who are compassionate from weakness,
the truly merciful will never, as it were, interfere with the divine
government of men by substituting mercy for justice regardless of
the state of mind of those who are meant to benefit by such a course.

Mercy can be exercised toward those who have no claim against us

Now we must turn to the second dimension of mercy: its
exercise with regard to such men as are not our debtors and to
whom we owe no specific service. For, wherever such a specific
obligation is present — founded, for example, in ties of family or
friendship or wardship — it is self-evident that the wretchedness
of such persons, whether it be illness, need or a deep sorrow, should
concern us. Here our fellow being has a claim to our active help
and our full solicitude. There is consequently no room here for the
actualization of mercy as such.

Not so when we are faced with the distress of a stranger whose
fate is formally no concern of ours: a wounded man whom, like the
good Samaritan, we meet on the roadside; a person in the throes
of despair, whom we happen to come across; the unknown poor
who entreat us to help them — and other similar cases. Here is a
situation to which the primary and adequate response is mercy: the

overflowing love, the charity that bends down to heal; the sovereign surpassing of the measures of strict justice; the indefectible eagerness of the merciful heart to rescue the miserable from their misery and raise them up to itself.

Hardheartedness is the extreme antithesis to mercy

Of the several attitudes opposed to mercy, the extreme one is hardheartedness or callousness: the attitude of an explicit cold indifference to the misery of one's fellows. It is characteristic of a soul completely imprisoned in pride and concupiscence. The callous man is moved by nothing; he knows no compassion, let alone mercy. In his barren and stubborn lovelessness, he is liable to pass from mere indifference to something akin to positive cruelty: for any appeal to his mercy is likely to evoke on his part not only no sympathetic response but a definitely hostile reaction.

Indifference is a lesser antithesis to mercy

Another less extreme type is that characterized by indifference proper. In a person who represents this type, there is less emphasis on pride; but his bondage to concupiscence stifles in him all aliveness to the misery of others. He is not so much hard or cold as blunt, dull, and torpid. His complete lack of awakeness and responsibility — his incapacity ever to break away from the spell of his personal interests — renders him insensible to the suffering of his fellows. He is the rich man of the Gospel who, revelling in his wealth, lets Lazarus starve.

Delighting in another's indebtedness is opposed to mercy

There is, further, among the types of character deficient in mercy, the sort of person who delights in his superiority, in his prerogative of power, as it were, derived from another's indebtedness to him. He may not be very keen on the content of his claim, nor find it too hard to renounce a material advantage. He is above all anxious to preserve his ascendency over others; to keep them dependent upon him. He will, therefore, not so much insist on his claim being satisfied as he will emphatically maintain that claim; nay, endeavor to bring as many people as possible into the situation of owing him something. He enjoys the consciousness of having them in his power. He loves being beset with entreaties; he savors the idea of others trembling in expectation of his decree.

This attitude, again, is specifically opposed to mercy. For mercy not merely remits the debt of a miserable one, lest his misery should be increased: it is at the same time intent on relieving him from the pressure of his sense of indebtedness.

The ungenerous character, on the contrary, never forgets a wrong suffered nor integrally writes off a debt owed him in a way that eliminates all sense of inferiority on the debtor's side. He enjoys his position as a superior and exploits his advantage over his subordinates. He always takes care to emphasize and to have acknowledged whatever kind of superiority he can boast of. Whether it is a superiority in the moral, the intellectual, the economic, or the social order, he will see to it that those below him do not forget their inferiority for a moment and he will take pleasure in their consciousness of it.

This attitude is primarily the opposite of generosity, but since there can be such a thing as generosity without mercy (in a good pagan, say) but no such thing as mercy without generosity, it is *a fortiori* opposed to mercy.

Generosity is essential to mercy

For it is implied in mercy to be generous, as well as to be concerned about the misery of others, and ready to help them. It is implied that we avoid taking advantage of our superior position unless it be definitely necessary for the sake of an objective value.

Whenever we have to deal with a person laboring under any kind of inferiority, whether it is moral depravity or intellectual debility, vital deficiency or lack of culture, a misshapen body or grievous poverty, or any sort of social disability — we must not only *not* enjoy our advantage but painstakingly avoid letting our partner feel his inferiority in any fashion. In charity we must draw him to ourselves so as to extinguish in him all sense of oppression and inferiority.

This is not to say that we should not inwardly keep to the obligations inherent in our superior position: for we are not free with impious hands to level a hierarchy of values which has not been created by us but imposed by God's distribution of His gifts. Otherwise we should also reject the opportunity to help the other which God has offered us by placing him and us in our respective positions. Yet, by every means we must avoid making him feel his weaker position — except in special cases where the latter is required by our consideration of his spiritual welfare.

Mercy is more than the proud fulfillment of juridically formulated obligations

Lastly, another specific antithesis to mercy is embodied in the attitude of those who recognize moral obligations only inasmuch as they are in some way capable of a juridical formulation. Such a man will perhaps punctiliously watch over the welfare of a person formally entrusted to his care; one not so entrusted, however, simply does not exist for him.

He is emphatically *correct*; his only preoccupation is to aver himself irreproachable before his own conscience. It gratifies him to have accomplished whatever could be required of him according to the strict standards of legal justice. Not a step further will he go.

He takes no interest in the realization of something important in itself; he knows no genuine love for his neighbor. His only real concern is the ultimately proud one of acquitting himself of his obligations so as to be proof against any definite accusation and able to look upon himself as a being without blemish.

Should a stranger in distress cross his path, he will shrug his shoulder: "This is no concern of mine; I have not pledged myself to provide for him." He may even quietly look on without interfering (though it were in his power) while a fellow creature rushes to his ruin: "Ah well," he would say, "if his affairs had been confided to *me*, things would not have come to such a pass." Nor will our "correct" man ever feel inclined to remit a debt. Why should he? Nobody can by rights ask him to renounce a rightful claim.

Mercy far exceeds a bureaucratic concern with obligations

Akin to this pharisaical type of man, though considerably less repellent, is the purely legalistic one, characterized by an infatuation for the idea of right, untarnished, in this case, with the motif of self-complacency. We might also call it the bureaucratic type. The morality of such a man is genuine and estimable, yet sorely defective. Though his mind is not warped by pride, he is entirely devoid of warmth of heart and therefore in an essential sense morally crippled. He simply lacks comprehension for any *should and ought* that is outside the range of legal obligations.

Whatever he is in justice bound or explicitly engaged to do he will do with eager readiness and conscientious thoroughness; but to perform any good work beyond that would never occur to him and indeed make no sense to him. "Am I formally obliged to do this?" is the one question he always asks himself without bothering about anything else. In possession of a claim upon someone who suffers from some misery, he, too, will be disinclined to renounce it: for so to act is not a precise and stringent duty.

Summum jus, summa injuria ("the strictest justice may mean the greatest iniquity") is the well-known adage in which the essence of this attitude has been condensed.

The man of mercy, on the contrary, is loath to overemphasize the distinction between what is and what is not strictly obligatory. Not that he would, in ever so slight a measure, trifle with a duty or a commitment; but he in no way recognizes these as a limit to his endeavors for serving his fellows. Mercy thrives in the souls of those alone who visualize everything *in conspectu Dei*; who, in full awakeness, measure everything by supernatural standards.

Mercy presupposes true inner freedom

It also presupposes an inward suppleness and fluidity; a thoroughly melted, quickened, liberated heart. Every inward scar, as it were — every *hardening*, every *incrustation* brought about by an experience we have failed to rectify before God — dams up the flux of mercy. Nay, the path of mercy is thwarted by every kind of inner unfreedom: by our bondage, for example, to anxiety or to disgust; to the rancor evoked in us by an insult; and in general to every overemphatic preoccupation. For everything that stunts our freedom tends to make us self-conscious and to deprive us of the capacity, implied in mercy, of taking our stand above the situation.

He alone who has attained the supernatural sovereignty that results from true freedom and is reserved for those who seek only the kingdom of God and His justice, who expects nothing of his own forces but everything of God — he alone can participate in the specifically divine virtue of mercy.

None but those who have burst through the narrow limits of ego-life, and in full openness and awakeness centered their lives in Christ, can truly respond to the *miseria* of others and — beyond all mere compassion — perform the act of that redeeming loving kindness which conveys to the wretched a breath of the love of

God and lifts them from their misery, "Lifting up the poor out of the dunghill, that he may place him with princes, with the princes of his people" (Ps. 112:7-8).

Mercy presupposes humility

Nor is this holy sovereignty possible without humility. He alone who is deeply humble is blessed with true inward freedom and fluidity; he alone is free from all impeding hardness. The general significance of humility as a condition of all participation in the divine life stands out in particular brightness when it is a question of mercy. Our possession of the highest *human* virtue (which is humility) constitutes the necessary foundation for our progress towards sharing the specifically *divine* virtue of mercy. We must die to ourselves so that the mercy of Christ may fill us. With St. John the Baptist we must say: "He must increase; but I must decrease" (John 3:30).

Our mercy toward others is the measure of our life in Christ

Mercy, the specifically supernatural virtue, thus provides a touchstone more infallible perhaps than the test of any other virtue for a life conceived and molded in Christ. Hence, the question whether we have been merciful must play a decisive part in our examination of conscience. Many are the occasions for mercy which we miss. Only too often do we, as did the Pharisee, pass by a wounded one — clinging to our personal concerns, circum-scribed by our lack of freedom.

Yet, the virtue by which we live hourly is precisely the one of which we ought to be most mindful. And the mercy of God is what we live by. It pervades our lives integrally; it is the primal truth on which the whole being of a Christian rests. "For his mercy endureth forever" (Ps. 135:1). Indeed, the light of which the Psalmist says, "The light of Thy countenance, O Lord, is signed upon us" (Ps. 4:7), is *His mercy* who "maketh His sun to rise upon the good and bad" (Matt. 5:45) and who "spared not even His own Son" (Rom. 8:32) in order to redeem us.

The way to attain the virtue of mercy lies in our constant awareness of being encompassed by mercy: of the fact that mercy is the air we children of God are breathing. May the mercy of God, of whom the Church says: "With eternal love did the Lord love us, wherefore He drew us, raised from the earth, to His heart in commiseration" (Office of the Sacred Heart of Jesus) — may this mercy of God pierce and transform our hearts. May it draw us into the orbit of its all-conquering, liberating, suave power, before which all worldly standards collapse.

For according to the words of the Lord's Prayer ("Forgive us our trespasses, as we forgive those who trespass against us"), only insofar as we become merciful ourselves may we harvest the fruits of His mercy and taste, on a day to come, the last word of His mercy "that eye hath not seen, nor ear heard: neither hath it entered into the heart of man" (1 Cor. 2:9).

"Blessed are the merciful: for they shall obtain mercy."

16

Holy Sorrow

AS HAS been pointed out on several occasions, supernatural life represents something radically new, apart from other new aspects it introduces, in that its fullness reveals certain vestiges of that *coincidentia oppositorum* — that union of apparently irreconcilable opposites — which is a privilege of divine life. Qualities which cannot subsist in a person simultaneously so long as he has not relinquished the standpoint of nature — such as patience combined with fervent zeal, or again, peacefulness and an eager readiness to fight for a good cause — appear to achieve an organic mutual penetration in the character of the saints.

The greater our participation in divine life, the more enhanced is the possibility for us to actualize, in one single attitude, a diversity of virtues which in the natural perspective cannot but exclude one another.

Earthly man suffers the tension of *becoming*

This notwithstanding, a certain essential duality, an irremovable division as it were, remains inherent in our terrestrial situation as such. Of this duality the Christian consciousness must inevitably take account.

Again, that duality or breach manifests itself under two aspects. First, man in his earthly existence is a *mixed act*, as scholastic philosophy puts it; he is partly *in act*, partly *in potency*. In other words, we constitute actual, accomplished, fulfilled reality on the one hand; potentiality and *becoming* — unfulfilled beings — on the other.

Only God, who is absolute Being, is pure act — full and infinite Reality, to which no shadow of mutability attaches.

In eternity only shall we, too, be *accomplished*: not *pure act*, to be sure, for even there our being will be dependent on God; but sharers in the immutability of God insofar as we shall no longer contain any element of mere potentiality but have our whole being realized in one eternal moment. There (and there alone) we shall be past all becoming, having attained to a being free from all changeableness. All values in us will have matured to full actuality, with no room left for any potential ones. All that we are will be set out in its definitive shape.

It is not owing to original sin alone that in our earthly existence we are subject to the law of becoming. The state of man in the Garden of Eden, too, was no *status finalis* but a *status viae*. Man with his nature still unsoiled by sin was also meant to develop and was confronted with a task. He was meant to mature in knowledge and to supplement creation with a spiritual culture of his own devising; and again, to people the earth with his progeny. Yet, this was to take place in an undisturbed organic order — without any disharmony, labor or suffering.

But for original sin, there would have been no death. Instead of the painful and terrifying separation of soul and body, mankind would have known only an uncatastrophic passing on to a higher form of being — that *status finalis* in which "God is all in all."

Nevertheless, immense as is the contrast between the state of the fallen world and a paradisiac mode of existence, the latter too would have borne the sign of that duality which lies in the *mixture* of act and potency, and which essentially sets apart the *status viae* from the *status finalis*.

Earthly man suffers a tension between original sin and his redemption

Owing to original sin, however, earthly life is subject to the law of duality in yet another sense: a duality which even subsists after Christ's redemption of the world. On the one hand, we still suffer from the effects of original sin; on the other hand, we are redeemed beings: "reconciled to God," that is, through the most sacred Blood of Christ. By holy Baptism we are given participation in the life of Christ. So long as we remain in the state of grace, nothing can separate us from God: but yet we are still wanderers in a valley of tears.

As members of the Mystical Body of Christ, already on earth we are in an ineffable fashion united with God, participating in the divine life of the Holy Trinity: "seeing" and yet not seeing, "face to face" but "darkly as through a glass" (1 Cor. 13:12). We have not yet attained to an eternal and irrevocable communion with God. We are *no longer at the epoch of Advent*: for the eternal Word of God has become flesh, and wrought our redemption. Nevertheless, we are still in a phase of hope — a stage of expectation. As measured by the eternal glory which awaits us, our *status viae* still means an *Advent*.

Jesus said to us: "In the world you shall have distress: but have confidence. I have overcome the world" (John 16:33); but again He said: "Watch ye therefore, because you know not the day nor the hour" (Matt. 25:13). We still walk in the valley of tears, afflicted with crosses of all kinds. We still have to "fill up those things that are wanting of the sufferings of Christ, in my flesh, for his body, which is the church" (Col. 1:24); and yet we know "that the sufferings of this time are not worthy to be compared with the glory to come" (Rom. 8:18). We are still burdened with tasks; we must still hurry on from one moment to another; we are still caught in the movement of time; we are still constrained to activity — and yet, already on earth, contemplation forms the deeper and more important part of our life.

Already we have found the pearl of the merchant of the Gospel; we are no longer unquiet seekers — for "already our hearts are at rest in God" (St. Augustine, *Confessions*). Already we may say with St. Paul, "Buried with him in baptism; in whom also you are risen again" (Col. 2:12) — and yet we are still dependent on hope and filled with longing, crying out with St. John, "Come, Lord Jesus" (Rev. 22:20).

Unless we always keep in mind this dual character of our situation, we cannot dwell in truth fully and adequately. We must never, under the spell of the relative reality of present life, lose sight of the proper and absolute reality of the life to come; but neither must we forget that we are as yet citizens of the earth. To think or behave, in a sense, as though we no longer were *in statu viae*, is as false as to take our earthly passage for ultimate reality.

Man's dual aspect can be known by natural reason

Even our natural understanding — an understanding not guided by the light of Revelation — may discern this dual aspect in the features of earthly existence. The truly great among the non-Christian thinkers, such as Plato, were well aware of it. Without knowing about original sin, they saw the breach that runs through the world and ourselves. They perceived that man, according to his essence as a spiritual person, is ordained to the Good and destined to rise towards greater heights; but no less clearly did they perceive the downward drift in man's nature: his natural proclivity towards bad things. They beheld both the primacy of the spiritual and the rebellion of the flesh against the spirit; both man's faculty of spiritual concentration and his proneness to abject dissipation. They understood that the Good is more proper to man, more adequate to his inmost meaning: yet at the same time, that evil comes easier to him — that as soon as he relaxes his vigilance and yields to self-indulgence he will infallibly gravitate towards the nether regions. The beautiful myth in Plato's *Phaedrus* of the two horses pulling in opposite directions expresses this truth forcefully enough.

These great minds grasped both the truth that the genuine, perennial values herald the higher reality which we surmise to be our homeland proper, and the complementary truth that on this earth, inversely, evil prevails. The deeper and more awake a mind is, the more it will penetrate, even by its own natural lights, the basic duality of our earthly situation.

Materialists overlook the duality in man

Who, on the other hand, are farthest remote from the truth? Those who, without bothering about their metaphysical situation at all, are blind to objective values as such and entirely imprisoned in the world of their daily concerns; and again, those who are unaware of the scissure in our terrestrial being inasmuch as they only grasp its inferior aspect and content themselves with it.

The first of these two categories are the men without yearning, entirely fascinated by material goods and seeking no satisfaction except in these. By the second category, we mean the explicit materialists, who are convinced that man is nothing but a brute with a particularly well-developed brain. They deny all ordination of man to higher ends as well as all absolute values. They do not do so in a spirit of resignation or pessimism: rather, taking such a world deprived of all higher meaning and value for granted, they try to make it out as something cheerful and acceptable. In ignoring all higher values, they overlook the disharmony inherent in this world. To be sure, this implies an illusive effort to pass over or to explain away — or again, to represent as essentially curable — all ineluctable suffering of mankind as long and as far as it seems in any way possible.

Superficial optimists think we can eliminate all disharmony by secular means

Another false attitude is that of optimistic illusionism proper. Those who profess this error do acknowledge objective values; they are not satisfied with a purely subjective well-being nor exclusively busied with the pursuit of their interests. They are enthusiastic about moral values and capable of zeal in the service of ideals.

But they live without any reference to an eternal destination of man; they talk and behave as though man stood in no need of redemption at all. They would make us believe that there is no such thing as a radical flaw in our terrestrial constitution; that the earth could, by purely natural means, be changed into a paradise. They are superficial optimists — typified by thinkers like Jean-Jacques Rousseau.

These people, then, fail to recognize the character of earthly existence as a *status viae*. They are bent on interpreting terrestrial life as a self-sufficient and definitive reality, and to this end attempt to relativize all suffering and disharmony in the world to a level of mere accidentality. By sheer progress within the framework of this world, we *must* be able to get rid of all disharmony! — such is their contention.

And, clinging to the presupposition of this shallow confidence, they — like thoughtless children — pass by the abysses of human nature; the laws of suffering and death, constitutive for man's earthly state; the primacy in man's mundane life of evil and of brute force. To sum up, by comparison with the first discussed category of dull or complacent naturalists they may be said to have caught some glimpse of the truth; yet they, too, are a prey to illusion and fundamentally unaware of the character and meaning of terrestrial reality.

Metaphysical pessimists see misery as our ultimate destiny

Others, again, see exclusively the suffering and disharmony abundant in the world. They feel overwhelmed with the immensity of injustice, oppressed with the shackles of the body. They can no longer grasp the promise of a higher reality in values, so they develop into complete pessimists. Though sufficiently alive to the fact of disharmony, they, too, fall short of understanding the cleavage in our terrestrial world. True, they know and appreciate the higher values; but the metaphysical relevancy of value — its being a mark of our ultimate ordination and destiny — escapes them. In despair or resignation, they believe value to be nothing but a fine illusion. Lower reality is *reality proper*; to its massive laws we are integrally and inexhaustibly subjected; briefly, misery is our real and ultimate destiny. These metaphysical pessimists are also a species of illusionists. Erecting the disharmony of earthly life into an absolute, they in their turn fail to recognize the character of earthly life as a *status viae*. We may say that though they are aware at least of our need of redemption, they disbelieve in its actual possibility.

Some see the duality, but think human effort alone can overcome it

Of all minds unenlightened by revealed religion, those — as has been hinted above — come closest to the truth which have grasped the double aspect of human nature, the cleavage between its ordination to value and its tendency to break away therefrom. These are neither optimists nor pessimists; their outlook takes account of the ineliminable duality of earthly existence. They recognize both the primacy in man of the spiritual element and his oppressive dependence on the body and its urges.

Aware, in some way, of the proper destiny of man as well as of how unrealizable it is here on earth, they penetrate the character of earthly existence as a *status viae* — as something provisional, imperfect, and charged with a meaning which points to a reality outside its range. Thus, they neither ignore man's need of redemption nor despair of its possibility; however, their vision stops short at the necessity for that redemption to be wrought from above. With Plato, they still believe in a Godward evolution immanent to man. They fail to fathom the depth of the abyss, unbridgeable by all human effort, which separates us from God. Man's need of a *Divine* Messiah is what they have failed to comprehend.

The Jews saw man's need for a divine Redeemer

An entirely new position, by contrast to those discussed above, is the one represented by the Old Testament. The chosen people, to whom God has revealed the true situation of man, know that mankind, fallen through original sin, is marred by a mortal wound which only God can heal. Indeed, the chosen people, the depositary of the Old Testament, were in possession of the key to truth. They saw the split in man's situation and knew about its cause. They were aware of man's need of redemption by a Divine Messiah; on the strength of God's promise given to Abraham, they *awaited* in wistful hope the coming of that Messiah.

He came: the "eternal Word has become flesh"; and with that, our situation has fundamentally changed. The gulf which separated mankind from God is bridged; the debt of Adam is paid; our reconciliation to God is achieved. Man is redeemed: he has been offered a new supernatural community with God. By virtue of a free gift of divine mercy — a gift surpassing all concepts and all expectations — he may, in Christ and through Christ, participate in the divine life of the Holy Trinity. The path is open for him to eternal, blissful perfection and sanctification.

Even after the Redemption, the duality in earthly life remains

Even after the Redemption, however, earthly existence has remained a *status viae*. In many respects, the painful duality inherent in our earthly situation endures unchanged. Nay, while in one sense overcome, in another it has increased; for a new division has arisen: the duality of those *redeemed*, those already inexpressibly united with God — and those still in the state of hope, still on their pilgrimage towards perfection proper.

And on this higher plane, in the light of the full divine revelation, the danger of overlooking that irremovable duality of things terrestrial, and of confining one's vision to either of the two aspects of man's metaphysical situation, appears again. (We are speaking here, to be sure, of truly religious Christians only: not of Christians engrossed in earthly concerns to the point of growing all but forgetful of man's eternal destiny.)

Some Christians overlook the hope implicit in the Redemption

There are Catholics upon whose minds the tangible reality of terrestrial life, with all the disharmony implied in it, so much obtrudes itself as to make the reality of the Redemption — and of the supernatural community that unites all members of the Mystical Body of Christ with God — pale in significance.

Their gaze is fixed upon the ocean of human suffering, and the incertitude of our eternal fate. They are entirely filled with the thought of how "fearful a thing" it is "to fall into the hands of the living God" (Heb. 10:31). "With fear and trembling" (Tob. 13:6) do they walk along their lives' path. Their sins and the specter of their failure continually haunt their vision.

Well as they know that Christ has redeemed us and pronounced the words, "I am the resurrection and the life" (John 11:25), their minds dwell almost exclusively on the remoteness of mankind from God, the power of evil, the multitude of daily insults to God; on the helplessness of man and his dependence on the brute forces of nature; on their own weakness, the impotence of the human will, the tragic character of all terrestrial life.

Other Christians overlook the disharmony still remaining after the Redemption

Others, on the contrary, overlook the fact that we are still *pilgrims in the valley of tears*. They tend to behave as though Redemption meant that we are already in our heavenly home; as though we no longer had to fear anything; as though all disharmony were removed from the world; as though life no longer had any laborious tasks in store for us but was meant to be one everlasting feast of jubilation.

"Blessed are they that mourn..." comforts the afflicted

Both these classes of Christians respond inadequately to the duality which, even after the Redemption, remains in our terrestrial situation, according to the words of Our Lord: "Blessed are they that mourn: for they shall be comforted" (Matt. 5:5), which should be considered, here, side by side with these others, spoken by the Apostle of the Nations: "Rejoice in the Lord always: again, I say, rejoice" (Phil. 4:4).

In the beatitudes (Matt. 5:3-11), the way Our Lord refers each time to a heavenly reward is meant to indicate the eminent value of the quality praised. As regards the words "Blessed are the merciful," "Blessed are the peacemakers," or again "Blessed are the clean of heart," this is evident enough. But the meaning of "Blessed are they that mourn: for they shall be comforted" is less easy to understand. Why should *they that mourn* be called *blessed*? Can it be that a particular value is attached to sorrow as such?

To be sure in this case it is not only the value of the attitude in question which the blessing is meant to convey. This word is destined to *comfort* "all that labor and are burdened" (Matt. 11:28): it is a manifestation of divine mercy. To all those who have to suffer on earth — the oppressed and disinherited, the sick and the poor, the lonely, the downcast, the afflicted — this word reveals that the valley of tears is not reality ultimate and definitive. It implies that they are to come into their own in that final home where "God wipes away all tears."

It is a ray of light piercing through earth's darkness and brightening up the path of the weary and despondent, of those beset by despair. It is addressed, above all, to "them that" still "sit in darkness and in the shadow of death" (Luke 1:79): it eminently represents the *Eu angelion*, the joyful tidings of Christ. This word by itself modifies the terrestrial situation of man. It opens the gates of eternity. It reveals to mankind that earthly life is but a *status viae*.

Mourning in this life is blessed insofar as it represents a yearning for union with God

In addition to that, however, this beatitude does refer — like all others — to the high value of one particular attitude. For one thing, it declares blessed the sorrow of those who still abide in the *Advent*: those not satisfied with earthly reality. Blessed are, indeed, those who yearn for redemption: who, roused from the slumber of self-contained earthliness, are aware of the disharmony of a fallen world and experience the vestiges of original sin as a heavy burden.

Blessed are they whom no earthly happiness can deceive about the essential inadequacy of the present world; whose thirst cannot be quelled by terrestrial goods. They shall be comforted, because they long for what only eternal community with God can give them — whereas those who set their hearts on earthly treasures and seek for happiness in an unredeemed world are the truly and ultimately miserable ones.

Yet that word in the Sermon on the Mount is not addressed to them alone whose sorrow is the *Advent* sorrow. Even for souls fully responsive to the grace of Redemption, the present world remains a valley of tears. The inconceivable gift of the Incarnation of God and the redemption of man by His death on the cross have not wholly ended our separation, on earth, from God. Earthly life has remained, not only a *status viae* — even a paradisiac state, free from all disharmony, would be that — but a state of *dolorous* longing and unfulfillment.

Already, as members of the Mystical Body of Christ, we are in an inexpressible fashion united to God and may participate in the life of the Holy Trinity. We still, however, possess God according to the mode of *belief* only, not according to the mode of *vision*. If we really and truly love God, this "seeing through a glass in a dark manner" cannot but pain us. Whoever feels no sorrow at this relative separation from God and does not yearn to see God face to face, is not yet filled with that supreme love of God which speaks from St. Paul's words: "Having a desire to be dissolved and to be with Christ" (Phil. 1:23). "Blessed are they that mourn" for not having attained yet to the beatific vision.

Mourning must be understood, here, as the feeling of privation that accompanies a hope for future contentment and fulfillment: the suffering, that is to say, of wistful love. For we are still imprisoned in time, compelled to hurry endlessly from one object to another. The hour has not yet struck which will allow us to abide undisturbed with Him who constitutes our beatitude. Though redeemed, we still live by hope. We are still pilgrims who cannot know whether we will persevere to the end; who are still beset by dangers of all kinds; in whose midst "the devil, as a roaring lion, goeth about seeking whom he may devour" (1 Peter 5:8).

Our community with God is not yet a *definitive* one but still an object of hope. We are still, as it were, running for a prize. For those who love God, this implies suffering. "Blessed are they that mourn": they, that is to say, who feel the gravity of our terrestrial situation, are aware of the abyss between our *status finalis* and our *status viae*, and consciously bear the cross which lies in the fact that our union with God cannot on earth be a definitive and indestructible one.

Mourning has value as a sign of our love of God

This sorrow is precious in the eyes of God: for it proves, on the one hand, that our vision is adjusted to the perspective of truth and guided by supernatural light — that our faith is a living one; and reveals, on the other hand, a glowing love of God in our soul which prevents us from being satisfied by anything less than the sight of God and an eternal, indestructible community with Him. What, after all, should we think of a lover who endures without grief a separation from his beloved — no matter how sure he is of her love?

Mourning is appropriate because of mankind's failure to love God

For one more reason is sorrow a mark of the elect of God. Blessed are those who suffer from the multitude of insults to God: the fact that "Love is so little loved." Whoever truly loves God and his neighbor cannot without suffering know that "the world knew him not" (John 1:10); that so many men "remain in the shadow of death" and, "not knowing what they do" (Luke 23:34), jeopardize their salvation. The more our hearts are filled with a holy joy about the *magnalia Dei* ("the splendid works of God"), the more we shall bemoan the ingratitude of the world and the folly of those who reach for *stones* while spurning the *bread of eternal life*.

But then, do *we* not deny Christ again and again; do *we* not fail seven and seventy times a day? Was Christ not crucified by *our* sins, too? When Christ's word on the cross "I thirst" (John 19:28), penetrates into our heart; when we perceive the call of the God-Man who wills to be *loved by us*; when the inconceivable mercy of God impels us to fall on our knees in adoration — how should our hearts not bleed at the thought that we respond to that call so sluggishly and that it evokes so little response in the world; that there are so many who forfeit their salvation! All saints were filled with this sorrow; St. Francis walked, weeping, through the woods because "Love was so little loved": "My love is crucified."

The man who, knowing nothing but joy on this very earth, does not suffer from the terrible disharmony of the fallen world, loves neither God nor his neighbor truly. He "abides," as it were, "in death."

Sorrow in this sense is inseparably linked with hunger and thirst for justice. Those referred to in the words, "Blessed are they that hunger and thirst after justice: for they shall have their fill" *must* mourn in this world, where Christ is daily nailed to the cross anew.

We should mourn because of the suffering Jesus endured

In the measure in which a Christian lives by his ties with the supernatural, he will sorrow, above all, over *the sorrows of Christ*. The words: "My heart hath expected reproach and misery: and I looked for one that would grieve together with me, but there was none" (Ps. 68:20b), will pierce his heart. With the blessed Jacopone da Todi he will exclaim: "Mother, fount of love the purest, make me feel all the anguish thou endurest, to mourn with thee" (*Stabat Mater*).

However felicitous one may be in one's personal life, this pain must never be allowed to die away. How could we forget — though the joys we experience be ever so genuine and ever so great — the suffering of the "Lamb of God, that taketh away the sins of the world": the suffering which has redeemed us and is the key of our eternal happiness? Far from it. He who is wounded by the love of Christ will pray: "Let me be wounded by his wounds, let me become inebriated with the cross and the blood of Thy Son." It is, in the first place, "they that mourn" *for this cause* whom the Lord means when He says, "Blessed are they that mourn: for they shall be comforted."

We should mourn because of the sufferings of mankind in this world

But His word also refers to those who cannot pass by with indifference the ocean of suffering that fills the world. A man so absorbed by his personal happiness as to remain completely untouched by the multifarious suffering that surrounds him is evidently shallow and heartless. From the life of a true Christian — regardless of his personal lot — this sharing of the world's burden of suffering cannot be absent.

At every moment an infinity of heart-rending things happen in the world. The fact that this earth is a valley of tears never remains hidden even in anyone's immediate environment, unless his eyes are blinded. To everyone who loves, and in the measure in which his love is a living one, the words of St. Paul apply: "Who is weak, and I am not weak? Who is scandalized, and I am not on fire?" (2 Cor. 11:29).

Blessed are those who suffer from the disharmony of the world; who from charity help the rest carry their heavy burden; whom the accident of their good fortune does not prevent from being aware of the nature of a fallen world. These — the yearning, the waking, the loving ones — will be comforted in eternity, where "God shall wipe away all tears."

We are all called to take up our cross

But more — the Cross as such towers ineluctably over the life of every Christian. Through Christ, suffering has acquired an entirely new meaning. What was merely an inexorable *consequence* of original sin before Christ has now assumed the character of a fruitful *penance* and *purification* — a manifestation of love. Suffering love has redeemed the world. The cross stands forth as the symbol of redemptive and expiatory suffering freely accepted by merciful charity.

No one who is unwilling to take up his cross can truly follow Christ. In the life of every Christian, that cross is there. Not unless he embraces it with eager readiness — perceiving in it the call of God and accepting it as a means of his mortification — can he be transformed in Christ.

To evade the cross is to evade Christ. Whether we try to escape from it in fact, to hide it from our eyes, or to bury it under a layer of shallow pleasures and peripheral interests — it is Christ from whom we thus separate ourselves. "But it behooves us to glory in the cross of Our Lord Jesus Christ: in whom is our salvation, life, and resurrection: by whom we are saved and delivered," the Church sings in the Introit of the Exaltation of the Holy Cross. Again, in Passion Week: *O Crux, ave spes unica, hoc Passionis tempore* ("Hail Cross! thou only hope of man, Hail on this holy Passionday!"), *Venantius Fortunatus, Vexilla Regis*.

Only he who "lives by Christ" can fully bear his cross

Our nature, to be sure, struggles against the cross: we seek to flee from it. Sometimes we achieve this purpose to a degree by keying down our life to a lower standard, and appeasing our desire for happiness with more trivial goods.

If, on the one hand, this success in eschewing the cross can never be but a partial and largely an illusory one, on the other hand it again requires a great deal to experience one's cross to the full. He alone who "lives by Christ" is able to bear the whole weight of a heavy cross — to endure it integrally; to realize all the suffering it implies. He alone, above all, is able so to cling to it as to make the cross, as it were, *carry him*. He alone is able to carry it in full inward peace and unity: without recalcitrance or despair, without even the bitterness of emphatic resignation.

For to him, and him only, it means the gift of a participation in carrying the holy Cross of Our Lord. He endures crucifixion with Christ. He hails the cross as a possibility of expiation for his own and also for others' sins, a means of the purification he is allowed to undergo by God's mercy. To die to himself in order to be reborn in Christ is what he desires. He knows that all death is painful — that without the cross and suffering he cannot die to himself. For the Lord has said: "If any man will come after me, let him deny himself and take up his cross and follow me" (Matt. 16:24).

Properly bearing our cross unites us with Christ

Such a true Christian may not, as did certain saints, seek for suffering. This requires a special vocation. The cross that God sends him, however, he must in love be ready to welcome: *O Crux, ave spes unica*. He may pray that he be spared the cross, saying with Jesus, "My Father, if it be possible, let this chalice pass from me" (Matt. 26:39), but not without adding as Jesus did, in a spirit of ultimate acquiescence in the will of God: "Nevertheless, not as I will but as Thou wilt."

For it is out of love that God sends our cross to us; and it is destined to prepare the way for a deeper love for God. So long as

457

God does not take the cross from us, we must feel it as a participation in the Cross of Christ, as a costly treasure, as a divine gift of mysterious fruitfulness. In bearing our cross, we are placed in contact with Christ suffering out of charity. We should bring ourselves to recognize in *our* cross *the countenance of the suffering Savior*; to experience the nearness to Christ implied in its acceptance. Blessed are all those who bear a cross, for they shall be comforted: as St. Paul says, "As you are partakers of the sufferings [of Christ], so shall you be also of the consolation" (2 Cor. 1:7).

"Blessed are they that mourn: for they shall be comforted." These words illuminate the holy paradox of our terrestrial situation. Blessed are, *not* those unaware of the cross, *not* the spoiled children of fortune absorbed by a life that is all sunshine and enslaved to a gigantic illusion even to the moment of death — but those who recognize, and suffer from, the strife between God and the world; who embrace their cross and share in the Cross of Christ, the Conqueror of that strife.

Yet, God's existence should fill us with overwhelming joy

And yet it is holy joy which must fill us above all. We must bring to full fruition in us the words of St. Paul: "Rejoice in the Lord always: again, I say, rejoice." Indeed, even in our torn state on earth we have more reason to rejoice than to grieve. For God, the Sum of all values and Paragon of all glory, is also Reality absolute, and the primal Cause of all being.

Our response to the world is a false one unless it is adequate to the true order and hierarchy of being. Many as are the things in the world which demand as an adequate answer the response of sorrow, the absolute and ultimate reality, preeminent above everything else, demands on our part the response of joy.

So infinitely high does the fact that God exists rank above all the rest, that our response to that fact, too, must infinitely surpass in weight all our other responses. As all finite being is a mere empty shadow of Being infinite and absolute, so also does all imperfection and disharmony of this valley of tears shrink almost to nothing if viewed in the perspective of the infinite glory and harmony of God. Thus is our cause for joy incomparably greater than for sorrow. Therefore, we understand that notwithstanding the cross and all sorrows inherent in earthly existence, the Apostle says, "Rejoice in the Lord always."

God's redemption of mankind is a further reason for overwhelming joy

But this holy joy, overshadowing all sorrow, which prompts the Church to sing in the *Gloria in excelsis*, "We praise Thee; we bless Thee; we adore Thee; we glorify Thee; we give Thee thanks for Thy great glory" — this jubilant rejoicing could never blossom in our souls unless the gulf that separates us from God were bridged by God; unless the burden of guilt that weighs down man (whose nature is tainted by original sin) were removed by the mercy of God.

Our redemption by the God-Man Christ, who has burst our chains and restored us to communion with God, is what provides us with an actual warrant for our joy.

Nor must this holy joy over the incarnation of God and our redemption — this bliss which finds its highest expression in the *Exsultet* of Holy Saturday but pervades the entire Liturgy in innumerable variations — ever leave us. For the many things that evoke in us a justified sorrow, taken all together, are nothing if contrasted with this blissful reality. Our cause for this holy joy always retains its central and paramount position in relation with all things, nor can it ever become a matter of secondary interest. Therefore the Apostle says, *Iterum dico vobis, gaudete* ("Again, I say, rejoice").

Though our redemption is a necessary condition of our delight in the glory of God, though only the redeemed can properly give thanks for it — *Gratias agimus tibi propter magnam gloriam tuam* — the primary *object* to which our joy adequately refers is not our deliverance and elevation, but God Himself, His glory as such, His infinite goodness which reveals itself to us in Jesus' face.

But in the second place, our redemption and our undeserved privilege of being called to an eternal communion with God justify, on our part, an indestructible holy joy — a supernatural joy which is to fill our eternity. "Thou hast redeemed us, O Lord, in Thy blood, out of every tribe and tongue and people and nation, and hast made us to our God a kingdom. The mercies of the Lord I will sing forever" (Introit of the Feast of the Most Precious Blood of Our Lord).

We should also rejoice about God's gifts of grace to mankind, and for the Church

We have, further, an occasion for unending joy in every one who has been transformed by grace, who can say of himself with St. Paul, "The grace of God was not without effect in me"; who bears the seal of Christ on his forehead and in his whole life. Therefore does the Church sing in the Introit of All Saints and of all great feasts of the saints: "Let us all rejoice in the Lord, celebrating this feast."

We must also rejoice in God's gifts of grace, which change even our earthly habitation into a forecourt of heaven: notably, the Sacraments, and above all, the Holy Eucharist. "He fed them with the fat of wheat, alleluia; and filled them with honey out of the rock, alleluia, alleluia, alleluia" (Introit of the Feast of Corpus Christi).

Again, do we not find an enduring cause for joy in the existence of the Holy Church, the Bride of the Holy Spirit; in her infallible doctrinal authority; in the supernatural community of the Mystical Body of Christ? In these things, every Christian must take constant delight, however heavy his cross, however much his personal life may abound in suffering. All terrors and all the woes of the world are powerless to destroy these goods; the joy they inspire soars victoriously above all sorrow.

Christian hope infuses even our sufferings with joy

Yet, evidently an objection might be raised. Is not our incertitude as to whether we shall persevere and partake in the fruits of Redemption, a drop of wormwood which might poison all this joy? Had we not better bear in mind the words of St. Augustine, "He who made thee without thee will not justify thee without thee"? True enough, the hour of eternal holy joy — joy pure and untroubled, joy unceasing and indestructible — has not yet struck for us. The Lord has not yet spoken to us the words: "Well done, thou good and faithful servant: enter into the joy of thy Lord." We still dwell in this life, and our situation is still fraught with the character of duality.

However, all our sufferings are transfigured by a ray of light; a light of vivifying solace is spread about everything that would, in itself, legitimately fill us with anguish and sorrow. That light is hope. It is our right, it is our duty to hope: for hope is one of the three theological virtues which are to inform a Christian's life. Hope, illuminating everything like a shaft of light that pierces through darkness, rectifies and sweetens all sorrow in its innermost core.

So long as we are *in statu viae* we still live in hope. This means that the eternal morning has not yet dawned: that we have not attained the Goal but are as yet on our pilgrimage. But it means, also, that we already possess hope itself: that, in other words, joy has already virtually conquered all suffering. For we do not hope in

461

the sense of a vague, obscure, halfhearted expectation. Ours is a *radiant* hope, a firm hope founded on the word of God and the fact of Redemption. And the possession of this Christian hope — a response to the goodness and the revealed truth of God — is in itself an incomparable treasure of happiness.

Therefore, although there is plenty of reason for sorrow, and although our sorrow is not only excused but exalted: "Blessed are they that mourn," a Christian on his earthly pilgrimage must never live "as though he had no hope." In the first place, since there is an infinitely greater reason for joy than there is for sorrow, joy must keep its primacy over sorrow. Secondly, the cross of earthly life — all pain and all sorrow, that is — should be illumined and transfigured by hope. "That you be not sorrowful even as others who have no hope," says St. Paul (1 Thess. 4:13).

We should rejoice even about the natural gifts of God

But neither must the suffering we have to undergo in this valley of tears prevent us from gratefully enjoying the numberless natural gifts of God, particular to us and common to all, with which our lives are blessed. Neither our own suffering nor that of others must be allowed to blind us to the splendor of sunlight, to the beauty of the sky and the stars; to the bliss of loving and being loved; to the greatness of the truths we may penetrate. It would be ungrateful of us, and an unfitting answer to the liberality of the "Father of all lights," were we to abstain from delighting in all the grandeur and beauty in the world which tells us of God and is destined to elevate us to Him.

Let us admit, though, that God may burden us with a cross — such as the loss of one who is dearest to us — which withers up *all* joy about creaturely things in our heart, and transforms our life into a pure *via crucis*. Even then, however, our supernatural joy because of God and because of the glory that awaits us in eternity and is the object of our wistful hope must remain alive in us, and keep its primacy.

In the life of St. Francis of Assisi, we find this grateful joy at every gift of God wonderfully united to a deep sorrow over the disharmony of this valley of tears. His attitude expresses in an exemplary way the right response of man to the dual aspect of terrestrial life. The same one who shed so many tears over his sins and whose heart was pierced by pain because "Love is so little loved," with his eyesight almost gone and his body all but completely broken, was to write the *Canticle to the Sun*, that superb pæan of joy.

Christians must interweave their lives with true sorrow, but with even greater joy

It would be a great error, then, to deny that a Christian should be glad of the creaturely goods, too, which he owes to God's munificence: as though the precariousness of our situation on earth and the ocean of sufferings in the world forbade us to enjoy the blessings God has accorded to each of us. No, we should always display a full and adequate response to God and to everything He sends us.

Is it suffering; is it the cross? Let us readily acquiesce in His holy will, yet always sustained and consoled by hope, and aware "that the sufferings of this time are not worthy to be compared with the glory to come, that shall be revealed in us" (Rom. 8:18).

Again, if joy is what falls to our lot, we should appreciate it gratefully, and take an unrestrained delight in the bounty of God, without however allowing our happiness to make us forgetful of the unchangeable gravity of our earthly situation.

In brief, a true Christian must not live in a way as though Christ had never spoken the words, "Blessed are they that mourn," but even less in a way as though He had not also said to His disciples,

463

"Be glad and rejoice, for your reward is great in heaven." The Christian knows: "Pain and suffering are only there for the sake of joy." (Father Heribert Holzapfel, O.F.M., *"Freude"*)

The tissue of a Christian's life must be interwoven with threads of true joy and threads of true sorrow alike, because we have not yet arrived at the point "where God shall wipe away all tears." But it is joy that must have the primacy: for, after the *lumen Christi* has brightened the world, even on earth there is incomparably more cause for bliss than for sorrow. Joy must be the deeper, the decisive element, the form of our life, as it were. For that which warrants our joy is the supreme reality, the ultimate word in the universe. The sufferings of this world are essentially transitory. Happiness, eternal and indestructible, awaits all those who follow Christ.

However dark the griefs and terrible the sufferings a Christian may know, over and above them soars the triumphant luster of joy. This is the spirit of the Liturgy. With all its mournfulness, Passion Week leads up to the definitive and ultimate reality of Easter: the soaring beatitude transcending all time; and from the latter is derived the keynote of the Liturgy of the whole year. The seasons of *alleluia* far outweigh those in which *alleluia* is not sung. Even during the time of Advent and of Lent, a ray of hope, and with it of joy, is never absent.

To the Church, which sees everything in the light of eternity, joy is the superior and consummate reality. "So also you now indeed have sorrow; but I will see you again and your heart shall rejoice; and your joy no man shall take from you" (John 16:22).

17

Holy Sobriety

Therefore, let us not sleep, as others do:
but let us watch, and be sober. (1 Thess. 5:6)

IF WE examine the lives of the saints we shall find that —
notwithstanding their fervor, notwithstanding an intoxication
with Jesus — they also possess a trait that may best be described as
holy sobriety.

Their hunger and thirst after justice, their *obsession* with God,
their overflowing charity towards God and their fellow creatures,
their unlimited confidence in God — these traits are apt to make
them appear fools in the eyes of the world. However, they are far
removed from illusory exaltation and bloodless idealism.

Holy sobriety is marked by genuineness and simplicity

They bear the stamp of genuineness, of truth, of a classic
simplicity. Their boldness in overcoming the world is free from
romanticism, from any attempt to deny man's weakness or his
bondage to earthly things, from any contempt for the dangers to
which our fallen nature is exposed. It is entirely lacking in the
artifices of embellishment or the rhetoric of fictitious importance

in interpreting human things. Their lives are pervaded by a holy sobriety, which is as distinct from the vulgar sobriety of the so-called realists as it is from romantic illusionism.

Vulgar sobriety is blind to values and to the supernatural

Vulgar sobriety or *common sense* represents rather something negative. The people we so describe are such as refuse, either explicitly or at least by their concrete behavior, to recognize the reality of value and of the spiritual universe.

The first species — that of the ideological deniers of the power of values — includes all those who profess a distrust of all higher and sublime things, and would allow for the reality of nothing except the palpable and the trivial. Although they might not deny the existence of a spiritual world, they would by no means rely upon that world. They consider all men who do as victims of illusions. They are prone to attribute all actions and feelings of their fellow men to low and prosaic motives.

Behaving, for their part, on more or less consistently utilitarian grounds, they pride themselves on being *realists* and flaunt their superiority above the *idealists*, who draw from them a smile of pitying condescension. Even more do they distrust the world of the supernatural. What they can touch and grasp with their hands appears to them the only solid reality.

Obviously, sobriety in this sense is a defect, since it springs from the failure to grasp what is ultimate reality: the supernatural, and all the hierarchy of the universe. Such people are wrong in believing themselves realists; for they take their departure from a distorted and impoverished vision of reality: certainly they are not illusionists who mistake phantoms for realities.

They are, however, as far from the truth as are the illusionists — inasmuch as they are blind to a large section of reality, and the most important section at that — clinging invariably to their earthbound speculation in considering everything *à la baisse*, in the direction downward. They are always disposed to believe that that which ranks lower in reality is more sound and certain.

Exclusively "practical" men are sober in a negative sense

As has been hinted above, this negative type of sobriety also appears in an even more strictly implicit, an entirely unideological form. We observe it in these humdrum people devoid of all sublimity, all luster, all poetry. Their *ethos* is not informed by the breath of the realm of values; their mental complexion shows no trace of the luminous inspiration which emanates from that realm. Not that they deny the sphere of things spiritual and supernatural; they recognize it as a reality and their actions may be determined by motives pertaining to this realm.

But even in such cases, their *ethos* remains gray and dull. Even though deriving their motives from that superior sphere, they somehow treat it as if they were dealing with the sphere of utilitarian purposes. Their *ethos* will never transcend the range of a commendable righteousness and efficiency. They pragmatize everything they lay hands on: even their prayer assumes the character of a useful activity. The world of practical things — the sphere of everyday necessities — remains the *causa exemplaris* after which they fashion their vision of all things and their response to all objects.

This form of pseudo-sobriety, too, is something completely negative. It is, indeed, incompatible with sanctity. People who are sober in this sense, too, are impervious to the world of the supernatural. Even though formally aware of Christ and ready to serve Him, they are not inwardly penetrated by the light of His countenance and the breath of His spirit. This negative sobriety is as definitely antithetic to the Christian attitude of *sancta sobrietas* as is all illusionary exaltation.

Holy sobriety avoids illusions about human nature

The latter, again, occurs in several varieties. Its most obvious type is presented by those idealists who — wanting in that salutary mistrust of human nature which the Fall has made necessary — light-mindedly abandon themselves to the autonomous strain of their natural enthusiasms. Whether, in a sort of Rousseauian optimism, they make a principle of believing everything natural to be *ipso facto* good, or whether they merely follow the momentary inward aspect of their experiences with a blind and uncritical confidence — they inevitably fall a prey to illusions. Unmindful of the Psalmist's warning, "Every man is a liar," they glibly run into situations fraught with grave dangers.

Convinced of the purity of their own nature and the conquering power of their good intentions, they discount or underestimate the snares of the evil Enemy. They feel themselves pure, selfless, and charitable; and mistake this deceiving, subjective feeling for the objective reality of possessing these virtues. Briefly, such people refuse to take account of original sin. They turn a deaf ear to St. Peter's admonition, which the Holy Church repeats daily in the Compline: "Be sober and watch: because your adversary the devil, as a roaring lion, goeth about seeking whom he may devour" (1 Peter 5:8).

This illusionism constitutes a fatal obstacle to our transformation in Christ. One tainted with this disease necessarily lacks true self-knowledge and is unlikely to escape any of the traps set for him by the Enemy. Being more or less unaware of man's need of redemption, this type of idealist cannot conceivably possess the true readiness to change. Though aspiring to perfection within the limits of his nature, he knows little of the necessity of dying to oneself and being reborn in Christ.

For all his well-intentioned efforts, he abides in a world of illusions; even the incontestably good actions he may accomplish are not free from a certain taint of speciousness, a mark of things ungenuine and inadequate. What warps his virtue is the lack of holy sobriety.

Holy sobriety rejects illusions caused by interpreting natural things as supernatural

Another form of illusionary exaltation consists in the tendency of many of us to misinterpret this or that purely natural and all too human attitude or state of mind as a manifestation of supernatural origin and dignity. This vice mostly betrays itself by a habit of *idealizing* all things, and a mincing aversion to call them by their proper names.

One such person, for instance, will mistake an emotional dullness in him, which may in fact be the consequence of chronic fatigue, for a sign of religious serenity. Another will believe himself devoured with a holy zeal for the House of God, whereas in fact it is a purely natural urge for correcting and admonishing others, a pedantic or governess-like disposition, which prompts him continually to upbraid and to preach to his fellows. Another, again, will misconstrue what is simply his healthy temperament, his vitality, his sanguine vivacity, as an outflow of his imperturbable confidence in God. Even the rash blunder of mistaking one's purely natural depression for the *caligo*, the *dark night* of the mystics, is by no means an unheard of occurrence.

Holy sobriety calls us to blunt truthfulness about our nature

Yet, our transformation in Christ requires precisely that blunt truthfulness which is eager to call everything by its proper name. In order to become a true *Christian*, I must first say with the honest *pagan*: "I am a man, and know that nothing human is alien to me."

We cannot be constituted in a true relationship with God nor dwell *in conspectu Dei* unless we consider man in his true reality and guard against all illusive interpretations. For whatever is specious and spurious in us cuts us off from objectivity and humility, falsifies our response to values, distracts us from God and thwarts the path of our transformation in Christ.

Holy sobriety remains constantly mindful of our terrestrial status

An ordinary fellow who, aware of how subject he is to material things, preserves his sanity and common sense, is likelier to awake some day to a full supernatural life than is the muddle-headed illusionist of false sublimity who is busy decking human and natural things with pompous but false tags and deceiving himself along with others. Indeed, he who makes a habit of transposing natural things of everyday occurrence into an idiom of faked interiority or solemnity, and thus (deeming himself a saint while in reality his motives are entirely of this earth) leads an existence based on illusions, not only falls short of any progress towards true holiness but actually insults God.

A danger of religious illusionism attaches, in particular, to some Christians' proclivity towards disregarding — leaping over, as it were — the reality of man's terrestrial situation. To be sure, our glance *should* be directed to eternity; we *should* consider everything *sub specie æternitatis* and accord a primacy to everything that is relevant to eternity and extends to its sphere. Indeed, we must ask with St. Aloysius, "What does this mean to eternity?" Yet, we must not take on a pose of dwelling already in eternity, nor simply pass over the *status viae*. For we must always abide in truth, which we cannot do unless we realize our metaphysical situation as a whole, taking into account both our being ordained to eternity and the fact that as yet we are dwelling on this earth.

This disregard may produce its bad effects in two alternative directions. Either our mode of experience becomes ungenuine, and we dwell in a *pseudo-sublimity*; or else, we fall into debasing and banalizing the supernatural: we drag it down, unintentionally, into an atmosphere entirely of this world — a danger which has been discussed earlier, in the context of false simplicity.

Holy sobriety respects the stages inherent in many earthly relationships

The error of skipping the terrestrial phase is typified by the attitude which some Christians take towards the cross. They imagine it to be particularly virtuous or pious behavior if, at the death of a beloved person, they remain entirely calm and evince little or no pain — since the deceased has won eternity, and chosen the best part. They do as though they were themselves already dwelling in eternity.

Again, the alternative holds: either they will develop a kind of false, morbid, foggy idealism; or else, they fall into a shallow, matter-of-fact resignation, a banal routine composure (a cheap substitute for true Christian serenity and peace of mind), becoming thus wholly insensible to the gravity and greatness of death.

The fact is that they have lost the sense of the true proportions of our metaphysical situation, the true correlation of earthly life to eternity. The false familiarity they affect with eternity will either seduce them into a thin and pale idealism, an attitude of invariably *floating in the heights*, or it will lead to an implicit desubstantialization of the meaning of eternity, a short-circuited assimilation of its aspects to the sphere of earthly affairs. In either case, the distinction is blurred between eternity and the earth, and a denatured idea of the supernatural replaces its true conception. Instead of our actual transformation into a supernatural mode of being, it is the supernatural that we bring down to the level of natural concerns.

The same law applies in this case as applies in all other great things in our life. Such things have their proper dimensions to traverse. This is a condition of their proper realization. Attempts to pass by these dimensions will lead us to a merely ostensible attainment of our end. A love-relationship, a work of art, a great undertaking like the foundation of a new religious Order — all these imply, of necessity, a period of maturing.

There are certain successive stages which must be traversed; certain stages which must be actually covered. If we ignore this rhythm which is a law of being; if we attempt to skip over the proper course of things and to secure the final result at one blow; if we even try to force the maturing of some great plan — we fatally deprive that great thing of its depth and its inward weight, and substitute for it a mere counterfeit, bearing the stigma of flat artificiality. It is only by the paths which God has marked out for us that we can reach the high peaks of spiritual being.

Holy sobriety remains conscious of the gulf that separates us from God

In regard to the interrelation of earth and heaven, too, this truth holds. Only by developing along the proper lines in the framework of earthly life can we mature for eternity. We must consider the immeasurable distance that separates us from God: and hence, neither believe that we can part with our earthly condition at one bound and soar above everything as though we were angels, nor approach God with too much familiarity and haul down the supernatural into the banal atmosphere of our everyday life.

It is by directing our glance in unquenchable longing upwards to God, by maintaining a permanent attitude of *sursum corda* throughout the varying actions and situations that constitute our life, that we shall more and more outgrow the limits of earthliness and incorporate ourselves in the world of God. In this manner the supernatural will become, in actual truth, the determining and shaping principle, the *forma* of our life. "Seek the things that are above, where Christ is sitting at the right hand of God: mind the things that are above, not the things that are upon the earth" (Col. 3:1-2).

Holy sobriety avoids an exaggerated estimate of our own experiences

Religious illusionism may also take the form of our persuading ourselves that we are burdened with a heavy cross, which we bear with heroism — whereas in fact we have no opportunity at all to practice such a heroism, for the *heavy cross* exists only in our imagination.

Suppose someone outspokenly draws our attention to certain defects we possess. Instead of gratefully accepting his criticism, we feel sorely misjudged and consider our endurance of the injustice we have suffered as a heroic sacrifice. We appear to ourselves as an exemplary Christian, a silent martyr who for the sake of Christ's love refrains from remonstrating against a wrong. Yet, all this is mere illusion: the truth is that we fail to perceive the real invitation of God offered by the criticism, and delight in a lofty pose which lacks any real foundation.

Or again, some slight privation, slighter than those other people suffer a hundred times a day, impresses us as a heavy cross and an occasion for exceptional heroism. Little do we surmise that, as a matter of fact, this semblance of heroism is but the product of a ridiculous self-pampering. No, we wallow in self-pity, and complacently enjoy our power of heroic endurance. We do not apply the same measure when estimating the situation of others.

Instead of reflecting that in fact we are not doing too badly and had better thank God for His bounty, instead of pondering the smallness and insignificance of the burden we feel so irksome when the burden is compared with what others have to bear, we indulge in a heroic posture which is justified by no objective condition and therefore lacks inner truth.

We should keep on our guard against all such illusionism, and always be eager to abide in the truth and to see things as they are. Let us never read into our experiences any artificial profundities; let us not put a supernatural construction on what is simply human nature, and often enough, human frailty. Especially, let us not fall into the habit of assuming, without sufficient factual foundation, that something extraordinary and sublime has happened to us.

We must keep in mind that sublime experiences are rare gifts of God, and if the question arises we should reverently and soberly examine whether He has really accorded us such a gift. Thus, for example, we must beware of rashly assuming that God has blessed us with the exquisite gift of a holy love in Jesus uniting us to another person. For this, in particular — the ultimate mutual awareness of love in Jesus — is a unique bliss as rare as it is sublime.

As has been pointed out on an earlier occasion, we must look upon such a love as an entirely special and extraordinary gift of grace, a thing one must never expressly seek nor expect to obtain (in contraposition, say, to a happy marriage as such); for it is possible in very specific conditions only and reveals a very specific call of God. If, therefore, we feel inclined to believe that such a gift has been awarded to us, we should in holy sobriety examine whether the conditions for it are really present in our case.

The true supernatural attitude implies that we recognize the gifts of God in their real character, and appreciate them according to what they objectively signify — independently, that is to say, of our desires. First, then, we must in holy sobriety establish the pure facts about the thing in question, considering it exactly as what it really is. Having thus gained a clear and sane view of its primary reality, we must next seek to penetrate its deeper meaning and to perceive the call of God it is meant to convey.

Certainly we must embrace the gifts of God in full receptivity; but on the other hand we should not, prompted by an illusive idealism, impose on them an interpretation derived from our desires and, like Don Quixote, mistake an inn for a castle. We should humbly leave to God what He might really deign to give us. The wealth of supernatural reality is such, the decrees and the blessings of God are so mysterious and so great, that all the illusions hatched by our fantasy can never measure up to them and would only flatten out the depth and beauty of the spiritual cosmos. "We should live soberly, and justly, and godly in this world, looking for the blessed hope and coming of the glory of the great God and our Savior Jesus Christ" (Titus 2:12-13).

Holy sobriety is cautious about private "illuminations"

A further domain of religious illusionism which requires mention is that of so-called personal *illuminations*. Some people believe certain ideas and fancies which are either mere products of their unconscious desires or at any rate purely natural impressions to be illuminations sent them by God — the voice of God, as it were. Likewise, they may mistake a phantasm for a vision, or again, mistake their thoughts during prayer for private revelations.

Keen caution and a salutary self-distrust are necessary here. Real illuminations and revelations by God are things so sublime and exceptional that reverence alone should prevent one from easily assuming their presence.

A final conviction in this sense should never be formed without the sanction of one's spiritual director. He alone may decide whether the illuminations and revelations one claims to have received are really such, or mere illusions — if not trickery of the devil. Even the great St. Teresa of Avila distrusted the mystic graces she was receiving until the fact had been confirmed by her confessor. She tells in her *Life* that once, at her confessor's behest, she

475

went so far as to snap her fingers at Christ who had appeared to her in a vision; and that the Lord then told her nothing was more pleasing to Him than such a spirit of true obedience. Indeed, every Christian must recognize the objective proceeding of ecclesiastical authority and the instructions of the Church as the authentic standard by which all private revelations are to be measured.

Holy sobriety relies more on factual evidence than on inner voices and feelings

But the necessity of a prudent distrust of ourselves is not confined to cases where the question is whether or not we have been distinguished by an exceptional gift of God. It also arises whenever we believe that we perceive a clear and unmistakable inner voice speaking in us: whether it suggests to us to do a certain thing; or that we should regard something as our duty; or that we have discovered our principal defect; or again, that we have gained some decisive insight into the character of others.

In the face of all inner voices, feelings and sensings unsupported by experimental and rational evidence, of all intuitions suddenly arising and upsetting the whole of our previous knowledge of a situation, the utmost reserve is advisable. It is often all too tempting and easy to feel that, for instance, somebody loves us or has something against us, or again, that he has changed his attitude towards us. It is somehow alluring to believe oneself deeply understood, grievously misunderstood, or persecuted.

A person thus inclined will accept for irrefutable witnesses these purely subjective impressions, unsupported by any clear indication in the facts, and on their basis he will form stubborn convictions. In the face of all rational objections, he will stick to his instinct as the more trustworthy criterion of truth.

This proud illusionism is a great evil. The truth is that factual indications definitely deserve greater trust than do all sorts of inspirations, which are only too apt to lure us into illusions and deceptive imaginations. It is a commendable practice to submit such impressions to the judgment of our spiritual director. We must then steadfastly believe in that judgment rather than in our subjective fancies and in our interpretations of other people's acts as suggested by these emotional prejudices.

Holy sobriety humbly admits human limitations

Holy sobriety is closely linked to humility and to the Christian principle of abiding by the plain truth. *The root of all "mystical" illusionism lies in pride.* The *mystical* man, who contemns ordinary reason and common sense, is reluctant to admit his bondage to terrestrial shackles, his frailty and fallibility. He prefers not to be subject to the universal laws of fallen nature. At least he feels his task is to grapple with problems of a unique character, and an exceptional brand of difficulties. Holy sobriety, on the contrary, implies a humble admission of the fact that we, too, must pay our tribute to universal human weakness.

The sober man is free from the obsession that he must needs be something unique and extraordinary, and is free from all narrowing crampedness. He takes account of reality as it is — of the *whole* of reality, to be sure, not (as does the self-styled realist) of its crude and base aspects only. He is aware that by himself he amounts to nothing but that he may say with St. Paul, "I can do all things in Him who strengtheneth me" (Phil. 4:13). He knows that God can and will regenerate him if he cooperates. He knows that Christ has redeemed him and communicated His holy life to him.

The "natural idealist" is blind to human weakness

His spiritual impetus, therefore, is entirely different from that of the natural idealist. The idealist inclines to overrate the power of the human spirit as such; he believes himself able to rise above his human weakness by purely natural means: that is to say, by sheer moral effort. He is prone, also, to overlook man's bondage to earthly conditions in general; to interpret the frailty inherent in man's constitution as a merely accidental shortcoming.

Thus, his lofty mood involves a certain divorce from reality; his bold perspectives are never free from a trait of anemic thinness and of reckless illusionism. He would storm the skies by flight, like Icarus — instead of humbly ascending step by step the narrow, steep, and laborious path that leads to eternity. His attitude has something forced and high-strung about it. His enterprise is doomed to failure, for it rests on a gigantic illusion concerning human nature, whose dismal abysses he hardly even suspects. He fails, in a word, owing to his ignorance of man's need of redemption.

The saint builds his hopes on confidence in God

Of a wholly different kind is the spiritual *élan* that characterizes the saint. Humbly aware of his own weakness, clearly conscious of his need of being redeemed, in an unrestrained avowal of man's frailty and enchainment to earth, he looks up to God and prays: "God, come to my assistance." He would not, then, start building the tower without knowing the foundations.

But again, full of insatiable longing he looks up to Christ, and unreservedly follows Him who spoke the words, "If any man thirst, let him come to me and drink" (John 7:37). With the Apostles, he responds to the Lord: "Thou hast words of eternal life."

He builds his life not on *ideals* but on the supreme and ultimate reality, the Being most real, the *ens realissimum*: on *God*. He cooperates in being lifted above his nature by Christ, and unites his will to grace, hoping that grace may not work in him in vain.

His *élan* is a response to the Lord's call, "Follow me": a fruit of his faith in Christ, who has turned a Saul into a Paul, and whom

St. John in the Apocalypse heard pronounce the words, "Behold, I make all things new."

His *élan* is a fruit of his hope based on the transforming power of grace, which made a band of simple, ignorant fishermen into luminaries of the Church; a fruit of his love for Christ, whose most holy countenance has drawn him into its orbit of light. Therefore, it has nothing superficial and anemic, nothing romantic and unreal about it; it is genuine, strong, and victorious. The saint dwells in the truth fully; he alone takes account of the whole of reality.

Holy sobriety permeates the Liturgy

This spirit of holy sobriety permeates the entire Liturgy, which exhibits no trace of a tendency to cover up painful things, but looks integral reality in the face. No prudishness whatsoever, no illusive denial of human nature is encountered there. But all things are seen in their highest light, and every good is grasped according to its meaning in the order of creation. Human frailty, the dangers which encompass us, all chasms and crevices of our fallen nature — we see them inexorably contrasted with the infinite glory of God and with all values envisioned in their reference to the order of creation. The tension between our fallen nature — the reality we start from — and the goal we are ordained to reach, our rebirth in Christ, is manifested without reserve or concealment.

Holy sobriety is essential to our transformation in Christ

Not unless we rid ourselves of all illusory exaltation, not unless we keep dwelling in the truth, can we attain to a veritable union with God. For God is Truth. Therefore, we must relentlessly clear away whatever illusions still survive in us. Holy sobriety should form the basis of our life. We must gladly recognize our limitations and firmly free ourselves of any imaginary claim to qualities or accomplishments we do not really possess. Nor must we yield to despondency when we meet with failure or come to discover our defects; when, perhaps, all of a sudden our task appears to be too difficult and we see nothing but darkness around us.

Advancing along the steep path of our transformation in Christ, we shall inevitably come across obstacles and have to pass through phases of the "dark night." Then must our implicit faith in the light we once saw — our *fides* in the strict sense of the term — reassert itself; then must the luster that once shone upon us from Mount Tabor brighten up our night.

We must treasure in our heart the great Call we have received and the promise of comfort we hold. We must in holy sobriety expect in advance the manifold limitations of our nature which are sure to appear, and be prepared for the "dark nights" that will come. True self-knowledge, freedom from all illusions, and a clear recognition of our metaphysical situation are indispensable conditions of our transformation in Christ.

It is, then, holy sobriety that seals with the stamp of truthfulness, of genuineness, and of full reality all the Christian virtues — such as confidence in God, the readiness to change, contrition, hunger for the kingdom of God, simplicity, patience, meekness, mercy, love of God and one's fellow creatures.

Not only is holy sobriety *compatible* with a life inspired and sustained by Faith, with that supernatural ecstasy — that *drunken* love of Jesus — which makes the saints appear as fools in the eyes of the world: it is a necessary presupposition of these things. The rapturous love of Jesus, which a St. Paul or a St. Francis of Assisi had, necessarily springs from the soil of that holy sobriety which the Church, in the hymn *Splendor paternae gloriae*, praises thus: "Joyously let us drink the sober drunkenness of the Holy Spirit."

18

True Surrender of Self

AT THE beginning and at the end of the road we travel in the process of our transformation in Christ, we hear Our Lord speak these mysterious words: "He that shall lose his life for me shall find it" (Matt. 10:39). They convey to us the demand that we die unto ourselves and the promise of a new life derived from and centered in Christ.

But the phrase *to lose one's life* (indeed, as it is sometimes translated, *one's soul*) implies another, more particular element besides that renunciation of one's natural self whose various aspects have been set forth in the preceding pages. It is the holy paradox of Death and Resurrection that flares up in these words — the mystery of dying with Christ, and awakening to life again with Him. Our study of the theme of *transformation in Christ* may therefore properly be terminated with a consideration of this aspect.

Surrender to the call of natural values prefigures our surrender to Christ

Even on the natural plane, there is to be found a reflection of the truth of these words in the Gospel. For what determines the spiritual measure of a man, the inner wealth of his personality? Obviously, it is the degree of his awareness of values and the intensity of his adequate response to values. The more aware of values one is, and the more able to display an adequate response to every value, the more he participates in the world of values. In every act of conforming to a true value, there lies a union of our mind with this value. Yet, this conforming involves a kind of *surrender*: a certain detachment from our self, a certain subordination and abnegation of self.

This surrender involved in our response to values constitutes the only possible way to inward growth; it is in this way alone that we ourselves shall be endowed with values. And this surrender contains something of the losing of one's life enjoined by Christ upon His followers. It represents, as it were, a natural prefiguring of that loss of life.

Our supernatural transformation presupposes our free surrender to God

Man is in his innermost essence specifically ordained to God. **"Thou has created us** *for Thee*," says St. Augustine (*Confessions* 1.1). In the measure that man submerges himself in his adoration of God, his personality becomes ampler and richer, and adorned with higher values.

Inversely, in the measure that he is concerned with his own self and the consideration enjoyed by that self, he becomes poorer, narrower, more arid, and jejune. That is why, as the example of the holy Curé d'Ars shows, even a man of scant natural gifts may develop into a great and rich personality, if only he gives himself fully and unreservedly to God; whereas, in comparison with such a man, a person who is endowed with the highest natural talents, but who shuts himself off from God, will emanate a barren and oppressive atmosphere.

To be sure, we receive supernatural life, just as the natural one, as a free gift from God's hand, without any contribution from our part. Yet we cannot become transformed in Christ unless we lose ourselves in our vision of Christ. Only if we immerse ourselves in a loving adoration of Christ, can we be transformed in Him.

Our supernatural life will not expand automatically without our contribution. It cannot spring into full blossom unless Christ becomes for our conscious experience, too, the actual center of our life — in such a fashion that all our life is directed to Christ and is pervaded by our adoring love of Christ. For the unfolding of supernatural life, again, a self-surrendering response to value — referred, here, to God through the medium of the God-Man — constitutes an indispensable precondition.

Yet, evidently, *losing one's soul* in this proper use of the term means more than the surrender implied in every genuine response to value. We must, in a stricter sense, die unto ourselves and become empty so that Christ may unfold His holy life within us. Likewise, our surrender to Christ must far exceed all our other responses to value: it must be an *integral* surrender of self, such as is possible and proper in relation with the absolute Lord only, "in whom all fullness of divinity dwells." The motif of losing one's soul acquires then, here, an entirely new — a much more literal, un-equivocal, and definitive — meaning.

Surrender to God does not obliterate our selfhood

However, it would be a grave error to interpret this concept of dying to oneself or losing one's soul as an extinction of selfhood in the crude sense of a depersonalization or neutralization.

Certain religious theorists today seem to assume that one can only get rid of narrow egotism and become imbued with a truly theocentric attitude if one ceases to attach any weight to one's relation with Christ insofar as this relation is experienced by one's own consciousness. They would express their theories something like this: "What am I; what are my longings and my love for Christ — is not all this much too small and unimportant to be something in the eyes of God? The only thing that matters is for us to keep step with the great objective rhythm of the holy Church, and, without thinking of our personal problems and situations at all, dedicate ourselves exclusively to the great community of the Mystical Body of Christ; for the latter alone, and surely not our petty little ego, means something to God." The more I succeed in effacing my own personality, the more, they would say, my attitude must become an *objective* and *theocentric* one.

It is these speculations also that have brought forth an attempt at dividing the saints into those having a predominantly *objective* outlook and those having a predominantly *subjective* outlook — as though the idea of a saint of subjective outlook were anything but a contradiction in terms.

Only a full, personal self can give himself freely to God

The error that underlies this conception is the more dangerous as it corresponds with the anti-personal spirit of the age, which tends towards a glorification of the collective as such. The propagators of this error give proof of their shallowness of mind by equating personality with subjectivity and measuring objectivity by the standard of impersonality. They forget that God, the Origin of all objective reality and validity, is a Person. They attach the derogatory label of *subjectivity* to *ethos* and even to the personal conscious mode of being. In fact it is *a certain kind* of *ethos* only that is infected with subjectivism. They are blind to the fact that God *is Love* — in which we participate according to the measure of our own supernatural love.

They disregard the basic truth that it is only by confronting myself with God, by establishing myself in an *I and Thou* relation with Christ, by my loving adoration of Christ — and *not* by any consciousness of being a mere part of a big Whole — that I can transcend the narrow limits of my ego.

At bottom, their doctrine smacks of pantheism; for it tends to confuse qualitative height with quantitative width and comprehensiveness. It tends to substitute an absorption of the person into a vaster human unit for the surrender of man's ego to the divine *Thou*. True surrender is properly and eminently a *personal* act, and the only one by which a person can rise above his inherent limitations. They forget the moving grandeur and eternal importance of every immortal soul. St. Teresa of Avila says, "Christ would also have died to save one single soul."

If it were true that the individual means nothing, the community would not mean anything either. A community — a State or a nation, for instance — if imprisoned in its economic and power interests, is just as subjective and narrow as an individual so imprisoned. Like the individual, the community can only outgrow its narrowness and subjectivity if it is directed to ends that are important before God.

What defines a *mere private interest* is not the fact that it is the interest of an individual rather than of a group, but the qualitative circumstance that it expresses a pursuit of mere subjective gratification instead of a purpose important in itself and objectively valuable. The humblest and most hidden concern of an individual, once it has moral value, is no longer a mere private concern.

Inversely, the pure interests of a community as such are, in fact, private concerns. As soon as the purpose in question is important in itself and objectively valuable, it transcends the framework of mere subjectivity and acquires an importance before God, a relationship to eternity. Whether it concerns a single person or a group of persons is not the important point.

The error of anti-personalism has today infiltrated even into some Catholic circles. It can be found, for example, in certain enthusiasts of the so-called *liturgical movement*. These liturgists are prone to regard distrustfully the mystic and ascetical elements in religion. Any intense emotional attitude towards Christ — any *I and Thou* relationship with Him — appears to them suspect, subjective. In all depersonalization, on the other hand, they are inclined to see religious progress.

Yet, in truth, every religious progress in our life means a higher stage in our becoming, *qua* persons, transformed in Christ and participants in His holy life. This life, again, means love — charity unconfined and unending towards God and one's fellow persons. The index to our transformation in Christ consists in the measure of our participation in His love for God and for men. By becoming depersonalized and neutralized, however, we become incapable of such a participation.

Depersonalization is incompatible with love of God and transformation in Christ

What does God, above all, demand of us? *Our love.* What is the question Our Lord puts thrice, emphatically, to Peter in that great hour when He entrusts him with the care of His flock? It is the question as to his love. "Simon, son of John, lovest thou me?" (John 21:16).

Those men err who believe it to be our supreme goal that we become pure instruments of God. Certainly — and particularly, insofar as we fill a post in the hierarchy of the Church — we are *also* meant to be tools of God. But our proper and ultimate vocation is to be transformed in Christ: that is, to become saints. "For this is the will of God, your sanctification," says St. Paul (1 Thess. 4:3).

So long as we are a mere channel for the flow of God's will, so long as we are nothing but an impersonal tool in the hands of God, so long as we have no desire other than to discharge a certain function in the universe according to the plan of God, we cannot be transformed in Christ. The attainment of our proper supernatural aim presupposes an entirely different attitude on our part. It requires that we surrender ourselves to Christ by an act of love which is nothing if not eminently personal. It demands that we thus help the divine life unfold in us.

Christ must become the center of our thought, our yearning, and our will. Our every act must be stamped, as it were, with His seal. In all our conscious being we must become imprinted with the Christ-stamp. It requires, indeed, our having that *drunkenness with Jesus* which was present in the great saints.

Only think of these — of a St. Paul, a St. Francis of Assisi, or a St. Catherine of Siena! What a full personal life it is that pulsates in them! Do they not represent the utmost antithesis to any impersonal and neutral mode of being, yet at the same time, to any subjectivistic narrowness? The secret of their being both at once lies in St. Paul's words: "I live, yet it is not I who live but Christ who lives in me"; in St. Francis': "My God and my all"; in St. Catherine's: "That Thou be, and I be not." This is the meaning of "He that loses his life shall win it."

The saints do die to themselves, in the sense of being absorbed by their love of Christ, losing themselves in Christ, and only thus do they find their true selfhood — their self as intended by God.

We must give ourselves unconditionally to Christ

Our integral relationship with Christ — the Head of the Mystical Body which encompasses and sustains us, and works within us — necessarily implies, then, an express confrontation of our *I* with the divine *Thou*. True self-surrender consists in our giving ourselves to Christ absolutely, in a spirit of loving adoration; in our full renunciation of our sovereignty; in our becoming empty with regard to all other things. It means that we make no reservation whatsoever; that no province subsists in our personal world over which we still want to reign in our own right or in which we still are somehow asserting ourselves.

So long as we still draw the line somewhere in us (even though we do not expressly formulate that limitation), so long as we, however tacitly, at some point still utter a *ne plus ultra* which opposes a barrier to the extension of the Lord's empire in us, we have not given ourselves to Christ in a way that is a true self-surrender. We must really push our skiff from off the shore; burn the boats behind us. The important thing is to do away with all conditions and reservations, overt or hidden. In this matter, *very much* is of little avail: it has to be *all*. It is only by the totality of our surrender, the heroism — unspoilt by any proviso — of our leap in the dark, that we achieve the loss of our soul.

In true self-surrender, we experience ourselves being possessed by God

But there is one more aspect to this loss of self as implied in true self-surrender: namely, that state of being possessed which we experience when dimly aware of a power stronger than ourselves taking hold of us. In such moments we feel as though, like Habakkuk, we were taken "by the hair of our head" and lifted above ourselves.

Plato has seen — he develops it in his *Phaedrus* — that all great things are somehow done in a state of *madness* (the term meaning here, not of course a pathological condition of insanity, but our being entranced by something greater than we are). Then we thrust off or become enchanted away, as it were, from the secure base which we have laboriously established for ourselves and on which we have built our ordinary life.

These are the moments, then, in which a great thing bursts into our life and shakes its hitherto solid framework. The firm ground on which we have formerly moved securely, able to govern and to order rationally all our affairs, is drawn from under our feet. We no longer have, as we had before, a sense of sovereignty over the situation. That is why Plato attributes a specific value to being in love: for being in love essentially implies a kind of soaring above the normal level of our life, a certain rapture.

Whenever anything thus causes us to soar above the habitual plane of our life, whenever we are possessed by something that overwhelms us not by its mere dynamism but by its objective superiority, we also become delightfully aware that it is precisely this renunciation of our sovereignty which makes us really free.

Only, we must carefully maintain here a keen distinction between two things which resemble each other superficially but in reality are separated by an immense difference. One is a state of mind towering above our normal level of life, the other a condition in which we sink beneath that level.

This is not the only instance of men's aptness to mix up the supra-normal with what is in fact inferior to normality. Thus, there are not a few who fail to see the difference between purity and lack of sensuality. So also some cannot discern the difference between the peaceful serenity of a saint and the emotional obtuseness of a Stoic — only because they are both opposed to the unstable type, swinging to and fro between the poles of jubilation and of excessive grief. And yet the two are much farther from each other than either is from the normal temperament of a person of warm emotions.

Possession by God is the opposite of abandonment to passion or to mass psychosis

To return to our topic, an essential distinction must be established between one's being swept off one's feet by the impact of a dynamic passion as such, and one's being possessed by something not only *stronger* but intrinsically *higher* than oneself. An untrained mind, it is true, will easily overlook that difference.

Many a strong passion may overpower us to such a degree that we no longer know whither we are carried by its wave. Now, what is most characteristic of this state of being swept off our feet is the *discarding of our responsible self* implied in it. Our central personality, which normally controls our decisions and governs our conduct by its consents and its vetoes — by sanctioning, or withholding its sanction from, whatever course we incline towards — is put out of court; our decisions are taken over its head, as it were.

This is accompanied by a consciousness in us of losing our freedom, of being gripped, dragged about, and dictated to, by something that is not ultimately ourselves. A dynamic influence, stronger but of a lower nature than our habitual set of motives, has dethroned our inner sovereignty and reduced us to a state of dependence. A sort of depersonalization has indeed taken place here, though no neutralization takes place. Our inward integrity and dwelling with ourselves — the *habitare secum* — is destroyed.

Sensual passions are not the only factor that can produce such effects; men often fall a prey in a very similar manner to mass psychosis in its manifold varieties. Any large group of people, given certain circumstances, may easily form into a mass, responding to some demagogic slogan with a surge of cheap enthusiasm or indignation. We may expect its members, then, to be carried away by the motion of the collective mind, with their rational selves (their moral and prudential consciousness) being obliterated and their center of sanction passed by. The individual feels relieved from responsibility. He is delivered over to an impetuous wave of energy which sweeps aside his self-control and determines his behavior as an irresistible automatism.

No clumsier error could be imagined than to consider this contagion of a *sub-personal* effervescence as something greater than what originates in one's personal selfhood. All more highly organized natures that have for a time fallen under such a spell will later, when restored to the use of reason, feel ashamed of yielding to an illegitimate emotion even qualitatively so far below the habitual level of their lives. What a stultifying effect does such a mass psychosis usually exercise on the brains of its victims; how pitiably it depresses the mental standard of the individual!

A psychic rapture of this kind also exhibits the characteristic trait that the subject is not only enslaved by the fascination of the motive that sways him but also enjoys the *fact* of his intoxication itself, the very *condition* of morbidly being possessed.

True self-surrender, on the contrary, implies that we are entirely centered upon the object in which we lose ourselves. The value of that which holds us, and by no means the pleasure of being held, dominates our consciousness. One who seeks that pleasure for its own sake errs just as they do who yearn for the thrill of love rather than thinking of the beloved person, and hence never attain real love at all.

There is no point in our longing to lose ourselves in general. What we should long for is exclusively to lose ourselves in Christ. Let us never forget that, though an intense love or enthusiasm as such is undoubtedly a great experience and a fine sight, its value essentially depends on *whom* or *what* we love; on the person or thing that evokes our enthusiasm.

Yet, the supreme difference between the two forms of being possessed remains this: that true self-surrender is a sanctioned act, ratified by the free and conscious center of our personality, whereas the state of being swept off our feet implies a specifically unsanctioned mode of behavior, implies a disconnection from or an overriding of our personal center of sanction.

We can freely sanction the loss of our habitual sovereignty over self and circumstance

One reason why this mistake so frequently occurs involves the widespread omission of another, no less significant and necessary,

491

distinction: that between a sanctioned attitude as such and a sovereign attitude in which the subject, entrenched in his securities, maintains himself, as it were, above the situation. To state the exact nature of this difference again requires some explanation.

In our ordinary, natural life we take our stand on a kind of firm ground, propped, mostly, by an elaborate system of conventions. We have devised a framework for our life in which we assign its place to everything that we meet. We are anxious always to maintain our sovereignty over the situation; we seek to preserve, in regard to everything, the consciousness that *we have it* and are *not had by it*. We take heed lest anything should grow too large for us to cope with. We keep at a distance from all things we suspect of a tendency to possess us, and accordingly endeavor to diminish great things by emasculatory interpretations, so that they might no longer become dangerous to us. In a word, we fear losing that firm ground under our feet.

And, in fact, we do so justifiedly insofar as it is a question of things that represent no higher reality than we ourselves do; things that may not, on the strength of their objective content and quality, legitimately claim to possess us. Such are, notably, all mere passions: for example, the effect of certain narcotics, or again, the imperious automatism of some kind of professional activity, which tends wholly to absorb us.

The error, however, lies in identifying this routine tendency to remain sovereign over the situation and to preserve the solid ground under our feet with the sanctioning as such. *A bold dedication of self, too — a relinquishment of the solid ground on which we feel secure — can be an act sanctioned by our central personality.* Faith itself is nothing less than an immense venture: the venture of advancing beyond the naturally ensured base of our cognition. God invites us to engage upon this heroic venture.

Supernatural life as a whole requires us to depart from that firm natural terrain. The Apostles, indeed, left that solid ground when in response to Christ's *sequere me* they left everything behind and followed the Lord unconditionally; when they spoke, "Lord, to whom shall we go? Thou hast the words of eternal life" (John 6:69).

Yet, they did so, *not* in an unsanctioned way, yielding blindly to a compelling urge, but in the blissful consciousness which we find in the words of St. Paul, "For I know whom I have believed" (2 Tim. 1:12). They gave themselves wholly to the absolute Lord over life and death, from whom they had received everything. Their departure from the framework of their former lives — their losing of self — bore the most express and most complete personal sanction a human act can bear. Any self-surrender that lacks such a sanction lacks ultimate validity. We must, then, *never abandon ourselves to any unsanctioned impulse.*

The true state of dwelling with ourselves, again, presupposes what we have called the *sanction*. But the endeavor to shun all risk and flee all danger of being possessed — to carefully preserve the firm ground under one's feet — is not consonant (and is even inconsistent) with the true *habitare secum*, though it represents a kind of illegitimate counterfeit thereof. It is the source of all philistine mediocrity. It is doubtless better to abide on the firm ground of one's well-ordered natural life than to allow oneself to be swept off one's feet; but again it is infinitely better to lose oneself in Christ and to be seized by Him than to keep smugly within that secure natural framework.

Not only is such seizure better — it is *necessary* for us if we are truly desirous of being transformed in Christ. Our abandonment of self is an indispensable condition of the full unfolding in us of supernatural life. For Our Lord says, not only "He that shall lose his life for me shall find it," but also "He that findeth his life shall lose it."

We must, then, *lose our soul so as to find it.* In other words, we should renounce all vain effort to incorporate Christ into *our* life, but endeavor wholeheartedly, with the full sanction of our central personality, to transpose our life into Christ and entrust it to Him; indeed, to be possessed by Him.

True self-surrender is the antithesis of depersonalization

True self-surrender constitutes the extreme antithesis to depersonalization. In fact, only through such a surrender can we attain the full actualization of our proper personal life — in comparison to which our ordinary self-centered life is but a kind of somnolence. On the other hand, the surrender implied in being carried away by a superior dynamism means a submersion of personality in the vital sphere, an intrinsic degradation of the soul and thus (though not in the sense of becoming a coldly functional instrument of outward aims) it is eminently a process of depersonalization.

True self-surrender clarifies and deepens our vision of things

Furthermore, true self-surrender by no means generates a state of mind in which all things other than those which possesse us fade into obscurity, as though immersed in a sort of fog, with their outlines blurred and their distinctions disappearing. Rather, in the new vision bred of true self-surrender, all inferior things are surpassed. The mind is raised into a brighter light, which makes everything enter into its proper place. The depersonalizing type of surrender throws us, on the contrary, into a turmoil, a dull twilight of the mind in which all higher classes of things lapse into oblivion and invisibility. This kind of experience has the dark lethargic tint of a narcotic trance.

It is true that in the highest form of being possessed — in mystic ecstasy — the mind tends to be aware of nothing besides God. Here all creaturely things may seem plunged in darkness, but this is still an exuberant manifestation of their being surpassed, not a sign of their obliteration. Therefore, as we know from the evidence of the mystics, the mind after its awakening from ecstasy has a clearer and deeper vision of all things as fitted into their proper places under the dispensation of God.

The submersion of all creaturely things in the vision of a soul entirely lost to Him of whom the Apostle says, "Of Him, and by Him, and in Him are all things" (Rom. 11:36), never means a confusion or subversion of the divine order and hierarchy of the universe. This surpassing of all things created, though in the moments of actual ecstasy it seems to amount to their obliteration, leaves their order wholly intact and not only respects but confirms it. It manifests it in a more perfect fashion. After the passing of that transitory stage of darkness, created being will stand out in clearer and brighter outline than ever. The mind that has given itself altogether to God acquires a more penetrating vision of all things.

We should prepare ourselves for possession by God

We can never bring about of our own volition this state of being possessed by and lost in what is greater than ourselves. It can only come to us as a gift of God. But on our side we must develop an eager receptivity towards such a gift, should it be granted. We must have an unhampered readiness to embrace it. We must combat our habit of anxiously clinging to our natural security and attain the boldness needed for a relinquishment of that secure natural base. Joyously and without reflecting on ourselves we should let grace elevate us above ourselves.

Possession by high natural goods will prepare us for possession by Christ

Nor should we cultivate this readiness in view of the exceptional moments only when a special grace of God may call us

495

directly, and the sweetness of Jesus touch our heart. Whenever a sublime beauty in nature or art is offered to us; whenever a great love in Jesus might unite us with a fellow person; whenever the beauty of another soul (its inmost meaning and vocation, the unduplicable thought of God it represents) manifests itself to us and enraptures our heart; in all such cases, too, we should desist from anxiously keeping at a distance and laboring to adjust this impressive thing, once again, to the dimensions of our normal life. Rather we must try to understand the call of God which lies in such gifts. We must lay ourselves open to the impact of the great thing in question.

Here, too, we should not seek to avoid being possessed. But there must be a possession sanctioned by our center of rational orientation and evaluation, and incorporated in *the one great possession that is to rule our life: our possession by Christ*. Our love and admiration for noble creaturely things will, if thus conceived, also become a path leading us to an ever-increasing unconditional surrender to Christ — by helping us, notably, to overcome our attachment to our secure natural base, our contentment with a medium of petty and familiar safety, our fear of risk and venture.

Every act of giving ourselves to what, even though it has no supernatural connotation, approaches us from above, will help to thaw our heart. It will, ultimately, further our progress towards that state of blissful freedom which is the privilege of those living by Christ — the freedom St. Augustine thus puts into words: "Love, and do what thou wilt" (*Treatises on 1 John* 7.8). How timid many Christians are; how cautiously they fence round their hearts! Yet, not only does God *ask* to penetrate into our hearts; it is also His will that His way into our hearts shall be paved not only by the direct operations of grace, but also by great experiences on the human plane, too, provided that these be anchored in Christ.

A true Christian, then, *must* display this readiness to be possessed which always presupposes his personal sanction. He must be able, in holy courage, to leave the firm ground of familiar securities; he must rejoice in the state of being possessed. But he must not insist on *deciding all by himself* whether a specified experience may be upheld before the face of God but should make his sanction depend on his director's decision.

On the other hand, whenever God places in his path anything of great beauty or any other high good which claims to possess him, if, having confronted it with God, he feels justified in according it his full sanction, he should be equally ready to give himself to that elevating force without restraints or preoccupations.

For it is a duty of gratitude to be responsive to the word of God wherever it reaches us: to "keep it in a good and perfect heart" (Luke 8:15) rather than let it "fall upon a rock" (Luke 8:6). It is extremely important for us to profit by the moments when God draws us nearer to Him, when He allows us to be possessed by true values — and so loosens the fetters of our trivial system of petty self-protection and invites us to an act of ultimate audacity and freedom.

To such moments apply these words of St. Paul: "Behold, now is the acceptable time: behold, now is the day of salvation" (2 Cor. 6:2). To be sure, all such possession by high natural values must be *ordained to our true surrender of self to Christ.* If this is not the case, we do not hear the call of God; nay, we even abuse His gifts.

If all our life is thus incorporated in Christ so that we consistently seek — and find — Him in every created value, then our *being held* by the latter implies no submersion in darkness. On the contrary, it helps us to collect ourselves and to realize that true freedom which comes to us from above. It is in such moments — not in the trivial common sense attitude we have to display in our everyday occupations — that our vision is given a valid perspective. It is then that we see the true countenance of things, which we must engrave in our mind so as to evoke it even at times of interior dryness.

In such moments of being possessed by a genuine value, all things shine forth revealing their deeper meaning and their secret ties with superior Reality. In these moments we experience something of what the Scriptures call "the passing by of the Lord." Then do we rise to an awareness of our true metaphysical situation, and start to see everything *in conspectu Dei*. This is precisely the infallible test of our being held by a high and authentic created value, a great human love in Jesus, for example.

Then all conventional points of view suddenly fade into insignificance, all our little attachments and shackles of habit — all that we otherwise make so much fuss about and are so unwilling to dispense with — fall from us as if by magic. Then no disorder arises, but on the contrary, all real values become more clearly visible, and are seen even more deeply in their mutual harmony. Everything thus moves into its proper place and manifests the true order of things *in conspectu Dei* — whereas, when we are enslaved by a mere passion, we see all our world plunged into confusion and disorder.

Again, it is a proof of our basic decision to become a new man in Christ: to cast from us uncompromisingly everything that cannot maintain itself before the face of Christ or is somehow out of keeping with this new life in Christ, no matter how pleasant and familiar it has been to us as an appurtenance of our accustomed life — when we experience a legitimate state of being possessed as a joy-bearing gift; when we yearn to lose ourselves in Christ and say with the Bride of the Canticle of Canticles: "Stay me up with flowers, compass me about with apples; because I languish with love" (Song of Sol. 2:5).

Reference must be made to another dimension of the loss of self, an entirely new one which is confined to the mystic states of mind. The *inward death* depicted by St. John of the Cross in his *Dark Night* far exceeds that dying to oneself which we have met with as an aspect of our transformation in Christ. It amounts to a *dying of the soul* comparable to the experience of being immersed in complete darkness — a negative prefiguration and token of our future *total* rebirth in Christ. Here, the concept of losing one's self acquires a greatly enhanced, a very much more literal meaning. The life in Christ which grows out of that surrender implies an immediate experience of Christ, a *sensing* of the fact St. Paul describes in these words, "I live, now not I; but Christ liveth in me."

This supreme aspect of our transformation in Christ, a classic treatment of which can be found in the writings of many mystics, particularly of St. Teresa of Avila and St. John of the Cross, does not enter into the scope of the present work. It suffices to remark that this phase of man's transformation in Christ, too, constitutes an essential aspect, in a sense, the crowning aspect of the Vocation expressed in these words of the Lord: "But he that shall drink of the water that I will give him shall not thirst forever" (John 4:13).

Our consideration of the theme of *transformation in Christ* has now come to an end. In its course, we have measured the full meaning of the vocation that resounds in the words, *sequere me*. We have envisioned the countenance of "the new man who is renewed unto knowledge, according to the image of Him that created him." We have caught a glimpse of the new supernatural beauty, that reflection of the holiness of the God-Man, which fills the "prisoners of Christ" and radiates from their souls to light up the world of mankind: "That you may declare his virtues, who hath called you out of darkness into his marvelous light" (1 Peter 2:9).

We have surveyed the attitudes in which the fundamental principle of *dying with Christ and rising to life with Him* is unfolded. We have discussed the nature of the great assent which is the precondition, on our part, of our transformation in Christ: the assent that is to pervade, shape, and illumine our whole life until the coming of the hour that sounds the call, "Behold the bridegroom cometh: go ye forth to meet him" (Matt. 25:6); the assent sublimely expressed in the Psalmist's prayer: "Uphold me according to Thy word, and I shall live: and let me not be confounded in my expectation" (Ps. 118:116).

Suscipe me — receive me, O Lord, into Thy holy Law; receive me into Thy Love; receive me into Thyself. *Secundum eloquium tuum* — for Thou hast said, "You have not chosen me: but I have chosen you; and have appointed you, that you should go, and should bring forth fruit" (John 15:16). All my weakness, all my defeats, all the darkness in my soul fail to discourage me. I take refuge in Thy arms; I throw myself upon Thy Heart, *the desire of the eternal hills*. I *know* that Thou receivest those who give themselves to Thee wholly. *Et vivam* — I shall live, then: live by Thee, even Thy true divine life, to which all fullness of natural life is but a dwelling in death; the life of which Thou hast said: "This is eternal life, that they know Thee, the one true God, and Him that Thou has sent, Jesus Christ." This is the life that I long for, the life which like a stream flows over into eternity; the everlasting, never-ceasing blissful life which is one with Thyself and Thy never-ending Love. Let me not be confounded in my hope. O Lord, *salus in te sperant-ium*, Thou hast never yet disappointed those who put their hope in Thee and deliver themselves wholly to Thee. For Thou alone, in whom is the fullness of divinity, canst fill our hearts to the full. I have heard Thy Psalmist cry out: "Taste, and see that the Lord is sweet." I hear the voice of Thy Apostle: "Eye hath not seen, nor ear heard, neither hath it entered into the heart of man, what things God hath prepared for them that love him" (1 Cor. 2:9). And Thou hast Thyself promised to those who follow Thee that one day they will hear Thy voice: "Come, ye blessed of my Father, possess you the kingdom prepared for you from the foundation of the world" (Matt. 25:34). *Suscipe me, Domine, secundum eloquium tuum et vivam, et non confundas me ab exspectatione mea.*

Biographical Note

Dietrich von Hildebrand (1889-1977)

HITLER feared him and Pope Pius XII called him a "twentieth century Doctor of the Church." For more than six decades, Dietrich von Hildebrand — philosopher, spiritual writer, and anti-Nazi crusader — led philosophical, religious, and political groups, lectured throughout Europe and the Americas, and published more than 30 books and many more articles. His influence was widespread and endures to this day.

Although he was a deep and original thinker on subjects ranging across the spectrum of human interests, nonetheless, in his lectures and in his writings, von Hildebrand instinctively avoided extravagant speculations and convoluted theories. Instead, he sought to illuminate the nature and significance of seemingly "everyday" elements of human existence that are easily misunderstood and too frequently taken for granted.

Therefore, much of von Hildebrand's philosophy concerns the human person, the person's interior ethical and affective life, and the relations that should exist between the person and the world in which he finds himself.

Von Hildebrand's background made him uniquely qualified to examine these topics. He was born in beautiful Florence in 1889, the son of the renowned German sculptor, Adolf von Hildebrand.

At the time, the von Hildebrand home was a center of art and culture, visited by the greatest European artists and musicians of the day. Young Dietrich's early acquaintance with these vibrant, creative people intensified his natural zest for life.

In Florence, von Hildebrand was surrounded by beauty — the overwhelming natural beauty of the Florentine countryside and the rich beauty of the many art treasures that are Florence's Renaissance heritage. Pervading this Florentine atmosphere was Catholicism: in the art, in the architecture, and in the daily life of the people. These early years in Florence quickened in von Hildebrand a passionate love of truth, of goodness, of beauty, and of Christianity.

As he grew older, he developed a deep love for philosophy, studying under some of the greatest of the early twentieth century German philosophers, including Edmund Husserl, Max Scheler, and Adolf Reinach. Converting to Catholicism in 1914, von Hildebrand taught philosophy for many years at the University of Munich.

However, soon after the end of World War I, Nazism began to threaten von Hildebrand's beloved southern Germany. With his characteristic clearsightedness, von Hildebrand immediately discerned its intrinsic evil. From its earliest days, he vociferously denounced Nazism in articles and speeches throughout Germany and the rest of Europe.

Declaring himself unwilling to continue to live in a country ruled by a criminal, von Hildebrand regretfully left Germany for Austria, where he continued teaching philosophy (now at the University of Vienna) and fought the Nazis with even greater vigor, founding and editing a prominent anti-Nazi newspaper, *Christliche Ständestaat*.

This angered both Heinrich Himmler and Adolf Hitler, who were determined to silence von Hildebrand and to close his anti-Nazi newspaper. Orders were given to have von Hildebrand killed in Austria. Although his friend and patron, Austrian Premier Engelbert Dollfuss, was murdered by the Nazis, von Hildebrand evaded their hit-squads and fled the country just as it fell to the Nazis.

It is characteristic of von Hildebrand that even while he was engaged in this dangerous life-and-death struggle against the Nazis, he maintained his deep spiritual life, and managed to write during this period his greatest work, the sublime and highly-acclaimed spiritual classic, *Transformation in Christ* (Cf. pp. xiv-xvii).

Fleeing from Austria, von Hildebrand was pursued through many countries, ultimately arriving on the shores of America in 1940 by way of France, Switzerland, Portugal, and Brazil.

Penniless in New York after his heroic struggle against the Nazis, von Hildebrand was hired as professor of philosophy at Fordham University where he taught until his retirement. Many of his best works were written during this period and after his retirement. He died in 1977 in New Rochelle, New York.

Dietrich von Hildebrand was remarkable for his keen intellect, his profound originality, his prodigious output, his great personal courage, his deep spirituality, and his intense love of truth, goodness, and beauty. The rare qualities made Dietrich von Hildebrand one of the greatest philosophers and one of the greatest men of the twentieth century.

Index

Stages of development, 328 - 330, 403, 471
Stoic indifference, 316, 400
Strength, and meekness, 412
Stupidity vs. simplicity, 78
Suffering
    See Afflictions; Misery
Sulking, 409 - 411
Superficiality
    See Frivolousness
Superiority, 434
Surrender of self, *Ch. 18: 481 - 500*
    See God, surrender to

T

Tenderness, 402, 405 - 408
Time
    contemplation and, 123 - 125
    decisions/action and, 328 - 330
    God's sovereignty over, 326 - 327
Transformation
    contemplation and, 234
    factors necessary for:
      free cooperation with God, 250
      God's grace, 232
      holy sobriety, 479
      personhood, 484 - 487
      surrender to God, 243, 482, 487
    free will and, 222, 228, 247 - 249
    means to achieve:
      ascetical practices, 243
      contemplation, 236
      orderly life, 245
      prayer, 250
      response to things, 231
      seeing things *in conspectu Dei*, 241 - 243
      work, 246
    obstacles to:
      frivolousness, 91 - 93, 106, 141, 245

    instrumentalizing values, 233
    wrong motives, 238
    values and, 236 - 238
    virtues/acts in relation to, 222
Triviality
    See Frivolousness
Truthfulness, 469

U

Unity, inner, 71, 153, 360
    true simplicity and, 74 - 76
    value-response and, 101

V

Value-blindness, 151
Value-response, 231, 276, 285
    habit and, 289
    humility and, 155
    self-complacency and, 170 - 171
    transformation and, 236, 495 - 498
    true consciousness and, 62
    true freedom and, 219, 296 - 298
    See also, Values
Values
    contemplation and, 121
    contemplative delight in, 237
    faith and, 99
    inner peace and, 362
    instrumentalization of, 233
    patience and, 325
    possession by, 495 - 498
    simplicity and, 93, 99 - 103
    surrender to, 481
    transforming effect of, 237
    unity engendered by, 101
    See also, Value-response
Vanity, 174
Virtue
    acts and, 222 - 224, 239
    contemplation of own, 175 - 180

free will and, 218, 223, 229 - 231
response to values and, 231
work and, 246
Voices, inner, 476

W

Wakefulness, 65 - 67
Wickedness, 363
Will, free
   See Free will
Work, 246

Y

Yearning for good, 324
Yielding vs. mercy, 430

Z

Zeal, 412
   See also, Justice, hunger for

SOPHIA INSTITUTE PRESS

Sophia Institute is a non-profit institution that seeks to restore man's knowledge of eternal truth, including man's knowlege of his own nature, his relation to other persons, and his relation to God.

Sophia Institute Press serves this end in a number of ways. It publishes translations of foreign works to make them accessible for the first time to English-speaking readers. It brings back into print many books that have long been out-of-print. And it publishes important new books that fulfill the ideals of Sophia Institute. These books afford readers a rich source of the enduring wisdom of mankind.

Sophia Institute Press makes high-quality books available to the general public by using advanced, cost-effective technology and by soliciting donations to subsidize general publishing costs. Your generosity can help us provide the public with editions of works containing the enduring wisdom of the ages. Send your tax-deductible contribution to the address noted below. Your questions, comments, and suggestions are also welcome.

For a free catalog, call:

Toll-Free: 1-800-888-9344

SOPHIA INSTITUTE PRESS
BOX 5284
MANCHESTER, NH 03108

Sophia Institute Press is a tax-exempt institution as defined by the Internal Revenue Service Code, Section 501(c)(3). Tax I.D. 22-2548708.